How Social Movements Die
Repression and Demobilization of the Republic of New Africa

How do social movements die? Some explanations highlight internal factors such as factionalization, whereas others stress external factors such as repression. Christian Davenport offers an alternative explanation where both factors interact. Drawing on organizational as well as individual-level explanations, Davenport argues that social movement death is the outgrowth of a coevolutionary dynamic whereby challengers, influenced by their understanding of what states will do to oppose them, attempt to recruit, motivate, calm, and prepare constituents, while governments attempt to hinder all of these processes at the same time. Davenport employs a previously unavailable database that contains information on a black nationalist-secessionist organization, the Republic of New Africa, and the activities of authorities in the U.S. city of Detroit and state and federal authorities.

Christian Davenport is professor of political science and faculty associate at the Center for Political Studies at the University of Michigan and Global Fellow at the Peace Research Institute Oslo. He is the author of *State Repression and the Promise of Democratic Peace* (Cambridge, 2007) and *Media Bias, Perspective, and State Repression: The Black Panther Party* (Cambridge, 2010), which won an award for the best book in racial politics and social movements from the American Political Science Association. He is a coeditor of *Repression and Mobilization* (with Carol Mueller and Hank Johnston, 2004) and *Paths to State Repression: Human Rights Violations and Contentious Politics* (2000).

Cambridge Studies in Contentious Politics

Editors

Mark Beissinger *Princeton University*
Jack A. Goldstone *George Mason University*
Michael Hanagan *Vassar College*
Doug McAdam *Stanford University and Center for Advanced Study in the Behavioral Sciences*
Sarah Soule *Stanford University*
Suzanne Staggenborg *University of Pittsburgh*
Sidney Tarrow *Cornell University*
Charles Tilly (d. 2008)
Elisabeth J. Wood *Yale University*
Deborah Yashar *Princeton University*

(*continued after the Index*)

How Social Movements Die

Repression and Demobilization of the Republic of New Africa

CHRISTIAN DAVENPORT

University of Michigan, Ann Arbor
Peace Research Institute Oslo

CAMBRIDGE
UNIVERSITY PRESS

CAMBRIDGE
UNIVERSITY PRESS

32 Avenue of the Americas, New York NY 10013-2473, USA

Cambridge University Press is part of the University of Cambridge.

It furthers the University's mission by disseminating knowledge in the pursuit of education, learning and research at the highest international levels of excellence.

www.cambridge.org
Information on this title: www.cambridge.org/9781107041493

© Christian Davenport 2015

First published 2015

A catalogue record for this publication is available from the British Library

Library of Congress Cataloguing in Publication data
Davenport, Christian, 1965–
How social movements die : repression and demobilization of the Republic of New Africa / Christian Davenport.
    pages cm – (Cambridge studies in contentious politics)
Includes bibliographical references and index.
ISBN 978-1-107-04149-3 (hardback) – ISBN 978-1-107-61387-4 (paperback)
1. African Americans – Political activity – History – 20th century.   2. Black militant organizations – United States – History – 20th century.   3. Social movements – United States – History – 20th century.   I. Title.
E185.615.D3837   2015
323.1196´0730904–dc23   2014022609

ISBN   978-1-107-04149-3   Hardback
ISBN   978-1-107-61387-4   Paperback

To Juliet "Ndidi" Seignious
The freest and most beautiful human I know
Mother, mentor, miracle

Contents

Tables

Figures

Acknowledgments

As people who know me would readily attest, I am fond of saying that "it takes a village to" do a wide variety of things. This is definitely true with regard to writing a book – especially one that has taken nearly a decade to complete and that has followed me to numerous institutions and parts of the United States. While working on this manuscript, I received a hundred and one kindnesses and a few bruises along the way. This said, some individuals and institutions provided a bit more consistent assistance than others as I repeatedly came back to them for a clarifying point, yet another reread, some coffee, a meal, a distraction, or a brilliant insight. I wish to acknowledge them here and give them their props.

For the majority of the time that I was working on what became the current book, three individuals provided amazing input: Imari Obadele and Chuck Tilly as well as Mark Lichbach. Early on, these scholars-mentors-advisors saw something in the project that most did not and encouraged me to pursue it. They did not tell what to do but merely suggested what might be lucrative topics in which people might be interested. One institution in particular proved invaluable: the Walter Reuther Library in Detroit. This is that rare institution where no question was too stupid or too small to merit full attention and assistance. Such an attitude was encouraging and refreshing – especially after some not-so-nice interactions with librarians on an earlier book. Two individuals came to provide some much-needed companionship as I wallowed through document after document, as they were doing some wallowing of their own: David Cunningham and Gilda Zwerman. They immediately understood what I was trying to do and served as a constant source of inspiration, letting me hear about what they were going through and how they continued amid the problems that emerge in a large research project.

When I was at the University of Colorado, I received a grant from the National Science Foundation that proved invaluable for scanning and coding the various documents that I came across. During this time, I had the amazing luck of working with four graduate students who helped me figure out what was there and what could be done with it: Heather Frazier, David Reilly, Glen Galaich, and Claudia Dahlerus. Also during this time, my colleague Scott Adler introduced me to his father, Sheldon Adler, who had served as a lawyer in Detroit during the period of my investigation. These contacts turned out to be extremely useful, in part because they taught me a great deal about who would speak to whom and about what.

Later, I moved to the University of Maryland, where I had two amazing colleagues who consistently provided valuable input: Jillian Schwedler and Marc Howard. Through the workshop on Conflict and Contentious Politics and numerous conversations, their interventions opened me up to the implications of the case for other societies (i.e., the Middle East and Europe – their areas of specialization, respectively). They also prompted me to think comparatively, which I was not always inclined to do. During this time, I also came across two undergraduate students who provided over-the-top assistance with coding: Gabrielle Birnberg and Yael Kletter. They always put everything they had into the work that they did, and seeing this made me even more interested in the topic as the interest of yet another generation reenergized me.

There were useful comments provided to me within diverse workshops around the United States where I discussed the case, my argument, and some of the evidence used. These included two locations in particular and specific individuals: the Contentious Politics Workshop at Columbia University, with Vince Boudreau, and the Order, Conflict, and Violence Workshop at Yale University, with Elisabeth Wood, Nicholas Sambanis, and Stathis Kalyvas. I was challenged at these venues in ways that pushed me further into the examination in ways that I did not foresee.

With support from the National Science Foundation and the Center for Advanced Study in the Behavioral Sciences at Stanford University, I was able to obtain a fellowship for a year to write up my thoughts. The amazing staff at the center were invaluable in helping me track down hard-to-find material, submitting dozens of Freedom of Information Act (otherwise known as FOIA) requests, and locating individuals throughout the United States. Additionally, two other Fellows, Rose McDermott and Lani Guinier, and my colleague and dear friend Sarah Soule (also at Stanford University), provided insights into my subject that not only made me see the subject in new ways but created an atmosphere within which I could actually write. This was a bizarre combination of space, support, and energetic engagement. I am thankful for that.

I must admit that the project began to wear on me after a while, but a final push came from a variety of individuals. I was blessed to have some incredibly insightful as well as giving colleagues at the University of Notre Dame: Ernesto Verdeja and Cat Bolten (WTPA!). They listened, prodded, probed, attacked, thought, and rethought topics that were always useful. Additionally, I was able to bounce some ideas off participants at two workshops: one on "Peace and Conflict" and another on the "Study of Politics and Movements." Especially noteworthy here were Kraig Beyerlein and Rory McVeigh (colleagues and friends in sociology) as well as Cyanne Loyle and Chris Sullivan (former students, friends, and now colleagues).

Perhaps my last and most useful pushes came from three individuals who read the last version of the manuscript and provided extremely useful comments (after my arrival at the University of Michigan). One such individual was Keffrelyn Brown, who always sought the narrative voice. Another was Errol Henderson. Errol engaged the work with the seriousness and care for which one can only wish. We did not always agree, but his critical eye was always a truthful one that had to be engaged. Finally, there was Ragnhild Nordås. In a moment of kindness or madness, Ragnhild went through the final manuscript with such a close look that even I (the author) had to go back and wonder about what I had written. It was amazing to have this careful evaluation, because by the time she approached it, I felt I really did not have anything left in me. Encouraged, engaged, and insightfully guided, I was able to finish the book and actually like it, which writers know, after working on something for a while, is quite an accomplishment. Many thanks to her.

Now, with all these thanks and acknowledgments, I do not want anyone to think that any faults with the current work lie with anyone but myself. I take full responsibility for what you are about to read. Of course, I would also like to take some of the praise, but I will leave that for you to decide.

Peace,
Christian Davenport
(Nom de Guerre)

Introduction

Met Any American Communists Lately?

Between 1919 and the late 1950s, the Communist Party of the United States of America (CP-USA) engaged in a wide variety of challenges directed against the U.S. government and its economic system. Because of this, many aspects of the organization became well known to the American public. Indeed, in their day, the names of the organizational leadership (i.e., William Foster, Earl Browder, and Eugene Dennis) were as popular as any at the time. Bent on dramatically transforming U.S. political-economic relations, the Party attempted to raise awareness regarding the evils of the American political-economic system and engage in numerous struggles against it. The activities put forth toward these ends were as numerous as they were varied, from editorials to unionization to political campaigns to mass protests. The locales varied as well. Focused initially on major cities, efforts began to emerge seemingly everywhere. Within the context of international conflict with the former Soviet Union, which was believed and later found to have supported the Party financially as well as ideologically, the behavioral threat presented was very real. If the Party achieved all that it wanted, nothing would be the same in the United States.

In response to the activities mentioned earlier, the U.S. government engaged in a similarly wide variety of repressive strategies to identify, constrain, and destroy the "commies." By most accounts, this was the most thorough initiative of its kind in American history. Over the period of the challenge, the American Communist Party was officially banned, and government agents throughout the country assembled lists of members as well as their activities (real and imagined). In turn, suspected and real activists were harassed, detained, questioned, arrested, beaten, deported, and, in rare cases, executed. Equally important, U.S. civil society participated in the persecution of Communists, as private citizens informed on suspected communists and corporations identified as well as fired suspected members and sympathizers. Name lists were also distributed to different organizations and individuals throughout the country so that none of the blacklisted could be hired or given places to live or rent. In effect, the Red Scare led to the Red Purge.

The outcome of the search-and-destroy mission led by U.S. political authorities was seemingly no less than a devastating removal of all things Communist in American life (e.g., Goldstein 1978; Schrecker 1998). Over time, membership in the Communist Party decreased to a small number of hardliners and the number of spinoff organizations increased and then declined, as did the number of newspapers and the activities of the relevant dissidents associated with them. By the 1960s, if one was Red, then one was essentially dead – jobless, friendless, shunned, and scorned. In this context, repressive behavior appeared to work exactly as planned: upon being targeted by the American government, the challenging organization basically ceased to exist along with the activities, individuals, and many elements of the ideology associated with them.

Now, although repression appeared to play a major role in the destruction of CP-USA, this has not been the only explanation offered. For example, some, like Lipset and Marks (2001), argue that what accounted for the demise of the Communists (and the Socialists, for that matter) was not persecution but the fact that Americans simply did not find their message attractive. Here the strengths of and opportunities within the U.S. political-economy offered to many a piece of the American pie, thereby decreasing the necessity for and interest in the leftist organization. Others noted that the movement was essentially devastated by developments within the USSR and its violent totalitarian practices, which led to significant disagreements in the Communist Party about whom they should and should not be affiliated with and what they should and should not do. Here, confronted with the reality of actual Communism, many just stopped working for and affiliating with the cause, splintering into different factions and later disengaging from contentious politics altogether.

What is important about these alternative explanations for the decline of CP-USA is the fact that they move away from the singular possibility that it was repression that did the Communists in toward a broader consideration of multiple factors at the same time where repressive behavior was merely one among several associated with the challengers' demise.

The Surge Worked, Didn't It?

More than once, presidential candidate John McCain berated his opponent and future U.S. president Barack Obama with the question, "You admit that the surge [i.e., the enhanced counterinsurgent effort in Iraq during 2007] worked, don't you?" By "worked," he meant that the violent behavior undertaken by insurgent Iraqis associated with al-Qaeda diminished following U.S. action. After a few attempts at trying to contextualize his opinion about war in general as well as other issues that he wished to highlight (most notably the economy and the Bush administration's numerous shortcomings), Obama conceded that "yes, the surge worked." This concession was important. McCain and Obama would go back and forth several times on various issues, but on this point they would join with many others arguing that government repression had weakened al-Qaeda in Iraq (AQI).

The basic point was simple. Prior to the surge, AQI violence was on the rise. Before this time, al-Qaeda seemed able to do what they wished, hitting targets all over the country, even those believed to be difficult (i.e., within zones of control held by the United States). After the surge, however, AQI violence decreased. The impact was seemingly a clear one: repression hindered AQI's ability to recruit, train, and engage in operations, similar to the situation with the U.S. Communist Party. With this realization, McCain, Obama, General Petraeus, and Rush Limbaugh made their case for effective counterinsurgent policy.

But did the surge "work"? Over time, a small but growing opinion began to emerge, suggesting that the surge might not be the cause of the decreased violence in Iraq (Inman and Davenport 2012). Some noted that the surge came *after* and not before the decrease in violent behavior. Some noted that AQI violence might have decreased because a large number of people had left the area, leaving fewer individuals to kill. Some noted that the earlier violence was severe enough that worthwhile targets could not be found. Some noted that AQI was not weakened and incapable but that they were simply waiting for the occupiers to leave and major counterinsurgent efforts to dissipate; here the situation was one of abeyance, not defeat. The differences are important because, again, we find that repressive action was merely one among several explanations for the end of a dissident organization. Additionally, we find that (once more) it was not clear what role it played and how much of the explanation it accounted for.

Secession Interrupted?

In 1968, a group of African Americans came together in Detroit to form the Republic of New Africa (RNA). The objective of this organization was simple: secede from the United States, claim five states for the new nation, obtain hundreds of millions for reparations for the damage done by and since slavery, and have a plebiscite of all African Americans to see whether they wanted to join. The objectives were ambitious and the tactics associated with them bold: Afro-centric education, repeated conferences on nation building, and standing up to police raids. Initially, the group received a significant amount of attention from local, state, and federal media. There was also a significant buzz among the African American community. By 1968, black nationalism had risen in popularity over the more moderate civil rights movement, and African Americans began to flock to organizations like the RNA.

Along with the increased activity and attention of the media and black population, however, came the attention and action of diverse government agents. Lumped under the general category of black nationalism or hate groups, the RNA was subject to a wide number of repressive activities, including physical and electronic surveillance as well as informant and agent provacateur raids, mass arrests, and shootouts. The rate and intensity of government action was nothing at the level of an organization like the Black Panther Party, which was heralded as the most dangerous organization in the United States at the time, but nevertheless the behavior directed against the organization was not inconsequential.

Over time, like the membership of the Communist Party and al-Qaeda, the number of RNA members dwindled, and their activities decreased in frequency as well as scope. What accounted for the organization's demise? On one hand, it seemed that government behavior was directly responsible for the RNA's end. How could a challenging organization persist under such scrutiny and negative sanctions? On the other hand, it seemed that the RNA itself was responsible. How could a challenging organization continue to advocate and pursue an ambitious goal such as the one they were pursuing on a shoe-string budget and with such a wide variety of strong-willed individuals pulling in distinct directions? The answers to these questions have been unclear, with researchers, former RNA members, and observers maintaining diverse positions.

The present volume is interested in shedding some much-needed light on this topic – specifically with regard to the RNA but generally with regard to all institutions behaviorally challenging political authorities. To go forward on this journey, however, we must first go back.

The Puzzle, Research Question, and Motivation

In many respects, the subject of this investigation is an old one. As long as nation-states have existed, groups of individuals have emerged to challenge political and economic leaders, institutions, and the practices associated with them. Toward this end, people have come together in social movement organizations,[1] they have articulated changes that they would like to see

---

[1] Others are interested in "terrorist" and/or "insurgent" organizations where it is generally the case that such institutions are banned by law. In the case of social movement organizations, although legally facilitated in many countries (especially in democracies), the organizations can still be subject to a variety of different sanctions from political authorities. To be clear, I am interested in social movement organizations (i.e., "a complex, or formal, organization which identifies its goals with the preferences of a social movement or a countermovement and attempts to implement those goals"; McCarthy and Zald 1977, 1218) as opposed to either social movements (i.e., "a set of opinions and beliefs in a population which represents preferences for changing some elements of the social structure"; McCarthy and Zald 1977, 1217) or social movement "industries" (i.e., which represent a constellation of organizations; McCarthy and Zald 1977, 1219). The three are related but distinct.

(i.e., they put forward claims), and they have engaged in specific activities to signal their dissatisfaction to those in charge, prompting some effort toward their desired objective (i.e., they participate in claims making). In response, agents of the state have sought to protect political and economic leaders, institutions, and policies through the application of coercion including, but not limited to, arrests, beating, harassment, agents provocateurs, targeted assassination, raids, torture, disappearances, and mass killing. Repression may not be the first strategy employed or the one used most frequently, but historically, it has been among those receiving the most attention as well as the one people most fear.

While the action-counteraction identified is essentially ubiquitous within modern nation-states (partially defining them, in fact), something else is also commonly observed but less commonly discussed. Here I am referring to the fact that many (if not most) of the challenging organizations, the individuals associated with them, the tactics they employ, and/or the challenges they advocate seemingly die off (i.e., go away, disappear, are withdrawn). That is, people making a specific claim (claims makers) stop coming together, group objectives (claims) are no longer pursued, social movement organizations (institutions that represent the claims makers) cease to exist, and the behavioral challenges used to reach the specific ends are no longer undertaken.

What is the reason for the death of a particular behavioral challenger? As noted earlier, and in line with advocates of protest policing and counterterrorism and insurgency as well as those who discuss political order and state failure, one explanation concerns the repressive efforts taken by governments against the challengers. In the face of expected or actual arrests, beatings, mass killing, and so forth, it makes sense that individuals seek to diminish the possibility of such activity by leaving the targeted organization and ceasing to engage in collective action deemed problematic for those in power. Demobilizing would likely reduce the sanctions imposed against them as they would no longer be threatening. In this case, *repression kills social movement organizations*.

It is also possible, however, that movement organizations die off for other reasons. For example, people engaged in social struggle might simply get tired of each other. They might get fed up with the seemingly endless meetings, unattended events, and underappreciated effort. Members might get turned off by endless debates and basic disagreements regarding what should be done, when, where, and how. In this case, *social movement organizations kill social movement organizations*.

Although I am interested in what impact both explanations have on challenger demobilization, I frame my discussion in a way that privileges the first, asking, *What role does repression play in ending a social movement organization in conjunction with/juxtaposed against other factors?* There are several reasons for such an approach.

First, the interest in efficiently using the coercive power held by nation-states is among one of the longest held in international and comparative politics. Indeed, it is intricately connected with definitions as well as theories of the nation-state itself (e.g., consider the work of Hobbes and Weber). In this framework, government wields a monopoly of coercive power that offsets the development and use of nongovernmental coercive power within civil society by social movement organizations and other challengers (e.g., terrorists and insurgents).

Second, exactly how government functions in the capacity of societal protection is not well understood, although by one metric, governments do quite well. For example, most nation-states persist over time, and regime change, revolution, and significant modification to a national political-economy are rare. If one were to consider the relevant scholarship regarding specific acts of coercion or general coercive behavior directed against those challenging governments, however, the findings are quite mixed. For example, evaluating the influence of repression on dissident behavior, every single finding, including no finding, has been identified. Within this work, repression increases dissent (e.g., Francisco 1996, 2004; Lichbach and Gurr 1981); decreases dissent (e.g., Hibbs 1973); initially decreases and at higher values increases dissent (e.g., Muller 1985); and decreases dissent over time (e.g., Rasler 1996) and it is alternatively negative or positive (e.g., Gupta and Venieris 1981; Moore 1998); has varied effects depending on the type of repression and aspect of dissent (e.g., Koopmans 1993; Earl and Soule 2010); and has no impact whatsoever (e.g., Gurr and Moore 1997). This is highly problematic from the view discussed earlier, because if part of the reason for repression is so that governments can fend off challengers and reduce behavior that could adversely affect authorities as well as the political-economic structure that relies upon it, then they do not do well at all.[2] Finally, when confronting one of the largest and one of the rarest challenges to the state, armed insurgency, governments seem to fare better, but this worsens over time. For example, civil war researchers find that for much of the post–World War II period, governments generally vanquished rebels in their confrontations, but after the Cold War, these engagements generally ended in negotiated settlement.

While useful in getting a general idea of what repression might do, the research is generally limited, for it does not consider alternative explanations for the death of a single challenging institution. Specifically, it ignores what is taking place within the dissident challenge itself, which might also account for the demise of those in opposition to government.

To address the topic, my effort initially juxtaposes the external (repression-oriented) explanations, where social movement organization demise is determined by the repressive efforts of governments only, against internal (challenger-oriented) explanations, where the demise of a social movement organization has nothing at all to do with repression but with the social movement organizations themselves. Such an inquiry allows us to understand how effective governments are at performing one of their oldest, most important

---

[2] This presumes that increased dissent is bad for the political-economy.

and highly controversial functions. While considering the two rival explanations, I introduce a third: *that the demise of social movement organizations involves an interaction between social movement organizations and the efforts put forth by governments to counter or destroy them.* This essentially takes one of the most widely supported findings of the social movement literature – that emergence has something to do with the character of the environment as well as something to do with the character of the movement institution – and uses this insight to explain why social movement organizations die (or terminate).

To conduct my analysis, I construct and then evaluate a unique database concerning both *external repression* undertaken by federal, state, and local police against a U.S. black secessionist movement organization, the RNA, including overt as well as covert activity, as well as *internal organizational dynamics* within the RNA, including discussions, meetings, conferences, and protest. These activities took place between 1968 and 1973 (discussed further later). The results of this research are quite informative. Specifically, I find that both external repression and internal movement dynamics played a role in RNA demobilization, decreasing individuals (members), ideas (claims) associated with the initial claims-making effort, institutions (formal organizations), and interventions (actions). For example, the investigation reveals that overt repression (e.g., arrests, raids, and trials) generally depleted the RNA below a certain threshold but only for a brief amount of time. In contrast, severe repression (i.e., violent and/or large-scale activity) diminished organizational functionality (e.g., participation, discussions, optimism, and behavior) for a longer period, but this did not deliver the fatal blow, and in certain circumstances, these activities served as a rallying point (a "backlash"). Viewing a tactic much less considered in the relevant literature, the research further discloses that covert repressive action (i.e., RNA fear of infiltration and surveillance) significantly weakened the social movement organization. In many respects, I maintain that it had a more profound influence than overt behavior.

These latter influences are especially interesting because even though the RNA was aware of the deleterious impact that repressive action would have on them, and there was some willingness to initially trust those in charge of the dissident institution despite immense risk, the organization's capacity to counter the government's effort was undermined by two factors that were largely internal to the movement and that preceded the repressive behavior directed against them. First, the RNA was unable to deliver on the objectives that it set for itself (e.g., establishing a new government with an active citizenry as well as landmass in the United States of America). Second, the RNA was unable to accurately comprehend what repressive action would be directed against them (expecting overt as opposed to covert activity). Both of these problems reduced the trust of those within the RNA, which further undermined their ability to function and made them vulnerable to subsequent repressive activity. Small, fractionalized, distrustful, and generally struggling, the group was an easy target.

Although it is difficult to assess the precise causal sequence, it is clear that sequence matters. As a consequence, there is no discussing the termination of movement organization without addressing movement organization initiation and dynamics. Specifically, I argue that the contradictions in group ideology that developed at the founding set the RNA on a specific path, which, after the RNA experienced repression, increased the likelihood of specific types of movement demobilization. This is largely attributed to the organization's understanding of repressive behavior, how it would likely be targeted, their preparation for such behavior, and the match-mismatch between the organization's expectations and the reality of what they actually experienced. Great divergence in opinion and difficulty in overcoming relevant differences (e.g., owing to factionalization) facilitated demobilization, whereas divergence in opinion and flexible adaptation in addressing problems diminished it.

Why should we care about this topic? There are several reasons for such an inquiry.

First, if repression has no impact at all on social movement organizations or if it makes dissident behavior more radical in terms of what dissidents ask for and/or what dissidents do, then this represents a strong indictment against those who advocate the use of government coercion, state repression, and/or human rights violation in all its forms (i.e., protest policing, counterterrorism, and counterinsurgency). As international and domestic laws, assorted treaties, and popular perceptions throughout the world have increasingly moved against such behavior, research on this topic could not be more perfectly timed. Despite this context, however, through discussions of states of emergency, states of "exception," and legal derogations, governments have repeatedly been able to justify and receive widespread support for their use of repressive behavior. If it is shown that government coercion is not effective at doing what it sets out to do, however, work leading to this conclusion would represent an important critique of government coercion and the arguments used to support it.

Second, the investigation of repression's influence on social movement organizations would further bring together two areas of inquiry that have largely been ignored, improving our understanding of both: (1) the study of behavioral challenge(r)s to political authorities (e.g., rebellion, insurgency, dissent, social movement organizations) and (2) the study of state repression against behavioral challenge(r)s (e.g., counterinsurgency or terrorism, protest policing, and human rights violations). The former research has generally been concerned with how social movement organizations are created and sustained. Indeed, I would maintain that this is where the bulk of the research on the topic can be found. Comparatively little effort has been directed toward why they are ended. Indeed, this is one of the areas in need of serious research. Similarly, although attention is given to government action taken against challengers (general policing of protests and protesters, such as arrests of individuals engaged in behavioral challenges), many government actions (covert behavior, such as torture and disappearances, as well as informants and agents provocateurs) are relatively ignored. The latter research tends to neglect the targets and victims of state repression, focusing instead on what repressive activity is selected, how it is implemented, and what political-economic contexts are most likely to prompt specific forms of it. While this has made sense given the objectives of this research program, it leaves us in a situation where comparatively little effort is extended to understanding what impact repression has on the individuals subjected to it or on the broader society in which these actions take place.[3]

Third, the simultaneous consideration of both social movement organizations and state repression is important, for the combination will provide a more realistic assessment of both. For example, by paying more attention to the dynamics and problems within social movement organizations, repression and its impact on behavioral challenges will be better understood. Similarly, by paying more attention to the dynamics and problems with repressive applications, social movement organizations and their susceptibility to government action will be better understood. Indeed, it is my intention to show that only certain types of social movement organizations at certain periods in their existence will be influenced by repression in a manner that will influence their demobilization. In other contexts, repressive action might not have any impact at all, or it might even have the opposite effect of what political authorities would expect, strengthening resistance and rebellion.

By adopting an approach that considers both governments and repression as well as challengers and dissent, I will also be able to show specifically how particular movement-countermovement origins and processes lead to particular outcomes. In short, I address how certain paths to termination involve distinct patterns of birth and upbringing. In telling the story of the grave, therefore, one has to tell the story of the cradle, middle school, adulthood, and so forth.

Toward a Better Investigation of Demobilization

Typically analyses of social movement death are based on detailed historical analyses, which may not be especially clear about issues of definition, operationalization, and systematic evaluation of propositions but which are well adept at identifying causal mechanisms as well as providing the raw material for theory building. Alternatively, researchers drawing conclusions from detailed statistical examinations, which are better in terms of definition, operationalization, and testing rival hypotheses, often infer relationships from highly aggregated (frequently at the nation-year) or poorly measured data (proxies that are quite distant from the thing they are supposed to measure). These

---

[3] Although there is some research directly related to the current book, referred to as the conflict-repression nexus (e.g., Lichbach 1987), there are many limitations with this work that, aside from inconclusivity, preclude its usefulness (discussed briefly later in this chapter and in greater detail within the next few chapters).

might obscure causal mechanisms and ignore factors such as group discussions and emotional experiences, which bear directly on how social movement organizations are supposed to be influenced by state repression and are notoriously difficult to measure. Prior research (especially quantitative work) also tends to treat all relationships as if sequencing and timing were irrelevant, ignoring the fact that specific sequences or events that happened earlier might have important influences on what takes place later.[4]

Fundamentally shifting the approach used to examine the influence of repression on dissent, however, I argue that perhaps one of the best ways to study the topic is to systematically evaluate discussions, actions, and relationships between members of social movement organizations in day-to-day dissident gatherings (e.g., meetings, conferences, and workshops as well as protest events, doing so in a way that facilitates nuanced evaluation and interpretation). Here one can gauge the impact of repressive action and social movement behavior on movement demobilization as well as the dynamic interaction between these two factors. Indeed, it is my argument that the effect of repression on social movement organizations is conditioned by the challengers' attempts to prepare its members for repressive behavior (what I call *reappraisal*) and to sustain organizational *trust* while governments are trying to undermine both of these efforts through *overwhelming* (doing more than what is expected), *outwitting* (doing something different than what is expected), and cultivating *distrust* (doing things to reduce a person's willingness to put his or her life in someone else's hands). Without addressing these issues, one simply cannot understand what repression is or is not doing to or within challenging institutions. To understand (de)mobilization, therefore, one must address the meso (dissident organizations) and micro (individual challengers).

Although repressive behavior can prove damaging to social movement organizations, limiting resources and effective action, it is not until the movement organization can no longer prepare for repression and sustain trust that demobilization proves likely. Relationships here are not only dynamic but also context specific. The sequences of activities and counteractivities are important to highlight. After significant efforts to prepare for its influence, repressive behavior is less likely effective than that which takes place before challengers have been able to develop a response. A form of repression that is different from that discussed or prepared for (outwitting) is more disruptive on an SMO than a form that is discussed or prepared for but is greater than anticipated (overwhelming). Similarly, repressive action has different effects on challenging organizations where a significant amount of trust has been cultivated as opposed to challengers where trust does not exist.

The approach put forward in this book is distinct from what is traditionally found in the literature because I am not explicitly going to test a particular argument, nor am I going to provide some case history and extract some

---

[4] For important exceptions, see Davenport (1996) and Loyle et al. (2012).

theoretical insights at the end. Rather, I outline my theoretical argument and expectations, derived from a detailed reading of the literature, and then use close scrutiny of a unique and relevant data set viewed through the prism of the argument presented. This is closer to the approach where detailed case history is used to better understand causal mechanisms, but I am also identifying at the outset that I believe specific mechanisms are possible and acknowledge the fact that alternatives might exist.

To be clear, I readily note that the approach suggested here is not easily adopted, because the data requirements for such an inquiry are somewhat high (which I think needs to be improved in the discipline), necessitating access to the innermost workings of a behavioral challenge. For the data to be useful, we need to know who is present in a social movement, what they say, what they do, and with whom, and we need to know about the actions in which authorities engage: when, against whom, and where.

Toward this end, I use a database of daily activity for a black nationalist and secessionist group, the RNA, which existed in the United States roughly between the years 1968 and 1971 but was based in Detroit for most of its history. This unique collection, which includes federal, state, and local government documents; media reports from national and local sources; and records from the RNA itself, allows us to peer inside the social movement organization, evaluating group and individual behavior and how members felt about what the government was doing against the challengers. The records also allow us to ascertain what government was doing against the group, who was involved, what they did, and against whom.

With approximately ten thousand pages of information, I have selected five different periods in the history of the RNA to examine the diverse ways that internal social movement dynamics and external applications of state repression influenced dissident survival, independently and in tandem:

1. the founding of the RNA in Detroit in March 1968
2. RNA movement into Ocean Hill–Brownsville, Brooklyn, in October 1968
3. the shooting and raid at Detroit's New Bethel Baptist Church in March 1969
4. the development of a faction during November 1969
5. the shooting, raid, and arrest of numerous members in Jackson, Mississippi, in August 1971

Specifically, I look at two months before the specific event in question, the full duration of the event itself, and then two months after the event in question, by the day.

Although the subject of social movement demobilization has received little attention, the RNA has received even less. Like many social movement organizations, the RNA is clouded in mystery and myths, exacerbated over time. The information one finds on the organization is quite limited and eclectic: a chapter in an edited volume here (Jeffries 2007), a chapter in a general overview of black resistance there (Kelley 2002), some references in books about Detroit here (e.g., Spreen and Holloway 2005), and an undergraduate honors thesis there (Zeile 2006). Within this work, attention is given to a few specific individuals, some brief discussion of the organization's overall objectives, and mention of at least one of the two high-profile shootings noted earlier. Exactly where the individuals associated with the organization came from, how the RNA came into being, what they did – precisely – how they did it, how things evolved over time, and what tensions appeared to exist within the organization are not generally addressed.

Regardless of the organization's popularity and the awareness of the U.S. government's campaign against it, the RNA is an ideal case in many ways, but not for reasons that are normally provided. For example, the group is not the largest of the period within the black community, they do not engage in the largest number of contentious activities or the most violent, and the attention they receive from diverse authorities does not appear to be extensive compared to the Black Panthers, for instance. This said, while the number of members is not large, there is enough information for us to reasonably claim that there was a serious and sustained claims-making effort against the U.S. government and that this organization was responded to by political authorities in a serious and sustained manner. While the number of actions is not among the largest or most violent, numerous activities were undertaken, and several involved violence. As expected, the latter received extensive local, regional, and national attention. The total dead from the conflict involving the RNA was far less than the one thousand battle death threshold conventionally maintained by many social scientists as worthy of attention, but the number killed in actual state-dissident confrontations should not detract from the seriousness with which the challengers pushed their claims or with which the relevant political authorities took such claims. Although the RNA did not receive a high degree of sensationalized attention, broadcast loudly and prominently in venues that would likely resonate widely throughout the American population, therefore, they did receive attention on a consistent basis across distinct sources, including their own.

But this distracts from the point. I maintain that what makes the RNA important is not their uniqueness but their representativeness of the time, which has largely been ignored. As with many black nationalist groups, the RNA had members who earlier participated in the civil rights movement but who also had connections with other black power groups in Detroit (e.g., UHURU and the League of Revolutionary Black Workers) as well as other parts of the United States (e.g., the Black Panthers and the Revolutionary Action Movement [RAM]). Membership drew from many parts of the African American community: teachers; phone operators; construction workers; printers; salespeople; shipping clerks; drafts people; stock clerks; pastors; postal workers; grocery clerks; messengers; lawyers; cashiers; students; electricians; taxicab, truck, and ice cream car drivers; social workers; car washers; assembly-line autoworkers; self-employed artists; and the unemployed. This type of membership was quite common throughout the United States during the period in question. Although the goals of the RNA will now seem extremely radical, at the time, many elements of their platform were shared by other organizations. For example, control over the black economy, local and neighborhood government, and participation in schools that were all black were supported by organizations like the Nation of Islam under Elijah Muhammed, Malcolm X's Organization of African American Unity (OAAU), Maulana Karenga's US organization, RAM, the Student Non-Violent Coordinating Committee under Stokely Carmichael (later Kwame Ture), and the Huey Newton faction of the Black Panther Party. Aboveground and underground activity was advocated by the All African People's Republic, OAAU, RAM, and SNCC under Ture. Indeed, it is hard to find any element of the RNA platform that did not have at least one other black nationalist organization that supported it. This said, the particular configuration of the RNA's platform was unique. No other black nationalists advocated everything that they did. Thus, while broadly capturing the sentiment at the time, they did have a somewhat different take on things – a niche, as it were.

Representative of the time (i.e., among black nationalists), the positions advocated by the RNA were not broadly representative of the black community writ large. For example, most African Americans did not overtly advocate control over the economy, participation in black-only organizations, "buying black," replacing "slave names," (names traceable to slavery and slave masters) or separating from the United States and establishing a separate nation. Some did advocate such things at relatively small percentages of the black population (e.g., 4 to 8 percent, depending on the item), but this number is not insignificant if one considers what damage small numbers of people could do. Such a number was not deemed insignificant to whites in Detroit or in Washington, D.C., during the period. This acknowledges that it only takes a few to create a problem for a nation-state. Timing is also important because the dynamics present when the RNA was around were very different from the period before it. In a sense, the black nationalists like the RNA emerged at the end of a broader conflict cycle stretching back several decades. This is important, because by the RNA period, the agencies involved in repression had largely worked out various issues with regard to policies, practices, and personnel. To address state-dissident interactions in such a context, it is important to acknowledge these issues.

The last reason for using the RNA example concerns the extensive amount of detailed material that is available about the organization and what was done against them through something that amounts to a perfect storm of data release and discovery (i.e., lawsuits, hoarding, and systematic archiving). Discussed further later, the available documentation provides an unprecedented window into both what governments have done and also what challengers have done, what they plan to do, and what they did after governments took action. Indeed, I would say that the RNA archive sits among other important historical discoveries in terms of the insights it can provide into repression and mobilization (e.g., East Germany's STASI files or Guatemala's secret police files).

Why, historically, do we know so little about the RNA? There are several reasons. First, despite the inevitable release of information concerning the group for most of its history and afterward, there was simply little that was available to those individuals who were not intricately involved with and aware of these movement organizations. Until recently, much of the trace evidence about the group and the actions taken against it was not available to the public. Indeed, to know something about the RNA, what they did, and what happened to them, one either had to have been in the organization; hailed from a particular part of Detroit; been really into the black political movement; or working with a federal, state, or local organization that had an explicit interest in radical organizations. Second, the organization did not achieve its goals. A great many challengers are never heard about again after their challenge, and these tend to be the ones who *did not* get accommodated by political authorities or receive some degree of recognition. Third, the organization was composed of African Americans, and historically radical, black social movement organizations have not been studied as much as moderate ones. Indeed, outside of the American civil rights movement, few black social movement organizations have garnered attention from researchers of conflict and contentious politics.[5] Recently, there has been a growing trend to publish about groups from the period, largely by African American scholars (e.g., Van deburg 1992; Tyson 1999; Woodard 1999, 2003; Hill 2006; Joseph 2006, 2007). Despite this attention, however, the RNA has not been one of the groups highlighted. Fourth, the RNA existed in Detroit, a city that is largely neglected in U.S. history; existing scholarship tends to focus on the East and West coasts or on the South (especially during the 1960s and 1970s), ignoring the Midwest. Fourth, the RNA engaged in a highly controversial claims-making effort not favored by whites, or by many African Americans, for that matter. As most individuals tend to study groups that they and/or others like, this would decrease the chances that they would be examined. Lastly, the group received press coverage, but not as much as the more confrontational, sensational, and overtly violent Black Panther Party. Consequently, the RNA was less likely to enter the awareness of many Americans.

Although the records of the group involved are unique in many respects, I believe that the activities of different U.S. agents documented within the records *are not unique*. The type of information available on the RNA likely exists for every challenging organization that has existed after the development

---

[5] A targeted Google search on "the civil rights movement" reveals approximately 5.5 million hits, whereas a search on "the black power movement" reveals approximately 700,000. Obviously not definitive, this is suggestive of the varied importance of the two.

of modern government record keeping protocol (post–World War II or I). For example, numerous scholars have revealed that the U.S. government in particular (e.g., Goldstein 1978; Donner 1980; Cunningham 2004; Davenport 2005) and other political authorities in other countries (e.g., Koehler 1999; Cohen 2010) have engaged in significant surveillance of groups that challenge them. Accordingly, all these sources reveal that the government tracks who is involved with behavioral challenges, what they do, when they do it, and why, as well as what is done against them. Most of these records are not known to the public, however, and thus what they reveal about social movement organizations as well as the governments who track and attack them has largely been left undisclosed.

The situation of data impoverishment is no longer the case with the RNA.[6] Through a series of lawsuits, donations, disclosures, and other means, several thousand documents were obtained and are now housed at my Radical Information Project,[7] a depository of information regarding contentious politics and conflict processes. This has provided unparalleled access to the daily inner workings of the social movement organization and insight into what influenced the organization's activity as well as its demobilization. Discussed in greater detail subsequently, these records give us the necessary information to ascertain what influence, if any, repression has independent of and in conjunction with internal social movement dynamics.

Outline

Acknowledging that people might be interested in this book for a variety of different reasons and drawn to it from very distinct orientations, I have tried to accommodate these differences as much as possible. As a result, it is possible (and even suggested) for individuals to read selections, focusing on the particular components in which they are most interested.

For example, with political scientists and sociologists in mind, as well as those interested in the theoretical arguments generally used to understand social movement demobilization, I begin in Chapter 1 with an evaluation of the influences that emerge from outside *or* inside the relevant social movement organization. In Chapter 2, I suggest that demobilization is best understood through the simultaneous intersection of external *and* internal explanations. This work would also be of interest to the same group identified earlier.

Principally for people interested in political science, sociology, and history (American as well as African American, concerned with repression, counterinsurgency or terrorism, civil liberties restriction, and human rights violation,

---

[6] A few organizational records have been comparably well recovered. For example, consider the archive concerning monitoring of the Student Nonviolent Coordinating Committee in the United States or the STASI's records in Germany.

[7] This is accessible at http://www.radicalinformationproject.com.

investigated at local, regional, and national levels), Chapter 3 describes the U.S. government's general approach to dissidents in the late 1960s and early 1970s as well as the specific tactics used against African Americans in Detroit. Chapter 4 presents information for those interested in the diverse source material used to document, analyze, and understand the internal workings of the RNA and the state repression used against them. Such information should appeal to those interested in rigorously examining social movements, mobilization, and overt and covert repression as well as the process and politics of information and data generation. The chapter is important because it identifies not only what governments collected and why but also what the media as well as RNA themselves collected. One might consider such topics dated in the world of blogs, tweets, and Instagram postings, but even in an age where increasing attention is being given to social media and machine coding, there will still be interest with what can be done with complex archival material – what some are now calling "big data." For historians of civil rights, black power and nationalism, those interested in the origins and dynamics of black nationalist organizations, or those generally interested in mobilization, Chapters 5 and 6 take us from the first organization created by the individuals involved in what would become the RNA up through the founding of the RNA. I do this to situate the subsequent detailed evaluations of organizational emergence, dynamics, and termination. Such an approach is intentional because I maintain that one cannot simply begin a discussion of black nationalist social movement organizations, or any social movement organization for that matter, with the first day that they had members, for this does not address how they mobilized, how they think about topics in general and repression in particular, who their members are, and how much trust is held between them at the outset. Such a starting point is also bad for understanding state repressive practices, as these are generally established before the specific challenging institution comes into formal existence – modified accordingly to fit the situation. One must begin a little before the beginning and move from there.

Chapters 7 through 11 present detailed micro- and meso-level examinations of the five periods in RNA history identified previously. Within each, I discuss the two-month period leading up to the event discussed, noting individuals, institutions, ideas, and interventions (or behavior) undertaken by the RNA. I then discuss the event of interest and conclude by discussing the subsequent two-month period, noting changes in individuals, institutions, ideas, and interventions as well as whether and in what way repression and/or internal dynamics explain what occurred. These chapters should appeal to political scientists, sociologists, and historians, among others.

In the conclusion, I reflect on the specific death of the RNA. I also address the implications of existing research for students of state-dissident interactions, outlining research questions and methodological suggestions for future investigations. These insights should be of interest to those focused on understanding social movement organizations, state repression, human rights violation, counterterrorism and insurgency, and state-dissident interactions, and how such topics can be examined.

Before leaving, I wish to offer a brief disclaimer. To be clear on what will be found here, this book is focused on understanding why and how a group of individuals who created and/or joined the RNA continued in this effort over time (i.e., it is about their survival as an independent challenging institution). Accordingly, I am not interested in understanding black nationalism writ large (e.g., Joseph 2006, 2007; Dawson 2013); in exploring differences between or within federal, state, and local authorities in their repression of the group (see Goldstein 1978; Cunningham 2004); or with nationalism generally conceived (e.g., see Brubaker 1996). While deemed interesting and worthy of attention, these topics are beyond the scope of the current research, and some quality research, referenced earlier, achieves these objectives quite well.

PART I

THEORY

I

Killing Social Movements from the Outside *or* the Inside

When we contemplate what we know about why social movement organizations (SMOs) are ended, we have to acknowledge rather quickly that we have just begun to scratch the surface on the topic (e.g., Edwards and Marullo 1995; Klandermans 1997; Nepstad 2004). As Koopmans (2004, 26) correctly summarized, "to date, the explanation of protest decline is perhaps the weakest chain in social movement theory and research." Part of the reason for the difficulty in addressing the topic is that different scholars in sociology and political science use different labels to refer to the same phenomenon or, at least, seemingly related phenomena, for example, "decline" and "contraction" (Koopmans 2004), "(dis)continuity" (Taylor 1989), "termination" (Downton and Wehr 1991), "disbanding" (Minkoff 1993), "demobilization" (Edwards and Marullo 1995; Weinstein 2007; Humphreys and Weinstein 2007), "decay" (Jenkins 1998), "outcome" (Brandt et al. 2008; Lyall and Wilson 2008), "mortality" and "survival" (Edwards and Marullo 2004), and "decapitation" (e.g., Byman 2006; Cronin 2006; Jaeger and Paserman 2009; Jordan 2010; Price 2010).

I prefer the label *demobilization*, and I will use this to refer to (1) official termination and/or significant alteration of the formal *institution* engaged in challenging authorities; (2) departure of *individuals* (members) from relevant organizations – especially the founding and/or core members that participate most frequently; (3) termination of or significant reduction in dissident *interventions* (behaviors); and (4) a fundamental shift in the *ideas* of the challenger (particularities of the claim) away from what was earlier established. Although any of these on its own signals demobilization, normally several are present at the same time. In this chapter, I discuss the more prominent explanations of social movement demobilization and the results of rigorous investigations into the topic.

Understanding Demobilization

Given my preceding definition of demobilization, it is clear that there are several ways that this may come about. Many of these are connected with the idea of movement "success" (i.e., achieving new advantages to the SMO and/or getting acceptance by elites as spokespersons for a cause) (e.g., Gamson 1975; Button 1978; Steedly and Foley 1979; Goldstone 1980; Frey et al. 1992; Giugni 1998). For example, a formal SMO might be terminated and its members might leave when dissident behavior ends and/or goals are no longer pursued because it is believed that the claims-making effort has been accommodated and/or incorporated into the existing political economy.[1] In short, winning (even partially) ends the need for SMOs, and thus, in its wake, claims making as well as claims makers go away. It is important to understand that I am not interested in demobilizations of this nature – what we might refer to as *positive demobilization*. Rather, I am interested in those in which the relevant SMO is generally believed to have collapsed or imploded (because of internal reasons) or was significantly hindered or exploded (because of external reasons). Specifically, I am interested in SMOs that are essentially killed, which I refer to as *negative demobilization*.

My guiding assumption is that all four components of demobilization (institutions, individuals, interventions, and ideas) are necessary to have a social movement. Without an institution, the efforts that did exist would be less organized, less stable, and less sustainable. Without individuals, there would be no one to engage in anything at all. Without dissident interventions, there would be nothing to compel the powers that be to change their ideas, policies, practices, and institutions. Finally, without ideas, there would be no claims, goals, or direction regarding how the designated objectives could be achieved. Another guiding assumption is that the focal point of countermobilization has been the challenging organization and the behavior undertaken by its members. Consequently, I am most focused here. This is because governments seem to acknowledge that there will always be individuals dissatisfied with the status quo. They also seem to acknowledge that subversive ideas will exist that (if realized) would fundamentally alter the status quo. These are generally viewed as the price of doing business as a nation-state. When these individuals and ideas are brought into an institutional context, however, and they begin to engage in collective action, this is where threats are really posed and government action is likely.

Considering what has been written on demobilization, existing research generally takes us in two directions: (1) SMOs are killed from outside, with a

---

[1] The expectations of social movement demobilization are not uniformly supported here. For example, work on terrorism suggests that government concessions initially increase violence because the accommodative policy satisfies only the moderates in the SMO, prompting those left within the movement (the radicals) to increase their use of violent activity (Bueno de Mesquita 2005). This is similar in nature to the dynamics Della Porta (1995) discussed.

focus on things that exist external to dissident organizations, and (2) SMOs are killed from inside, with a focus on things that exist internally to dissidents and their institutions (for an early and influential example on this line of inquiry, see Zald and Ash 1966).[2] A third explanation sits at the intersection of these two, however, part of the larger "organizational turn" in the study of social movement organizations (e.g., Davis et al. 2005; Connable and Libicki 2010; McLaughlin and Pearlman 2012). Each is discussed before moving to my extension of the last, which is undertaken in the chapter that follows.

Although I discuss several ways that SMO death could be brought about from the outside, I especially focus on state repression as a strategy for killing social movement organizations (i.e., protest policing and counterterrorism/insurgency). There are several reasons for this: (1) the state's use of repressive behavior and its impact on social movement organizations are core aspects of the modern nation-state; (2) repression is one of the most common responses used by governments against those that challenge them, and a significant amount of scholarly, popular, journalistic, and government attention has been directed toward this subject, but despite this attention, little is known about its influence; and (3) repressive behavior is a form of state activity believed to be worthy of detailed identification and examination. Let us discuss the full range of alternatives before focusing our attention.

Killing from the Outside

It is commonly believed that some force or combination of forces emerging outside of the dissident organization of interest is responsible for the challengers' demise. Exactly which factors are involved, how they contribute to ending social movement organizations, and just what existing evidence tells us is the subject of much debate. In the following, I discuss three factors that vary with regard to the clarity of their connection with demobilization, the amount of attention that has been given to them, and the amount of empirical support the arguments have received. The first two (resource deprivation and problem depletion) have not been the focus of explicit, detailed, systematic analyses, but they have been examined in a wide variety of cases. The third (state repression) has been examined quite frequently in a rigorous manner; unfortunately, this has not improved our understanding of its impact on SMO death.

Resource Deprivation
One of the most obvious explanations for movement demobilization is the systematic hindering of SMO efforts to generate the human and financial resources

---

[2] Interestingly, this piece lists many of the factors that I highlight, but they ignore two issues: (1) state repression and (2) that the two factors can intersect to influence movement organizations. The first point is countered by later literature, whereas the second has not been dealt with in any substantively important way.

necessary to continue engaging in challenging behavior (e.g., Jenkins 1983; Galaskiewicz 1984; Haines 1984; Minkoff 1993; Tarrow 1994; Edwards and Marullo 1995; Cress and Snow 1996; Weinstein 2006).[3] Drawing explicitly on work concerned with resource mobilization (e.g., Oberschall 1973; McCarthy and Zald 1977; McAdam 1982; Jenkins and Ekert 1986), this argument maintains that whereas the desire for protest is more or less constant, the resources available for such behavior vary. When resources can be found, SMOs will flourish.[4] With them, dissidents can pay rent; travel; offer decent salaries, training, seminars, and workshops; obtain equipment, food, and medicine; and engage in a wide range of dissident activities, such as strikes, demonstrations, petitions, sit-ins, teach-outs, terrorism, guerilla warfare, and insurgency. When resources are difficult to come by, however, then SMOs are more likely to demobilize.[5] Unable to pay rent, they are evicted; unable to travel, they miss meetings and training; unable to offer salaries, they never hire or fail to retain valuable members; unable to acquire equipment, they are outgunned.

While existing research across a variety of behavioral challenges is attentive to the fact that resources are crucial to the continuity of an SMO, it is less attentive to the fact that those controlling the purse strings have something of a stranglehold over dissident organizations. As a result, there have been no efforts to systematically examine resource allocation from the perspective of those actors directly trying to control social movement organizations, and few attempts have been made to identify the specific circumstances under which SMOs acquire resources.[6]

Perhaps one of the only consistent findings relevant to the topic of interest that has been explored is that moderate SMOs (aimed at reform and nondisplacement of leaders) are likely to receive resources from funding organizations, such as government agencies. For example, in an examination of financial support to black activists during the American civil rights movement, Haines (1984) shows that when "radical" black organizations emerged and/or engaged in dissident behavior, large amounts of resources were directed to the more "moderate" wings of the civil rights movement. This presumably allowed the latter to continue to exist while compelling the former to demobilize under the strain of daily existence. Unfortunately, Haines is content with identifying the distribution of resources and then speculating about the resource holders'

---

[3] Cress and Snow (1996) provide a useful list of the different types of resources that exist.

[4] Now, one may argue about whether resource acquisition is a measure of success (Giugni 1998, 13), but clearly resources are necessary for continuity.

[5] A different but related argument concerns organizational ecology (Dimaggio and Powell 1983; Hannan and Freeman 1989). Here it is maintained that "organizational characteristics that improve a group's legitimacy [being able to convince powerful actors about the validity of what is being done] ... [improve] its bargaining position and continued activity" (Minkoff 1993, 888).

[6] Most efforts are indirect. For example, Minkoff (1993) argues that reform-oriented SMOs are more likely to be supported. This degree of support, however, is not explicitly part of her model. Others maintain similar types of assumptions.

motivations. He made no effort to understand how or why resource holders determined which SMOs could survive and which should be pushed toward the dustbin of history.

Similarly, in their classic study of American farmers, Jenkins and Perrow (1977) note that the general successfulness of SMOs is connected to their sustained ability to generate outside support. Again, this obscures the control and debilitating effect of the external actors. There is no attempt to identify those who wish to control behavioral challenges, what they would find acceptable, and how they would manipulate resource allocations to get there. In a sense, one is left drawing one's own conclusion.

Perhaps Piven and Cloward's (1979) seminal work comes closest to acknowledging the problems of reliance on external support and the use of this support to control claims making.[7] These authors note that the more centralized, stable, and reform minded an SMO is, the weaker it becomes, because it is rendered more susceptible to the influence of those who control the means of resource allocation. Tied to external support, activists become unable to push for what needs to be done in a manner deemed appropriate.

Recent scholarship on the interdiction of funding for terrorists is definitely in line with the resource deprivation approach to killing movement organizations (e.g., Gunaratna 2000; Lee 2002; Barron 2004; Council on Foreign Relations 2002; Pieth 2006). For example, focusing on the use of external funding by al-Qaeda, one report identifies that

as long as Al-Qaeda retains access to a viable financial network, it remains a lethal threat to the United States... It raises money from a variety of sources and moves money in a variety of manners. It runs businesses operating under the cloak of legitimacy and criminal conspiracies ranging from the petty to the grand. The most important source of Al-Qaeda's money, however, is its continuous fund-raising efforts. (Council on Foreign Relations 2002, 1)

The implications of the work here are clear for those wishing to "kill" the relevant challenge: identify and cut the purse strings of supporters as well as the way that al-Qaeda gets money, and the challengers will at a minimum be severely damaged and maximally eliminated entirely.

Similar attention has been given to rebel insurgencies and the topic of "lootable" resources as well as illegal trade (Collier 2003). For example, numerous revolutionary groups fund their activities through drug-related profits. Such groups have included but are not limited to the Nineteenth of April Movement (M-19; Colombia), the Burmese Communist Party (Golden Triangle area of Southeast Asia), the Contras (Nicaragua), the ETA Basque separatists (Spain), Moslem *mujaheddin* (Afghanistan), and the Tamils (Sri Lanka).

---

[7] For a decent discussion about different examinations of Piven and Cloward's argument, see Giugni (1998).

A different but related tale is offered by Weinstein (2005). Within his examination of various cases, according to Ron (2005, 448),

he finds that insurgents can ... suffer from a resource curse, chiefly in their recruitment efforts. Rebellions blessed with plentiful resources are flooded with low-quality, opportunistic recruits seeking easy gain, and many of these fit the "rebel as criminal" profile. Poor insurgencies, by contrast, mobilize support by relying on an entirely different type of recruit, including individuals with more education, ideological commitment, and ethnic solidarity. As a result, these tend to be more effective and disciplined rebel forces.

Paradoxically, in this case, those interested in killing social movement organizations have an interest in not blocking extremely successful dissident resource acquisition: poorer insurgents are more likely to put up more of a struggle and be more careful about everything that they do, including fighting more efficiently.

Regardless of the inconsistency with which the holders and distributors of resources are addressed and the frequently limited way that relevant connections are examined, the point still remains that numerous government leaders, SMOs, nongovenmental organizations, and scholars believe that the fate of an SMO is in part determined by the good graces of someone external to the movement who supports it. In this argument, the life and death of a social movement are determined by outsiders giving (or not giving).

Problem Depletion

Whereas the key to resource deprivation is to starve an SMO by withholding much needed support, the key to problem depletion lies in removing (1) the perceived need for the movement and/or (2) the perceived relevance of the claims-making effort within the relevant population (e.g., Blaufarb 1977; Joseph 2007; Berman 2008; Biddle 2008; Fitzsimmons 2008). In the first case (decreasing need), to kill a movement, somewhat similar to resource deprivation, one would keep resources away from challengers. In the second (decreasing movement support), one would eliminate the challenger's reason for existence. Again, there are diverse paths to these ends and variable levels as well as qualities of research on the topic.

For example, one can view the creation, support, and perceived success of moderate SMOs as a mechanism of problem depletion as it communicates to more radical challengers as well as their supporters that no other claims-making effort is necessary to address a specific issue (McCarthy and Zald 1977; Meyer and Rowan 1977; Hannan and Freeman 1989; Elsbach and Sutton 1992; Suchman 1995). Through propaganda and "soft repression" (Churchill and Vander Wall 1988; Ferree 2005), governments can try to convince individuals that there is no problem or that the challengers are intricately connected with its continuation. It is possible that the challenger wins and takes over the government by force. In both cases, the very weight of a problem is diminished as those most likely to benefit from the success of the SMO in question come to believe that they have someone working on their behalf. Such a belief removes the likelihood that other citizens would join and/or support the particular challenger or a different SMO as the issue has already been somewhat depleted and it would not be worth the effort. In a sense, the logic is, "If it's broken but someone is working on it, don't rock the boat further." This plays directly to the self-interested motivations generally presumed to work within collective action problems where the general predisposition is to free ride on others (e.g., Olson 1965; Lichbach 1995).

A variant on this theme is to create and support "front" SMOs (i.e., organizations that actually represent the status quo's interest but that maintain the veneer of a challenger) so that they can compete with the organization that is believed to be problematic or threatening.[8] This makes it seem as if the relevant problem will never be addressed because of the inefficiency and violent nature of the dissident organization that was the initial target (i.e., the one now caught up with fighting other SMOs). The outcome of this is that it appears that the problem just needs to be lived through, that collective action is not possible, and the social movement does not gain any adherents.

Although I suggested earlier that I was not interested in actual movement success, it is clear that the perception of success or, more likely, moving in that direction could have the same impact. Here, speeches, meetings, the establishment of committees, investigatory panels, and the like from political representatives (which Gamson 1975 would call "accommodation") could serve as mechanisms of problem depletion. Alternatively, it just might be the presence of other SMOs dealing with the same or similar problems (e.g., Minkoff 1993, 1999; Soule and King 2008). Again, this approach reduces the likelihood that citizens would join and/or support an SMO because it would not seem necessary.[9]

Perhaps the area of research most relevant to the problem depletion approach is that associated with counterinsurgency (CI). According to one review of this work,

if all (the) principles (of CI) were reduced to a single central theme it would be that success and failure depends [*sic*] on the resolution of the political conflicts underlying the military hostilities. According to this line of reasoning, the application of military force is not nearly as efficacious as in more conventional warfare. Rather, the contest between insurgents and counterinsurgents is seen as a competition for the prevailing sympathies of the noncombatant populations where conflict is taking place. In one of the classic works of this literature, Mao Tse-tung famously observed that the relationship between insurgents and the broader population in which they operate is akin to fish and water,

---

[8] The FBI created numerous organizations during the 1960s with this objective in mind, and more recently, there is the case of "astro turf" organizations, that is, concerning the identity of who sponsors a political message.

[9] This is plausible, but its operationalization is highly problematic, as one would need to ascertain the sincerity of the actor or action as well as the potential for and reality of change.

such that guerrilla warfare basically derives from the masses and is supported by them, it can neither exist nor flourish if it separates itself from their sympathies and cooperation. (Fitzsimmons 2008, 2)

The key to winning confrontations thus resides in winning the hearts and minds of the relevant population or, in Mao's conception, "draining the sea" so that guerillas have nowhere to swim or hide.[10]

With this in mind, one path to problem depletion is a war of words or propaganda. In this case, ordinary citizens and government opponents are bombarded with information indicating that they should not support challengers and that the dissidents are losing the confrontation, generally suffering amazing losses along the way to this conclusion. A different variant of this theme proposes that one of the keys to winning the hearts and minds is to provide some measure of "good governance" (Fitzsimmons 2008). Bard O'Neill (cited in Blaufarb 1977, 171–72) is clear on this point when he argues,

Popular support [for insurgency] from the elites and especially the masses stems primarily from concrete grievances concerning such things as land reform, injustice, unfair taxation, and corruption. It is over these issues that the battle to win hearts and minds is most directly enjoined. History suggests that a government can most effectively undercut insurgencies that rely on mass support by splitting the rank and file away from the leadership through calculated reforms that address the material grievances and needs of the people.

In short, meet the needs of the people (or enough of the population), and their perception of the need for behavioral challenges and challengers will be gutted.

Of course, this presumes something about the nature of the behavioral challenge. As Biddle (2008, 348) discussed, some work

assumes that insurgencies represent a contest for the loyalty of a mostly uncommitted general public that could side with either the government or the insurgents; success requires persuading this uncommitted public to side with the government by winning their hearts and minds via provision of superior goods and services, including government-supplied security.

To the degree that this fits the case, problem depletion will be quite effective. To the degree that this is not the case, however, and the public is already committed, problem depletion will not kill SMOs.

---

[10] Interestingly, in work more directly relevant to social movements, one could apply a certain version of identity theory in a similar manner (e.g., Stryker 2000). For example, a government could attempt to construct an identity (of a citizen) such that any effort to challenge the collectivity (the state) would result in the challenger as well as those associated with him or her (1) shunning, ostracizing, or exiling them from sociopolitical relations; (2) prompting others to treat them with derision and distrust; and (3) compelling them to stay loyal or at least appear this way.

State Repression

Finally, we come to those coercive actions undertaken by political authorities directed against someone challenging their beliefs, institutions, and actions or the context or conditions within which the government exists. Interestingly, the work on SMO demobilization identified previously (at least that which examines the topic systematically) has essentially ignored the importance of this factor. Indeed, I am only aware of one study of SMO survival where a measure of state repression was included (Soule and King 2008). Within this work, the authors employed a summary score concerning the presence of the police at movement events during a particular year. The motivation for including this variable was clearly in line with the preceding discussion. Repressive behavior was believed to have a debilitating impact on the subsequent existence of the SMO (i.e., imposing costs of a wide variety – hindering resource acquisition and recruiting through bans and beatings), with those subject to it folding under pressure. This impact, however, was not supported by the empirical investigation.

In political science and sociology research concerned with the influence of repression on dissent, commonly referred to as the *conflict-repression nexus* (Lichbach 1987), more attention has been given to the topic over time, but there has been a shift. In the conflict-repression nexus, the concern is generally with the dissidents' ability to engage in protest and not with sustaining the formal existence of a dissident organization. It is useful to address this research explicitly, for it offers the best insight into what students of conflict believe resides at the core of understanding the impact of repression on challenges and challengers.

One of the oldest arguments of the conflict-repression nexus maintains that repressive action increases the degree of fear experienced by dissidents as they generally do not want to be subject to harassment, beatings, arrest, torture, and/or death (e.g., Olson 1965). In an effort to avoid such actions, dissidents do what would most likely reduce the possibility of such an experience: they withdraw from the social movement organization and avoid all behaviors, individuals, and ideas that would prompt the undesirable outcome. Here *repression kills a movement.*

Not everyone accepts the negative influence of repression on dissidents and dissent, highlighting instead the importance of anger (e.g., Gurr 1970). In this context, repressive action does not provoke fear within those subject to it. Rather, it provokes anger within the targeted group as dissidents believe that the government's activity is unjust. After all, the challengers are merely trying to be heard on a particular grievance, and for that they are subject to yet another abuse, another grievance. This compounded injustice (an insult after an injury or an injury after an injury) provokes anger and an increase in dissident behavior as the targeted seek to strike back. Of course, this could provoke additional repressive action, which then sends the conflict into an upward spiral until one of the actors is vanquished – normally the dissident challenger, if history is consulted. In this view, *repression breathes new life into a movement*, at least for a while.

Somewhat more complex arguments exist where researchers allow for both fear and anger to exist, but generally not at the same time. For example, identifying an inverted-U-shaped relationship, some researchers maintain that at low and high values of repression, those subject to coercive government action are not bothered by its application in a negative sense but become enraged by the consistent application, and dissent is increased. At middle-range values (which suggests inconsistency in state coercion), those subject to repressive action are scared off because it is not quite clear what is going to happen. Here the effect of repression on dissent varies depending on the magnitude of the repressive behavior itself.

Others step away from the emotional factors highlighted earlier and maintain that repression compels dissidents to reflect on their experience and evaluate whether their approach is effective at achieving the desired outcome (e.g., Lichbach 1987; Moore 1998, 2000; Francisco 2004; Pierskalla 2009). Here, when subjected to repressive activity, challengers generally conclude that the act provoking government coercion is ineffective, and in response, the challenging behavior most closely tied with is decreased and other forms are increased. Here repression kills some aspects of a movement but breathes life into different aspects.[11]

Still other researchers maintain that targeting repression more precisely can result in the end of social movement activity (e.g., Mason and Krane 1989; Kalyvas 2006). Here, when government coercion is specifically targeted against dissidents directly, it is likely to lead to demobilization, as those subject to the coercion are scared off, imprisoned, or killed and newer recruits are less likely drawn to the movement. In this context, fear generally works as suggested in the first explanation for SMO demise, with the only difference being that the locus of the fear being discussed is shifted from dissidents to ordinary citizens and potential recruits. Here it is assumed that those who are not targeted will avoid situations where they could be targeted. This argument says essentially nothing about those already engaged in the challenging institution, but it can be concluded that without popular support, challengers are not likely to continue for very long, or at least are not likely to be successful in overthrowing the government and compelling authorities to concede to their demands without popular support.

In contrast, when repression is diffusely targeted against seemingly anyone who might be associated with the relevant SMO, then ordinary citizens are more inclined to cast their lot with the challengers so that they can get some measure of protection from the fear-inspiring state (Kalyvas 2006). In this case, fear is not paralytic but is instead provocative, compelling ordinary citizens to

---

[11] Note that this says nothing about altering the desired objective; it merely addresses the issue of not being sanctioned in some way.

join an SMO. With the influx of new members, it is expected that the SMO and its behavior could continue. It is not clear if this would lead to an increase in dissident behavior or simply a continuation of whatever level was previously undertaken. Regardless, as a result of diffuse targeting, *repression (again) kills specific aspects of a movement while breathing life into others.*[12]

Relative to the two explanations for social movement termination discussed earlier, the impact of repression on dissent has been examined the most consistently as well as the most thoroughly across space, time, contexts, and measures. At the same time, however, as I identify within quantitative work principally based in political science (Davenport 2007, 8),

the results [of this research] are highly inconsistent. Sometimes the impact of repression on dissent is negative (Hibbs 1973); sometimes it is positive (Francisco 1996, Lichbach & Gurr 1981, Ziegenhagen 1986); sometimes it is represented by an inverted U-shape (Muller 1985); sometimes it is alternatively negative or positive (Gupta and Venieris 1981, Moore 1998; Rasler 1996); and sometimes it is nonexistent (Gurr and Moore 1997).

Reviews of both quantitative and qualitative work based more in sociology make similar comments, revealing greater complexity (Hess and Martin 2006, 250–51). Integrating quantitative, qualitative, and theoretical scholarship in political science and sociology, Ortiz (2007, 219–20) captures well the interdisciplinary confusion, noting that

proponents of resource mobilization and political opportunities theories suggest that repression is a key determinant of political violence, since rebellious groups in the context of high repression are restricted in their ability to mobilize for collective action of any kind, and may be severely penalized for trying to do so (Eisinger 1973; McAdam 1982, 1996; McAdam, Tarrow, and Tilly 1996; Tarrow 1989). This proposition is frequently tested with the inverted-U hypothesis, where moderate regimes experience the highest levels of collective violence, while regimes with low levels of repression do not motivate violence and highly repressive regimes render mobilization difficult (Fein 1995; King 1998; Muller 1985; Regan and Henderson 2002).

Other scholars argue quite the opposite, that intense repression actually ignites collective violence (Carey 2006; Einwohner 2003; Francisco 1996; Khawaja 1993; Kurzman 1996; Lichbach 1987; Loveman 1998; Mason and Krane 1989; Moore 1998; Olivier 1991; Rasler 1996; Weede 1987). These studies suggest that people resort to desperate solutions when they are in desperate situations. As Gartner and Regan (1996, 278) suggest, "too much repression might leave the opposition little alternative to revolt." The backlash hypothesis, however,

---

[12] The difference between selective and indiscriminate violence is largely attributed to state capacity. If governments have the resources and knowledge to identify challengers, then they will do so. If they do not, then they will not. Informing the targeting discussion, however, capacity is not really addressed in the rest of the literature relevant to state repression and its impact on political challengers or challenges.

has found only mixed empirical support. The hypothesis seems to work well in some cases but not in others (see Lee et al. 2000).

Relatively recent theoretical developments (Goldstone and Tilly 2001; Goodwin 2001; White 1989) suggest that the capacity of the state to effectively repress and to pose a significant threat to protesters might be the key to determining why some revolts are defused by mounting repression, whereas others seem inflamed by it. Following this principle, few studies show that effective perception of strong military power directly affects political repression (e.g., Davenport 1996), but such studies generally do not test the military's influence on collective political violence. Therefore, amid varying contexts, methodological approaches, and model specifications, different findings abound.

Killing from the Inside

Up to this point, I have focused on explanations for SMO demobilization that originate outside of dissident organizations. I have tried to identify exactly what was involved (i.e., how a specific environmental factor influenced SMOs, who engaged in relevant activity, and what motivations lay behind it) and what existing research into the relevant factors revealed about possible influences (i.e., how frequently dynamics were analyzed and whether the hypothesized relationship was supported).

Although it was important to identify how dissident organizations could be killed from outside the relevant institution, it is clear that movement organizations could be demobilized from inside as well. As is clear from the discussion, the reasons for internally oriented SMO death vary significantly, as does the frequency with which these issues have been considered and exactly what has received empirical support. Unlike the work on external influences, however, the work on internal influences does not contain any efforts that explicitly and rigorously examine relevant factors across cases, time, methodologies, and measurements. Mostly what are found are theoretical arguments and/or single case studies, which are not up to the same standards of investigation. From this research, five factors are commonly identified: burnout, factionalization or polarization, lost commitment, membership loss, and rigidity. Each is discussed in what follows.

Burnout
One of the most frequently identified issues with regard to internal demobilization of a social movement organization concerns the fact that dissidents often become weary of the conversations, arguments, deprivations, and lost opportunities involved with SMOs – that is, the daily grind of social struggle (Klandermans 1997; Carson 1981; Poletta 2002). In a sense, those engaged in SMOs become burned out and decide to disengage from the life of a challenger in an effort to escape the stresses of participation and to recover economically, physically, and psychologically.

The reasons seem straightforward enough. As Klandermans's (1997, 103) examination of labor activists reveals,

being a union activist is a time-consuming job. On average activists spend 4 hours a week (half of it on their free time, half of it their working time) on their union, and a fair proportion even 5–10 hours a week. It is not only a time-consuming job, it is also stressful. Union activists can get caught between many fires, company management, union officials, members, colleagues, spouses. As a consequence, many of them report overload and role conflicts. One-third to half of the activists feel that they have more tasks than they can manage. Half to two-thirds report conflicting expectations from their employers and their unions. A quarter to one-third experience contradictory demands from their colleagues, fellow-activists, or constituencies. Yet, interestingly, these are not sufficient reason to quit. But, for some activists such stressful experiences produce burnout and burnout *is* a reason to step down.

Of course, Klandermans (1997, 104) then goes on to reveal that we do not really know much about burnout and how it works. Indeed, it is possible that people build strong social ties that close them off from the outside world, which makes leaving the SMO problematic. Understanding of this process has not improved that much over time, as few have attempted to pick up where he left off, but the insight from the argument noted earlier is nevertheless clear: challenging political authority is difficult, and after a while, most engaged in such behavior will just get fed up and quit. Here *social movement organizations kill social movement organizations*.

Factionalization or Polarization

Some research relevant to internal demobilization highlights the process of factionalization, noting that dissident members sometimes hit a point beyond which they refuse to go – at least collectively (e.g., Hirsch 1986, 1990; Nepstad 2004; Pearlman 2008–9). In this work, there are various reasons for this development. For instance, there may be a difference of opinion regarding the objectives being pursued (revolution or reform) or the tactics employed to get there (violence or nonviolence). Here dissidents find that they can no longer work within the confines of the existing SMO, and they decide to pull out.[13] While this often signals the birth of a new organization, it also signals the death of another. The major difference between factionalization and burnout concerns differences in the former's emphasis on contrasting opinion about *how* to engage in dissent, whereas burnout concerns differences with regard to engaging in challenges *at all*.

Clearly factionalization is a problem endemic to social movement organizations. Within all SMOs, there is a group of strong-willed individuals who believe that through their direct engagement, they can change some aspect of

---

[13] For example, Lahoud (2010) finds something similar with regard to splintering for doctrinal reasons.

the world and that the SMO is in conflict with another party (generally the government) that they see as being hell bent on stopping them. Given this context, it makes sense that at some point, all of this could result in a conflict within the dissident organization about what needs to be done as contexts change. Related to this, examining Columbia student protestors Hirsch (1990, 245) find that

polarization is often seen as a problem since it convinces each side that their position is right and the opponent's is wrong; this makes compromise and negotiation less likely (Coleman 1957). Since it leads each side to develop the independent goal of harming the opponent, movement participants may lose sight of their original goal.

The confidence with and manner in which SMO participants hold their positions and their willingness to stand up to those that disagree with them suggests that having once been polarized, it is possible for them to be polarized again. As the group had the interest and ability to create one organization, one should not be surprised if they do it another time.

Now, this deviates from our common conception of how social movement organizations function and generally makes them seem a bit less firm, fixed, or stable. However, it likely reflects reality more closely, especially for activism for which risks and emotional content are much higher. As Gupta (2002, 1–2) argues,

regardless of elite rhetoric that creates an image of a cohesive, resolute people united in their aims and desires, this creation of "hard" boundaries around the perimeter of (an SMO) at most minimizes or distracts from potential internal cleavages that might exist within that group (Barth 1969; Brass 1994; Duara 1996). In fact, nationalist movements (as but one form of challenge) are rarely, if ever, homogenous and internally cohesive; among other possible cleavages, nationalist movements and organizations often fragment internally along radical and moderate lines over what constitutes appropriate means and desirable ends (Tarrow 1998). A quick survey of regional nationalist organizations in Western Europe, for example, reveals that in many cases, two or more groups compete to carry the banner of the nation, with those groups split on matters of tactics, goals, and degree of bargaining flexibility over ultimate aims (Müller-Rommel 1994; Lynch 1998). If we broaden the focus to include not just formal organizations, like political parties, but include other kinds of social movement organizations, such as interest groups, cultural associations, university clubs, youth groups, and terrorist cells, the picture that emerges is one of considerable complexity and diversity, with groups taking up positions all along a moderate-radical spectrum.

With such an understanding, this shifts our attention from how movement organizations are able to engage in dissent to how they are able to keep themselves together long enough to engage in dissident behavior. Unfortunately (again), we know very little about factionalization (for newer insights, see Wood 2003; Weinstein 2007; Pearlman 2008–9; Cunningham 2011), how it develops, and what factors are associated with it. As Gupta (2002, 2) is quick to note, despite the common occurrence of radical/moderate splits...there have been few systematic attempts to study their political effects, particularly on the goals, tactics, and success rates of different organizations in disparate movement environments...Few studies do more than document the possible sources of intra-movement fissure.

Nearly a decade later, things have not changed much.

Lost Commitment

In their consideration of social movement demobilization, some researchers highlight the impact of lost commitment whereby group members lose their emotional attachment to the SMO, no longer fear the cost of departing, and no longer feel a moral obligation to continue in the struggle (e.g., Allen and Meyer 1990; Meyer and Allen 1991; Downton and Wehr 1991; Edwards and Marullo 1995; Klandermans 1997; Nepstad 2004). With diminished commitment, the risks and forgone opportunities of continued engagement become unacceptable, leading to withdrawal from the movement institution.

Like all of the other internally oriented mechanisms of social movement organization death, this one also emerges from dissident engagement with SMOs. Exactly what is expected, however, varies by the aspect of commitment that one is considering. Returning to Klandermans (1997, 97), it is argued that

affective commitment more than...other...dimensions seems to be dependent on interactions with the organization one is a member of. The more satisfactory their interactions are, the stronger the affective commitment. Therefore, attempts to make contacts with the movement more satisfactory are instrumental to the maintenance of affective commitment. Continuance commitment is dependent on investments made and the perceived attractiveness of alternatives: The more members have invested and the less attractive alternatives appear to them, the stronger their continuance commitment will be. Therefore, sacrifices required from members or other attempts to increase members' investments, derogation of alternatives, and attempts to convince members of the superiority of their own organization are ways to maintain continuance commitment. Normative commitment depends on long term processes of socialization. There is little a movement organization can do in terms of influencing processes of long term socialization, but through frame alignment (Snow et al. 1986) it can try to increase the degree of congruence between the values of the organization and those of the individual.

Again, there is a difference here from burnout that is worthy of mention. Commitment concerns a connection to a belief structure as opposed to burnout, which simply refers to exhaustion from continual engagement in seemingly mundane activities. To lose commitment to a cause, belief, calling, or idea is thus very different from losing tolerance with conversations and endlessly licking envelopes.

Membership Loss

Recruitment and retention are additional problems for movement survival (Hirsch 1986, 1990). As commonly understood, dissidents frequently put forward efforts to get new individuals to join their movement as others depart. This includes leafleting, holding rallies, placing ads or setting up a table, directly talking to individuals on the street, and, in extreme cases, putting a gun in someone's face and/or killing a person's family before informing the individual that he or she is now a member. Such efforts are related to social movement death, because if the SMO is not able to replace those who leave, then its numbers will dwindle, perhaps resulting in an inability to perform diverse functions, which is one aspect of death identified earlier. Alternately, recruitment might be relevant to social movement termination, not because the organization fails to replace members (who may not leave), but because they cannot increase membership, thereby allowing the organization to undertake new tasks that might be required for its survival.[14] Different from burnout and lost commitment, membership loss is less about why people leave[15] then about the mechanics and relative efficiency with which challengers can acquire as well as retain enough members to keep the organization going.

Rigidity

The last explanation for SMO death from the "inside" concerns what is referred to as rigidity. Organizationally oriented scholars highlight the inability of SMOs to adapt to change as the primary reason for decline (Greenhalgh 1983). Here, because of an organization's structure, it develops a certain degree of functional "stickiness." Decisions become centralized around a smaller number of individuals, and communication tends to become one way as information is provided to those in control but little is provided back to those outside of the core. Finally, faced with numerous problems and no real time to reflect on what would be best, leaders tend to rely on what they believed had "worked" in the past, and they become less willing to experiment with new as well as seemingly different approaches to problems. This rigidity reduces the organization's ability to modify its tactics and/or objectives in accordance to change. Lacking this ability, the social movement organization crashes and burns – often quite dramatically.

---

[14] Clearly there is a separate element to recruitment that concerns individuals unconnected with and outside of SMO who decide if they wish to involve themselves and, if so, at what level of participation. It is possible that an SMO interests a nonaffiliated individual but only at the level of light support and not at the level of physically joining. I believe that this support resides outside of the SMO and involves what was discussed above regarding external factors.

[15] Although I am less interested in why recruitment works than noting that it is an important phenomenon for SMO survival, some have argued that the key to successful recruitment resides in drawing on preexisting ties (e.g., Pinard 1971; Snow et al. 1980; Oberschall 1973; Morris 1984; Hirsch 1986; Passy and Giugni 2000). These ties (familial, social, economic, and political) not only bring members into an organization but they have been found also to keep them there (Passy and Giugni 2000, 121). Such overlapping provides meaning to activism. Another vein of literature focuses more on hiring individuals to engage in dissent as the key to success in recruitment and retention (e.g., Collier and Hoeffler 2002). Here participants would stay involved as long as the pay was reasonable relative to what else was available.

Now, one could highlight the fact that an organization's rigidity is connected to its ability to adapt to something that may be inside or outside of the SMO itself. Unfortunately, organizational adaptability as it relates to social movement death has not been examined in any real detail. The closest that one comes to it is a suggestion that some structural characteristics proxy for it (e.g., the hierarchical nature of the institutions or the type of leader an organization has; i.e., Francisco 2004; Bob and Nepstad 2007). It is presumed that relevant behavioral dynamics (retrenchment and inflexibility) naturally are associated. What matters in this work are the characteristics within the relevant organization that facilitate adaptation (e.g., Edwards and Marullo 1995, 910). Similar arguments have also been made in evolutionary and coevolutionary terms (e.g., Oliver and Myers 2002; Koopmans 2005; Davenport and McDermott 2011).

Summary

Within this chapter, I have identified the predominant ways that researchers have historically attempted to account for the demobilization of those who challenge political authorities. As conceived, two paths have been taken toward this end. In one, challengers are killed from outside the organization. In another, challengers are killed from within. Although literature has tended to explore these explanations in isolation, in the next chapter, I explore their interactive influence.

2

Killing Social Movements from the Outside *and* the Inside

Although research has advanced our understanding of demobilization a great deal, existing scholarship has not really acknowledged that the factors outside of social movement organizations could interact with factors inside SMOs to kill them (e.g., Connable and Libicki 2010; for important exceptions, see Martin and Dixon 2010; McLaughlin and Pearlman 2012).[1] Within this chapter, I wish to develop this newer, third way to think about how social movement organizations are demobilized. To guide this discussion, I initially overlay the two types of influences described in the last chapter (three external and five internal). Doing this reveals fifteen distinct combinations, which will be discussed here. The combinations most relevant to the current book are those involving state repression. These combinations are important not only for what they tell us about how SMOs are influenced; they also serve to guide us in what we should look for when examining the topic, because most of those involved in challenging governments have some idea of what these combinations are and develop countermeasures to offset their negative effects. Similarly, in an effort to counter the countermeasures, governments engage in activities to weaken social movement resilience to their efforts, thereby facilitating social movement demise. As I discuss, not all efforts put forward by the different actors "work" (i.e., achieve their objectives – at least in the short term), and thus the interaction continues back and forth until one side has the advantage. The chapter concludes by outlining different scenarios as well as the dynamic interplay between state and challenger activities and counteractivities. Additionally, I identify some likely trajectories of challenger survival and demobilization.

---

[1] Other research suggests that there are interactive effects between repression and social movement organizations (e.g., Martin and Dixon 2010). These authors do not highlight the same factors that I do, but the argument is largely consistent. Similar work by McLaughlin and Pearlman (2012) concerns movement fragmentation, which is a relevant but distinct topic.

TABLE 2.1. *Intersections of External and Internal Sources of Demobilization*

	Internal				
	Factionalization	Exhaustion	Lost Commitment	Departing Member	Rigidity
External					
Resource deprivation	I	2	3	4	5
Problem depletion	6	7	8	9	10
Repression	11	12	13	14	15

Killing Movements

As conceived, most of the intersections between internal and external factors in social movement demobilization identified in the following are straight-forward (Table 2.1). Moreover, most of them are explicitly intended by political authorities who attempt to exacerbate perceived limitations within challenger institutions. This does not mean that governments are all powerful and succeed in these efforts. Indeed, unintended consequences are more than possible. Rather, it means that the relevant authority intends to facilitate those internal-external intersections.

For example, situations may exist where resource deprivations (the top row of the table) take place at the same time as a faction develops within a dissident organization (intersection 1). In this context, SMOs are forced to deal with two potentially deadly forces concurrently. The difference between this and the separate appearance of these factors discussed earlier is not simply in their simultaneous existence but also in the mutually negative reinforcement they provide. For example, a faction may form around the issue of resource deprivation and what should be done about it, or a faction may simply be worsened by the resource problem as the different sides of the division weigh in, adding yet another dimension to the internal strife. Deprivation may provoke or occur along with SMO exhaustion as dissidents grow weary of having to go from door to door and fund-raiser to fund-raiser in pursuit of support (intersection 2). Challengers may also grow weary of the disheartening conversations associated with financially deprived institutions. Deprivation and commitment loss may overlap (intersection 3). Here an inability to pay rent, buy equipment, or financially support members intersects with a reduced willingness to sacrifice for "the cause," resulting in demobilization. The struggling institution undermined by deprivation may prove to be a difficult environment to recruit into, and the organization might not have many resources to address the relevant problem leading to people disengaging and membership declining (intersection 4). In the final cell for the row, deprivation and rigidity intersect (intersection 5). Here, in an effort to develop an appropriate strategy to meet financial crisis, the challengers might tighten control over operations and operatives – resulting in greater rigidity as well as fewer opportunities for participation and communication that lead to demobilization. Alternatively, an already rigid institution might be hit with resource deprivation. Note that deprivation frequently serves as a catalyst to internal problems, but it need not. Internal problems may already be apparent (because of some other reason), only to be worsened by the external factor.

Intersections with problem depletion (as another form of external influence) work in a similar manner to those discussed earlier (the second row in the table). For example, a reduced sense of organizational support may provoke, exacerbate, or exist along with factionalization and polarization in an SMO as individuals attempt to address the threatening change in the environment, resulting in even greater dissension (intersection 6). In this context, it may become exhausting for participants to justify to themselves as well as others the reasonable nature of what they are doing, which results in demobilization (intersection 7). Engaged in a largely less supported enterprise where it seems as though someone else is addressing the relevant constituency (i.e., trying to work on something that has seemingly been resolved), group members may lose commitment (intersection 8) and/or prefer to remove themselves from the situation entirely (intersection 9). Such developments may not just compel individuals to leave; they may also prevent others from joining. Finally, in an effort to redirect the organization toward some new problem (trying to provide a new reason for existing in the face of a resolution), leadership may become more rigid, compelling individuals to leave because of the organizations' increased internal restrictiveness (intersection 10). It is also possible that a rigid organization will have a harder time shifting objectives in situations of problem depletion. The intersection thus proves to be especially vexing for behavioral challengers trying to survive.

Most relevant for the current research, we come to the third row in the table, the intersections involving state repression. For example, it is common in the aftermath of repressive action for SMOs to factionalize with regard to how the movement organization should respond to state action (intersection 11); this is the basic dynamic behind the frequently discussed but seldom examined "radical flank effect" (e.g., Gupta 2002; also discussed by McLaughlin and Pearlman 2012). Again, factionalization might precede the repressive action, but the latter should simply worsen the former. Similarly, in the face of repressive action, challengers may become exhausted by the constant fear of arrest, an endless series of trials, physical harassment, and/or incarceration, while simultaneously trying to figure out what to do as well as engage in claims-making activity (intersection 12). In the context of repression, commitment to the SMO (intersection 13) and membership (intersection 14) may also decline, resulting in demobilization. Faltering commitment and problems with recruiting should also be exacerbated by repressive action. Last, it is not uncommon

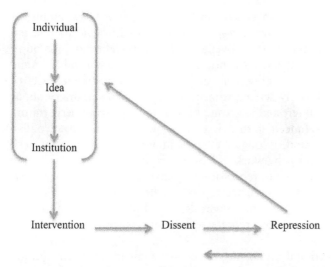

FIGURE 2.1. Basic dynamics of mobilization, dissent, and repression.

to find that organizations subject to government coercion become more rigid in their efforts to survive the ordeal (intersection 15). This becomes an especially difficult situation for SMOs because, despite being under pressure, it is unable to adapt because of its structural inflexibility.[2]

As conceived, therefore, we have external repression targeting social movement organizations and interacting with individuals, ideas and interventions (practices), and institutional characteristics. This is depicted in Figure 2.1. In my model, individuals generate ideas, and these ideas result in organizations being created and actions being taken. Repression directly affects and is affected by dissident behavior as police beat, arrest, and kill protestors, but repressive action also influences the internal dynamics within SMOs, which is what was discussed previously.

Now, what is interesting about the intersectional approach advocated here is that all of the external-internal combinations need not result in the SMO being killed. Indeed, there are several where the relevant influence could go in different ways. In large part, this is determined by what the actors involved do about the specific interactions.

In some research, the effects of repressive behavior are related to an SMO's ability to recruit and replace members who depart from the organization (e.g., Zwerman et al. 2000). This is most relevant to intersection 14 in Table 2.1. Here we see the relevance of both fear and anger (as discussed earlier), but both emotions exist simultaneously, and it is the relative balance within SMOs that

---

[2] Resource mobilization and problem depletion might also be associated with the interest of some external agents in disrupting or eliminating a behavioral challenge, but these areas are not historically as long standing or as intricately connected with state policy.

determines whether they survive as a dissident organization. For example, in Zwerman and Steinhof (2005), repression provokes fear within those subjected to it, prompting victims to leave the movement. Despite the effect of disruption and destruction, however, the SMO is not killed because new members come into the organization. These individuals are either unaware of the costs of participation or are not only willing to accept the risk but are angry about what was done and are interested in getting back at the repressive perpetrators for their prior activities. Indeed, in this view, the movement is able to stay alive despite government coercion, as long as it can maintain a steady stream of fresh blood. This is reinforced by the work of Davenport and Sullivan (2014), who find that those directly subject to repression stay involved in dissident activity, those who did not directly experience repression flee, and a new cohort of activists is brought in to replace those who leave, which is in part drawn by the news coverage of the previous repressive behavior as well as by resistance to it.

A different intersectional argument concerns the enhanced (re)integration of preexisting members into a social movement; this would be most relevant to intersection 13 in Table 2.1 (e.g., Opp and Roehl 1990). In this case, the impact of repressive action on a behavioral challenge is determined by three types of factors within the dissident organization: (1) moral incentives – norms of the group that favor protest; (2) social incentives – group sanctions against nonparticipation; and (3) public goods incentives – grievances regarding what the organization would like to change. Within this work, if members are well integrated into SMOs and there are strong norms as well as group sanctions for non-participation, then regardless of state repression individuals will be willing to continue. Indeed, here dissidents would believe that it is their duty to do so. In contrast, if members are not well integrated into the SMO, norms are limited, and there are no group sanctions for nonparticipation, then repressive behavior would send individuals away.

What is also interesting about the intersections noted earlier (especially those concerning state repression)[3] is that both governments and SMOs know that they exist, and both governments and SMOs make efforts to offset the effectiveness of the other's activities to influence them. These tactical countermeasures and counter-countermeasures are not frequently discussed at the same level of consistency or depth as the dynamics of dissent and repression themselves, but they do exist and should be incorporated into any discussion of demobilization. Both actors and their behavior will be discussed subsequently.

SMO Countermeasures

On the challenger's side, two strategies are undertaken to reduce the impact of external and internal threats to organizational survival (these are depicted

---

[3] There is less of a possibly that intersections 11, 12, and 15 are associated with opposite effects.

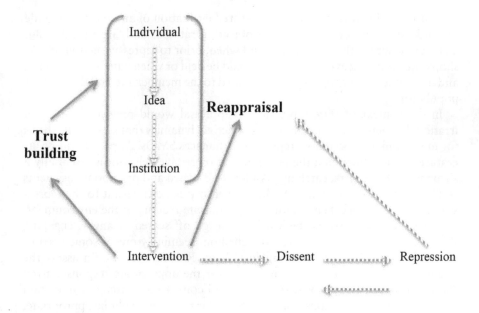

FIGURE 2.2. Social movement organization countermeasures.

in Figure 2.2). Although the two overlap in important ways, one principally concerns external factors, whereas the other focuses on internal ones.

Reappraisal
Challengers of political authorities are well aware of the negative impact that external factors like repression can have on them. Acknowledging this, dissidents engage in efforts to prepare members for repressive behavior, thereby insulating themselves from the worst impacts. In something comparable to what is called "reappraisal" in the field of psychology (e.g., Scherer 2001; Aronson et al. 2005),[4] SMOs train themselves to identify what is taking place around them, putting the experience into the appropriate category, which then serves as the basis for subsequent action. Here challengers attempt to provide

---

[4] Similar arguments seem to be found in organizational literature on learning (e.g., Edmondson 1999) and crisis management (e.g., Pearson and Clair 1998).

"an attitudinal heuristic [that] uses a stored evaluation of an object as a guide for understanding the actions of the object" (Pratkanis and Greenwald 1989, 251). Evidence for this would be found when, prior to repressive action, workshops and conferences on repression would be held or when pamphlets, articles, and magazines on the topic were distributed to the membership and the broader population.

In the context of state repression, reappraisal would prevent the type of irrational, reactive, and potentially destructive dynamics that serve as the basis for most thinking about how repression influences SMOs. At present, most literature seems to maintain the position that repressive behavior is essentially a surprise to challengers, catching dissidents off-guard and prompting dissidents to feel and/or do something, anything, even if it is not relevant to the repression directed against them. With the appropriate reading of the environment, however, dissidents would be less likely to go off scared or angry, engaging in discussions, meetings, protest, or rebellion, seemingly out of some need to respond to what was directed against them. Rather, they would assess the situation and evaluate the circumstances for the appropriate response, given the organization's objectives, resources, and comparative strength. In certain contexts, discussions, meetings, protest, and/or rebellion might be appropriate, but only if in line with the SMOs' general plans and preparations. Additionally, the type of repression directed against them might be a determining factor in the challengers' response.

Such a perspective raises some interesting issues. For example, although the appropriate response for the assassination of a dissident leader might be the assassination of a government leader, it might be more prudent for the SMO to flee or go underground, to find a better way of hiding the organization's hierarchy and/or simply to restructure in the aftereffect of the violent action. Existing research, however, views simple repetition of prior dissident behavior as an indication of repression's overall success/failure (i.e., continuity of behavioral challenge and demobilization, respectively) or organizational continuance. Similarly, what is the appropriate response to a raid on a social movement organization's headquarters? Is it a raid on a police station and military outpost or the hiring of a lawyer? What is the appropriate response to detection of a wire or of a mass killing? These issues are not addressed within existing research, but they bear directly on what we study and how. Reappraisal compels us to explore these issues directly, for I would maintain that if a challenger is prepared for repressive behavior conceptually (i.e., the challenger has an idea what is involved as well as what is a reasonable and effective response to what was done), then actual repression should not be as disruptive to the challenging organization. As such, reappraisal should reduce many of the internal problems that plague repressed challengers. For example, there should be less factionalization as to how to respond to repression because this would have been worked out ahead of time. Individuals would be less likely to leave or depart because they would have some idea of what could happen. Indeed, in many respects, prepared SMOs should function as they had before repression. Unprepared SMOs, however, might behave as existing literature seems to suggest. These organizations would simply be reacting with little understanding of what is going on and what they are doing.

Now, I am not suggesting that reappraisal concerning state repression is the only response pursued by challengers to offset what can and does happen to them. Indeed, I think that it is likely that other forms of reappraisal exist as well, for example, ideological and organizational. In the former, group members evaluate how "the movement" should act relative to how it does act. In the latter, group members evaluate how they, the members, believe the organization should act relative to how it does act. Excessive differentials in these could have deleterious aftereffects for social movement organizations. Within this book, however, I maintain that repression has influences on these other forms of reappraisal as well, and thus it should be the focus of attention.

Trust Building

Another approach to counter the potentially demobilizing effects of the interaction between external and internal factors (especially those involving state repression) is to build trust within the challenging organization. Consistent with existing work, I define trust as the willingness of one to be vulnerable to another based on the belief that this other is (1) competent, (2) open, (3) concerned, and (4) reliable (Mishra 1996, 265; also see Tilly 2005, xii). Accordingly, to try to build trust challengers would attempt to efficiently, transparently, and consistently attend to general issues of interest to the behavioral challenge or challengers in a way that displays both concern and conduct befitting the institution. It is important to acknowledge the risk of such an enterprise to the "malfeasance, mistakes, and failures of individual members" (Tilly 2005, 4), but the acceptance of this risk and the leap of faith involved that things will work out are the stuff of trust and trust building itself. Evidence for such behavior could involve making decisions in public, revealing the logic behind decisions as well as allowing discussion on the relevant points, holding meetings when they are planned and conducting meetings in a way that reduces acrimony, generally attending to matters in a way that does not appear corrupt and completing what is set as the organizational objectives.[5] The risk involved concerns the fact that the leaders or facilitators of the challenging institution could be inept, disinterested, or, worse, completely against their followers, resulting in their harassment, arrest, torture, or death. This is one of the reasons why the publicly distributed information and transparency of the actions mentioned earlier are so important.

Why is trust essential for a challenging institution? In short, trust makes SMO-related work possible by reducing transaction costs; it enhances solidarity; it reduces uncertainty about the future; and it even provides a little

---

[5] Clearly democracy is involved, but it is not exclusive to the definition.

insulation from distrust and suspicion. In short, it helps undermine many of the factors that kill SMOs from the inside.

For example, factionalization is generally believed to arise when members of an SMO reach a point of incompatibility, requiring that the organization separate or split in some manner. Trust counters this in various ways. First, trust tends to reduce arguments from reaching a "boiling point," as it would be expected that when all the members are interacting, they will have the organization's best interests at heart. This will lead participants to attempt to reconcile as opposed to going their separate ways. Second, once there is a rift of some sort, an extensive attempt would be made to repair it (e.g., Robinson et al. 2004). Third, even after a betrayal within a trustful organization and a division of some sort occurs, trusting social movement participants would be more apt to ignore it or underestimate its severity. Trust attempts to overcome exhaustion as well. As conceived, burnout is an unwillingness to continue on with an SMO because of fear, disappointment, and so forth. Trust works against this in the sense that trusting social movement participants will be less apt to leave if they believe that the other members have their best interests at heart. Indeed, trust involves a willingness to make oneself vulnerable. This is not to say that trusting individuals forget or ignore what transpires (an arrest, beat down, or killing). Rather, this is to say that when they trust, they are willing to accept uncomfortable situations more easily than others and make allowances when others might not.

Perhaps no factor is as important as commitment within a social movement, and trust is relevant here as well. As discussed earlier, commitment refers to one's sense of belonging with others (solidarity incentives), the pursuit of benefits related to SMO activity like a salary (material incentives), and being part of a solution to a pressing problem (purposive incentives). Clearly trust is important for those who are challenging political authorities. One element of the definition itself bears on this: concern. It is expected that trusting individuals believe that someone (the leader at a minimum or all members at the maximum) is interested in them as well as in their well-being. With that concern manifest, they are encouraged to establish and maintain a commitment to the relevant SMO and stay with it. Indeed, trusting individuals should be highly committed and resistant to most things that might try to deter them.

There is clearly a relationship between the two SMO measures. For example, reappraisal is important for trust building, and I posit that ineffective attempts at the former will reduce the latter. If a dissident organization proves unable to identify what type of repression might be used as well as what can be done to offset its negative aftereffects, then SMO participants will come to view the organization as well as its leaders as incompetent, unreliable, and unconcerned with their best interests. Hence they will lose trust and withdraw, hoping to reduce the possibility of further damage, which they see as increasingly possible. In contrast, if a dissident organization proves able to identify what happens repressively as well as what can be done to offset its negative aftereffects, then

SMO participants will come to view the organization as well as its leaders as competent, reliable, and concerned with their best interests. In these contexts, challengers will extend trust to the others in their institution and will likely continue to participate in the challenge, putting themselves in potentially risky situations but not seeing them as such because of the group's perceived effectiveness.

Obviously an ability to identify and counter repression is not all that challenging institutions are expected to do. For example, I would argue that an organization's ability to progress toward the stated objectives would go a long way toward building and sustaining trust. This said, it is essential for challengers – especially those of a radical nature – to keep their organization afloat by appropriately dealing with state repressive behavior. Being able to enjoy other successes presumes that one is alive to enjoy it.

Government Counter-Countermeasures

Challengers are not the only ones who understand the interactive consequences of external and internal dynamics as well as the fact that action can be taken by SMOs to recover from them. For example, political authorities do not sit idly back and allow the targets of state repression to regroup, restructure, and repair themselves. Rather, when the dissidents are deemed threatening enough and governments are both willing and able, authorities attempt to systematically weaken the techniques applied by social movement organizations that are used to counter government coercion; in short, they engage in counter-countermeasures. How is this done? The approach is twofold (depicted in Figure 2.3).

First, in an effort to counter reappraisal, governments attempt to either *overwhelm* an SMO by applying one form of repression to a level that was not expected or to *outwit* an SMO by applying forms of repression for which the dissident organization was not prepared. Each approach has distinct influences on challengers, and thus each has a different impact on killing social movement organizations.

For example, *overwhelming* SMOs counters reappraisal by subjecting dissidents to more repression than anticipated (e.g., greater scope and/or lethality). Examples here abound. Expecting selective harassment, members are harassed in groups; expecting to be questioned and released for brief amounts of time, dissidents are placed in holding cells for long periods of time and questioned for days or weeks; expecting small-scale violence at the home base or at an event, the organization is killed en masse. The key here is to subject challengers to an experience that significantly deviates from the perceptions of the group established by their approach to reappraisal. This leads individuals to feel that the dissident organization is unprepared, prompting them to experience the raw emotions discussed earlier. As a consequence, government countermeasures lead individuals to have an unpleasant experience with the

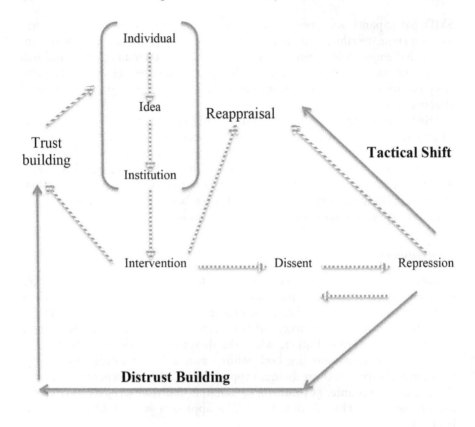

Legend:
- solid line:
  relationships
  of interest
- dashed line:
  previously
  highlighted
  relationships

FIGURE 2.3. Government counter-countermeasures.

movement, prompting burnout, lost commitment, factionalization, and departure or exit.

Similarly, *outwitting* leads to demobilization and an undoing of the challengers' countermeasures, but in a different way. In this case, the idea is not to do more of something anticipated by the SMO's approach to reappraisal but to systematically deviate from expectations entirely through unexpected tactics. If the dissidents are expecting a raid, for example, outwitting involves infiltrating the organization with an informant and/or agent provocateur; if challengers are expecting the leaders to be assassinated, then governments arrest them and drag them into court; if challengers are expecting sustained violent exchanges after Sunday public meetings, then governments randomly target activists during the week with random questions. This leads to an unpleasant experience, as does overwhelming, but of a different sort. Here, assuming that individuals like their world to be as orderly and consistent as possible, the outwitting approach to state repression undermines order and consistency, prompting challengers to reevaluate their actions and beliefs and the ability of the organization to protect them.

What determines the government's tactical selection? I argue that the choice is influenced by intelligence in general (i.e., information about the challenger's strategy out in the public domain) and domestic spying (i.e., using physical and electronic surveillance and informants as well as agents provocateurs). If an SMO is known fairly well (i.e., who is in it, what the organization seeks, what tactics are used to get there, and what strategy of reappraisal is employed), then outwitting is most likely. If an SMO is not known well, then the government is more likely to try to overwhelm their opponent and see what happens.[6]

Second, in an effort to counter dissident trust building, governments attempt to weaken the very bonds that make behavioral challenge (i.e., collective action) possible. Though the objective is clear, the approach adopted is not. For example, I think that it has generally been believed that massive and violent state repression eliminates trust among social movement activists, as it was expected that those group members subjected to this repression would come to focus on themselves and their own physical survival, ignoring the collective. I believe this has changed. Newer work shows that even amid the worst forms of state-sponsored political violence, dissidents are able to find ways to act collectively in resistance (Francisco 2004), and some have even discovered that the bonds of trust are strengthened, not weakened, under such circumstances (Zwerman and Steinhoff 2005).

What is really consistent (but admittedly understudied), however, is the belief that perceived infiltration by informants and agents provocateurs uniformly reduces trust within an organization (e.g., Marx 1974, 1979). The logic here is straightforward. With infiltration, a challenger is not quite sure if the individuals with them in the room at a meeting, on the street at the protest, or in the hills during insurgency are friends or foes (i.e., if they are actually "with" them). As the essence of trust is a willingness to make oneself vulnerable to those who are believed to be working on their behalf, even the perception of infiltration will directly weaken that trust. Indeed, it is possible within compromised situations for challengers not only to mistrust others but also to stop trusting themselves for not being able discern who is and who is not trustworthy. Once that happens in an SMO, challengers are likely to withdraw by not participating or by departing from the organization entirely. Again, as noted in

---

[6] Such a strategic decision is comparable to research concerned with selective as opposed to indiscriminate violence.

TABLE 2.2. *Context and Contention*

	Government Advantage	Dissidents Advantage
Democracy	↑ Overt repression	↓ Reppraisal
	↑ Outpacing	↑ Trust
Radicalization	↑ Overwhelming	↑ Trust
Movement openness		↑ Reappraisal; ↑ Trust
Goal clarity	↑ Overt repression	
Hierarchy	↑ Overt repression	
First strike	↑ Outpacing or overwhelming	↓ Reappraisal or trust

the discussion about undermining reappraisal, the dynamics here take time to develop. What is important to identify is that while an SMO is trying to build trust, the authorities are trying to destroy it. The fate of the organization lies in the balance.[7]

A difficulty arises with distrust building and suspecting informants, and agents provocateurs in particular, in part because of observability. Informants and agents provocateurs do not really announce themselves within a movement. I maintain that it is the suspicion of their existence within a movement organization that is believed to function as the disruption that reduces trust. Now, governments can let it be known through false letters or newspaper articles that a particular group has been infiltrated, but (herein lies the crucial point) the challenging group itself needs to acknowledge that such a thing is possible for the impact really to be felt. In a sense, infiltration is only real if it is believed to be real by challengers. Only then will trust be influenced.

Contextualizing Countermeasures

It should be clear from the preceding discussion that I do not believe that all state-dissident interactions are alike and that all interactions (all moves and countermoves) are likely to push an SMO toward life or death. Rather, I am arguing that the processes involved are largely contingent on the characteristics of the actors and the choices they make in conjunction with the broader political, economic, and social contexts in which they occur – which provides either governments or dissidents with advantages. Toward this end, in the following, I identify several factors that I believe have an influence on the state-challenger interaction and give one actor the advantage over the other (see Table 2.2).

---

[7] This point about reciprocal adaptation is comparable to earlier work about coevolution put forward by Oliver and Myers (2002) and Moore's (1998, 2000) strategic adaptation. The only difference here is that I suggest that adaptation could take place at multiple levels. There is the fight between governments and dissidents. There could be a fight within dissident organizations themselves. There could be a fight within government as well (e.g., Simon 1994).

Government Characteristics

System Type

To begin, I believe that authoritarian governments will generally have an advantage over democratic ones in killing SMOs. The former have greater freedom to infiltrate and engage in a wider variety of negative demobilization-related activities. The latter are constrained in many ways and are forced to hide what they are doing, cloaking relevant activities in the law and using generally less violent methods because they fear exposure. Because of these general constraints on democratic political authorities, I believe the degree of trust within SMO participants in democracies increases as they develop an inflated sense of their own possibilities and are able to bond with one another in a relatively easy way with few consequences. This perception of relative democratic passivity also increases the possibility that reappraisal will be improperly specified and that the government need only deviate from expected patterns a little to bring about the desired result of ending the targeted SMO.

Confronted with some aggression, I would expect that most challengers in a democracy would fold, not being prepared for such behavior. As a consequence, generally in line with existing research, I would expect there to be more challenges in democratic countries than in autocracies and for SMOs in democratic systems to display greater variability in survival rates. That said, given that democracies are more likely to apply covert techniques because of their fear of exposure, I would expect that targeted social movement organizations are more likely to be destroyed by infiltration and reduced trust than by excessive use of more overt and aggressive methods. Given the variety of state agents in a democratic context, I would also expect that outwitting efforts are a greater possibility than are overwhelming efforts to undermine reappraisal. This leads to the second factor.

Repressive Disposition

Also relevant to state-dissident activities is the government's prior response to behavioral challenges. As conceived, earlier responses of political authorities to behavioral challenges are informative for those challenges that come later. Earlier toleration of a particular form of challenge is likely to invite challenges of the same sort from those that follow, whereas earlier repression is likely to invite challenges of a different nature. Earlier approaches of government help to establish standing operating procedures. This will likely influence future decisions about what could or should be done when similar situations arise, depending on government willingness to listen as well as its ability to convey its evaluation of the situation in a compelling manner.

Hierarchy

Regarding political authorities, the structures of the organizations involved in repression are important to identify, as the top-down versus bottom-up

orientation is crucial. For example, it is generally known that top-down organizations (e.g., totalitarian political systems) are better able to perform simple
as well as large tasks, but bottom-up organizations (e.g., free-standing terrorist
cells) are better at small and more complex activities that require on-the-spot
adaptation. If challengers stay with one approach, then government can get
away with a hierarchical institution and will likely have an advantage. This is
especially true if the authorities attempt to overwhelm the challengers. If the
challengers shift tactics frequently, however, and the government adopts an
outwitting strategy, then government would be better off with a more bottom-
up orientation.

Challenger Characteristics

Radicalism
I believe that dissident organizations espousing radical objectives and with
fewer connections to existing polity members are the ones against which the
most repressive behavior will be directed (i.e., when overwhelming is most
likely). This leaves the state with the advantage regarding the impact on reappraisal, for the state is able to employ a larger amount of coercive behavior.

Connections to and affiliations with the existing government are fairly
straightforward.[8] As Tilly (2000) suggested, there are five actors that one
needs to identify and track to understand who is or is not in a political system:
(1) agents of the government (i.e., the police, military, court officials, and politicians), (2) polity members (i.e., recognized actors enjoying access to government and its resources), (3) challengers (i.e., recognized actors lacking access),
(4) subjects (i.e., those not currently recognized but part of the territorial unit),
and (5) outside actors (i.e., those outside the polity).[9] The relevance of this
categorization for state repression is clear. Polity members are, by definition,

---

[8] It may seem that connections to or affiliations with governments by challengers is distinct from
radicalism, but I maintain that radicalism cannot be viewed without such a concern because
it influences how someone is likely to be viewed or treated by authorities. For example, if the
relative of a country's president espouses political beliefs that call for the reform of a political
system, this challenge will likely be viewed in a very different way from the average citizen.
Although this could result in being perceived as more threatening, it is also possible that the
individual is cut some slack because of his or her relationship with the relevant authorities.
Radicalism thus incorporates the political distance between those in power and those outside of
power across the two dimensions.

[9] These characteristics are important, for as Tilly (2000, 4–5) states,

regimes vary, among other ways, in breadth (the proportion of all persons under the government's jurisdiction that belong to polity members), equality (the extent to which persons who
do belong to polity members have similar access to governmental agents and resources), consultation (the degree to which polity members exercise binding collective control over government
agents, resources and activities) and finally protection (shielding of polity members and their
constituencies form arbitrary action by governmental agents).

Radicalism is by definition found at the outermost edges of the polity.

acceptable to authorities and thus more likely facilitated (or tolerated) if they engage in challenges. Of course, it is possible that even polity members might be repressed if they engage in highly unacceptable behavior; in this context, however, some care would be taken in dealing with these individuals.

Challengers outside of the polity and lacking connections to polity members are more likely to be treated coercively and perhaps viciously to communicate a lesson to those generally under the coercive arm of the law.[10] In contrast, challengers with connections to polity members are more likely to be tolerated or facilitated, depending on exactly who and how good their connections are. If this group is repressed, it would be with relatively less covert or violent methods.

Although radicalization proves bad for behavioral challenges because it increases the likelihood of inciting the full wrath of state repression, I believe that radicalism also increases the degree of trust within a dissident organization, out of necessity or desperation. In claims-making efforts where the stakes are very high, dissident members literally hold the lives of their fellows in their own hands, as they could turn them or, through their poor behavior, have them end up arrested, tortured, or killed. This tends to increase the trust that radical challengers bestow on each other and to increase the bonds that connect them, making it difficult to turn members against one another or to deter them with threats. For the same reasons, the intensity of radicalization also increases the distance that individuals would fall if they were betrayed.

Openness

Related to the last point, I expect that relatively closed SMOs, such as terrorist cells, are better able to sustain their reappraisal and trust levels, but only with regard to covert repressive activity (i.e., infiltration), which is much less likely. These organizations might still suffer from reduced reappraisal and trust, but I would argue that this results from failed engagements with political authorities in overt contests (e.g., failed suicide bombings because of prior arrest or bombs being defused before detonation). Acknowledging this, given the importance of trust for closed and clandestine organizations, I expect the SMO to demobilize quickly once trust has been compromised. This is similar to arguments in the organizational literature. Additionally, Zwerman et al. (2000) identify that because of their insular nature, closed dissident groups are more likely to develop psychological problems that invariably weaken the institution. Cut off from others outside of the highly closed SMO, members lose a sense of the real world, inaccurately estimating their own significance and even the status of their actions for society. This disjuncture puts the organization on a

---

[10] Differing from Foucault's (1995) suggestion that modern governments try to hide their coercive activities, I maintain that these political authorities are more likely to overdo it when they apply repressive behavior to commonly perceived enemies (i.e., legitimate targets). This serves as a lesson to others.

path to repeated unsatisfying experiences – experiences that often reach tragic proportions before demobilization occurs – and eventual demobilization.

Goal Clarity

Paradoxically, groups that are clear about exactly what they are pursuing should be easier to disturb than those with less clear objectives. Although this seems counterintuitive, my argument is as follows: if the goals are simple and well understood (e.g., the single-issue movement organizations Gamson 1975 favorably discussed), then authorities will have a better idea of what they need to prevent, and trust will be reduced when the organization is not able to achieve these goals. In contrast, less clear goals do not provide a clear target for government preemption, thus favoring dissidents.[11] At the same time, however, if the SMO's goals are too elusive, movement participants will be frustrated in a different way, again leading to dissatisfaction and eventual demobilization.

Hierarchy

The structure of the dissident organization is also important to state-dissident interactions. Specifically, I believe that a hierarchically organized SMO provides authorities, as do clear goals, with a clear target in the chain of command. As a result, I expect that hierarchical organizations are the ones most likely to suffer from reduced reappraisal and trust under repression. In this context, authorities would simply have to disrupt the organization's leadership (through harassment, detention, or elimination) and the rest of the SMO would feel the impact, eventually collapsing. This dynamic can be offset by the organization having an explicit plan about what to do when the leadership is disrupted. As in the current U.S. War on Terror, more diffuse organizations generally have a better chance of surviving and avoiding the negative effects of repression. Indeed, when lacking a leader, or at least an easily identifiable one, these types of organizations are better able to sustain themselves in their confrontations with authorities.[12]

General Dynamics

With these elements in mind, I argue that a common state-challenger trajectory would involve the following. In the beginning of a challenge, the dissident

---

[11] These expectations appear to diverge from the work of Gamson (1975), who suggests that single-issue groups are less likely repressed and more likely accommodated – of course, controlling for the degree of radicalism involved. This also deviates from the work of Hannan et al. (2007), who seem to suggest that unclear identities and goals would be more likely to lead to state repression. As these authors do not explicitly address repressive action, this is merely speculation, but it appears to be consistent with their work and thus merits attention.

[12] Though the different conditions and characteristics have been examined individually, it is possible that they occur simultaneously or develop in sequences. Although this is possible, we are not yet at the point where such issues could be laid out and systematically evaluated. Indeed, the discussion here is the first to outline the components of what is involved.

organization decides on its objective (i.e., the overall goal, goal clarity, and level of radicalization). This will in part be a function of the existing government's structure (i.e., how democratic and open it is), its revealed predisposition toward repression (i.e., earlier tolerance regarding behavioral challenges of a similar sort),[13] and the structure of the challenging organization (i.e., how hierarchical it is in terms of leadership, how open it will be to new members and information). The movement comes into existence with some level of trust among participants as well as some understanding of what government is likely to do with regard to the designated behavioral challenge. Trust is expected to be higher for organizations that are highly selective in recruiting members, crafting the organization, and reappraisal is expected to be clearer when activists have had some prior experience with state repression.

The structure of the challenging institution will generally influence the government's initial response to the challenger in conjunction with the initial tactic and/or goal selected by the challenger, prior repressive action, and the influence of repressive organizations (i.e., their habits and predisposition as well as their ability to act independently). Governments with more extensive covert approaches might be more proactive in nature and use informants as well as agents provocateurs.

The first round of interactions between government and SMO leads the challenger to reflect on its approach to reappraisal as it thinks about the difference between what they had lived through previously expected and compared to what had been imagined or prepared for. The greater the difference between the two, the greater the potential negative impact on organizational trust and the greater the movement toward demobilization will be. The magnitude of this effect will be determined by the amount of effort undertaken by the challenger to adjust to the difference encountered over time and the reservoir of trust held at the beginning. Highly adaptive organizations can do "damage control" and overcome the problems with diminished trust. Less adaptive organizations cannot.

As noted earlier, governments do not sit back and allow challengers to adapt without additional activity. The more general strategies of repression (overwhelming or outwitting) can have an impact on dissident organization adaptation, the less effective challengers will be. For example, political authorities can overwhelm challengers by engaging in activity that exceeds the imagination and capability of the challengers. This is best achieved when capabilities are known in advance through domestic spying. Without this, capabilities can still be determined with experimentation, but governments in this context must be prepared to try different approaches (e.g., engaging in arrests, raids, or violence) and to assess these influences on the challengers (e.g., increasing trust,

---

[13] Some have argued that disposition might be best conceived as being part of system or regime type – arguing that these correlate with authoritarianism and democracy – but earlier research of my own (e.g., Davenport 2007) as well as the work of others (e.g., Bueno de Mesquita et al. 2005; Conrad and Moore 2010) has shown this not to be the case.

behavior, or attendance). Alternatively, political authorities can try to outwit challengers by engaging in activities that significantly deviate from challenger expectations. Again, this is best achieved with inside information about expectations, but it can also be determined by experimentation, evaluation, and subsequent behavioral change.

The mechanisms of influence change. For example, covert repressive activity, such as through informants, bugs or wiretaps, false communication, and agents provocateurs, disrupts the organizational calibration discussed previously for two reasons: (1) it provides very little information to the challengers about government activity and (2) it undermines trust within the organization by misdirecting and impeding communication and collective action. Alternatively, political authorities may engage in more overt strategies, such as physical harassment, arrests, raids, and grand juries, and disrupt the organizational calibration discussed earlier by compelling SMOs to redirect investment (e.g., putting money into lawyers instead of printing leaflets or paying for bail instead of traveling) and by imposing excessive costs (e.g., physically removing leaders).

After initial rounds of interaction, challengers and governments move against one another tactically until one or the other demobilizes or some accommodation or victory is made. Historically, I would argue that this normally involves challengers being demobilized.

With these general dynamics in mind, a challenging group is more likely to survive and not demobilize not only if it can sustain the costs of repressive action (e.g., fines, beatings, deaths) but also if it begins with and sustains an appropriate understanding of state repression as well as a level of trust within the organization. I think that both can be built during the process of mobilization, but this is not easy to do consistently. I also maintain that, properly cultivated, these can go a long way to helping an SMO survive state repression – at least in some form. Additionally, though reappraisal builds trust, I do not believe that trust builds reappraisal. The latter involves an ability to predict outcomes and match responses with those predictions. Trust involves an evaluation of a relationship, but it does not mean that individuals become better at observing the world because of it. In contrast, a challenging group is more likely to fail and be demobilized if governments are able to frustrate attempts at reappraisal as well as undermine trust among organizational members through overwhelming and outwitting or by hindering the group's broader objectives.[14]

---

[14] Principally, I view my argument as being consistent with other work that is coevolutionary in nature, with the different actors responding to one another in a mutual fashion (e.g., Oliver and Myers 2002; Koopmans 2005). My argument differs from this other work in that the other models are simply concerned with what I will call "first-order interactions"; that is, they focus on the dissident behavior of challengers and the repressive behavior of governments. This work ignores what I will call "second-order interactions," that is, the internal maintenance being undertaken by challengers to offset the negative impact of the first-order interactions as well as the domestic spying and counterintelligence activities of governments to undermine these efforts. Without considering both at the same time, one cannot really understand the impact of repression or internal movement dynamics on SMO demobilization.

Summary

Within this chapter, I attempted to identify exactly how external and internal factors interact to influence social movement demobilization – outlining an intersectional approach. Following this, I discussed the variety of ways that challengers (aware of the intersection discussed in the first section) try to counteract the negative influences through *reappraisal* and *trust building*. I then discussed how governments attempt to counteract the countermeasures through *overwhelming* (exceeding challenger expectations), *outwitting* (deviating from challenger expectations), and *distrust building* (undermining social movement participants' willingness to believe in the other participants). The last part of the chapter attempted to identify what conditions influence state-dissident interactions leading a conflict in favor of one actor or the other.

In Part II, we move to address the history of protest policing and state repression in the United States, specifically in Michigan and Detroit, relevant to the RNA (Chapter 3). Following this, I discuss the particularities of the database being relied on to conduct the historical overview, with a more detailed examination presented in Chapter 4. The former chapter is undertaken to situate the anti-RNA effort within a broader discussion about state repression and then a more detailed discussion about how this specific counteraction involved diverse agents of the state. The latter provides a brief overview of the records collected by various political authorities regarding the RNA and my method for examining this information within the current research. This is done to develop a reasonable understanding of what is included and what such a compilation could and could not tell us about SMOs and state repression.

PART II

CASE

3

Repression and Red Squads

What is the role of the government in the context of behavioral challenges to authorities, and what is the role of the government in the specific context of Detroit and the Republic of New Africa (i.e., how is government involved with the repressive policies used to subdue the organization, what exactly does it do, and what type of information is collected to assist with these efforts)? As I attempt to contextualize the US-RNA interaction into literature concerning state repression and to discuss what information is used to evaluate the argument put forward earlier, these are the questions that I address within the current chapter.

Why Repress?

Although several different reasons for state repression have been advanced, none has the resonance or standing of the desire to counter behavioral challenges. Indeed, it seems uncontroversial to say that governments are interested in keeping challenges and challengers within parameters that they deem acceptable (see Tilly 1978 for useful discussion). Although this varies somewhat from place to place and time to time, I would argue that several elements of this process are fairly stable. For example, political authorities consistently like to keep the goals of any challenge or challenger as moderate as possible (i.e., not advocating the overthrow of the existing political-economy and/or removal of individuals associated with it), the behavior of these challengers nonviolent, and the number of participants in relevant activity small. Now any deviations from one of these preferred states may communicate to authorities (as well as to the mass citizenry) that there is a "threat" to political order. Indeed, any one of these may threaten the perception that the existing government is in control of the relevant territory and that all those under their jurisdiction can exist without the fear of something bad happening to them or their interests (e.g., their property being damaged or destroyed and their lives taken or irreparably damaged).[1] If several of these dimensions are present at the same time (e.g., there is a radical transformation proposed and the challenge is violent in nature or the challenge is violent and the number of participants is significant), then the magnitude of the threat will be increased. If all three dimensions are present, then one has a situation of civil war and/or what many would call "anarchy" or "state failure," situations where some centralized authority has failed in its attempt to wield coercive control over a specific territorial jurisdiction.

The methods for dealing with behavioral challenges include a relatively long list of government activities that are unfortunately now quite familiar to citizens throughout the globe. In an effort to contain and/or eliminate challengers and their challenges, authorities may employ informants, agents provocateurs, verbal harassment, arrests, pepper spray, water hoses, water boards, or targeted assassination; ban political organizations; or engage in disappearances and/or mass killing (e.g., Churchill and Vander Wall 1988; Boykoff 2006).

Of course, authorities may also apply methods that are more accommodative in nature, possibly influencing behavioral challenges by bringing the challengers "inside" the system (e.g., Gamson 1975; Tilly 1978; Moore 1998; Shellman 2006; Walter 2006). This could be achieved by making the challenger a representative in government or perhaps assigning the challenger to some kind of consultative position. The idea here is that, once on the inside, challengers will stop challenging the status quo, to which some refer as "channeling" (Earl 2003). Authorities may also co-opt behavioral challenges simply by paying off those in opposition. For example, leaders of SMOs might be given bribes to keep their followers in check and off the streets. The idea here is that once paid off, leaders will (in turn) control their own constituents, bringing their aspirations and activities to levels acceptable to those in government.

Alternatively, authorities may try to manipulate the articulation, understanding and framing challenger objectives through propaganda and persuasion, influencing what people understand to be the goals of the challenge, the means selected to achieve these goals, and the likelihood of success in such efforts. Essentially, the government here makes the challenger's objectives seem unattainable or insane, the means illegitimate or illegal, and the possibility of success limited or impossible.

Finally, authorities may ignore the behavioral challenge and let the dynamics present within the challenging organization as well as the broader society (e.g., counterprotestors) limit the effectiveness of the challenge. Here governments do nothing other than letting the difficulties with generating and sustaining mobilization take their toll.

Despite the reality that more than one method may be applied simultaneously by government, few scholars have considered this possibility. Typically,

---

[1] This concerns threats other than from the state itself, which is another matter entirely.

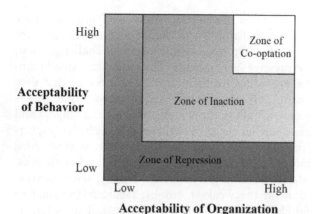

FIGURE 3.1. Understanding government responses to dissent.

researchers examine repression independent of the other techniques of control, or they study accommodation in isolation, and so forth (for important exceptions, see Gamson 1975; Moore 1998, 2000).

Tilly (1978), in his seminal book *From Mobilization to Revolution*, did consider a broader repertoire of government strategies and, equally important, when one particular technique would be expected to predominate, and this proves to be quite useful (shown in Figure 3.1). As conceived within this work, the government's response to a behavioral challenge was determined by two factors: (1) the *acceptability of the action taken* (i.e., the number of challenges, their duration, the geographic range involved, the size of the organization, and the magnitude of violence) and (2) the *acceptability of the group involved* (i.e., openness to the organization's beliefs, its objectives, and its members as well as their connections with the existing power structure). Acceptability in this case means tolerance or a lack of perceived threat worthy of repressive action. The placement of a specific challenger and its behavior on the two dimensions just identified determine how authorities would treat them. Generally, dissidents using unacceptable tactics and those whose organization was deemed unacceptable to the authorities would be the ones most likely to be repressed. Those challengers that used acceptable tactics (e.g., nonviolent activities) and whose organization was deemed acceptable by government leaders (e.g., who advocated reforms within the existing political economy) would be the ones most likely facilitated. Those falling in between the two would most likely be tolerated.

Now, Tilly did not believe that all types of government responded to the same challenges in comparable ways. Rather, he believed that different types responded in different ways. Behaviorally, he identified four types. For example, *repressive* governments view the largest number of groups and actions as unacceptable across both dimensions. Consequently, these political authorities repress the largest number of challengers and challenges, and they tolerate a reasonable number of challengers and challenges but facilitate very few. *Totalitarian* governments also repress a large number of challengers and challenges but fewer than repressive governments. They tolerate a small number of challengers and challenges but facilitate a great number so that they may co-opt and channel them. *Tolerant* governments, those we would generally conceive of as "democratic," allow the widest range of challengers and challenges, and they repress a smaller range of challengers and challenges, certain actors, and certain types of groups. Compared to repressive governments, these governments facilitate a larger number of challengers and challenges, although far fewer than do totalitarian governments. Finally, *weak* governments focus their repression on the weakest groups, facilitate the smallest number of challengers and challenges, and tolerate the most. This is largely explained by the fact that they do not have the wherewithal to either repress or co-opt.[2]

From this perspective, if one were trying to understand what governments do in situations of political contestation, the key would be to identify the type of government as well as the acceptability of the challenging activity and the group undertaking it. With this information, one could estimate what the relevant government would do and, in the specific context of this book, what type and what degree of repression might be employed.

Why Repress in Detroit? The "Red Squad" and the Policing of American Radicalism

Although Tilly's model in particular and the literature in general is useful for generally understanding why governments repress (which has been given a great deal of attention) and against whom such behavior is directed (which has received comparatively less attention), there are some limitations with the approach. Perhaps the most important problem with existing research is that it tends to homogenize the unit of observation to the nation-state quite frequently at yearly aggregations, explicitly lumping together all challengers and all parts of government.[3] As a result, the diversity of claims makers present at any given time (which likely vary in terms of both tactics and ideological orientation and objectives) and the diversity of government agents involved in their suppression (which may also vary in technique and objective) have been generally lost. This said, I believe that one could adopt the same model identified previously to

---

[2] In later work, Tilly (2005) steps away from the general relationships articulated here, arguing instead that the influence of dissent on repression is likely to vary according to the presence or absence of diverse mechanisms.

[3] Indeed, it is only in the last few years with subnational conflict studies and the microfoundational turn in this work that such an effort has been substantively challenged (e.g., Kalyvas 2006). Within this work, however, only I have attempted to address the topic with regard to state repression (e.g., Davenport and Stam 2003).

understand repressive action in one particular part of a country or in the current book, within a single city: Detroit. Such an evaluation should not ignore other levels of aggregation and simply consider the lowest-level jurisdiction (i.e., the street address, village, city, or region) at the lowest temporal unit (i.e., hour, day, week, or month). Quite the contrary, researchers have to assess what is taking place at the national, state, and local levels simultaneously as they are potentially connected with one another and reinforcing or disconnected and isolated. Accordingly, each level of government in the U.S. government's response to the RNA is discussed in the following section.

U.S. Federal Repressive Policies Around 1968

At the founding of the RNA, the United States was undergoing a transition of political orientation at the national level, from an approach that was somewhat more tolerant of dissent to one that was increasingly and obviously repressive.[4] The earlier approach, generally associated with the periods of civil rights, the Great Society, and the War on Poverty, was characterized by a relative openness at the highest levels of government. Here dissent was broadly permitted to take place and authorities attempted to work with those in the streets to resolve their problems in a noncoercive manner. This approach characterized the presidencies of John F. Kennedy and Lyndon Johnson, especially during the years following Kennedy's death.

All was not rosy, however. One author (Robert Goldstein), who is associated with perhaps the most detailed evaluation of repression during the time, maintains that

those who received the major benefits of the Kennedy administration's largesse were those liberals who had been unfairly smeared with the communist brush during the McCarthy period and dissidents who did not really question the fundamental directions of American foreign and domestic policy (such as the peace marchers who were given coffee and cocoa). The few truly radical groups that existed or developed during this period, such as the [Communist Party], the [Socialist Workers Party], the Fair Play for Cuba Committee and the Advance Youth Organization, continued to suffer severe governmental reprisals, and even liberal groups such as Women's Strike for Peace and the Pacifica Foundation came under investigation by congressional committees, presumably as a warning to other groups not to get too far out of line. (Goldstein 1978, 425–26)

Though this relative tolerance for "acceptable" groups and behavior applied to seemingly all dissidents, African Americans (from which the RNA exclusively recruited) held a special place in this period. During the two presidencies of

---

[4] Some elements of the federal government were clearly repressive before this time (e.g., the FBI, which had a somewhat longer trajectory of antiradical coercive action under way; e.g., Goldstein 1978; Cunningham 2004), but even these organizations were not as open or as aggressive as they would be at the time the RNA came into existence.

interest, there was a degree of sympathy for the black situation as well as access to and even accommodation for African Americans engaged in struggle, which represented a sea change from the period before it. For example, Johnson's War on Poverty was unveiled during his January 1964 State of the Union speech, quickly followed by the passing of the Economic Opportunity Act, which allocated both attention and resources to the plight of America's most needy, especially African Americans. This said, reinforcing Tilly's point, only certain African American claims-making efforts were tolerated and responded to in a noncoercive manner by the federal government. As long as the claims were for integration as well as civil rights and the tactic employed was nonviolent as well as nonaggressive, then overt, state-sponsored repressive activity was limited. However, when African Americans turned toward aggression, violence, and radicalism, the government responded with significant repression.

All of this changed after Kennedy was assassinated and several years after Johnson assumed the presidency. Indeed, as Goldstein (2000, 429) well summarizes,

during the 1965–1975 period...the United States went through a period of political repression, which, at its height in 1967–1971, exceeded in intensity any other time in the twentieth century with the possible exceptions of the 1917–20 and 1947–50 periods. The social setting for this intense period of political repression was a background of political turbulence, dissent and violence unmatched in American history since the Civil War.

The "background" being discussed included the Vietnam War and the resistance to this effort, the "worst series of racial disorders in American history" (Goldstein 2000, 429), enhanced black militancy, skyrocketing rates of violent crime, and the growth of a countercultural movement adopted by many of the youths of America that transformed their language, behavior, and ideological orientation for many years to come. In the face of these developments, the general position and tactics of the national government shifted in important ways.

During this period, shepherded by President Johnson himself, greater coercive power was given to the executive through the Omnibus Crime Control and Safe Streets Act of 1968. In this context, red baiting increased, and under federal jurisdiction, the diverse agents of the state stepped in line to restrict varied rights throughout the nation. For example, in April 1968, Congress outlawed the communication of the idea of rioting across state lines and of advocating the overthrow of the U.S. government. In the same legislation, for the first time in U.S. history, the government legalized the use of federal wiretapping and eavesdropping. Directly related to this, the activities of various agents not normally associated with U.S. repression were increased (e.g., the CIA, the National Security Agency, and the U.S. Army). The reins were also fully taken off the FBI, which was more traditionally associated with American repression, and the organization was essentially allowed to engage in surveillance and the disruption of social movement organizations with impunity, most notably within the Counter Intelligence Program (COINTELPRO).[5]

Again, African Americans held a special place in the government's planning and activity. In particular, there were two reasons for this. First, the nature of black SMOs had shifted, and accordingly, so did the focus of the government. As Goldstein (2000, 447) notes,

by 1965, reporting requirements were increased to encompass *all* civil rights activity, whether involving "subversives" or not, as agents were directed to supply "complete" information regarding "planned racial activity, such as demonstrations, rallies, marches or threatened opposition of this kind," including full coverage of "meetings" and "any other pertinent information concerning racial activities." In late 1966, FBI field offices were instructed to begin preparing semi-monthly summaries of "existing racial conditions in major urban areas," including descriptions of the "general programs" concerning the "racial issue" of "civil rights organizations" as well as "black nationalist," "Klan" and "hate-type" groups, with a focus on indications of "subversive or radical infiltration," identities of "leaders and individuals involved," minority community "objectives" and the "number, character and intensity of the techniques used by the minority community."

The second reason for focusing on African Americans concerned the largely black, urban riots of the mid- to late 1960s, which had increased each year leading up to 1968 (Myers 1997, 99). The responses to these activities and the fear of future black militancy were as varied as they were significant. Immediately, there were extensive hearings convened involving the highest political bodies in the land, most notably the National Advisory Commission on Civil Disorders (i.e., the Kerner Commission). These sessions were held to compile all the information regarding what took place so that the guilty could be punished for illegal action and so that individuals could be prevented from such activity in the future. There was also an effort made to discover the radical roots of such behavior. Again Goldstein (2000, 450) captures the spirit of the time rather well:

in September, 1967, Attorney General Clack directed the FBI to "use the maximum resources, investigative and intelligence, to collect and report all facts bearing upon the question as to whether there has been or is a scheme or conspiracy by any group of whatever size, effectiveness or affiliation to plan, promote or aggravate riot activity".... In direct response to this pressure from Clark, the FBI expanded its COINTELPRO in early 1968, initiating a "ghetto informant" program (which reportedly reached 4,000 operatives by 1969) designed to develop sources among people who lived and worked in a "ghetto area" who would report on such topics as "black extremist organizations," the names of "Afro-American type book stores" and their "owners, operators and clientele" and all indications of efforts by foreign powers to "take over" the Negro militant movement.

---

[5] Prior to this time, the organization did not have an explicit mandate granting it carte blanche to do as it desired.

The founding of the RNA (in 1968) thus occurred within a national political context that would not only draw the attention of the federal government but would further prompt them to coercive action with little consideration for alternative strategies. Indeed, at the birth of the RNA, the U.S. government was actively concerned with and trying to undermine foreign as well as radical connections to and developments within SMOs in America. The government was also actively trying to diminish the occurrence of racial disorder, antiwar activism, and all expressions of militancy. With the RNA's connections to individuals such as Malcolm X and Robert F. Williams, who were connected with radicals and communists and socialists both throughout the United States and abroad, the organization would clearly be viewed as threatening to the U.S. government. The RNA's desire for separatism and nationhood would identify it as a significant threat in most contexts, but in the siege-like mentality of the Johnson and later Richard Nixon (referred to as the "Law and Order") administrations, this perception would likely have increased even more. In addition to this, with the insidious statements of the Malcolm X Society during the Detroit riot/rebellion of 1967 (discussed later) and the overlapping membership with the Revolutionary Action Movement (RAM), which advocated urban guerilla warfare and discussed sabotage as well as the destruction of American cities if their demands were not met, it is clear that the RNA would be targeted. Finally, although the antiwar part of the RNA's message was limited, it did take a position similar to that of the Black Panther Party that Africans in America should be exempt from being compelled to fight for a nation that did not respect or protect them as citizens. This further antagonized the U.S. government and prompted it to consider and implement coercive activities to the exclusion of other techniques. However, although identified as threatening, given the perceived infeasibility of the RNA's plea, the perceived concentration within one state (e.g., Michigan), and the limited number of participants, repression of the institution was generally left to lower-level government actors, to which we now turn.

State Repressive Policies in Michigan

With regard to the state of Michigan, around 1968, there were some direct parallels to the national level, which led to a largely reinforcing position. At the same time, there were some differences that increase the importance of looking at this level of government. For example, several states (including Michigan) took to heart diverse presidential initiatives for addressing the issue of African American civil rights identified under U.S. Presidents' Roosevelt, Truman, and Kennedy, attempting to reduce some of the more egregious activities undertaken against blacks (such as those of Michigan Democratic governors G. Mennen Williams, 1949–60, and John B. Swainson, 1961–62, as well as Republican George Romney, 1963–69). These efforts generally focused on eliminating inequality in employment, education, and housing (attempting to eliminate the root of the problem). Notably, these efforts did not explicitly address the issue of police–African American interactions.

The first topic (employment) was fairly straightforward, as it involved giving blacks a fair opportunity in the job market. Specifically, this concerned removing restrictive hiring policies that were still present at the time (e.g., white-only laws). The second topic (education) was a bit more difficult as it involved not only such things as physically placing African Americans in classrooms with whites but also informing resistant whites about the moral teachings of Christianity and about developments in federal law. The third topic (housing) involved finding, building, and/or facilitating the purchase of adequate living quarters for the rapidly increasing black population drawn to the area because of perceived improvements in employment. This was not problematic for the majority of citizens within the state. Most of the relevant community were concentrated in Detroit, which accounted for approximately 80 percent of the black population in Michigan.

Also similar to the national level, the support for these efforts was initially quite shallow at the top, but inevitably some bipartisan legislation emerged in support of the relevant policies. Unfortunately, like the federal efforts, however, the effectiveness of these initiatives was limited. For example,

by the end of the Romney governorship in 1969, there had been ... civil rights gains in Michigan with regard to access to public accommodations, government contracting, and the membership of the state civil service, [but] lesser gains in the (larger and more important) areas of private employment, housing, education[, and] law enforcement. (Fine 2000, 335)

At the same time, Michigan generally followed the national-level orientation toward repressive action against behavioral challenges. Possessing a highly valued and vulnerable economic infrastructure, the state was extremely responsive to any claims-making efforts by social movement organizations that directly threatened entrenched economic interests. This made sense. As stated in the early 1900s, by a researcher who had conducted by far the most comprehensive evaluation of the subject,

Michigan's vast network of factories, mines, farms and lumber camps depended on an efficient infrastructure of hydroelectric dams, power plants, railroads, bridges, tunnels, and Great Lakes shipping hinged on the [Soo Locks] and Detroit boat docks. The entire network was vulnerable to sabotage, or disruption from labor unrest. (Schertzing 1999, 99–100)

This tenuous security situation had expanded with the growth of industry, the ethnic and class diversity of the relevant population, and ideological orientations (i.e., communism and socialism).

Given this scenario, quite early in its history, Michigan political authorities (especially those in the Republican Party) were highly attentive to all contentious politics. As a result, the state was one of the U.S. leaders in anti-Red activity as a way to protect capitalism and capitalists and regulate workers. After the purging of the labor movement, ridding it of the most radical elements, and the 1935 passage of the Wagner Act, which gave "acceptable" labor organizations the right to unionize, heavy-handed repression directed against non-radical-oriented activists decreased significantly (largely out of reduced necessity and early success). Regardless of the shift, however, the infrastructure for coercion was in place, and this easily facilitated its reemergence and extension.

Specifically, two institutions emerged during this earlier period. On one hand, there was the development of the Michigan State Police (MSP).[6] Largely modeled on the FBI,[7] MSP developed to be "the premier law enforcement agency in the state with a widespread reputation for professionalism and innovation" (Schertzing 1999, 253). Essentially, their job was to "'guard against industrial sabotage or sabotage [at] military installations in Michigan,' investigate 'violations of laws against criminal syndicalism,' and cooperate with the FBI 'in its drive against communistic and subversive activities'" (Schertzing 1999, 306).

When labor was effectively dealt with (i.e., purged of its radical elements and decreased in overtly challenging behavior), the object of attention became political radicalism. The period leading up to the RNA was thus crucial for state repression. Noted by Schertzing (1999, 56),

during [MSP's] organizational phase of 1935–1965, the Michigan State Police achieved significant security, prestige, and expansion in terms of physical plant, manpower, and authority. Gradual improvements in selection and training standards, working conditions, pay, benefits, equipment, job security, and leadership enhanced state police morale and the department's appeal as a career opportunity, while the department's growing record of success in terms of criminal investigations, traffic regulation, domestic security, public relations and technological innovation enhanced its professional image and reputation.

Through a series of crises, the Michigan State Police crusade against the un-Americans evolved from the sporadic sideline of a few zealous detectives and vigilante groups

---

[6] As stated within Schertzing (1999, 56),

"state police" is an imprecise term when applied to American law enforcement. Many states maintain several, independent state-level law enforcement agencies which could be described as state police, or as having state police powers. Some have overlapping or duplicated jurisdiction. While some state police forces have the same authority for searchers, seizures and arrests as county sheriffs, others are limited to highway patrol, liquor or motor vehicle regulation, or to criminal identification. Some fall under the control of the governor or attorney general, while others are subject to an independent commission or to the state motor vehicle bureau. Some are semimilitary, uniformed forces, while others are comprised exclusively of plain-clothes detectives or special agents. For this study, each of these different types of agencies may be referred to as state police.

[7] In fact, it was commonly referred to as the Little FBI.

to an official, professional unit within the department. Far more institutionalized and sophisticated than during World War I, the state police counter-subversion program was legitimized by legislation, executive policies and red scare politics at both the federal and state levels, and by a broad social consensus for domestic security.

Conversely, there was the National Guard. Although federal in its inception, this institution was created to assist any locality in the state of Michigan with the establishment and preservation of domestic order when the relevant territorial jurisdiction proved incapable of providing such order themselves. This augmentation of police power would not go unused in the state generally or the city of Detroit in particular. Indeed, the National Guard was called out in Detroit as much as in any other American city.

Clearly both the state police and the National Guard developed an antiradical orientation relevant to repressive behavior employed within Michigan. This approach to governance largely emerged from former servicemen joining and leading the institutions. It also emerged from the indoctrination received in the training provided. Related to these issues, both organizations developed an antiblack orientation as well. In particular, this resulted from the fact that neither recruited African Americans. For example,

like the National Guard elsewhere in the nation [in the mid-1960s], only about 1 percent of whom were black, the Michigan Guard was essentially lily white – of the more than eight thousand Guard soldiers who served in Detroit, only forty-two were black. (Schertzing 1999, 58)

Further exacerbating the problem, the members of these institutions tended to view blacks as a major part of the reason there needed to be a state-level policing institution in the first place. For example, when someone asked a guardsman if the riot/rebellion of 1967 and his interaction with African Americans at that time had changed his opinion about them, he said, "Yes, I no longer consider Negroes civilized" (Fine 2000, 197). Conveying a similar sentiment, another guardsman remarked, "I'm gonna shoot anything that moves and that is black." Obviously, such statements and the behavior of guardsmen stationed in black communities did nothing to assist African American perceptions of U.S. coercive activity. As we will see later, such opinions were not isolated at the state level. Additionally, and perhaps more importantly, as we will see, state institutions were not nearly as active as others.

Local Repressive Policies in Detroit Around 1968

When one moves to evaluate how political authorities at the city level dealt with the challenge they confronted with the RNA, they can easily see the twofold dynamic present at the other levels: an earlier one for reform, incorporation, and tolerance of African Americans and a later one for hostility and repression. The pace and magnitude of the activities differ.

For example, largely following, but in other ways leading, national and state-level trends with regard to the improved treatment of African Americans, relatively early on, Detroit engaged in numerous efforts to address the various problems of racism. No single individual was more associated with this change than Jerome Cavanaugh, who, voted in by a coalition of liberal black and white residents, was mayor from 1961 to 1969. To address the relevant issues, develop some ideas of how bad the situation was, put forward some ideas about what could be done, and allocate some funds toward this end, numerous efforts were established. An important part of this initiative was the creation of various committees, commissions, and programs, including the Community Action for Detroit Youth (beginning in 1962), the Total Action against Poverty (beginning in 1964), and the Committee for Human Resources Development (beginning in 1967). There was also some effort made to revise the functioning of already established agencies.

Unfortunately, no matter which actions were taken, the pervasive nature of the problems confronting African Americans seemed to overwhelm the efforts put forward to resolve them. In short, racism was simply too deeply embedded in Detroit to be affected by the initiatives being put forward. Accordingly, remediation failed, and a conservative backlash emerged that turned the whole situation in the opposite direction – away from incorporation and accommodation and toward repression.

For example, in the area of housing, initially, numerous attempts were made to incorporate blacks into already existing neighborhoods or to develop new residencies (this occurred prior to Cavanaugh but escalated under his administration). Both, however, were blocked by a complex coalition of real estate brokers, housing developers, neighborhood associations, homeowners, and restrictive "covenants" (i.e., "clauses incorporated into deeds which had as their intention the maintenance of 'desirable residential characteristics' of a neighborhood"; Sugrue 2005, 44). This revealed a strong historical bias. As stated within one of the more thorough examinations of the topic:

Detroit's public housing was racially segregated. And the small amount of public housing built in Detroit was concentrated in largely black inner-city neighborhoods. The gap between blacks and whites in public housing grew even wider in the 1950s, as thousands of blacks were relocated for urban renewal and highway construction projects, while the admissions policy of the Housing Commission remained unchanged. (Moreover) Detroit was slow to desegregate its public housing projects, and offer housing facilities to blacks and whites.

... [Indeed,] not until 1956, after the Detroit Branch of the NAACP won a lawsuit that challenged the city's racial policy, did the city open all public housing to blacks, and even then desegregation was haltingly slow. (Sugrue 2005, 86–87)

Consequently, following World War II, an ever increasing number of African Americans came to Detroit to find themselves with an ever decreasing number of places to live, and even fewer that were deemed livable. Some were able to escape the spatial concentration and restriction by obtaining homes in transitional neighborhoods or places that whites had left completely, but most were left in the worst of the inner city (e.g., Sugrue 2005, 197–207; Farley et al. 2000, Chapters 6–7). With the poorest of the black community left in the poorest housing, with little to no maintenance and increased density, the situation was increasingly becoming problematic, to say the least.

Similarly, in the realm of employment, one can see that numerous city efforts were made to improve the situation for African Americans during the 1950s and mid-1960s. For example,

aided by personnel from other city agencies as well as private consultants, [Mayor Cavanaugh's] Committee for Community Renewal drew up a proposal for a community action program to confront poverty. The city's objective... was to develop programs that would "assist people in becoming self-sufficient and socially responsible citizens, generate greater participation in community life and problems of others, and build into the lives of the impoverished the skills and aspirations necessary for rewarding and useful lives." (Fine 2000, 73)

Again, these efforts represented an attempt to address the problems of African Americans and even proved to be successful in certain ways. However, they did not resolve the main issues confronting the majority of the black population in a substantive manner, especially the older and younger members of the relevant population who faced disproportionate levels of unemployment and underemployment.

Part of the reason for the failures was (again) simply continued racism. As Sugrue (2005, 92) stated, "racial discrimination in employment was an undeniable outcome of hiring processes in postwar Detroit." Another part of the reason for Cavanaugh's failure was that businesses were leaving Detroit in droves to go to the safer, whiter suburbs as well as to the South, where organized labor was weak, wages were low, and tax breaks were abundant. This had the effect of shrinking the overall size of the pie and increasing the competition for the jobs that were left. As it is impossible to squeeze water from a rock, it was equally impossible to provide jobs to the least skilled and least desired when there were hardly any jobs to allocate.

At a time of decreased assistance for African Americans; of increased white resistance to these efforts in schools, businesses, and neighborhoods; of increased economic hardship and emerging increases in crime and militancy, no topic proved to be as difficult to address as police–African American relations. Fine describes the Detroit Police Department during the period up to the mid-1960s:

As the only city officials present in the ghetto around the clock, the police, to the ghetto dweller, were the "most visible symbol" of white society, the "extended arm" of the city government that implemented the racial policies of the dominant white community. The result was that the police bore "the full brunt of the accumulated frustrations and hostility of the ghetto." (Fine 2000, 98–99)

Discussed later, this presence was far from neutral. The policing of the black community in Detroit had always been something of a problem within the city (e.g., Widick 1972; Farley et al. 2000; Sugrue 2005). Like the MSP and the National Guard, the police department recruited African Americans poorly. To make matters worse, along with private security firms, the police frequently recruited whites from the South, and they trained officers in a racially hostile fashion. Accordingly, the predominately white police force never looked on the increasingly larger black population in a favorable manner. Indeed, negative opinions appeared to rise along with the African American increase in the population. As George Edwards, the police chief during the beginning of Cavanaugh's administration, admitted, "recruits came into the police department with all of the prejudices, hatreds and hang ups contained in the general population" (Thompson 2004, 38). He continued, "[Ninety] percent of the 4,767-man Detroit Police Department are bigoted, and [a] dislike for Negroes is reflected constantly in their language and often in physical abuse" (38).

The pipeline was clear. After two years of studying police–African American interactions, Burton Levy, the head of the Community Relations Division of the Michigan Civil Rights Commission, concluded that Detroit had a faulty police system, not just a few rotten eggs. Rather,

[this system] recruits a significant number of bigots, reinforces the bigotry through the department's value system and socialization with older officers, and then takes the worst of the officers and puts them on duty in the ghetto, where the opportunity to act out the prejudice is always available. (cited in Fine 2000, 95)

This resulted in a very bad situation throughout the ranks. Taken from a survey around 1967, it was found (as reported in the *Detroit Free Press* in 1968)

that [white police officers] held "predominantly negative views of the black community." Lower echelon white officers saw Detroit's blacks as a "privileged minority... without real grievances, deficient in respect for law and order and ready to use violence to attain a still greater advantage vis-à-vis the white community.... Slightly more than 80 percent of the white patrolmen thought that the more blacks received, the more they wanted and the more likely they were to resort to violence to satisfy their desires. Detectives, sergeants, lieutenants, and inspectors largely shared these views.

Clearly there was some temporal variation. The situation was especially bad under the leadership of Louis Miriani, mayor from 1957 to 1961 (Cavanaugh's predecessor). He initiated and oversaw an unprecedented crackdown on the African American community, regardless of their involvement with criminal activity (which was presumably the reason for the crackdown). As recalled by United Auto Workers and Trade Union Leadership Council leader Robert "Buddy" Battle,

"the situation was [that] any Negro standing on the corner, coming out of the house to get in his car, going to the church, going into a store, coming out of a store, going into a nightclub or coming out of a nightclub" was likely to be harassed and arrested. (Turrini 1999, 12–13)

This practice continued after Miriani, however, expanding to even the black elite. As Thompson (2004, 40) notes,

even the wealthiest of Detroit's African Americans came to speak out against police excess as the 1960s unfolded. In 1965, members of the Cotillion Club, an elite black social organization, noted in a letter to Cavanaugh that police-community relations had deteriorated dramatically since 1963, when, in that year alone, "there were almost 500 cases of police-inflicted injuries; and 300 of these were in the five predominantly Negro Precinct areas." Indeed, according to city records, between May 1961 and February 1964, there had been 1,507 "altercations" between the police and Detroit citizens resulting in the injury of 1,041 citizens, most of them black. Of those citizen injuries, 690 were head injuries. In those same altercations, 580 police officers were also injured and, significantly, 303 of those injuries were to the officer's hands, knuckles and fingers.[8]

By most accounts, as the mid-1960s arrived, the situation was explosive. Prior to 1967, three separate reports of the community-police commission high-lighted the racial tensions in the city and the potential for violence, noting that the police were an especially significant problem and that the monitoring of civil disturbances had increased steadily with the creation of the Demonstration Detail in 1961.

Literature is also clear that antiblack sentiments and coercive treatment of African Americans were not contained solely to the police force. On more than one occasion, whites urged the mayor not to

further weaken the protection of Detroit's citizens against the daily rapes, robberies, knifings and murders by lawless members of the Negro community.... With the black man's switchblade at their throats, the white community wants a strong, resolute force of well-trained police officers. (Thompson 2004, 41)

Although white opinion was not uniform in supporting the increased coer-cive treatment of African Americans, this largely changed after the riots and rebellion of 1967. In this context, the liberal coalition that had attempted to alleviate the problems confronting most African Americans receded, and white acceptance of coercive action directed against this community (especially those engaged in criminal and/or disruptive behavior) largely increased.

The Ascendance of Repression in the Aftermath of the 1967 Riot/Rebellion

Despite discussion of rampant dissatisfaction, racially violent behavior in other cities, and racial tensions in their own city, Detroit's political leaders and polic-ing organizations were quite pleased with the fact that, up until 1967, their city

[8] Comparative data on police abuse for other communities and cities are very difficult as the collection of this material has only been institutionalized recently. That the topic was viewed to be serious enough, however, to merit not only government commissions and independent investigations but also the discussion of elite African Americans speaks to the seriousness of the issue within the relevant community.

had been spared. As a result, they were essentially blindsided by the eruption of the riot/rebellion that took place. By most accounts, this was an internationally covered outbreak that local and state authorities could not allow to be repeated. In addition to this, there was a pervasive belief among patrolmen that the "riots" were not disorganized; rather, it was believed that they reflected a coordinated strategy of black radicals, such as the Malcolm X Society and the RAM, to disrupt urban America.[9] Accordingly, the riot/rebellion was important precisely because it (re)emphasized the perception that blacks were a threat and whites were legitimate in their fear of this community. In many respects, the situation "convinced whites that Detroit was home to well-armed Black militants who were ready to kill whites, especially police officers – and, if given the authority to do so, Blacks would exonerate other Blacks who killed white police officers" (Farley et al. 2000, 45). This provided the motivation for additional white and job flight, and it provided the motivation and permissiveness for state repressive action of almost any type and level of lethality.[10]

As a direct result of the riot/rebellion, two important dynamics emerged. First, "racial conflict [moved to] the heart of all Detroit-based politics. For example, during the mayoral election of 1969, the white sheriff of Wayne County, Roman Gribbs, ran on a law-and-order platform, promising to use all necessary policing to forcefully crack down on crime [and general disorder]. His opponent – Richard Austin – the African American Wayne Country auditor, ran on a platform" advocating sound financial management and economic growth (Farley et al. 2000, 46). Gribbs won a narrow victory and quickly began to enact numerous policies regarding the policing of the black community and the protection of whites.

This signified a major shift in Detroit politics but also in the nation. In fact, in many ways, actions at the federal level actively promoted coercive action at the local level after federal funds were moved to confront the war in Vietnam and as federal, state, and local authorities prepared to confront growing antiwar, civil rights, black power, students,' and women's protests as well as violent crime. For example, on July 29, 1967, President Johnson established a National Advisory Commission on Civil Disorders to better understand what had happened over the past few years and what could be done about it. One of the primary conclusions emerging from this effort was that authorities lacked the proper information about what was taking place in society to prepare for future disturbances. As a result, there was an immense buildup in the political surveillance and policing machinery at all levels of the government. The riot/rebellion of 1967 kicked this effort into overdrive within the city of Detroit.

Second, the divide between whites and blacks grew larger, and in this breach, more militant policies were put forward. For example, on one hand, whites in

---

[9] Higher-level police officials attributed the riot to other factors, such as poverty.

[10] It was not contained by the extensive multiethnic coalitions or widespread media coverage that existed in other parts of the country, such as Oakland, California.

Detroit wanted protection from black criminals and the excesses of rioters and lawlessness. On the other hand, blacks wanted housing and jobs. Needless to say, black desires were not heard in the postriot context. Whites (along with the jobs mentioned earlier) largely moved out of metro Detroit to the suburbs, leaving the urban environment to the blacks and, interestingly, the predominantly white police department.[11] The out-migration was particularly problematic because the historically insulated policing institutions of Detroit were already engaged in a rather heated battle with Detroit's geographically isolated black residents. Of course, this was not a unique situation. As Donner (1990, 291) identified,

a number of cities, of which Detroit is a prime example, reflected in their police structures and target priorities a similar "urban pathology": a decaying Black ghetto,... the emergence of potentially violent Black and white groups, and the development among white policemen of a "siege mentality" against the Black community... after the ghetto riots of the late sixties, self-help and violence inevitably came to be regarded in both camps – police and ghetto – as a vital means of survival. "Law and order" became a coded battle cry as the police were transformed into an army defending white power and the status quo.

The "siege mentality" Donner identified was further reinforced by other factors. For instance, the police units that confronted the RNA were the ones most removed from ordinary police duties, and the various sections of the "Red Squad" had very little contact with other parts of the department and had essentially no oversight.[12] Such a pattern was continued after the riots/rebellions, as

[11] As Farley et al. (2000, 51–52) discussed,

following the urban riots of the 1960s, the Kerner Commission bleakly described what they thought the future held if the government failed to address the nation's fundamental racial inequalities: a nation divided into largely Black and impoverished central cities surrounded by largely white and prosperous suburban rings. They were wrong about New York, Los Angeles, Washington and other locations, since immigration from Asia and Latin America changed the composition of many central cities.... But they were correct about Detroit: economic changes since 1970, combined with continuing racial polarization and the longstanding movement of whites – but not Blacks – to the suburbs, make Detroit the polarized metropolis they predicted.

[12] This resulted from several earlier laws. For example, on September 24, 1950, the Michigan state legislature passed Public Acts 38, 39, and 40:

Act 38 strengthened the state law against subversion, while Act 39 appropriated funds for the personnel and operations of a state police subversive activities investigation division established by Act 40. Act 40 required the new state police squad to investigate and compile information concerning subversive activities in cooperation with military, federal, state and local authorities. The state police commissioner was empowered to maintain confidential political intelligence files which could be shared only with such other law enforcement or state agencies as he deemed necessary. The law deemed it a felony to publicly reveal any information concerning red squad personnel or expenditures. All state and local government employees were authorized to cooperate with the state police in subversive activities investigations, while sheriffs and local police were required to do so. (Schertzing 1999, 153) increasingly more aggressive special units emerged, for example, Stop the Robberies, Enjoy Safe Streets (STRESS) in 1971. These programs resulted in a large number of hostile black-police interactions, several deaths of African Americans, and increasingly higher profile inquiries from citizen and government committees.

In addition to this, leading up to the riot/rebellion, the Detroit Police Department was engaged in a bitter fight with Mayor Cavanagh to gain greater resources and autonomy, which it won. Feeling the neglect of Cavanagh's fiscal prioritization and many years' worth of scrutiny concerning the treatment of ever-emboldened protestors,

on January 18, 1966, the Detroit Police Officers Association (DPOA) was recognized by the City of Detroit as the representative of all patrolmen on the department (which) immediately began a strenuous campaign to improve officers' pay and working conditions, and as a result, a series of collective bargaining problems arose between the city and the police union. (Bopp 1971, 163)

Although extremely contentious at times (involving ticketing slowdowns; "sick-ins," where officers would call in sick on behalf of the police; and lawsuits en masse to prevent any disruption of law enforcement on behalf of the city), the mayor's office settled with the police right before the riot/rebellion, on terms as assorted as "seniority, grievance procedures, management rights, vacations, leaves (and union recognition)" (Bopp 1971, 172).[13] This hostile bargaining interaction with the mayor and the confrontation on the streets significantly increased the collective identity and bargaining power of the police. It was in this context, with an enhanced need to prove their worth and a lack of political accountability, that the police contemplated, planned, and implemented increased coercive activity.

All this is important to the case under investigation because the RNA came into existence at a time when federal, state, and local authorities were more than willing to (exclusively) engage in repressive activity against it. Indeed, the political futures of most of the politicians involved seemed to depend on the authorities containing and/or eliminating the black revolutionary threat that was intricately tied to conceptions of law and order. In addition to this, the liberal coalition that might have pushed for tolerance and accommodation was essentially delegitimized in the fires of the riot/rebellion that engorged the nation, Michigan and Detroit. These are the individuals who had not resolved the racial problem in the city, and these are the individuals under which violence increased. Cooptation was also apparently not possible, because there was effectively no one to co-opt, as liberal black leaders proved themselves to be as out of touch as their white contemporaries with what was taking place. Thompson (2004, 35) noted,

---

[13] Indeed, the issues of the settlement could not be finalized because of the riot.

Not only had many black residents begun to doubt their liberal leaders' progress, but just as seriously, they had begun to question the wisdom of their own civil rights leadership. As the city's black civil rights leaders became wedded to and excited by the Cavanaugh administration's anti-poverty efforts, many of the poor and working-class black constituents grew more critical of their involvement in these initiatives. It had not escaped Detroit's African Americans that even though middle-class black civil rights leaders became involved with the Cavanaugh leadership, brutal discrimination continued to flourish in the city.

Lacking a political middle, the battle was thus left to the extremes: with armed and coercively aggressive whites on one side and armed black militants on the other. Seemingly with no alternative approaches in sight, the stage for the contentious state-dissident interaction was thus set.

Summary

Within this chapter, I have endeavored to lay out the basic logic of why governments engage in repressive behavior generally and then why diverse political authorities were more than willing to engage in repressive action in the specific case of the RNA. This revealed the development of new preferences and dispositions, legislation, and institutions (i.e., Red Squads) as well as new (or rather expanded) activities. While presenting this information, I also discussed why no other policies of engagement were put forward to deal with the RNA's behavioral challenge.

In the next chapter, I move to exactly what relevant political institutions did to inform themselves about the RNA challenge as well as how the record serves as a principal source regarding, not only what governments did against the dissident challengers, but also how the RNA responded to such efforts.

4

Record Keeping and Data Collection

It is one thing to understand which actors and what actions are involved with challenger (de)mobilization and state repression. It is quite another to understand exactly what is involved with an analysis of such activity.

Essentially, I maintain that there are three elements to any analysis of challenger (de)mobilization. First, one has to have a challenger that can be observed from its inception to its demise. Second, one has to have information not only about what the challengers do in general but also against the authorities in particular as well as what happens inside of the challenging organization on a daily basis, before, during, and after any government action has been taken against them. Third, one has to have a detailed understanding of the different activities undertaken by authorities against the relevant challengers as well as some understanding of other external influences that might play a role in the particular organization's survival. Each is discussed subsequently.

Challengers from Inception to Demise

It might sound somewhat banal to say, but to initiate a study of political demobilization, one must begin at the beginning of the mobilization effort; in fact, it is actually better to start even earlier. Such a point of departure is essential for properly understanding who was in the organization, what were the original objectives being pursued and the tactics selected to get there, who supported the group, where and when those affiliated with the relevant challenger met, and how they communicated with each other. These are all important for identifying whether changes occur in an SMO as a function of developments within the organization as opposed to or in conjunction with those that take place outside of the institution (e.g., as a function of state repression). In effect, we want to establish a baseline from which different interventions can be assessed.

Exactly When Does a Challenge Begin?

Drawing on the preceding discussion, four elements are important to identify. First, mobilization begins when *individuals* come together on a consistent
basis; it cannot be some front organization or exist only on paper. Second,
the members must have some *idea* about what they want to do to change the
situation of interest (i.e., they must make an explicit claim against existing
political-economic leaders, practices, and/or conditions). Third, challengers
must engage in activities or *interventions,* the objective of which is to bring
about the desired change. And fourth, there must be some formal *institution*
created for the task of bringing the desired ends into existence. In short, people
must show up, have some concept of what to do, engage in something directly
relevant to the objective being pursued, and have some consistent organizational structure that brings all of this together. One could highlight each of
these individually. The founding documents and statements, an office, a list
of numbers, or some action might qualify. However, I would maintain that
several elements are required at one time.

Such an opinion is generally shared in the literature. For example, in social
movement research (a relatively low-level lethal action), challenges are begun
when dissident behavior is enacted, undertaken by some collectivity of individuals who have made a specific claim against some other actor (e.g., Tilly 1978;
Tarrow 1994; Earl et al. 2003). Similarly, in discussions of civil war (a relatively high-level lethal action), challenges are not designated as such until some
formally organized political challenger is able to field a military force and has
killed (or, at least, has the capacity to kill) some members of the government
(e.g., Sambanis 2004).

When Does One Know When One Challenging Organization Has Stopped and Another Started?

This is somewhat tricky, but the key resides in understanding the elements discussed previously. For example, if one can find that charters, members, locales,
objectives, and/or tactical approaches are all or in some combination distinct
from one another, it would be safe to say that the challenges are different and
unique. If, however, organizational charters are overlapping, members are similar, locales are the same, objectives seem comparable, and the same tactics are
employed at the same time, then it is safe to say that the challenges are related
and/or indistinguishable. Such evaluation is somewhat complex to make in the
US-RNA case because Detroit at the time represented a wellspring of political activism, with individuals playing different roles in different institutions.[1]
For example, one individual (Aneg Kgotsile) was a simultaneous member of
the Students for Non-Violence Coordinating Committee as well as the RNA,

---

[1] I would like to thank Errol Henderson for pointing this out to me.

and another prominent member of the RNA (General Gordon Baker Jr.) was leader of an organization called UHURU as well as of the Revolutionary Action Movement, which had diverse ties to the RNA. This was an issue not only for the Republic but also for other black nationalist organizations in Detroit, for example, the Black Panthers and the League of Revolutionary Black Workers/Dodge Revolutionary Union Movement. These groups shared ideas, institutions, interventions, and individuals, but not always to the same degree, and this allows us to draw some boundaries.

Along with my discussion earlier about the similarities and differences between the different black nationalist movement organizations in Detroit, it seems as if the main question is simply, was there enough distinct about the RNA to merit consideration on its own? Was there enough *there* to justify an examination of the RNA without simultaneously addressing other organizations at the same time? Part of the difficulty in answering this question is the fact that other organizational records do not exist to allow such an evaluation. Institutional independence is essentially an empirical question regarding a researcher's ability to parse one institution from another, and on this point the record does not exist – at least not in print or available to the public. At some point, some ethnographic work would be useful in teasing such issues out, but even this does not completely get us out of quandary set by the task.

This said, I feel comfortable arguing that the RNA was a distinct organization that was different from others around it. From the available literature and from discussions with various members as well as researchers of the period, it is clear that there was a distinct cohort of individuals that evolved from the Group on Advanced Leadership (GOAL), the Freedom Now Party, and the Malcolm X Society (all discussed later) into the RNA, which did not simultaneously exist in any other organization. There were also distinct ideas that were espoused, a distinct group of individuals, a unique organizational structure, a geographic base in Detroit, and a relatively uncommon combination of interventions (i.e., tactics). In the language of organizational literature, the RNA represented a distinct niche within a relatively full marketplace of black nationalism. Numerous entities in existence took up distinct spaces within this market, but nevertheless the RNA occupied a space that was unique and, for a time, coherent enough for us to consider them a distinct political entity. Perhaps the biggest piece of evidence for this is the fact that almost no other black nationalist organization openly took steps to secede from the United States, despite maintaining an interest in doing so. This was not a position that could be viewed as establishing an easy path for its members, and thus such a choice represents a significant degree of sacrifice as well as independence of thought and action. Another piece of evidence concerns the fact that there was a distinct compilation of observations taken by the police, the media, and the RNA itself about what this specific organization did, who was involved, and what was done against them that considered them to be a distinct entity from others around it at the time.[2] This is discussed further later.

Where Does Information About Behavioral Challenges Come From?

Historically, several potential information sources have been used by researchers relevant to identifying challengers and their repression and survival. For example, the RNA might have recorded its own creation, persecution, and existence by making a formal statement and issuing a press release. Alternatively, activists might recall such an occurrence in an interview. If the press were called, then it is possible that there would be a story contained in some archive somewhere. It is also possible that government took notice and issued a report. Although frequently used, these types of data suffer from a wide range of limitations, which must be addressed before they can be used (Davenport 2010).

Information on the activities of challengers, which is the second characteristic needed to assess my topic of interest, typically emerges from newspapers, government documents, legal records, and social movement reports within what is frequently referred to as "quantitative" work and/or from interviews, memoirs, diaries, and participant observation in "qualitative" research. Indeed, this is the stuff of which most studies in the relevant area of research are built. Information on the activities directed against authorities and against one another (e.g., recruitment, training, fund-raising, and morale boosting) is essential, for it is the claims-making effort (i.e., what I called interventions) that assists in classifying the political actor as a challenger in the first place.[3]

Information on behavior within the organization is also useful, especially for determining the general state of the challenger and identifying expressions of fear and anger as well as attempts at reappraisal and trust building. This type of information is generally much harder to get, and thus it has rarely been examined. Most SMOs do not keep detailed records of this sort. In a sense, most activists are too busy being active to be archivists. There is the occasional exception, like the records of the Student Nonviolent Coordinating Committee, which kept very detailed minutes, background papers, and the like (Carson 1981), but these were rare.

Interestingly, governments have frequently served as a source of information about internal challenger dynamics precisely because they have a vested interest

---

[2] Now, this is not to say the RNA did not have connections with other organizations and that it was not influenced by their experiences (in and outside of Detroit). Rather, it is to say that there was enough substance to the SMO (i.e., enough there) that it is reasonable to assume that the RNA's existence was independent enough to evaluate on its own.

[3] Without actual behavior being undertaken, a different type of organization is under discussion.

in understanding exactly who is in a challenging organization, what they are doing when they are there, and who is connected to whom (e.g., Churchill and Vander Wall 1988; Cunningham 2004). The problem with such records is the availability of the material to those outside of the government and the viewer's inability to determine exactly what was and was not collected. In fact, in an archive in its rawest form, these records are generally viewed as a compilation of snapshots, frequently disrupted by omissions (i.e., blacked out or redacted text) for "security purposes." It is very difficult to get a string of government surveillance information over the same place, people, and time because this reveals what the government was doing covertly, disclosing priorities and methods. One could imagine that, every now and then, governments of all types would like such information revealed to intimidate political challengers and foment suspicion, but they would not want this information revealed too consistently or in too much detail, for this might raise grievances and allow people to discern patterns.[4]

Given this situation, many researchers have consulted former activists through interviews (e.g., Poletta 2002). While useful in revealing insights into how challenging entities functioned and what participants did within them, such efforts must contend with the fundamental problem that what challengers remember and reconstruct is not necessarily an accurate record of what actually took place. Indeed, it is better to think of the recollection of contentious behavior as a different entity entirely from what actually took place. This problem becomes even greater as the distance between experience (the behavioral challenge) and retelling (or the researcher's interview or compilation) increases (e.g., Goodman 1994).

Understanding the strengths and limitations of different sources noted previously, for my research, I rely on a unique source of data regarding the RNA. The main source of information about this group, what they did and what was done to them, is a record compiled by a Detroit antiradical unit, or "Red Squad." Obtained through a combination of Freedom of Information Act requests, personal archives, and many court, police, and public records, the data used to investigate this case were compiled, scanned, and coded between 1999 and 2003 by myself and a dozen graduate and undergraduate students at the universities of Houston, Colorado, and Maryland (Davenport 1998, 2005). The records in the collection are quite extensive, in part explained by the increased mandate of as well as the increased resources allocated to the relevant government organizations over time.

As Donner (1990, 291) discussed, "the Detroit Red Squad underwent enormous growth in the sixties in response to New Left and black protest activities." He continues,

---

[4] This accounts for Edward Snowden's current difficulties after revealing too much about U.S. political surveillance.

Prior to the 1967 outbreak, the Detroit police had recognized the need to monitor the mounting civil rights demonstrations and for that purpose had formed a demonstration detail within the Special Investigation Bureau (SIB) that functionally overlapped the responsibilities of an established subversive unit in the Criminal Investigation Bureau. (292)

This shifted after 1967, however, as the units and their activities expanded. As for what was done, Donner notes that

the information collected by the squad concerning (relevant challengers) individuals or organizations was stored in master files, which bulged with inter-office memoranda, third party interviews (utilities, employers, landlords), newspaper clippings, documents and literature "lifted" by informers, and a variety of public records. Filed information included a subject's address, spouse, vital statistics, criminal history (if any), and a photograph when available. In addition, such personal information as "localities frequented," friends, personal characteristics, and traits were recorded. (295)

These records were compiled by diverse organizations, principally based within cities but extending up to state and federal levels, across government agencies. This includes police departments, judicial institutions (e.g., the Justice Department and district courts), intelligence organizations (e.g., the FBI, CIA, State Department, and U.S. Army), and the Internal Revenue Service.

The records themselves are composed of different types of documents, which contain different types of information.[5] For example, some are *informant* reports from several local (i.e., the Detroit Police Department – Special Investigations, Demonstration Detail, Intelligence Division, Inspectional Service Bureau, Security Unit, Detective Division, Criminal Division, Public Complaints Division, and Tactical Reconnaissance), state (i.e., the Michigan State Police – Special Investigation Bureau, Special Investigation Unit), and federal institutions (i.e., the FBI, the IRS, and the U.S. State Department). Here, as was common practice at the time, diverse government agencies had someone pose as a member of the RNA and provide information about what the person observed, heard, and/or read while operating in this capacity. This information would be told to some case agent, contact, or "handler," who would type up the testimony for distribution and filing. The identities of the informant and the principal contact in the police department are redacted in the documents, but all other information is available.

The records generally take the following form: at the top is the specific police division under whose jurisdiction the informant falls, the date of the report, and

---

[5] Do I feel that I have everything? Of course not, but this will never be the case, as relevant agencies may have either destroyed their files entirely or blacked out entries, especially information concerning the most controversial actions. Indeed, had it not been for the interruption of a few judges in Detroit and several police officers who deemed this information worthy for mass distribution, the files employed here would not have been made available.

DETROIT POLICE DEPARTMENT .

INTER-OFFICE MEMORANDUM
DETECTIVE DIVISION
SPECIAL   INVESTIGATION   BUREAU
                                    Date_____ August 5, 1969

To: ███████████████, Special Investigation Bureau

Subject: INFORMATION RECEIVED FROM SPECIAL INVESTIGATION BUREAU
           SOURCE ████

On Monday, August 4, 1969, the writer received the following information from Special Investigation Bureau SOURCE████

At 2:00 PM, August 3, 1969, the REPUBLIC OF NEW AFRICA held a meeting at 9823 Dexter, REPUBLIC OF NEW AFRICA office. There were about 40 persons in attendance. (Eight new persons became citizens of the R. N. A.: they arrived at the meeting in a new station wagon, license # CF 4460. Registration will follow on supplement when available.)

The following persons were identified by SOURCE at the meeting:

JOHN SAULSBERRY	VERONICA HIBBITT
JOHN DAVIS	RICHARD HENRY (Imari)
ALFRED HIBBITT (Alfred 2-X)	JUANITA HIBBITT
WARREN GALLOWAY	CHARLES THORNTON
CLEAM PEOPLES	ERNEST DENMON (Ernest L-2)
QUINN O.HATFIELD (Balagun)	LEROY LAWSON (Kenyatta)
MILDRED KOHLMEYER	BRENDA RALSTON
ROBERT WINSTON	ANDERSON HOWARD
JAMES MC HENRY	ROSA WINSTON

The meeting was chaired by Johnnie Saulsberry: Veronica Hibbitt (SISTER INSHA), daughter of ALFRED HIBBITT, was the Secretary.

The National Convention is to be held August 22nd, 23nd, and 24th, 1969, in Washington, D. C., --instead of August 15th, 16th, and 17th, 1969: RICHARD HENRY (Imari Obadele) is responsible for the change. SAULSBERRY has stated that it is HENRY's fault that the Co..vention dates conflict with the Cabaret party scheduled for August 23rd.

Free housing for at least 500 people has been obtained for those attending the Convention. The site of the Convention has not been revealed, although the Mayor of Washington has apparently given his approval.

Members going to the Convention are to contact SAULSBERRY, (who will attempt to rent a bus for this trip). There will be about 20 people from the Detroit Consul going to the Convention.

All National Officers are to be replaced--by election--during the Convention.

Form C of D-77-ME   D.P.D. 568 (12-63)   ℗e

FIGURE 4.1. Sample informant record. From Radical Information Project.

to whom the report was issued. Below this is the date of the event in question (e.g., a meeting, lecture, workshop, conference, or protest), the identity of the individuals present at the meeting who were known to the informant (by name), as well as an estimate of the total number of individuals attending specific events. By far, the bulk of the information identified in the records concerned the content of organizational meetings and events (e.g., protests and parties). Following this information is a chronological listing of exactly what took place. For example, records note who spoke (in order), what they said,

ERNEST DENMAN (Ernest 2-L) has been in New York City since early April, 1969. He has been working for the R.N.A. out of 125 Hopkins St., New York City. He has become a Muslum, and claims the Muslums will help the R.N.A. in any way that will not hurt their (Muslum) cause.

DENMAN (and 12 others) are going by bus to Chicago, Illinois on Saturday, August 9, 1969. They are to go to the Topographical Center for further study (maps, etc.).

RICHARD HENRY went to New York City last weekend and obtained money from from the New York Consul, --which was posted as bond for the release of RAFAEL VIERA.

  After VIERA's release, a party was held at the home of HAROLD P. JACKSON (Brother Sonnie), 145 Tyler.

ALFRED HIBBITT is now driving an old white over red Dodge, CF 9211. (Registratio will follow on supplement when available.)
At 7:00 PM on Mondays, Wednesdays, and Fridays, CHARLES THORNTON will conduct classes on "the building of a nation."

The Sphinx Club will sponsor a Cabaret party at 1775 West Forest, Masons' Hall, on August 23, 1969 (at 9:00 PM) for the benefit of the New African Educational Committee.

QUINN Q. HATFIELD (Balagun), who was arrested and charged with Attempt Murder--with the charge reduced to Aggrevated Assault#-has obtained a job at Dodge Main. #Louisiana arrest, 8-16-68).

JOHNNIE SAULSBERRY is now attempting to obtain work with the Board of Education. (The type of work is not known.)

JOHN DAVIS turned the National Citizenship files (from March, 1969 Convention) over to RICHARD HENRY at the meeting. HENRY requested the files for his use, prior to the convention.

READ AND APPROVED:

Special Investigation Bureau

Special Investigation Bureau

FIGURE 4.1 (*continued*)

what activities were being planned, and which had already been undertaken. While the majority of records were created by the Detroit Police Department, the second-largest number were created by the Michigan State Police, followed by the FBI. An example of an informant report is provided as Figure 4.1.

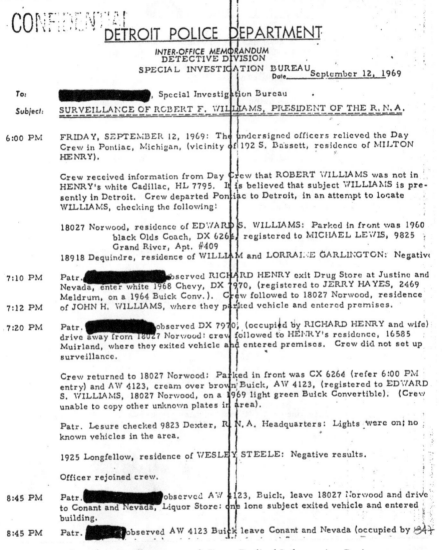

CON̶F̶I̶D̶E̶N̶T̶I̶A̶L̶

DETROIT POLICE DEPARTMENT

INTER-OFFICE MEMORANDUM
DETECTIVE DIVISION
SPECIAL INVESTIGATION BUREAU

Date_____ September 12, 1969

To: ████████████, Special Investigation Bureau

Subject: SURVEILLANCE OF ROBERT F. WILLIAMS, PRESIDENT OF THE R.N.A.

6:00 PM   FRIDAY, SEPTEMBER 12, 1969: The undersigned officers relieved the Day
          Crew in Pontiac, Michigan, (vicinity of 192 S. Bassett, residence of MILTON
          HENRY).

          Crew received information from Day Crew that ROBERT WILLIAMS was not in
          HENRY's white Cadillac, HL 7795. It is believed that subject WILLIAMS is pre-
          sently in Detroit. Crew departed Pontiac to Detroit, in an attempt to locate
          WILLIAMS, checking the following:

          18027 Norwood, residence of EDWARD S. WILLIAMS: Parked in front was 1960
                    black Olds Coach, DX 6264, registered to MICHAEL LEWIS, 9825
                    Grand River, Apt. #409
          18918 Dequindre, residence of WILLIAM and LORRAINE GARLINGTON: Negative

7:10 PM   Patr. ████████████ observed RICHARD HENRY exit Drug Store at Justine and
          Nevada, enter white 1968 Chevy, DX 7970, (registered to JERRY HAYES, 2469
          Meldrum, on a 1964 Buick Conv.). Crew followed to 18027 Norwood, residence
7:12 PM   of JOHN H. WILLIAMS, where they parked vehicle and entered premises.

7:20 PM   Patr. ████████████ observed DX 7970, (occupied by RICHARD HENRY and wife)
          drive away from 18027 Norwood: crew followed to HENRY's residence, 16585
          Muirland, where they exited vehicle and entered premises. Crew did not set up
          surveillance.

          Crew returned to 18027 Norwood: Parked in front was CX 6264 (refer 6:00 PM
          entry) and AW 4123, cream over brown Buick, AW 4123, (registered to EDWARD
          S. WILLIAMS, 18027 Norwood, on a 1969 light green Buick Convertible). (Crew
          unable to copy other unknown plates in area).

          Patr. Lesure checked 9823 Dexter, R.N.A. Headquarters: Lights were on; no
          known vehicles in the area.

          1925 Longfellow, residence of WESLEY STEELE: Negative results.

          Officer rejoined crew.

8:45 PM   Patr. ████████████ observed AW 4123, Buick, leave 18027 Norwood and drive
          to Conant and Nevada, Liquor Store: one lone subject exited vehicle and entered
          building.
8:45 PM   Patr. ████ observed AW 4123 Buick leave Conant and Nevada (occupied by 34)

FIGURE 4.2. Sample surveillance record. From Radical Information Project.

Some documents are *surveillance* reports (Figure 4.2). These records were
largely collected by the Detroit Police Department and the FBI. There are of
course different types of surveillance, but the records employed in this study
are of "physical" form. Here an officer observes either a place and/or an individual. Regarding places, these records identify who visited the locale under
observation and what they were driving (including the license plate number).
If nothing was going on at a specific target, then police would note this as well.

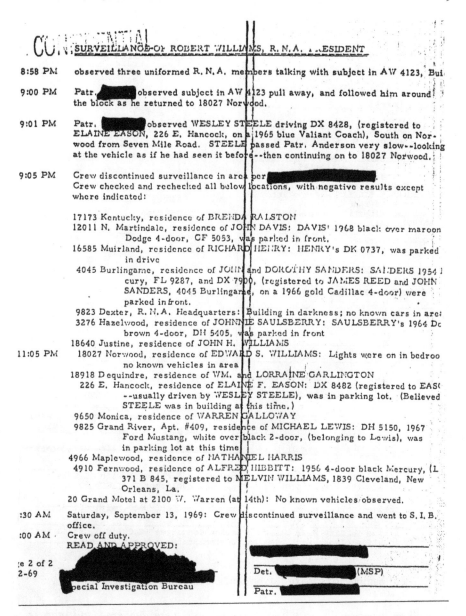

CONFIDENTIAL SURVEILLANCE OF ROBERT WILLIAMS, R.N.A. PRESIDENT

8:58 PM   observed three uniformed R.N.A. members talking with subject in AW 4123, Bui

9:00 PM   Patr. ▮▮▮▮ observed subject in AW 4123 pull away, and followed him around the block as he returned to 18027 Norwood.

9:01 PM   Patr. ▮▮▮▮ observed WESLEY STEELE driving DX 8428, (registered to ELAINE EASON, 226 E. Hancock, on a 1965 blue Valiant Coach), South on Norwood from Seven Mile Road. STEELE passed Patr. Anderson very slow--looking at the vehicle as if he had seen it before--then continuing on to 18027 Norwood.

9:05 PM   Crew discontinued surveillance in area per ▮▮▮▮.
Crew checked and rechecked all below locations, with negative results except where indicated:

     17173 Kentucky, residence of BRENDA RALSTON
     12011 N. Martindale, residence of JOHN DAVIS: DAVIS' 1968 black over maroon Dodge 4-door, CF 5053, was parked in front.
     16585 Muirland, residence of RICHARD HENRY: HENRY's DK 0737, was parked in drive
     4045 Burlingame, residence of JOHN and DOROTHY SANDERS: SANDERS 1954] cury, FL 9287, and DX 7900, (registered to JAMES REED and JOHN SANDERS, 4045 Burlingame, on a 1966 gold Cadillac 4-door) were parked in front.
     9823 Dexter, R.N.A. Headquarters: Building in darkness; no known cars in area
     3276 Hazelwood, residence of JOHNNIE SAULSBERRY: SAULSBERRY's 1964 Do brown 4-door, DH 5405, was parked in front
     18640 Justine, residence of JOHN H. WILLIAMS

11:05 PM   18027 Norwood, residence of EDWARD S. WILLIAMS: Lights were on in bedroo no known vehicles in area
     18918 Dequindre, residence of WM. and LORRAINE GARLINGTON
     226 E. Hancock, residence of ELAINE F. EASON: DX 8482 (registered to EASO --usually driven by WESLEY STEELE), was in parking lot. (Believed STEELE was in building at this time.)
     9650 Monica, residence of WARREN GALLOWAY
     9825 Grand River, Apt. #409, residence of MICHAEL LEWIS: DH 5150, 1967 Ford Mustang, white over black 2-door, (belonging to Lewis), was in parking lot at this time
     4966 Maplewood, residence of NATHANIEL HARRIS
     4910 Fernwood, residence of ALFRED HIBBITT: 1956 4-door black Mercury, (L 371 B 845, registered to MELVIN WILLIAMS, 1839 Cleveland, New Orleans, La.
     20 Grand Motel at 2100 W. Warren (at 14th): No known vehicles observed.

:30 AM   Saturday, September 13, 1969: Crew discontinued surveillance and went to S.I.B. office.

:00 AM   Crew off duty.
     READ AND APPROVED:

:e 2 of 2
2-69
▮▮▮▮ ecial Investigation Bureau

Det. ▮▮▮▮ (MSP)
Patr. ▮▮▮▮

FIGURE 4.2 (*continued*)

Regarding individuals, these records identify who the person is (by name, age, address, and some basic description), where the person went, how the person traveled there, with whom the person interacted, and how long the person stayed. Records also indicate when specific police details went on or off duty

LAST NAME	FIRST	MIDDLE	DETROIT POLICE DEPARTMENT

HENRY, RICHARD BULLOCK

Criminal Information Bureau

ALIAS
Imari Obadele, Sterling Grey

ADDRESS
16585 Muirland

TELEPHONE
Un.4-2501

AUTOMOBILE both use DK 0737   LICENSE NO.
'61 Cad.Conv. & '62 Blue Buick

FAMILY
WIFE: Octavia Vivian,nee Young
SONS: Frederick -5/11/'45
       Richard - 2/11/56
DAUGHTER: Marilyn-8/9/'52
BROTHERS & SISTERS -eleven including
Milton & Lawrence.
FATHER: Walter L. Henry -1135 19th. Philadelphia, Pennsylvania
Street, Phila.,(retired 1957 Post
           Office employee)
MOTHER: Deceased

BIRTH DATE	COLOR	HEIGHT	WEIGHT	HAIR	EYES
5-2-1930	Blk.	5'8"	165	blk	bro

INFORMATION SUBMITTED BY   DATE
3-30-'69

DPD NO.	CIB NO.
217423	

ASSOCIATES
Officers, delegates, & members of
Republic of New Africa.

FBI NO.	OTHER NOS. (SPECIFY AGENCY)
157 194 G	

FPC L 1101 10
M 1T01

LOCALITIES FREQUENTED

- - - - - - - - - - FOLD - - - - - - - - - -

MO SPECIALTY
Minister of Interior of R.N.A.

BUSINESS OR OCCUPATION
Former-Chrysler Tank Arsenal
Maybe employed as"Custodian"-Detroit
Public Schools Center Building,room#
                                 416

CRIMINAL HISTORY
Arrested   Traffic arrests in Detroit and Philadelphia

Arrested   3-30-1969 Assault w/Intent to Commit Murder (police officers)
       R.N.A. meeting at 8430 Linwood.

REMARKS:
1964: President of GOAL, rifle club organizer affiliated with Cleveland
Rifle Club (President-Medgar Evers). Publisher of " NOW " magazine.
Strong advocate of Malcolm X/

1965: Active in GOAL, RAM, Medgar Evers Rifle Club(MERC),participated in
forming the Fox & Wolf Hunt Club.

1967: Active in City Wide Citizens Action Committee (C.C.A.C.), still active
in rifle clubs practicing at Pontiac State Park rifle range.
                         (OVER)

FIGURE 4.3. Sample arrest record. From Radical Information Project.

as well as occasionally to whom these records were delivered and who read
and approved them (see an example in Figure 4.2).

In addition to surveillance records, *arrest* records are included among the
documents (Figure 4.3). These identify the arrestees' names ("slave"/legal
names as well as any "free" names or aliases), birthdays, color/race, height,
weight, hair and eye color, picture, mailing address, telephone number, automobile type and license number, the names of family members, associates

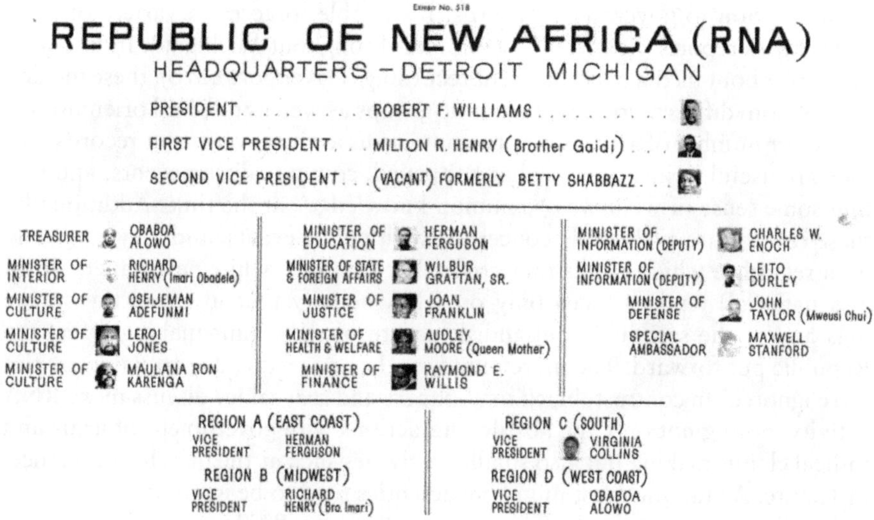

FIGURE 4.4. Organizational chart of leadership. From Radical Information Project.

within the black movement, the date of the report, the individuals' business or occupation, criminal histories, specific file numbers, and all organizational affiliations. Although the bulk of these records concern individuals in Detroit, there are documents from other cities as well.[6] Given the geographic distribution, it should come as no surprise that local, state, and federal arrest records are often included.

The files also include *ephemera* (which are less uniform but still extensive compilations). This includes interorganizational correspondence between different policing organizations (normally informational in nature), an extensive collection of newspaper clippings involving the RNA within local as well as national press and a wide variety of items that the police acquired about the group from raids, public gatherings, and theft from undercover operations. These include posters, flyers, letterhead, address books, planning documents, a novel, a coloring book, letters from supporters and other SMOs, directives from government officials to the RNA membership, executive orders from the president of the RNA to members, legal briefs, and synopses of "Constitutional Crises" and "National Conventions." Figure 4.4 reveals an organizational chart of the RNA leadership.

---

[6] This includes the following locales: Tuskegee, Alabama; Crittenden and Hughes, Arkansas; Compton, Georgia; Los Angeles, California; Chicago, Illinois; Lexington and Louisville, Kentucky; Metarie and New Orleans, Louisiana; Boston and Cambridge, Massachusetts; Ann Arbor, Michigan; the Bronx, Brooklyn, Manhattan, and Queens, New York; Columbus, Mississippi; Akron, Cincinnati, Dayton, and Cleveland, Ohio; Wilberforce, Philadelphia, and Pittsburgh, Pennsylvania; Memphis, Tennessee; and Washington, D.C.

In addition to government records, I was able to access a variety of local newspapers reports (i.e., from Detroit and throughout Michigan). In line with my book about media bias and event recording (Davenport 2010), these include papers from different locales and ethnic groups as well as political orientations. The sheer number of articles is not as numerous as the government records, but they are useful in identifying what happened, contextualizing events, and getting some sense of what was "common knowledge" at the time. Additionally, these records are exclusively concerned with public events, and they vary only with regard to which events they cover. For example, white newspapers (local and national) tend to focus only on RNA activity that involved the shootings and/or the seemingly outlandish nature of the claims-making effort the Republic put forward. The more mundane, less dramatic, day-to-day activities were ignored. In contrast, black newspapers and magazines discuss more RNA activity, noting not only the hostile interactions with government officials and radical claims making but also smaller activities such as the march, conference, or lecture. Again, the most mundane activities tend to be ignored.

Finally, I have obtained diverse records from the RNA itself. The form and content of records vary a great deal. Some records concerning *individual members* are rather detailed, including information about someone's name, address, and sometimes reasons for joining. Some records are *background reports* or *policy papers* concerning the RNA's position on a topic (e.g., nation building or the best type of economic system for African Americans). Some records concern *legal documents* that emerge from the RNA's legal system (e.g., lawsuits for slander or legal cases to ascertain the legality of a specific action taken). Some records are simply *announcements* about different events (e.g., political education classes, workshops, or organizational meetings). These records are also not as numerous as the government records, but they do provide an important source against what one can compare other sources.[7] Additionally, the records

---

[7] While social scientists use information like that identified above quite frequently, it is unfortunate that such use is not accompanied by reflection about the weaknesses as well as the strengths of the material utilized. Toward this end, I think it is useful to think about what each source likely provides as well as where they are probably deficient. This is done in the following.

For example, consider information from the U.S. government – generally, the police. Given the official mandate of the institution, I would expect that it would cover a large amount of RNA activity – especially that which was public in nature (i.e., out in the street and/or in a large meeting). I assume that its ability to acquire information would be reduced when the meeting size was smaller (as the likelihood of having an informant or some other source is decreased) but increased over time as agents became more knowledgeable. Clearly it is important to recognize that there are different institutions: federal, state, and local. In line with some of my earlier work (Davenport 2010) and much of the existing literature, many have argued that local sources provide the most detailed information, for they have the greatest access to the relevant challenging institution, have the largest number of opportunities to turn individuals into informants, and possess knowledge about the context and the people involved. In contrast, state and federal authorities, respectively, should have increasingly fewer of these characteristics and thus less information.

identified here are not as diligent about noting exactly who is or is not in attendance at individual RNA events but they do cover such things on occasion,

It is important to note distinct mandates of the different policing organizations involved as well. Local authorities were interested in identifying, countering, and/or eliminating challengers; state authorities were interested in preventing diffusion of activities and beliefs throughout the state in question; and federal authorities were interested in preventing national diffusion of relevant activities and beliefs. Additionally, agency-specific objectives might come into play. For example, during the period of the RNA, the FBI has been found to be more interested in appeasing J. Edgar Hoover than in responding to the situation on the ground (e.g., Cunningham 2004). They also had an interest in portraying challengers in the most threatening manner possible, thereby justifying their perception of the significant nature of the threat posed by radicals in general and African American challengers in particular. In source material provided by this organization, it is therefore important to recall the objectives of the records, the source (i.e., the individual field agent), and the audience or target (i.e., Hoover). With this consideration, it is clear that agents would be as detailed as possible with regard to who was doing what against whom and that there would be excessive discussion about criminal behavior as well as any actions taken that could threaten the U.S. political economy.

In contrast, local police in Detroit were under pressure to address the "black problem" left after the riot/rebellion of 1967. Although there was external pressure that one might expect to influence what emerges from the sources used in the present study, this is actually less problematic in the case examined here, for it was *not* standard policy at the time for records to be distributed outside of the relevant policing organization (i.e., it was assumed that only Detroit Police Department officials would have access to selected documents that were specifically requested). This is not to say that records would not be shared but rather that there was no standard policy that that would be the case. Such a position would reduce the amount of political posturing and would tend to focus the discussion on the matters at hand. As such, it represents a very different situation from that of the FBI, where records created in the field are expected to be distributed outside the immediate jurisdiction, up to the leader of the organization. As the individuals engaged in electronic and physical surveillance as well as informants and agents provocateurs had every incentive to identify every possible criminal offense or activity in which the RNA engaged, which could be useful later on in establishing a record that could be used against the RNA later in court, it is expected that a large number of activities would be noted – regardless of how small they seemed. Part of the reason for the broad sweep was that the police were not quite sure what they were dealing with in regard to the RNA. As a result, government agents tended to take down a tremendous amount of information.

Finally, during this time, state authorities in Michigan were largely following cues from federal authorities (lacking identity of their own), but there was no individual like Hoover or a practice of providing information like that found within the FBI. There was extensive coverage of events that they came across. This allowed them to respond to state-level concerns about the degree of radicalism found within their state. At the same time, lacking the extensive network of informants and agents provocateurs from within the more local policing agency, their coverage tended to be comparatively limited, focused on larger-scale activities and/or the most contentious groups flagged by federal authorities, where the RNA was not viewed as a priority.

My expectations and the orientation of most researchers regarding record keeping at the time were confirmed in many respects but differed in others. For example, the bulk of the records with information that was deemed codable and useful were local in nature (i.e., from the Detroit Police Department). These organizations pay far more attention to who did what to whom, when, and where. Sources further away from Detroit identified fewer events than the ones they focused in on tended to be larger, more violent, and relatively obvious. Interestingly, despite somewhat different organizational mandates, locales, and levels of effort, the sources presented information in similar ways. Indeed, the formulaic nature with which information was collected which is useful for comparison across source material. There is a division of sorts between Detroit-specific and non-Detroit-specific information. The bulk of the material concerns the RNA headquarters in Detroit, which was also the area from which the most consistent members came. The records here are very detailed (incredibly so) and seemingly address the smallest of events (e.g., meetings of three or four people or a bake sale to purchase land in the South). There are records concerning activities in other places as well, where assorted programs were held. These non-Detroit sources, however, tend to overlap with federal police information as they also tended to focus on the larger events, ignoring the more mundane, smaller actions. In total, there are more than ten thousand pages of information.

Case Selection and Data

Given access to various source material, I was able to address each of the elements required for an examination of challenger demobilization, as discussed previously. My method of analysis was somewhat distinct from that normally applied within the literature (mainly found in academic articles). Many researchers employ some correlational analysis, which identifies an impact of some independent variable (e.g., repression or burnout) on some dependent variable (e.g., subsequent political dissent). In line with this, I am currently working on numerous analyses with the provided data (Davenport and Sullivan 2014). Unfortunately, there are a great many reasons why a correlation of this sort might be found, and thus I've attempted to unpack the causal process and measure as well as analyze specific aspects directly, through detailed process tracing, not through proxies.

As opposed to selecting periods at random or some alternative method, I chose a within-case approach where the independent variables of interest (i.e., external as opposed to internal factors) varied and where I try to see how these influenced RNA participation and activity – my dependent variables of interest. Specifically, I consider five distinct periods that took place during the course of the RNA's existence and that contained records from the U.S. government, the media, and the RNA (all discussed later). Three periods involve

and put forward suggests a high degree of similarity with regard to training and procedure. Also interesting was the fact that there were far fewer references to criminal action than anticipated. I expected to see some mention of a weapon, marijuana, a planned bank robbery, or something on a repeated basis, but this was actually quite rare. I also expected to read about in-fighting more frequently, but again, this was rare. To be clear, I do not accept, and I suggest that the reader not accept, as fact all the charges levied against the RNA that are reported in the records employed. Many charges are found to be unsupported or entirely false, resulting in acquittal. Validating these claims is not the objective of the research. Understanding what authorities did and assessing the impact of its actions on the RNA (regardless of the actual merits of the charge) are the objectives. Similarly, I do not accept, and I suggest that the reader not accept, the charges levied against the United States by the RNA.

situations where there was no state repressive behavior employed against the RNA but there were significant internal debates/discussions within the dissident organization of interest. This includes 1 (the RNA Founding), 2 (Ocean Hill–Brownsville), and 4 (Factionalization). Two periods involve situations where there was repressive behavior at the time but limited internal turmoil, that is, 3 (the New Bethel "incident") and 5 (the raid/arrest in Mississippi). To gauge the impact of external as opposed to internal factors, I conduct detailed evaluations of the two-month period leading up to the event in question, comparing this to the period where the relevant event occurred as well as to the subsequent two-month period. These were essential for establishing baselines and controls, as the relevant periods tend to be quite different from the period of the event in question as well as the postevent period. This is discussed further in the next section.

Five Events and Five Periods

As noted earlier, I examine five discrete episodes in the history of the RNA, focusing on specific events within each. This includes the following:

1. the founding of the RNA in Detroit on March 28, 1968
2. the initiation of the first RNA campaign to create what was referred to as an "Open City" (a "free" space run not by the United States but by the RNA) in Ocean Hill–Brownsville, Brooklyn, on October 15, 1968
3. a police raid, arrest, and interrogation of the RNA, referred to as the "New Bethel Incident," at the first national conference in Detroit on March 28, 1969
4. the development of a faction within the RNA in Detroit on November 16, 1969
5. a police raid on the RNA's newly established capital in Jackson, Mississippi, which took place on August 18, 1971

The selected events not only represent some of the most important within the organization's history but also very different types of contexts, some explicitly repressive and some explicitly internal to the organization. This allows us to explore the impact of variation in the explanatory variables of interest (i.e., repression and/or internal disruption unrelated to repressive action) on RNA demobilization somewhat independently. I say "somewhat independently" here for varied reasons. First, although repressive action might not be present at a specific time, the group itself might still be discussing it, which could result in influencing subsequent behavior. Second, events take place in a sequence that may be extremely important for understanding what transpires. Existing research largely ignores this factor treating state-dissident interactions as though the course of previous events did not matter (for important exceptions, see Davenport 1996; Moore 1998; Loyle et al. 2012).

The approach adopted here is different from selecting events randomly or other methods, such as space or actor, that might not yield enough source material and/or capture the variation in the independent variables of interest. This is important (especially the former), for I have done my best not to rely exclusively on any single type of source without at least some corresponding evidence on part of the events in question. The events themselves and the context surrounding them are briefly discussed in the following.

Strictly speaking, before the founding, the organization as a distinct entity had not experienced repression in either overt or covert forms, as it did not yet exist, and thus we cannot speak of RNA repression at the beginning – as such. That said, individuals who became involved with the dissident organization had frequently experienced coercive government action prior to the creation of the RNA. As such, choices, ideas, actions, and institutions could be influenced by repressive action. Indeed, they have a specific conception of how they will likely be repressed (i.e., they had an approach to reappraisal that they communicated to potential and actual members). After the founding, there were some adjustments to reappraisal as well as trust building. Government efforts to undermine these efforts were limited at this time, but they did occur at some level because of agents provacateur who participated in the organization. After the creation of the RNA, the authorities unexpectedly took no overt action. Instead, they stood back, observed, and, using their numerous informants and agents provacateurs, probed and provoked the organization from the inside. These efforts were not known or even suspected, and thus mobilization was facilitated.

In contrast, during and after my second event of interest as well as the period of the event itself, the RNA decided to engage with Ocean Hill–Brownsville, Brooklyn. This decision was almost exclusively a decision made from within the RNA itself, with no direct connection to state repression. Here the RNA believed that the campaign would advance its cause of black secession, help energize the organization, and begin to get its message out. Of course, as I argue, even when repressive events are not undertaken, they are still present as challengers think and talk about what could happen and what has happened. Indeed, the study reveals that imagined repression is no less important than actual government activity. Clearly the evolution of African American nationalist thought played a major role in the Ocean Hill–Brownsville campaign as well. The concept of the black nation was the natural outgrowth of reflection about what had been previously pursued by the civil rights and burgeoning black power movement organizations. At this juncture, with a certain strain placed on the organization because of a lack of preparation for what was undertaken and the seeming deviation from the RNA's stated objectives, some initial effort at maintaining trust was made.

My third event and accompanying periods before and after explores the influence of a shootout, raid, mass arrest, and interrogation at the first anniversary of the RNA at New Bethel Baptist Church in Detroit, commonly known as the New Bethel Incident. This represents an overt form of state repression as a large number of organizational members and the core leadership were arrested en masse, questioned, fingerprinted, and held for numerous hours prior to being released. On one hand, the approach to reappraisal in this case was solidified as the RNA correctly anticipated the type of confrontation that it had. This reduced the degree of surprise and uncontrolled emotions highlighted in the literature, normally associated with reducing demobilization. On the other hand, however, the magnitude of the repressive operation with mass arrests, detailed interrogation, a national manhunt for members involved with the death of a police officer, the arrest of three members, and a long, drawn out court battle were too much for most to bear, "overwhelming" the RNA. Additionally, with the RNA suspicions about covert efforts being validated in the media, there was also some acknowledgment that the approach to reappraisal selected, with its emphasis on overt repression, might be inappropriate and that the repression had "outwitted" them. Though important, as it strained trust within the organization, this experience did not completely demobilize the organization. Indeed, in many respects, it increased its visibility as well as the degree of support from diverse quarters of the black community.

The fourth period of interest concerns the development of a faction within the RNA between the two leading figures in the RNA at the time: Gaidi Obadele (formerly Milton Henry) and his brother Imari Obadele (formerly Richard Henry). While the split was in part a function of differences that emerged within the RNA regarding dueling views about what should be done and how, there was also an influence of repressive behavior as well as the fear of overt repression that compelled the president, Robert F. Williams, and Gaidi Obadele to withdraw from the organization and prompted Imari Obadele and a younger cohort of activists to become more aggressive and step up their efforts to control the dissident organization. Again, it is not actually repression that has an influence but rather discussion and debates about it that influence the movement. This said, initially, reappraisal was ignored, as efforts were made to repair the sense of trust within the organization in part through a tightening of leadership, increased scrutiny of members and recruits, and a return to founding ideals. Only after some progress was made to redevelop trust was an effort made to reconfigure the organizational approach to reappraisal away from a focus on overt behavior and toward a focus on covert action, reducing the sense of being outwitted. I maintain, however, that the effort was too late, as the damage to the institution was too severe and membership declined.

My fifth and last period concerns another police raid against the RNA. This overtly repressive act involves the arrest of numerous individuals engaged in creating the first land base for the RNA, including the president at the time (Imari Obadele) and one of the vice presidents (Hekima Ana). Unlike the previous raid in Detroit, the action of interest here took place in Jackson, Mississippi, on August 18, 1971. As one police officer was killed during the exchange and another two were injured, this interaction was as violent as the last police-dissident standoff at the New Bethel Baptist Church. Regarding mobilization, the Mississippi raid was also a significant setback for the RNA, as it simultaneously disrupted the leadership (prompting a shift to another leader), reduced action on what was at the time their most important campaign, and embroiled the RNA in yet another form of repressive action for which they were not quite prepared: a large-scale effort to free their incarcerated colleagues from prison via a long court battle, which became known as the RNA 11.

With this crippling blow to the organization, trust was widely shaken. Efforts at reappraisal had anticipated the government's behavior (e.g., providing for a constitutionally mandated adjustment from one RNA leader to another in the case of captivity or incarceration), but these efforts represented a limited response, as it was assumed that all members of the RNA would simply follow the plan outlined. However, because of the complex effects of the raid, organizational cohesion was diminished, confusion was enhanced, a power struggle ensued among those remaining, and a downward spiral of demobilization engulfed the RNA. As earlier, a new organization emerged from the old. However, the group that was formed in March 1968 differed significantly in personnel, activities, ideas, and organizational structure that came following the Mississippi raid. In short, the RNA for all intents and purposes had effectively demobilized.

Units of Observation

To facilitate my discussion and in line with what has been outlined previously regarding demobilization, four elements of the social movement organization of interest will be discussed in detail as we move across the five periods: (1) *individuals* (i.e., who is present and what emotions they express while in the presence of other RNA members), (2) *ideas* (i.e., the objectives and selected means for achieving the desired objectives), (3) *institutions* (i.e., the particular structure of the organization created as well as enduring rules and practices within it), and (4) *interventions* (i.e., the actions taken by the dissident organization in its effort to reach its goals). Such an approach allows me to assess not only the quality of (de)mobilization at diverse points in time (i.e., before, during, and after relevant explanatory variables change) but also the effectiveness of challenger attempts at *reappraisal* and *trust building* as well as government efforts to undermine such activity: overwhelming, outwitting, and distrust building (these are operationalized subsequently). Specifically, I consider which impact a specific event has on the four elements identified previously and then consider lagged influences over the two months that follow.

As for my expectations of how the components fit together, the argument is fairly straightforward. If repression increases demobilization (as existing work suggests), then we would expect expressions of fear to increase at the time of the repressive event with very few efforts to counter this negative sentiment. Following this, I would expect expressions of doubt regarding what is being undertaken against the RNA. These expressions would lead to increased skepticism about what is being done, decreased numbers of individuals participating, increased changes within the institutional structure to deal with what is taking place (i.e., reorganization, rescheduling, and reprioritizing), and decreased attempts to continue the challenge (i.e., interventions).

In an effort to diminish this possibility of repressive behavior prompting demobilization, a social movement organization might try to counteract negative emotions. For example, a challenger might engage in "reappraisal" (preparatory activity concerning repressive behavior such as what to do if and when it happens) and attempt to make sure members of the RNA were ready for what they believed might happen to them and how they should deal with repressive events that do take place (e.g., keeping quiet and requesting a lawyer). A challenger might also try to develop trust. This involves particular types of activities that establish and build an emotional valuation favorable to members and mobilization, such as statements concerning a willingness to put one's faith into another's hands or believing that progress is being made toward objectives. If no emotional valuation was developed and members believed that the RNA was ineffective in pursuing its objectives, then trust would decrease. If an emotional valuation was developed and members believed that the RNA was effective in pursuing its objectives, then trust would increase. Clearly there is some overlap between the two dissident countertactics. If the RNA appeared to be prepared for what repressive behavior took place later, then trust would be established. If the RNA did not appear prepared, however, then trust would be diminished.

Different from how most literature frames the problem, the explicit awareness of the social movement activist is crucial to my argument. This is because, in my conception, challengers must be explicitly aware of what is being done to them (e.g., a raid or informing) and, with this knowledge, choose whether to respond. Now, this is very different than saying SMO mobilization is hindered because they once had a place to meet and then the landlord pulled the lease because of government action, such as being threatened by an IRS investigation, that they do not know about. I maintain that this is a relatively conservative position with regard to drawing conclusions from the information available, but I do this not to overreach from the source material consulted and encourage other scholars to follow suit. Quite frequently, we have to wait for an exceptional disclosure of some sort (e.g., government correspondence concerning the landlord in the preceding example), or we have to draw some conclusion from questionable sources. This hinders us from examining the topic, however, and thus I offer one way to proceed: one that I believe is both reasonable and valid.

Of course, as discussed earlier, interested in weakening behavioral challenges, governments might attempt to disrupt the counterefforts identified earlier. There are different ways that this could be done. The key to disruption of the challenger involves deviation from the challenger's expectations, which have been learned by efficient infiltration. Deviation occurs either by using repressive action that is not anticipated (i.e., when government shifts from using one technique to another), which was referred to earlier as "outwitting" (e.g., using raids when shootings are expected), or alternatively, when authorities arrest twenty individuals when the arrest of one was expected (when the sheer volume or severity of government action exceeds what has been found in the past), which was referred to earlier as "overwhelming."[8]

With these elements, challengers and political authorities engage in different activities until either the challengers (i.e., getting a voice in the existing system, obtaining some reform, taking over the existing system or in the RNA case seceding from it) or the government wins (i.e., eliminating and scaring away challengers, reaching a stalemate whereby no change is made or substantively altering the claim being made to something less threatening).

Creating the RNA-Authority Event Catalog

Interested in the various topics addressed earlier, I employed a fairly straight-forward strategy for analyzing the compiled material. As I conceived dissident behavior – the behavioral challenge – I coded the following characteristics from available material:

- the activity undertaken by RNA members (e.g., business meetings, fund-raising, shooting practice, demonstrations, social gatherings, political education courses, petitions, speeches, mock trials, rallies, the topics of discussion within meetings)
- the identity of specific individuals in attendance and their participation in the organization's activities – where mentioned (i.e., speaking, just sitting there, loading a weapon, taking notes)
- the estimated number of people in attendance at each group activity
- the geographic location of the action
- the target of the relevant action
- the date
- the time

Here, event type was subdivided into five mutually exclusive categories: violent dissent, nonviolent dissent, preparatory activity (e.g., shooting practice

---

[8] One could construct this process differently. For example, in earlier work of my own and others, it is argued that governments engage in specific activities to disrupt distinct parts of the mobilization process, for example, recruitment, retention, and resource acquisition. In this framework, researchers consider the influence of arrests or torture on subsequent mobilization. I don't believe this approach allows us to understand exactly what this does to government challengers, however – especially when each component of the mobilization process is not equally well measured and when challenger perceptions are not included. We end up seeing exchanges but do not know why any behavioral changes occur. My approach attempts to address this limitation through the application of tactical expectation and deviation.

or hand-to-hand combat), criminal action, and land acquisition. This is relevant for the current research because I am able to gauge the effects of arrests, raids, and instances when informants are suspected on not only the five areas of RNA activity but also how many people are present at RNA events, how many individuals speak at organizational meetings, and what they say.

In addition to the characteristics identified earlier, I also use the information to identify different emotions relevant to individual responses to repressive action. Specifically, expressions of fear include utterances like the following: "I don't want to get busted, man." I also identify expressions of anger (e.g., "Enough of this shit; we need to deal with these bastards" or "We should be cool until the heat goes away").

Additionally, in an effort to more systematically assess what was being said and gauge the general sentiment of the framing that takes place, I use the information contained in the records to code what Gamson and Meyer (1996, 285) refer to as the "rhetoric of change." As they state, "movement activists systematically overestimate the degree of political opportunity and if they did not, they would not be doing their job wisely" (285). To do this, however, activists must conscientiously monitor and counter discussions within their organizations to move people toward mobilization. Three strategies are identified within this work, each responding to a theme provided within the work of Hirschman (1970), who discussed the techniques that were employed by those who preferred inaction within an organizational setting.

For example, to counter *jeopardy* (the argument that by attempting some change, we risk losing achievements already won; Gamson and Meyer 1996, 285), activists engage in *urgency* (act now or the situation will remain the same). This could include a statement like "Come on, brothers and sisters, we gotta do this or we will remain stuck." To counter *futility* (the argument that there is no opportunity for change and that all action is a waste of time), activists engage in *agency*, discussing that there is a window of opportunity for change, for example, "The people are ripe . . . we have to take advantage of this change [in consciousness] or lose the whole thing." Finally, to counter *perverse effects* (the argument that attempts at change will simply make the situation worse), activists engage in *possibility* (the argument that attempts at change will make the situation better). This could include a statement like "One step toward the people is another step toward the revolution."[9]

Repression of the RNA was coded to include the following information:

- the type of activity undertaken by state authorities (e.g., instances of physical and electronic surveillance, wiretapping, the forging of letters by authorities, physical as well as verbal harassment, arrest, interviewing an employer, and/or conducting raids)

---

[9] Given the difficulties with coding these, I assigned one student to identify possible candidates. She would then code them and pass them to me for validation.

- the identity of the organizations involved (e.g., Reconnaissance Division, Criminal Division, and Special Investigation Bureau under the Detroit Police Department as well as the Michigan State Police and/or the FBI)[10]
- the number of actors involved in each activity
- the geographic location of activities
- the target of the relevant activity
- the date
- the time

Here event type is subdivided into two areas: overt repressive action and covert repressive action. The former is much easier to operationalize because records contain information about when and how many individuals were arrested, which readily conforms to our understanding of overt repression discussed earlier. In contrast, the records concerning covert behavior are somewhat more complex.

For example, although the records contain information about when a false letter was mailed, when an informant or agent provocateur attends a meeting, or when an individual was tailed, I do not expect that these would have an influence on the RNA because they would not be aware of such activity. Indeed, I expect covert action to work only when dissident organizations suspect such activity.[11] Accordingly, I use RNA statements regarding the possibility of an informant or agent provocateur being in their midst as an example of covert repressive action, but I also note the other activity, just to provide the information. In a sense, this makes the RNA members themselves the carrier or mechanism of its own repression.

What emerges from this collection of materials is a detailed accounting of both sides of the conflict. On one hand, we have what the RNA did and what they were planning to do, what they said, who was involved (by name), what they did, when things took place (by the hour and day), and where things occurred (by street address). On the other hand, we have what the U.S. government did (but not always what they were planning to do), who was involved (by agency), when things took place (by hour and day), and where (by street address).[12] Specific operationalizations of key concepts are provided in the following.

---

[10] Names of specific government agents were redacted from the material consulted, evidently to protect the identity of the political authorities involved.

[11] This does not mean that covert action has no impact, only that I am not as confident in my ability (or anyone's for that matter) to assess this impact – compared to the more explicit manner concerning challenger overt identification.

[12] The approach was taken to avoid as much of the polemics present within the discussion as possible. Clearly this is extremely hard to do. The RNA was interested in seceding from the United States of America and starting a new government because of the inadequacies and racism of the United States, thereby freeing and empowering African Americans. The U.S. government was interested in containing and/or eliminating an organization they characterize as highly threatening because they attempted to remove part of its territory as well as part of its citizenry.

Among my dependent variables, there are four: individuals, ideas, institutions, and interventions. Each is discussed subsequently, followed by a discussion of independent variables of interest.

The first dependent variable (*Individuals*) is largely behavioral in nature and is derived from the physical presence of an individual at an event noted in one of the relevant sources. As found, local police as well as Detroit-specific RNA records cover most activities by the RNA, including meetings, workshops and conferences, protests, travel, and personal meetings. Both of these sources have incentives to identify individuals, but for very different reasons. For example, local police track individuals so as to assist them with identifying and countering the relevant challengers and challenges. The RNA, however, track individuals because they need to plan their own actions.[13] Unlike media records,[14] which would tend to focus only on certain individuals (e.g., leaders), government sources would tend to be a lot more comprehensive to assist their disruptive and informational purposes.[15]

> In this context, all accountings of the relevant other – what they are doing and why they are doing it – are viewed somewhat suspiciously. Moreover, I have attempted to use some of the least problematic information contained within the source material about the respective actors and actions as well as the most reliable information I could obtain through triangulation across the source material to derive what is a relatively conservative accounting of RNA-government interaction. This may soften the encounter somewhat, such as when I discount a meeting when it is reported that the RNA brought in weapons and discussed a series of robberies because this came out of seemingly nowhere and it was never followed up again. Regardless, I feel it is the most defensible position to take with the information available.

[13] The RNA was obviously well aware of who was present at individual meetings and what they said, but they were not as diligent as the U.S. government in writing these down. Turnaround in new members was limited because of the partially closed nature of the organization. Consequently, I am able to identify how members participated and the frequent comings and goings of who was at a specific event for every single organizational event. To be clear, presence is identified by explicit mention within a particular record. If an individual is mentioned, he or she is identified as being present. If the individual is not mentioned in the record explicitly, he or she is not included.

[14] To a limited degree, specific activities are also covered by the black-and-white press (e.g., protest), but workshops and conferences are likely covered by the black press alone. By their nature, these events are public, and thus it is possible to identify individuals, but given the nature of the source, they do not identify all individuals present by name, and thus they have limited usefulness. In this regard, news coverage also decreases over the full-time period, as the RNA itself became less and less publicly visible and newsworthy.

[15] Additionally, informants were handled in such a way that led them to provide as much information as possible under punishment of being outed to the RNA, fired from the government payroll, punished by the authorities for some criminal offense, or some combination. Informants had every incentive to thus implicate as many individuals as possible while trying not to lie, and they were largely sent into an organization on something of a fishing expedition, focusing on who was present, what they said, what was planned, what was done, and whether explicitly illegal action was involved. Indeed, the only problem informants might have with regard to identifying individuals is when they were not known to the authorities or to the informant at the time of the report. This would be less applicable for higher-level members and individuals who continually participated frequently, for they would have likely been photographed earlier

Ideas (the second aspect of the demobilization) are more document oriented in that they emerge from policy statements and background papers but also within statements made by RNA members in meetings, press releases, news articles, interviews, and conferences or workshops. Documents are found within five sources: (1) federal, (2) state, and (3) local authorities – the volume decreasing across them, as well as (4) courts and (5) the RNA (both short and non-Detroit-specific). Again, different sources have their reasons for being relatively comprehensive, but also, again, they were distinct.[16]

The third aspect of demobilization concerns *institutional structure,* which is largely behavioral in nature as it concerns interactions and relationships between individuals (i.e., who leads and how, what the division of labor is). These are derived from almost the same sources as ideas, except the state police do not generally retain much information like this. What I found most useful here was derived from background papers, organizational directives, and meetings predominantly held by local police, the FBI, and the RNA.[17]

Interventions, the fourth and last aspect of demobilization, concerns the activities undertaken by the RNA that are directed toward the external world in an effort to change some political economic condition. This includes different types of behavior and different types of sources that are apt to capture it. For example, protest information is found most consistently in the records of the RNA and local, state, and federal police records, but it is also found in the press (black and white) and in court records. Along with the expectations of a relatively large amount of research, the less diligent sources cover events

---

and shown to the relevant individual for subsequent identification. Unfortunately, photos in the relevant file are not all time and place stamped. As a result, I anticipated and observed relative stability information about individuals, but not about those whose participation was unsteady. I not only identify whether individuals are present but also what they state.

[16] Authorities sought to compile information about the RNA to establish their radical, violent, and leftist orientation. This would lead them toward the more dramatic claims making of the RNA (i.e., seizing land for the new nation and reparations for all blacks). More mundane information about exactly how the varied ends would be achieved were found in the RNA records, but these compilations are sporadic – around when efforts were extended to create and/or significantly modify particular policies. One could potentially argue that this is where the two sources intersect. The repression directed against the RNA made it harder to create and keep material, thereby decreasing the likelihood that it would be available for me later – rendering RNA ideas harder to discover. I don't think that is the case, however, because the police were consistently confiscating RNA literature, address books, membership lists, flyers, and the like, putting it into their archive. Additionally, despite repressive action, the RNA also kept creating and using material in different formats to communicate with their audiences and the general American population.

[17] Though I am sure that some material is missing, the RNA was highly legalistic and detail oriented, in part a function of legal and literary backgrounds for some of the leaders. The outcome of this orientation is a significant amount of information about how the RNA was structured. Indeed, the excessive amount of detail about the inner workings of the RNA and a significant amount of the discussion about what should or should not be done, and how, yields a lot of organizational detail. This makes sense given the vacuum-like nature of government surveillance and informant activity.

that are larger, more violent, and/or involving highly contentious topics. These sources tend to miss more mundane activities, such as smaller and less violent protests. They would also tend to miss other forms of collective action that were not as public and/or as newsworthy, such as workshops or conferences and social gatherings. The reasons for the high amount of attention within the RNA and police sources again vary.[18]

We now consider the independent variables of interest. This includes variables involving the RNA as well as the government. Each is addressed in turn.

Reappraisal concerns those activities that are directed toward current members of the RNA in an effort to educate them about repression and what should be done when it is encountered. Given this, two sources are critical for identifying relevant activity: the RNA and the local police. I expect that the RNA would tend to discuss these activities as a matter of course – they were doing these activities and thus they should be discussing that at some point. Because the RNA discusses these activities, authorities should know them as well, getting them directly from the source. Some additional events were captured by physical surveillance where government agents were literally sitting across the street from them and came across something. This situation could have been problematic if I were not only interested in whether something had occurred. As I am not interested in understanding the various sides' opinions of such activity, this makes coverage a bit easier. I'm interested in whether someone mentioning whether repression could take place and what should be done if it does is supposed to gauge anyone's opinion about state repression itself, which would likely vary significantly according to the actor providing explanation.

Admittedly, *trust* and *trust building* are a bit more difficult to assess than reappraisal. This involves statements that reveal someone's internal world largely undertaken in the less public locales identified previously, covered most consistently by the RNA and the local police – again. Certain statements are explicit enough in this regard, but it is not clear if one could expect the RNA and the police to be equally sensitive to such utterances in the information they collect. Trust-building activities were expected to be and were much more frequent in coverage, and given that these are both provocative and on occasion open to the public, there are a greater number of sources that provide this type of information (e.g., black-and-white newspapers, courts, state and federal police, and nonlocal RNA members). Differing from reappraisal, however, these activities are more internally oriented and specifically taken in an effort

---

[18] The RNA would mention events less for distribution and circulation than simply because they are actually engaging in the relevant behavior. To do this, there is a certain amount of planning involved, and one aftereffect of careful planning and discussion is a clearly identifiable track record that can be employed later on. In contrast, police tend to cover RNA activities principally because they are monitoring all of their activity and conversations. In the course of this surveillance, events planned, undertaken, and in the past are consistently being discussed.

to improve intergroup relations. Trust building would also be achieved when the RNA appeared to do well in predicting when the government was going to do something against them, and how. This involves comparing the correspondence between preparatory messages establishing reappraisal and identifying its efficacy in forecasting subsequent repressive action.

Factors concerning the government are also largely behavioral in nature and public as well, thereby putting them into the category of better-covered events. For example, "overwhelming" is determined by the relative amount of overt government action: arrests, raids, targeted assassination, grand juries, random shootings, harassment both physical and verbal, as well as detention. When a significant number of events is put forward, an attempt to overwhelm challengers is revealed with too many activities, too many costs, and too many problems. These events are generally covered by federal, state, and local police; all sections of the RNA; and the media and courts. Indeed, I would argue that overwhelming is one of the easier things to identify in the US-RNA case in particular and political conflict or contentious politics in general. By contrast, "outwitting" concerns a change in government tactics. To do this well, sources would have to be equally likely to cover different overt techniques. Of the different tactics, sources are most likely to identify raids and mass arrests. Smaller arrests and those directed against less prominent members would be most likely covered by the police (especially locals) because there were specific documents for this. Grand juries would be covered in the media and by the RNA, whereas shootings and harassment would be almost exclusively covered by the RNA and newspapers most likely. Detentions (i.e., holding an RNA member in jail) – especially those for longer than a day – are the least likely activity to be covered. This is probably most often found in RNA material as it arises when they discuss bail and were seeking their release.

Distrust is more attitudinal in nature, like trust, and emerges from sources that more closely cover RNA utterances regarding how they feel about one another and the situation they are in. Unlike what we would expect, distrust building (if we could use such a word) is not undertaken by the police. I believe that informants and agents provocateurs as well as obvious physical surveillance are all employed to create distrust within an SMO, but except for the last, they are not expected to be identified; most of this is indirect in nature. In fact, as discussed, I maintain that distrust in the RNA is more likely to emerge from the RNA itself as they express suspicion about who was involved and why. Given that the police have an interest in such information, I believe that they will cover such utterances, and before beginning the research, I believed that this would be found more frequently. Interestingly, they weren't. Similarly, I felt that the RNA would tend to downplay such utterances in their own material, for several differences of opinion and suspicious activities reach particularly high levels, and the degree of discussion about these topics as well as the amount of paperwork they generated were quite voluminous. There weren't many of these, but when suspicions and the associated tempers arose, there was a lot said, correspondingly a lot written, and a lot remaining to be coded by my research team.

Summary

In this chapter, I have discussed the objectives and activities of the RNA as well as the objectives and activities of the U.S. government directed against this institution, across the distinct government units: federal, state, and local jurisdictions. Source material was compiled from both actors and the media, in Detroit as well as in distinct parts of the United States.

Specifically concerned with how to best analyze demobilization, I laid out some basic requirements for such an investigation and identified how the records employed in the US-RNA case provide an ideal opportunity for exploring the topic. After discussing what was and was not contained in the records, I discussed how this information was coded to allow even greater precision with understanding what could be as well as what was examined.

In Part III, I draw on a relatively thorough examination of primary and secondary documents as well as the information contained in the sources identified earlier to discuss the general background of the RNA (i.e., where they came from, who was involved, what they attempted to do, and why they changed), contextualizing the more detailed examination of the compiled database (in Part IV). Toward this end, we begin with some of the core individuals involved and then move to the first SMOs they created. We then consider the different institutions with which they were affiliated, ending with the creation of the RNA.

PART III

ORIGINS

5

We Shall Overcome?

From GOAL to the Freedom Now Party

To understand the RNA, one has to address the role of four people. On one hand, there were two biological brothers (discussed in this chapter), Milton and Richard Henry.[1] These two were the core around which the organization would form as well as the poles around which the organization would split and later dissolve. On the other hand, there were two spiritual "fathers" (discussed in the next chapter), Malcolm X and Robert F. Williams. These two, in their own ways, contributed to the complex and often contradictory vision pursued and the strategies adopted by the organization, including the RNA's approach to repressive reappraisal. As we attempt to understand the end of the RNA and what role repression played in its demise, we must first consider these individuals as well as those who associated with them. This sets the stage for an analysis of what happened to and within the Republic, which follows in Part IV.

Brothers in Struggle

At first glance, it seems strange that the Henry brothers (Edwin, Lester, Charles, Milton, Donald, Julian, Richard, and Laurence) would be associated with black power and nationalism as well as trying to secede from the United States, because for much of their lives, they seemed like the poster children for integration and the civil rights movement. Having grown up in Philadelphia, Pennsylvania, in the 1920s and early 1930s, they were born and raised in a working-class, two-parent household with a father (Walter Henry) who was employed by the U.S. Post Office for forty-three years (first as a deliverer and later as a clerk) and a mother (Vera Neville Robinson) who stayed at home to raise the children. All members of the family attended church routinely.

---

[1] The family had four sisters as well, but their importance for the RNA would be quite limited.

Indeed, the family was intricately linked to the erection of the first Union Baptist Church on Little Pine Street through their Great Aunt Susan, a fact that was a source of great pride. All of the boys were hardworking, but each moved in a distinct direction professionally. All would become interested in education to some degree and would achieve varying levels of success. Indeed, in almost every way, the Henrys were groomed for entry into the dominant white society, seemingly from birth. When, in the 1950s, the family was identified as the Detroit National Urban League's "Family of the Year," it would come as no surprise to anyone – especially them. They had literally worked for that recognition for years.

This situation was not unique to the Henrys. It appeared that the whole generation of blacks living in the United States around the 1940s and 1950s were being similarly prepared. Proper training and performance in a variety of areas would show whites as well as African Americans what the latter were capable of. Accordingly, blacks would excel at reading, writing, mathematics, science, philosophy, manners, and (although fitting a stereotype) sports as well; the race would be lifted with each achievement.

School was the principal vehicle for integration.[2] As Richard Henry (Obadele 1970c, 68) would later write,

with a fierce pride, the black teachers [in all-black Smith Elementary School where he and several of his siblings attended] strove to make us excellent, both so that we could achieve something in the world for ourselves and so that we would well represent them in the mixed schools to which we would go.

He continued,

[At all-black Smith], where the principal and all the staff were black, we might fear Mr. Lyle and Mr. Ager and Mrs. Shaw – because they would not hesitate to use the ruler on those who broke discipline – but we knew in essence that they loved us: we knew they were involved with us, they were us. They taught us many of the slave master's values; they taught us the white/nationalism involved in honoring his flag and his heroes... but they taught us racial competitiveness and racial mission. Everything they did, they made us understand, they did so that we would be able to compete successfully against the white man whom we were going out to meet in a white world. Everything they did, they did so we would be equipped to make things better not just for ourselves but for our race. (111)

Of course, the mission of preparation and proving one's merit was not exclusive to the realm of education. Indeed, during the relevant period, the entire black

---

[2] As Cone (1992, 16) suggests,

integrationists were (essentially) *practical.* They advocated what they thought could be achieved at a given time. They knew that justice demanded more. But why demand it if you can't get it? Why demand it if the demand itself blocks the achievement of other desirable and achievable goals? In their struggle for justice, they were careful not to arouse the genocidal instincts inherent in racism. Thus they chose methods which many whites accepted as reasonable and just.

community seemed like a womb with a mission for those within it. Inside, African Americans felt protected not only by immediate family but also by all those in the community. Inside, blacks felt that their best interests were being looked after by all they came across, whether teachers, doctors, lawyers, barbers, dentists, janitors, storekeepers, and librarians. In part, the comfort and trust were related to the shared mission of African American integration at the time, which predominated after Marcus Garvey's nationalist and separatist movement ended. By contrast, the world outside the womb was a harsh one filled with racism, white supremacy, and hopelessness.

The feelings of connectedness as well as the objectives of survival and empowerment would not be lost on the Henry brothers. Each left the womb to pursue integration in his own way. Milton's experience in particular had the biggest impact on the others, especially on his younger brother, Richard.

Milton, the Elder, Sets the Tone

It all began simply enough. After quickly moving through varied educational facilities in Philadelphia, Milton Henry attended Temple University, fulfilling his promise as a youth. At the time, Temple was viewed as one of the better educational institutions in the United States for anyone, but especially for an African American. Unfortunately for Milton, World War II interfered with his plans, and in 1941, he left school to fight for his country. The reason was simple. He believed that this was what he was meant to do (Obadele 1970c, 1). Additionally, being talented as well as ambitious, when called, Milton did not enlist in any regular unit. Rather, he attempted what had not before been tried: he joined the Army Air Corp, the Ninety-ninth Pursuit Squadron, where he trained to be a radio operator, an interest that he had had as a child when he (dis)assembled radios and record players. When he graduated in 1943, he had achieved the rank of second lieutenant.

This unit was far from ordinary. It was the first African American fighter squadron in U.S. history and would later come to be known as the Tuskegee Airmen. Consistent with the objectives of his childhood instructors, Milton joined what was believed to be the best that the black race had to offer the war effort at the time. Highly rigorous and, indeed, near-impossible entrance criteria assured that this was the case.

Although celebrated by African Americans, Milton's reception among the predominately white Army Air Corps was not a warm one. As Richard Henry (Obadele 1970c, 72–73) recalled,

from Chanute Field at Rantoul, Illinois, [Milton] and the other young blacks of the 99th Pursuit Squadron ... arrived starched and militarily erect at Maxwell Field, Alabama, and standing at attention in the sun heard the receiving colonel tell the white major who was over them: "Maddox, I don't appreciate you bringing these niggers down here." They were then summarily – with all their college degrees and years of schooling and dreams of light training and serving the U.S. Army as officers and gentlemen – put to sweeping streets.

This was not an isolated experience. Rather,

it was to be a thing of second-class almost all the way. There was segregation, not of their design, of course, but of the white racist oppressor's design, and the design was to facilitate discrimination and inequality. They could not use the facilities of white airmen, and the "colored" facilities were always a laughable imitation of the white. Finally, the Squadron went to Tuskegee Institute, the college in Alabama made famous by Booker T. Washington, where the Army had set up a flying field and school on the campus. Here the black student pilots set to training, using mainly white ground-crew and instructors, using finally, in advanced flight training, battered early-model P-40 fighter planes – several of which cost young black pilots their lives.

Such treatment continued throughout Milton's time with the Airmen, and as he moved upward in rank, the range of negative experiences magnified.[3] For example, although Milton technically was an officer, whites consistently refused to salute, and in fact they talked back to him about the unrealistic expectation that he would be treated as one of the "regular" (i.e., white) individuals of higher rank. The officer's club was not opened to Milton. Even townies harassed the best that the black race had to offer the war effort whenever they were given a chance.[4]

[3] The position of African Americans in the military at this time was pretty clear. As Reddick (1953, 195–96) notes,

At the end of World War II, it was still possible to characterize the policy of the Army by four generalizations. These were principles of operation that had persisted, with occasional exceptions, from the American War of Independence through the second World War. They were as follows:

1. The overall preference of the Army has been that there should be no Negroes in it at all but since this preference must be qualified by need, Negroes are to be used only when and where they are required by manpower shortages and by public pressures.
2. The overall preference of the Army has been that no Negroes should be in positions of authority in it but if they must be, they shall be limited and shall be over Negro personnel only.
3. The overall preference of the Army has been that its Negro soldiers shall be segregated not only from their non-Negro fellow soldiers but also from non-Negro civilians – especially women – at home and abroad.
4. The Army's overall preference has been that there should be no Negro heroes but if there must be awards granted to Negro soldiers for extraordinary endeavor, these should be, for preserving supplies and other military properties, for saving the lives of Army personnel – especially of white officers – rather than for heroic performance, under fire, against the enemy.

Also see Dalfiume (1969).

[4] The Airmen were not to be consistently beaten down. For ninety brief days, there was some relief from racist oppression when they were assigned to the Signal Corp Officer Candidate School at Ft. Mammoth, New Jersey. There they were treated as equals, acquiring a taste of what was possible. But, just as quickly as it began, they were returned to Tuskegee, where the discrimination and drudgery persisted, made that much more bitter by the New Jersey experience.

The story told here is different than what is normally told. The story of the Tuskegee Airmen is generally one of their overcoming racism – largely through ignoring it – and going on to outperform their white counterparts in battle (e.g., saving more aircraft during bombing raids). In this narrative, the blacks were "better" men who were able to transcend the narrow-mindedness of racism. This is not the only story, however, and this is definitely not Milton's.

In this case, Milton did what he was brought up to do and then a little bit more. Rather than ignoring discrimination, he fought back for what he believed was right. For example, upon perceiving something improper, he raised complaints with Air Corps headquarters at Billy Mitchell Field, New York, about not being saluted. While there, he complained about the separate facilities and the poor quality of those allocated to African Americans. He even fought with the townies on occasion. One such incident was recalled by Richard Henry (Obadele 1970c, 115–18) when a "white crew chief sergeant ... told [Milton], an officer, to fly a plane that [Milton] said didn't sound right. [Milton] told him to fly it himself and walked away."[5]

These struggles were not isolated ones that took place with no one watching and only Milton's little brother aware of what transpired – quite the contrary. Milton was known throughout the Airmen for his courageousness in not tolerating and directly confronting racism. One incident was recalled in the memoirs of Colonel Charles W. Dryden (2003, 167–68):

"I am ordering you to leave this officers club at once," said Colonel William L. Boyd to three United States Army officers on New Years Day (one of them being Milton Henry).

The place was the lobby of Lufberry Hall, the plush officers club at Selfridge Field located on the outskirts of Mount Clemens, Michigan, about twenty-five miles north of Detroit. Colonel Boyd was the base commander of Selfridge Field. The three officers were African Americans.

"Is that a direct order, Colonel?" Lieutenant Milton Henry asked. Lieutenant Henry was a courageous young officer, a graduate of Tuskegee Army Flying School who has challenged segregation and discrimination he encountered during his training there and in the surrounding area.

"That's right, Lieutenant, it is a direct order."

It was also an improper, illegal order that contravened an existing written directive. Army regulation 210-10, paragraph 19c, stated, in part, that officers clubs and messes had to extend to all officers on duty at the base the right to full membership.

The three officers knew this regulation. They and a large number of African American officers had done their homework as they planned strategies for the elimination of segregated facilities at Selfridge Field. They also knew that disobedience of a direct order from a senior officer could have dire consequences, especially in wartime when such disobedience was tantamount to treason – punishable by death. So they left Lufberry

---

[5] An African American died in that plane shortly after this exchange.

Hall, returned to the BOQ (basic overnight quarters), and conveyed to the rest of the officers what they had just experienced.

Another incident, told repeatedly like a folklore tale, concerns Milton's punching a bus driver in the mouth for asking him to use the rear entrance. It is noted that a group of British soldiers, also on the bus, quickly moved to save him after some angry whites from the local community started to make a fuss.

Given the historical uniqueness of the black fighter pilots and the adoption of the so-called Double V campaign for African Americans (victory abroad at protecting democracy as well as at home in extending it), Milton's exploits were frequently covered by black newspapers throughout the United States as well as a few white ones (e.g., Finkle 1973). Milton's younger brother, Richard, was a main observer and admirer of these activities, noting,

[We] had... begun to hear about [Milton's] troubles fighting discrimination in the Army, and in [his] last year at Barrett, 1943–1944, [Milton] was court-martialed for his efforts. He became a hero to us younger brothers back home; we followed the proceedings in the black newspapers, and we were rocketed away with joy as we read that during the court-martial he had told his tormentors: "All revolutions have been initiated by minorities. One day I may be in position to dictate to you!" (as cited in Obadele 1970c, 84)

Dismissed from the army, forced to leave the best of the black race for insubordination, Milton returned to his studies – this time at Lincoln University in southern Chester County, Pennsylvania, where he received a BA in political science and physics.[6] Milton then attended Yale Law School on a scholarship, graduating in 1950. It was during this time that he got his first taste of political engagement.

Initially, Milton worked for the Progressive Party in Henry Wallace's 1948 bid for the U.S. presidency against the Democrat Harry Truman and Republican Tom Dewey. In fact, he was made vice chairperson of the party in Connecticut. Like all third-party candidates in the United States, however, Wallace lost. What was more important for the history of the RNA, however, was that it was during one of his tours for the party that Milton met two prominent civil rights activists, Bayard Rustin and A. Philip Randolph. So impressed were they with the young man that Rustin and Randolph gave Milton authority to create a chapter of their League for Non-Violent Civil Disobedience against Military Segregation,[7] obviously something near and dear to his heart.[8]

---

[6] This is the school also attended by Langston Hughes and Thurgood Marshall.

[7] Such a program was previously (in 1947) known as the Committee against Jimcrow in Military Service and Training.

[8] There was wide support for this effort. As Reddick (1953, 199) states,

Almost every Negro newspaper endorsed the idea and the wide assortment of leaders who supported the movement included Dr. Carter G. Woodson, the Director of the Association for the Study of Negro Life and History, Dr. Alain Locke, the scholar, the Reverend W. H. Jernagin

The league would never have to do anything because the threat of political action, the unified front of African American leaders against the issue of military discrimination, and segregation and the upcoming electoral contest for the presidency prompted Truman to sign Executive Order 9981, calling for equal opportunity in the armed forces – a limited victory because of the conservative way in which its mandate was constructed, but a victory nevertheless.[9]

The experience with becoming involved and dedicating himself to challenging discrimination as well as the little taste of success in such an endeavor stayed with Milton, and in 1951, he moved to Pontiac, Michigan (a satellite of then smaller Detroit), with his wife, Marilyn. Milton had spent some time there when in the military, and he thought that the area would be a nice place to work and raise a family. In many respects, Pontiac was an interesting choice for relocation. In the post–World War II context, it was growing quite rapidly as a major industrial center and focal point for state politics. While Pontiac is important to our story, however, neighboring Detroit would come to play a more important role for Milton as well as the RNA. This is discussed more later.

In Pontiac, Milton worked as a defense attorney, filing one of the first desegregation cases outside of the South and later serving as a city commissioner (from 1954 to 1960). As for why he ran, Milton's reasoning was rather straightforward: "After getting out and finishing law school naturally I wanted to work in ... traditional areas. And ... the ... thing that I could do as a lawyer was to run for political office" (Obadele 1970c, 2).

Of course, this was not enough; Milton wanted to consider other ventures as well. If he was to do this, however, he would need some assistance. In this context, he decided to reach out to his brothers, Richard in particular, who joined his older brother both willingly and rapidly.

Enter Richard, the Younger

After moving to Pontiac in 1951, Milton had gone into business with a friend of his (Clarence Montgomery), and they were going to open a restaurant and sandwich shop. They wanted Richard to manage it for them. Richard was ripe for the invitation. He had failed to complete school at the University of Toronto, engaged in assorted jobs in Philadelphia (a postal worker and shop clerk), did some freelance writing, and busily worked on a love story.

of the Fraternal Council of Negro Churches, Dr. Channing Tobias, an "elder statesman," George S. Schuyler, a rather skeptical journalist, Mrs. Emma Clarissa Clement, the "American Mother of the Year" (1946) and the then immensely popular heavyweight champion of the world, Joe Louis.

An NAACP poll at that the time indicated that 71 percent of African Americans agreed with this effort (cited in a footnote in Reddick 1953, 202).

[9] The ruling was largely formalistic in nature with little investigation and/or enforcement.

Getting the invitation, Richard was thrilled at the opportunity to go work with his heroic brother. In a matter of days after the decision, Richard, his wife, Octavia (who was somewhat less excited about the prospect), and their two kids moved to Pontiac. Unfortunately, this venture did not work out. The restaurant and sandwich shop idea would quickly collapse. Despite the setback, however, the ever-hustling Richard found work as a laborer on highways, a drill press operator, a stringer, and, finally, a reporter with the Detroit *Michigan Chronicle* – a black weekly.

Years later (in 1955), Milton again asked for Richard's assistance. This time the idea was a bit more ambitious. While Milton was working as a commissioner, he had connected with another important political family in the area, the Cleages. One member of the family, Albert, would be especially important for what transpired, as his life as a minister provided a base in the church that become crucial for latter activism.

As with the Henrys, there were other Cleages: Henry (a lawyer), Louis (a doctor), Hugh (a postal worker and watchmaker), and three sisters: Gladys, Barbara, and Anna (none of whom had a specific profession, but they possessed a willingness to assist their brothers to the best of their abilities). Additionally, the Henrys and Cleages were joined by numerous others, for example, Jim Roberts (an attorney from the area) and Ted Barnes and Billy Smith (two individuals simply willing to help). They were all drawn together by a desire to do something to improve the situation for blacks in America generally and Detroit specifically, but they were not quite sure what that should be.

After months of persistent deliberation, this collection of individuals finally came up with an idea of what should be done. Reflecting on the existing media outlets (notably the Detroit *Michigan Chronicle*, where Richard was employed), they concluded that a new, more militant voice was necessary. Out of this discussion, they created the *Metro Newsweekly*, a publication to raise awareness and challenge individual and group conceptions of how things ought to be done. All of the individuals got involved, and at some level of sacrifice. For example, Albert Cleage handled layouts and editorials, Henry and Hugh Cleage quit their jobs to work at the paper for a time, and Gladys, Barbara, and Anna Cleage started working there to handle the day-to-day activities; Louis Cleage built a building on family land to house the project, and Richard Henry quit his job as a reporter to assume the position of managing editor. Milton sat aside on this one, thinking about his next move, but he served as a consultant and occasional contributor.

Like the attempt before it, within a year, this venture failed. After a series of mechanical and financial difficulties, the *Newsweekly* folded. Interestingly, this left Richard Henry with no other opportunity but to work for the military, which must have been an injury to Milton: the paper had failed and now his brother was compelled to work for one of the organizations that had disappointed him the most. Adding insult to this injury, in 1958, Richard went to work as an information specialist at the same Selfridge base where Milton had been stationed. Later, he transferred to the 403rd Troop Carrier Wing. In 1960, Richard passed the U.S. Foreign Service exam, but he was not deemed suitable for service, and in this context, he moved to the Detroit Arsenal (in the U.S. Tank Automotive Division) as a technical writer. After this, things started to look up for him professionally.

Meanwhile, fed up with the life of a black councilman, Milton Henry still looked for something to do. His reasons for leaving the council were clear:

I was one of seven City Councilmen representing a District... And I sat there and of course one out of seven [that was black and interested in assisting this community] I could see very readily that we really didn't have any ability to do much more than just trade on particular items... [The] municipal court remained almost completely white. The fire department was completely white. The police department had about four or five blacks on it and they felt they were doing their job. And the racism was rampant in the attitude of the place and... these are the things that you couldn't do very much about... I was just wasting time. I was a figurehead. I was there as a black man representing black people and I could see that in reality I had no power. I couldn't make any changes in the things that were important. They pulled me out for window-dressing. They'd have me sitting around at meetings talking, where most of the time they were trying to persuade me to vote for some nonsense that didn't have a damn thing to do with black people. So, I ultimately decided [that] I was going to walk off the Commission. (Obadele 1970c, 2–4)

Where did Milton walk to? Well, Africa, actually. Seemingly lost, he literally as well as figuratively picked up and traveled (back) to the "motherland," visiting Senegal, Liberia, Ghana, and Nigeria.[10] His trip was nothing but a revelation. As he states,

I saw the Convention People's Party, Nkrumah's organization and I saw that people were organized around trying to get control over their lives. Now they were in a bag as far [as] these white corporations were concerned and they were in a bag as far as not being able to get their lives really organized, but at least they [were] trying to build ports and they were trying to build roads and I realized as against what I had been doing, I have been trying to get pavements and garbage and all that kind of nonsense and that was the most routine aspects of life. It had nothing to do with be[ing] able to make life whole for our generation of people [African Americans] you see. And that's what I got in Africa. That people there even though they were poor and their standard of living was different they were working for a future and that gave some promise to their people. Real hope for a decent life and for freedom and liberation. (Obadele 1970c, 5)

When he returned to the United States, it was all very different for Milton:

When I came back... Martin Luther King... had the minds of everybody and everybody in this country was talking non-violence and lettin' your [black] blood flow and

---

[10] This may have been the first time that he interacted with Malcolm X. While traveling for Elijah Muhammad, Malcolm visited many of the same countries over the same period: Egypt, Ethiopia, Tanganyika (now Tanzania), Nigeria, Ghana, Guinea, Sudan, Senegal, Liberia, Algeria, and Morocco.

having these demonstrations . . . [Everything] hadn't dawned on me completely. It was a transitional thing. But I knew there was something wrong with people on . . . the street getting' their butt beat. (Henry 1970, 6)

It was on Milton's return that things also changed for the Henry brothers:

Once again Milton had an idea, developed with the Cleages as well as several others.[11] No longer content with small, half-hearted efforts with unclear objectives and partial solutions, the collection of individuals decided to create something of their own in order to address the most important problems of the day. Toward this end, in the fall of 1961, they created the "Group on Advanced Leadership" or GOAL. In many ways, the personnel, topics addressed, approach and structure of the RNA can be found in this first organization. It thus makes sense to begin here and move forward.

As for the leadership of GOAL, Richard Henry was made president, Henry King first vice president, Edward Brown second vice president, Vivian Broom corresponding secretary, and James Hurst financial secretary, with Albert Cleage, Henry Cleage, Milton Henry, and Octavia Henry serving as at-large executive council members. Milton was also director of the Urban Renewal Project, which aimed to achieve exactly what the title suggests.

   Though it was clear to these individuals that something needed to be done, it was less clear where to start. Detroit was beset with a wide variety of problems related to the condition of and opportunities for African Americans. There was no simple reason for the problems, however. The area of employment provides a good example of how difficult it was even to conceive of, let alone implement, a solution. As Sugrue (2005, 122) stated,

employers, hiring offices, and unions discriminated in so many seemingly unpredictable ways that even the most seasoned veterans of the labor market had difficulty figuring out the situation. The bewildering array of discriminatory practices and the range of

---

[11] Albert Cleage's connection was not simply political but also spiritual. As Dillard (2003, 162–65) stated,

   Blending theology, social criticism, and calls to action, during the late 1950s Central Congregational (then the name of Cleage's church) began to attract a large following of young professionals and working-class residents. He also began to attract a core of activists who would become influential in the theory and practice of black nationalist politics in Detroit. Attorney Milton Henry and his brother, Richard . . . both attended services at Central; as did James and Grace Boggs, local Marxists associated with the Detroit Branch of the Socialist Workers Party (SWP) and its various splinter groups; and Edward Vaughn owner of the city's largest black bookstore.
   The implications of this combination were important in terms of intellectual growth and political coalitions.
   Few . . . saw any ideological or political incongruities in moving from a SWP forum, to attending a talk by Cleage, to traveling to or otherwise supporting the Southern branch of the struggle. Rather, it was a fertile social and political space in which younger activists and older radicals were striving to make connections: between an "old left" and a "new left" one, between local, national and international struggles for justice.

motivations from the blunt to the subtle ensured that discrimination would remain an intransigent problem in the postwar city.

Compared to the situation prior to the 1940s, things improved a bit after World War II, but this was short-lived, with blacks being left on the bottom rung of the ladder. As one study notes,

[Detroit had] a long history of racial conflicts, often violent ones. Federal troops [had] been called out four times to put down black-white bloodshed: twice in the nineteenth century and twice in the twentieth. No other city has such a history. (Farley et al. 2000, 10)

Perhaps the single most important problem for the black community at the time concerned black-police interactions. According to one study of the period,

the Negroes in Detroit feel they are part of an occupied country. The Negroes have no rights which the police have to respect. It would appear that the average policeman looks upon the Negro as being a criminal. (Fine 2000, 99)

As a consequence of this situation, all black-police interactions were problematic: questioning, verbal and physical harassment, shakedowns, car searches, and home raids as well as beatings and a large number of cases of excessive violence. The issue of violence was especially noteworthy. The same report identified earlier goes on to suggest that "at one time in Detroit 'every Negro arrested somehow fell down' and suffered a cracked skull" (Fine 2000, 100). Even the police leadership at the time felt unable to control some of the activities. For example, during one interview with the police chief, George Edwards (during the period between 1961 and 1963), he remarked that he felt his job "was (essentially) to teach the police they didn't have a constitutional right to beat up Negroes on arrest" (Fine 2000, 103).

Set within this context, GOAL was interested in four areas (Group on Advanced Leadership [GOAL] 1964):

1. Schools:
   Equalizing class size;
   Using the same tests for all students;
   Firing prejudiced, lazy teachers; and,
   Getting truthful history and textbooks.
2. Justice:
   Ending Shoot-to-kill policies by the police;
   Firing "brutal" cops;
   Halting illegal search and arrest; and,
   Learning how to shoot a rifle.
3. Jobs:
   Installing the GOAL "full-employment" plan.
4. Economic Self-Help:
   Investing with GOAL to build a Negro-Owned bank.

As Fine (2000, 26) discussed, GOAL also had an interest in getting merchants to sell black products and organizing black workers in an effort to end discrimination in the skilled trades of Detroit. The first issue represented a growing sentiment that black identity was not reflected in the places where blacks were spending their money. While seeming to be somewhat less relevant to "self-help" than to self-expression, which is more connected with the black power movement, this issue was connected to the civil rights tradition because it dealt with gaining better representation within predominately white institutions. As the objectives were being pursued through boycotts, petitions, rallies, and lawsuits, the civil rights approach was clearly apparent. The second issue (black workers) reflected a longer-term interest in Detroit. Indeed, given the importance of trades to economic life within the city, there would be no survival for African Americans without such inclusion.

While the general technique for addressing diverse problems was relatively consistent with the broader civil rights movement and related organizations in Detroit, GOAL's approach was viewed as somewhat unique. The organization decided that it would not attempt to be a mass organization; this role was taken by the National Association for the Advancement of Colored People (NAACP) and the Trade Union Leadership Council. Instead, GOAL recruited carefully and developed a relatively small organization, drawing largely on those already familiar to the core grouping (the two families and their growing network). Despite the somewhat reclusive nature of the institution, however, their claim was that they were a relatively open and unbiased group. As they stated,

GOAL is an organization in which negroes of ALL political parties have a rightful place – so long as they are committed to black initiative, black dignity and black freedom. Our Executive Council contains Democrats (and others), Christians and at least one person who has professed the faith of Islam. Officially we are non-partisan – but we are NOT non-political. Members and officers are expected to have an intelligent awareness of the role of government (and therefore of politics) in our fight for Freedom, and they are free to express this intelligent awareness and to make their political preferences known. (GOAL 1965, 8)

Accordingly, in standard logic of organizational ecology, GOAL wanted to occupy a unique space (i.e., niche) among available African American institutions, trying to bring about change, serving as a vanguard – a "catalytic" institution that would lead by leading. In essence, GOAL intended to get things started and/or move things faster without dealing with issues like broader recruitment or implementation; something like a "chemical" spark (Dillard 2003, 163) or black think tank. On this point, they state that

GOAL leaves the fight for a political presence in government to the parties; GOAL's role is to make direct assaults on the practices and institutions that oppress [African Americans] – the lying textbooks, our own sense of inferiority and self-doubt, police brutality, job discrimination, school bias, business poverty, and so forth. And to mobilize in this effort all the members of the black community. (Richard Henry, as quoted in NOW! 1965, 8)

To facilitate such activities, the two most notable strategies involved their publication *NOW!* magazine and the GOAL radio show. The first was a highly stylized publication distributed in the greater Detroit and surrounding area that addressed a variety of topics but consistently served as a public voice for GOAL. It covered local, state, federal, and international news like social movement activism associated with civil rights, what Martin Luther King Jr. was engaged in, or what was happening in the war in Congo. They would also discuss social issues like the existence and role of blacks on television, provide pin-up girls that they called "Soulmates," provide information about art sales as well as other get-togethers, and always prominently highlight black products that were advertised throughout the magazine.[12] The second activity was a radio program on one of the first all-black-owned radio stations in the area, largely providing the same content as the magazine but taking advantage of the new medium. The show itself was part news, part editorial, and part talk show, prominently featuring members of GOAL, those affiliated with the organization, and selected others.

Given the objectives of the organization as well as the tactics selected to get there, the group compelled limited attention from political authorities – indeed, at this point, only local police paid them any attention. From existing records, it is clear that GOAL headquarters was under frequent surveillance. Many were photographed and identified coming to and leaving from the establishment (by name and position in GOAL). There was even some attempt to identify the vehicles that different individuals owned as well as where everyone lived. It was common to have a meeting or two monitored as well, for there were a few informants in the group who provided detailed notes about who was attending, when people met, and what individuals talked about, planned, and did. The objective here was surveillance and intelligence gathering. There was no overt action outside of the occasional placement of an obvious "undercover" agent outside an event or meeting. Accordingly, GOAL was largely not influenced by or even really aware of any repressive behavior.

[12] *NOW!* might be viewed as Henry's equivalent to the *Illustrated News,* which was largely associated with the Cleage family, especially Albert. As Dillard (2003, 162–63) stated,

In the latter part of 1961, Cleage, along with his siblings and a few friends launched their own bimonthly newspaper, the *Illustrated News.* Printed on bright pink newsprint and with a (self-proclaimed and potentially exaggerated) free circulation of 35,000, it appeared until 1965. How many persons actually read the family-financed paper is open to dispute, but during its brief existence, the *Illustrated News* was the chief public platform for Cleage and his associates. Cleage penned the majority of articles with frequent contributions from his brother, Dr. Henry Cleage, as well as Milton and Richard Henry. It was an outlet for their emerging black nationalist views and their often virulent criticism of the racial status quo.

Unlike the earlier ventures involving the Henrys and the Cleages, GOAL actually turned out to be fairly successful. In perhaps their most notable victory, in 1962, they attempted to get the Detroit school board to change their history books to be more reflective of African American life. Richard recalls the incident in detail, which reveals a great deal about how the group saw itself and how they went about their business. As discussed in one study of the period (Obadele 1970c, 117–18),

in the spring of 1962, in our first public affair, we brought J.A. Rogers – almost certainly the most prolific history researcher, black or white, of this century – to speak in Detroit. His appearance was a great success. We packed Central Congregational Church, and there was good coverage in the black press, but, more importantly, J.A. enthralled and inspired our small group and the audience, many of whom would subsequently become GOAL members, with his recitation of fascinating and little known facts about black history and about nefarious ways in which the white man had fashioned our oppression and created the myth of black inferiority.

With that as a stepping off point we opened a correspondence with Betty Becker, President of the seven-member Detroit school board which, at that time, had only one black member, Dr. Remus Robinson, requesting that the Board take immediate steps to integrate black people into the pictures used in Detroit textbooks. The correspondence was polite but fruitless: Mrs. Becker expressed her awareness and sympathy but pleaded helplessness.

In the meantime GOAL's tiny group of founders was working. We held lively meetings, working out our strategy and tactics. Ed Broom took several books being used in the schools and began to rough out new illustrations. Jim Hurst opened a correspondence with sources in New York City where a campaign for integrated illustrations in textbooks had already reaped some success. That summer [Richard Henry] picked up copies of the American history textbooks scheduled for use in Detroit schools' eighth grade in the coming fall term and began to review them. They were typical white super racist textbooks generally in use a decade ago. [He] extracted from these books 20 of the most egregious "errors, ill-founded conclusions, and significant omissions," taking these which best enabled [him], while refuting this material, to outline facts in black history which would most graphically illustrate the extent of the crime these books were committing against us [similar to the doll study in *Brown v. Board of Education*]. We presented this detailed study to the Board of Education barely a week before the opening of school. Moreover, we warned the Board, that we regarded the harm which these books would do black kids as so serious that the only remedy was to remove the books.

After being presented to the school board and Richard taking one of his kids out of school (for a sustained period of time – an action that would over time have forced the issue to go to court), the validity of GOAL's work was accepted and efforts were made to change the content a year later.

Although important in itself, what GOAL did not expect was the large amount of attention and support that they would receive from the black community following this event. The organization seemed to be on to something, and African Americans responded by coming to them in increasingly large numbers. Unfortunately, given the structure and general approach of GOAL, it really didn't have anything to do with or for the people trying to join. By design, it was not a mass-based organization. It thus turned them away.

Feeling the momentum of the education campaign, in summer 1963, GOAL moved to another direct action; this time A&P food stores was targeted for not having black products or any African Americans in management.[13] The campaign was short. After a series of small but well-publicized boycotts, GOAL again proved effective. Within a few months, A&P initiated a training program, hired some blacks, and increased the supply of selected black products. A related but smaller campaign in fall 1963 targeted Commonwealth Bank, noting that there were no African Americans working there and that there seemed to be no effort being made to court black customers. Again, GOAL threatened a boycott. The logic for the targeting was clear, revealing GOAL's emerging understanding of the situation. Part of the reason for gaining entry was to assist African Americans in obtaining loans for education, home purchases, and entrepreneurship. Without such assistance, blacks would continue to be disadvantaged. GOAL delivered on its threat and initiated a boycott. After a few days, the bank responded positively, putting a small program in place to reach out to and train blacks as customers and workers.

GOAL did not succeed in all their efforts. Interestingly, the least effective GOAL efforts were perhaps the most telling about the organization and what happened next in their history. Specifically, there were two examples.

First, there was "Operation Apply," which involved an effort to follow up on African American applications for jobs that traditionally they would not get, such as store managers, loan officers, and membership in the skilled trades. Stressing that without such opportunity, blacks would never be able to improve their economic standing or to acquire financial stability, GOAL appeared to have thought through this approach reasonably well. It is unclear, however, how frequently or how effectively they pursued it, but GOAL would go to various businesses sometimes just to have a meeting but other times to engage in boycotts. Unfortunately, there was little that could be done to convince the assorted businesses that they should care and no degree of pressure seemed to work. As a result, the initiative dissolved relatively quietly.

Second, there was GOAL's effort to curb antiblack police violence. They attempted this in numerous ways. Richard notes (as cited in Obadele 1970c, 128),

We dueled legally and verbally, employing mass rallies, picket-lines, press releases [and a $5 million lawsuit]...over the shooting in the back of a black girl, Cynthia Scott, by a vicious dog of a white policeman, Theodore Spicher, who, it appears, was either trying to force his illicit intentions upon her or illegally intimidate and rob her, or

---

[13] GOAL was not alone in this endeavor. Another group, Congress on Racial Equality (CORE), was engaged in a similar campaign against Kroger supermarket (Fine 2000, 72).

all three. [Additionally, our] legal department – manned not only by [Milton Henry], Les Molette and Bob Robbins but Eddie Smith and Myzell Sowell – moved quickly to defend the rights of a number of persons caught in the speedy machinations of injustice at Recorder's Court.

These efforts had no effect. Indeed,

in a letter to [Mayor] Cavanaugh, Congressmen Charles Diggs, Jr., asserted that as a result of the Scott affair and also the police slaying in a car chase on July 12 of an eighteen-year-old youth driving a stolen car, the progress in police-community relations (the last police Chief Edwards) had achieved could be "seen going down the drain." (cited in Fine 2007, 95)

This limitation was significant because of the magnitude of the problem. As mentioned earlier, at the time, there was seemingly no other topic deemed more important for African Americans than police brutality, which the president of the NAACP (known for its conservative and relatively optimistic view of black life in America) identified as "the single most important problem in the city" (cited in Fine 2007, 95). Harassment and arrest of African Americans from all walks of life were commonplace during this period and, in fact, for most of the city's post–World War II experience. However, it was the violence directed against blacks in the early 1960s that was especially highlighted by black leaders, in newspapers and in public opinion polls. In the context of countering increased state violence, GOAL's ineffectiveness seemed all the more troubling. Indeed, the more GOAL attempted to try and bring about change, the more limitations they saw in their approach.

Such an opinion was reaffirmed from Milton Henry's experience with trying to assist Republican George Romney run for governor of Michigan in 1962.[14]

---

[14] This was not as big a stretch as one would imagine:

A moderate Republican, Romney could point to an excellent civil rights record when he became governor. As managing director of the Automotive Council for War Production in World War II, he had been critical of segregation in defense housing. In a 1950 appearance before the Detroit Common Council as a member of the Citizens Housing and Planning Council, he protested the segregation in Detroit's housing program. While serving as the head of American Motors, he was one of the few corporation executives in Michigan to support the enactment and implementation of the Fair Employment Practices Act. In 1959 the Anti-Defamation League of B'nai Brith awarded Romney its Americanism citation. He further enhanced his civil rights credentials in 1961–62 as a delegate to Michigan's constitutional convention. (Fine 2000, 216)

Moreover,

In his first State of the State message on January 10, 1963, he declared that "Michigan's most urgent human rights problem" was racial discrimination – in housing, public accommodations, education, administration of justice, and employment. He called for increased funding for the FEPC's education program to enable it to add to its staff and to open new branch offices, legislation to prohibit discrimination by labor organizations and apprenticeship programs, and increased funding for the vocational training of the physically handicapped. He appointed Joseph Bell, Jr., to serve as Vice Chairman of the state Republican Party, the highest party

Acknowledging that blacks should not be overly concerned with political affiliation and should be more concerned with what the distinct parties were able to deliver to their constituents, Milton was approached by and assisted Romney in the latter's bid to win. Milton was clearly thinking strategically here. His actions would not only show Democrats that they should not take blacks for granted but would also show Republicans that if they delivered the goods, they could acquire African American support. At the same time, the action (if successful) would show blacks that they were able to sway political outcomes with their voting power.

Romney ended up winning, but Milton did not come out of this experience with any sense of victory. This was not because he went unselected for the various positions that Romney tried to fill. Rather, Milton and others "got together and... said, hell, you know [whites] are not going to react from the basis of [blacks] trying to influence some party either within or even you know without acting on the basis of trying to shift votes. What we needed was an independent party" (Obadele 1970c, 9).

Albert Cleage and those around him also came to a similar decision, albeit from a somewhat different path. In May 1963, Albert had joined with the powerful leader of the New Bethel Baptist Church Clarence LaVaughn (C. L.) Franklin (the civil rights leader, friend of Martin Luther King Jr., and father of Aretha Franklin). For a second, it appeared that the unification between the long-standing, charismatic, and popular religious leader with ties to the older African Americans (Franklin) and the newer, equally charismatic and increasingly popular religious leader with ties to the younger cohort (Cleage) would represent a serious challenge to the more established NAACP, which they both agreed had lost touch with common folk. Seeing the need for linking their concerns and efforts with the civil rights struggle in the South, they arranged the Walk to Freedom, which took place in Detroit on July 28, 1963. Aside from bringing together the largest civil rights demonstration in the United States to that time, with approximately 125,000 in downtown Detroit, it represented a crowning achievement for the burgeoning collaboration between the two leaders and their respective communities. The group was ignited with what would several weeks later be used in the "I Have a Dream" speech by Martin Luther King Jr. at the March on Washington, which occurred in Washington, D.C., on August 28. The event even brought out the NAACP and the mayor of Detroit, both reluctantly supporting the effort but both promising that the energy generated during that day would not dissipate.

Unfortunately, while the energy prompted by the Walk to Freedom may not have dissipated, the collaboration did. Planning for a follow-up event, a Northern Negro Leadership Conference or Regional Leadership Conference

position in either state party attained by an African American at the time. In March 1963 he appointed Leo Greene, a black Flint mortician, as the governor's special adviser on minority relations. (216, 217) was put forward and scheduled for November to map out the future of the struggle – in Detroit as well as nationally. Although things appeared to be going smoothly, Albert Cleage and Reverend Franklin differed on the selection of attendees. Albert wanted to include the younger, more radical groups. This was problematic because some within these groups were expressly critical of King, who, as I mentioned earlier, was a close personal friend of Franklin (Joseph 2006, 87). Albert also wanted to pursue an initiative begun at the March on Washington, putting together an all-black political party. More traditional in his orientation, but no less fierce in his pursuit of justice and equality, Reverend Franklin disagreed with this tactic, preferring the old integrationist effort to work within the existing two-party system. As a result, Albert left the group.

Following his split with Reverend Franklin, Albert Cleage and those with him once again teamed up with the Henrys to sponsor two activities: (1) the Michigan branch of the Freedom Now Party[15] (FNP) and (2) the Grassroots Leadership Conference. Each sent the group of activists on a different trajectory.

The FNP was created by a select group of individuals during the March on Washington. Led by William Worthy (from Boston), the basic logic of the FNP – the first all–African American political party to be placed on the ballot in the United States – was straightforward. First, they acknowledged that an all-black party could not dominate American politics because there were too few African Americans. However, their reasoning, similar to Milton Henry's logic regarding working with Republicans, was that they could swing votes in one direction or another. They pondered the implications of this idea:

What would happen to the Democratic party if they woke up one bright November morn and found that the Negro vote was no longer in their hip pocket(?) Or going on, what would happen to the Republican party if they started winning elections because Democrats no longer had the Negro vote. Now think a little further and try to imagine each of these parties seriously vying with each other for the Negro vote through "The Freedom Now Party." Do you think a few dixiecrats could tie up civil rights or any other issue concerning Negroes? What about appointments to high federal and state governmental agencies? On the supreme court they have a seat for a catholic, a Jew, and a southerner, but where is the seat for a Negro? With all of our political strength, there should be at least one. (Smith 1963, 1)

---

[15] This is close in terms of timing but different from the Mississippi Freedom Democratic Party (MFDP), which, in 1964, established itself as a nondiscriminatory, nonexclusionary competitor to the Democratic Party, which was blocking black participation. This was one of the initiatives associated with the Freedom Summer program, which had attempted to register blacks to vote so that they could influence the electoral system from within its existing structure. Unable to gain access, the MFDP attempted to get around it by directly gaining entry into the Democratic National Convention of 1964 by challenging the legitimacy of the official delegation, put in place by the restriction of black participation. They did not achieve their objective, and their effort was geographically restricted to Mississippi. Revealing that others were thinking in the same manner, however, the Freedom Now Party did persist for a while longer and on a national level.

A member of the party was even more direct on May 28, 1964:

The Freedom Now Party is a way of assuring Negroes that they can run for every elected office in [Michigan]. This is something that Negroes have never been able to hope for before because it cannot be done within the Democratic and Republican parties. (*Detroit Free Press*)

Second, while acknowledging that African Americans generally favored integration, they argued that whites generally did not, and this left blacks in an awkward and vulnerable position. Given the reality of the imbalance in existing political representation and power, the only way that blacks could look after themselves would be through an all-black political party. The reason: "power recognizes power" (Smith 1963–64, 2).

Third, the group explicitly acknowledged the fact that many do not believe that an all-black political organization could function well or could be meaningful for African Americans (Smith 1963–64, 2). The party quickly pointed out that there were already a host of all-black professions and institutions that had come into existence for the same reason that an all-black political party was necessary: as whites did not assist African Americans in taking care of various aspects of life, blacks had to create and sustain the relevant activity themselves (e.g., the black churches, schools, colleges, newspapers, doctors, lawyers, dentists, insurance companies, fraternities and sororities, barbers, beauticians, and undertakers). They then pushed the argument, wondering,

[If one got rid of] everything that is all black what do we have? Nothing, and this is just the point. Negro institutions have developed because of a very serious need and reason. We aren't wanted. We haven't been wanted in past history and we're not wanted now. Our only salvation is to build and nourish our own institutions. (Smith 1963–64, 2)

With this in mind, it was believed that the FNP would change all of this. An all-black political party would represent black people, meeting their most basic needs, which presumably they would understand best. A crucial element of the FNP's approach was to "bring civil rights complaints to the Civil Rights Commission created by the state Constitution" (Cleage, in a June 2, 1964, *Detroit Free Press* interview).

Because of the involvement of other states and the even more conventional nature of the claims-making effort, the FNP garnered a bit more attention from political authorities than GOAL, attention that was of a largely covert nature. Meetings were observed and dossiers of the affiliated were compiled, but nothing took place overtly against them (similar to GOAL's treatment by the authorities). The individuals in this group were thus largely left alone to do what they wanted. This is not to suggest that individuals and organizations, such as the Democratic Party, were not against them, but it is to suggest that U.S. political authorities did not employ their coercive powers.

As expected, the more integrationist blacks were against the FNP. Martin Luther King Jr. expressed numerous times that he was opposed to the all-black political party (*Michigan Chronicle*, March 28, 1964). In an even more aggressive move, churches such as the Dexter Avenue Baptist Church started closing their doors to the organization, claiming that segregation was just not the way to go. In this case, as would frequently be shown later, Richard Henry attempted to broker a peace, suggesting that the different sides come together and debate their differences, but this was not going to happen (*Detroit Free Press*, March 28, 1964). Some breaches, however, could not be overcome. Some collaborations could not be made.

Finally, fed up with the limitations of the two-party system and the piecemeal benefits that accrued to blacks from it, on October 11, 1963, the Henrys and Cleages joined forces with others to launch the Michigan chapter of the FNP. The usual individuals were involved, with slightly different roles. This time, Albert Cleage was the state chairperson and would run for governor, Milton Henry was Oakland county chairperson and ran for Congress (running against John Conyers), Henry Cleage ran for prosecutor, Louis Cleage as well as Helen Nuttal Brown ran for the board of governors at Wayne State, Grace Boggs (an important local activist) was state secretary, Ernest Smith was treasurer and campaign coordinator, Lamar Barron was executive secretary, Gwendelyn Kemp was Wayne County chairperson, and Charles Northington along with Reginald Wilson were field coordinators. Lacking the appropriate credentials and background for the effort, this time it was Richard who would sit out.

During the same period, Albert Cleage started to garner a great deal of negative press. For example, referring to his sermons, it would be common to read articles like the 1964 article "Does Cleage Teach Hate?" from the *Michigan Chronicle*. In answer to the question, Albert was clear:

Some people claim I'm preaching hate ... They're saying it because I'm preaching the Freedom Now Party, and they're concerned with what we're trying to do. Still, all Negroes in the US have been brainwashed and there's no getting around it. All their lives they've been taught to curry favor. Currying favor with the white man has been a means of survival for the Negro, and "good" Negroes are always taken care of. The white man will always take care of and reward good Negroes.

He continued, revealing an increasingly sophisticated and aggressive approach,

We've got to free men's mind ... The black man is as free as he wants to be, and our job is to rub raw the sores of discontent. We're fighting for freedom from white domination. "Freedom Now" will let everyone know we're living under a system of oppression.

Here any suggestion that blacks did not need to associate with whites was viewed as a hostile gesture and one worthy of scorn. The more distance from whites was advocated, the more negative press would be levied against the speaker.

Whites were not the only ones having a problem with what was being said. Although many throughout Albert's congregation and the city were supportive, not all blacks held favorable opinions regarding what was said. For example, there was a failed effort by members of his own church to have him censured because they felt that he was taking things too far and neglecting his congregation. The challenge made Albert seriously reflect about the choice that he had made, but, at least in the short term, it did not deter him. Freedom deferred was freedom denied, and it seemed increasingly so.

Summary

Within this chapter, we discussed the pre-RNA history of the Republic of New Africa. This was done through a detailed evaluation of the two individuals most central to its creation: Milton and Richard Henry, later Gaidi and Imari Obadele. The discussion was useful, for it revealed that the dissident organization of interest is only understandable through an understanding of the individuals who composed it. The chapter also revealed the reasons for the specific path taken by the relevant individuals as they created and terminated two organizations: the Group on Advanced Leadership and the Freedom Now Party.

6

We Shall Overthrow!

From the Malcolm X Society to the Republic of New Africa

Set on the path of activism, but beset with a series of personal as well as political issues, the Henrys and Cleages searched for a different approach. The inspiration for a new direction came from two individuals. On one hand was Malcolm X, perhaps one of the most important political thinkers, sources of inspiration, and organizational facilitators in U.S. history, whose influence was only hindered by his assassination. On the other hand was Robert F. Williams, today much less well known than Malcolm but, in his time, perhaps one of the most important African American leaders in the United States. This chapter tells the story of the influence of these two men and the formation of the RNA.

The Malcolm X Effect

On November 10, 1963, a month after the creation of the Freedom Now Party, the Henry-Cleage group pulled together a conference intended to counter the activities undertaken by the better-financed, better-publicized Detroit Council for Human Rights leadership conference run by the Reverend C. L. Franklin. This event drew on the actions and connections not only of the Henrys and the Cleages but also of others from the community, for example, Reverend Milton Galamison, leader of an employment nongovernmental organization in Brooklyn; Sam Jordan, a candidate for Detroit mayor; and William Worthy, the FNP national chairperson. No individual, however, would be as important as Malcolm X (the keynote speaker),[1] who had been drawn to the event by his friend Milton Henry.

Malcolm's connections with Detroit ran deep. As is now well known, he had lived in the city as a child and got into legal trouble pretty early. After he came out of prison, he initially spent time in Detroit with his sponsor in the Nation

---

[1] Adam Clayton Powell Jr. was the keynote speaker for the DCHR conference.

of Islam (NOI). As the NOI was founded in the city and its first mosque was located there, Malcolm was immediately steeped in the organization's history and strong ties to the community. Even after leaving Detroit to go to the NOI base in Chicago, serving later as a minister in New York as well as traveling nationally to create mosques all over the United States, he would repeatedly return to Detroit every now and then to see family, friends, and those who assisted him after prison as well as to interact with and recruit from the African American community that he perhaps knew best.

All of this was pretty well known, as many of the events were covered in the media, but it still merits noting that Malcolm's activities brought him increased attention from federal policing institutions like the FBI, which had been monitoring him since his first connections with the NOI. Again, this did not involve anything beyond covert observation, but it did represent another layer of attention from political authorities that was directed at the individuals who would become involved in the RNA.

It makes sense that Malcolm would come across and interact with the Henrys, in particular Milton, and the Cleages. Malcolm was notorious for "collecting" people (i.e., identifying and interacting with people whom he felt had potential as activists), especially African Americans with education and a willingness to engage in struggle. Milton clearly fit this bill as a black college graduate, Yale-trained lawyer, and Tuskeegee Airman. Moving in the other direction, Milton was equally as intrigued with Malcolm, as was most of America at the time. Richard and Laurence (the two youngest Henrys) were similarly enthralled when they met the NOI minister at the Shabazz restaurant in Detroit before the March on Washington and at a GOAL rally before John F. Kennedy's assassination.

As national spokesmen for the NOI, Malcolm became the voice of the awakening African American radicals of the early 1960s, who were disenchanted with the objective of integration and the reality of continued political, economic, and social discrimination. As Cone (1992, 16) suggested, if the basis of the integrationist approach was practicality, the basis of the nationalist approach Malcolm X epitomized was desperation. Belaboring the magnitude of the problem confronted by African Americans and the inadequacy of the dominant civil rights approach to address the various problems that blacks confronted, Malcolm's speeches were nothing less than revelations to those who heard them. At the time of his most inspirational speeches, however, his actions were limited by the NOI policy of nonintervention (i.e., not working with those engaged in social struggle and focusing on Muslims almost exclusively). Malcolm's willingness to succumb to this limitation would diminish over time as his awareness of other struggles and his disenchantment with the NOI increased. In this context, in late 1963, Malcolm began to build, and he was hungry for recruits. To create as many organizations as possible, Malcolm traversed the United States bringing inspiration and advice to any and all. For a select few, like GOAL and somewhat later the Revolutionary Action

Movement, he would provide not just inspiration but guidance and training to further their causes.

Malcolm's efforts at organizational development are less well known than what he said and what he did while with (as well as after) the NOI, but they are crucial for understanding organizations like GOAL and the RNA, who came to view themselves as the "Children of Malcolm." A large part of his impact on the Henrys and the others in Detroit was directly connected with Malcolm's speech at the Grassroots Conference, a speech that would become one of his most famous.[2]

As Joseph (2006, 91–92) states,

Malcolm's speech at the Grassroots Conference brought together two generations of activists gathered in Detroit to organize a national movement for Black Power. "The Message to the Grassroots" [speech] was the conference's crown jewel. Over the next decade the speech became a quintessential example of Malcolm's rhetorical genius and political complexity and was widely distributed around the country [it was recorded by Milton's recording company which stood as yet another venture for the entrepreneur]. Mixing black nationalism, anticolonialism, and self-defense with the now-famous allegory of House Negroes and Field Negroes, the speech showcased Malcolm's global vision before his break from the Nation of Islam (which took place four months after the speech).

In Malcolm's most political speech to date, the themes were clear. African Americans needed to unify and forget their religious and class differences, the latter being proxied by his analogies regarding "House Negroes" and "Field Negroes." There needed to be a political summit of all blacks to discuss their common difficulties, analogous to the Bandung conference of Third World nations in 1955, which unified all of those suffering under European colonialism. Malcolm also laid out the difference between a somewhat conservative effort where nonviolent African Americans tried to "sit next to white folks on the toilet" (i.e., the "Negro revolution" or what he referred to as a "begolution") and a more radical effort that attempted to violently acquire land for blacks to obtain freedom, justice, and equality as well as to pursue political independence and nationhood (i.e., the "black revolution").

Richard Henry was especially energized by the event as well as the speeches that accompanied it, but he admitted that he and the others were not quite ready for what Malcolm suggested. As he states,

by Malcolm's speech in November of that memorable year ... we knew, through struggle, of the immensity of the work that faced the black man in America if we were to be truly free. Through struggle we knew of our own limited resources and the great skill and care that would be required were we to support our revolution from these resources – and we were obliged to, unless we wished to be bought and owned by the

---

[2] This can be read at http://teachingamericanhistory.org/library/index.asp?document=1145.

enemy. We knew, through struggle, of the great pressures that operate upon the black man to make him doubt the need for revolution, to slow down and seek his liberation through a personal acquisition of gadgets and wealth . . . And we knew, finally, through struggle, that we needed something more than the hopelessly too-small-always first aid, the pit-of-the-stomach-empty reforms, of a civil rights organization like GOAL. *We needed power. Malcolm told us how – through setting up our own nation: that was our only real hope.* But we had to try something else first. (emphasis added)

That "something" that he spoke of concerned the Freedom Now Party, and with this acknowledgment, they pulled away from Malcolm, turning their full efforts to making the FNP work. Initially, circumstances seemed quite favorable. With an ambitious campaign, they received thirty-two thousand signatures, easily attaining more than the eleven thousand signatures in fifteen counties needed to be placed on the ballot. The election was to be held in November 1964, and with this as their objective, the membership went about the business of fund-raising and campaigning.

Although not directly involved with the FNP effort, Malcolm was never far from the efforts of those in Detroit. Before the November election, Malcolm returned on April 12, 1964, to participate in yet another conference and give perhaps his most famous speech, "The Ballot or the Bullet." This time, however, was different. This time Malcolm did not come as a member of the NOI. This time he could speak as he wanted. This time he came to build a broad-based organization. Again, Joseph (2006, 102) well captures the spirit of the event:

Braiding an analysis of self-defense, electoral politics, and Pan-Africanism with an assertion that America's civil rights struggles were part of a global movement, in this speech Malcolm defined his new political direction: "We need to expand the civil rights struggle to a higher level."

During his talk, Malcolm noted that the focus on civil rights had unnecessarily hindered the African American struggle by limiting claims making to the jurisdiction controlled by the United States. By shifting the effort to human rights, blacks could shift the venue of claims making and allow themselves to pursue alleviation of their grievances at the international level in such places as the United Nations. As Joseph continues,

in the "Ballot or the Bullet," Malcolm defined black nationalism as more than a simple call for unity or promotion of racial pride (like he had in "Message to the Grassroots"). Instead, black nationalism was part and parcel of the radical black self-determination, even in the face of ideological heresy, that Malcolm had been preaching for some time. (102)

Again, he discussed the topic of black unity. Again, he discussed keeping his religion a personal matter but his politics a highly public matter, suggesting that others follow suit. He again detailed his life as that of an outsider to American life, a "victim of Americanism" pondering what should be done:

should blacks use the "ballot" (i.e., vote and participate in the political system) or the "bullet" (i.e., revolution and dissident struggle)? This was where the topics began to change from the earlier Malcolm. Through a detailed discussion of the deficiencies of the two-party system, continued disenfranchisement, and gerrymandering, he concluded that American democracy had failed African Americans and that it would always do so until it was fundamentally changed.

What did blacks need? Well, he argued, they needed some friends and allies (preferably outside of the United States) as well as a new "interpretation" of the civil rights "thing." As he pointed out, civil rights are domestic issues, which are dealt with or not dealt with within the United States. Human rights, however, are international issues, which are dealt with within the international realm. This is crucial, for he argues that "when you take your case to Washington, D.C., you're taking it to the criminal who's responsible; its like running from the wolf to the fox. They're all in cahoots together. They all work political chicanery and make you look like a chump before the eyes of the world" (X 1964). Malcolm X went on to speak about guerilla warfare and the fact that this is perhaps the most effective way to counter a superior military power. He also identified that black nationalism (defined as African Americans controlling the politics and politicians, the economics and economic units of production, as well as the values within the black community) was already practiced by many within the Christian church, the NAACP, CORE, the SNCC, by Muslims, atheists, and agnostics. They just didn't call it that (and this was something noted by those who had been in GOAL earlier). In a dramatic change from his previous incarnation that suggested everyone join the NOI, Malcolm X argued that if an organization was practicing black nationalism, it should be joined. It didn't matter which one; all paths led to empowerment. As he said,

in this manner, the organizations will increase in number and in quantity and in quality, and by August, it is... our intention to have a black nationalist convention which will consist of delegates from all over the country who are interested in the political, economic and social philosophy of black nationalism. After these delegates convene, we will hold a seminar; we will hold discussions; we will listen to everyone. We want to hear new ideas and new solutions and new answers. And at that time, if we see fit then to form a black nationalist party, we'll form a black nationalist party. If it's necessary to form a black nationalist army, we'll form a black nationalist army. It'll be the ballot or the bullet. It'll be liberty or it'll be death. (X 1964)

Soon after this speech and specific violent events directed against blacks (such as the St. Augustine, Florida, riot on July 3, 1964, where a white mob attacked African American demonstrators), one could see Malcolm X's impact as GOAL began their calls for black self-defense in the form of rifle clubs. As Richard Henry stated in the *Michigan Chronicle* on July 4, 1964, "the St. Augustine incident [was] 'a stunning rebuke to the manhood of every black in this country... It is a harsh and final seal on the bankruptcy of Martin Luther King's doctrine of nonviolence. That technique is dead.'"

Moving somewhat beyond self-defense and representing an early version of what black power would come to discuss a few years later, Richard noted,

The rifle clubs would be "for going South in moments of siege" and for getting guns "into the hands of willing and needy blacks in the fascist South, when the time comes." The GOAL leader predicted that "proportioned underground warfare" by Negroes would come to the South. When that happens, [he] said, the northern rifle clubs would "back Negroes in besieged towns under attack by whites seeking to retaliate for the acts of the underground."

Interestingly, at the same time that GOAL was making this call to arms, the Civil Rights Act had just been passed (two days before), and the group was preparing to picket local grocery stores to deal with discrimination (*Michigan Chronicle*, July 11, 1964). The repertoire of engagement and the tactics deemed necessary had increasingly become more inclusive: they were trying everything but moving in the direction of greater radicalization.

A major blow was soon dealt to the elements of GOAL that favored working within the system. Despite the rallies, speeches, sermons, and editorials to raise consciousness as well as the persistence of diverse aspects of racism, the electoral returns on November 3, 1964, dashed the hope of the all-black political party in Detroit specifically and Michigan in general. For example, out of 1,642,302 votes for governor, Albert Cleage only obtained 20,000, and out of 136,489 votes for the first congressional district, Milton Henry only received 1,504 (*Daily Press*, November 5, 1964). Evidently, African Americans were not ready for and/or interested in all-black representation.

Shortly after the election, everyone tried to figure out what to do. Not all, however, were up to the task. Albert Cleage withdrew from the FNP, trying to diminish his disappointment with black voters[3] as well as with the overall strategy pursued, arguing that his church needed him and that he needed to spend more time with and working for his church, a truthful statement given the attempt at censuring he had confronted only months earlier (in June 1964). The other reason for Albert's withdrawal seemed to be a tactical difference with the Henrys (harking back to his tactical difference with C. L. Franklin). On one hand, Milton and Richard wished to reach out and form a broader organization that would include individuals such as Jackie Vaughn and Nicholas Hood, two local activists. On the other hand, Albert and Grace Boggs (two longtime activists) thought that this would simply dilute the party's message and impact. There was also some disagreement over a small proposal by Albert Cleage to change the structure of city council (called the Common Council)[4] from a nine-person committee to a twenty-three-person committee elected by wards

[3] In an article in the *Chronicle* (November 14, 1964), he maintained that the militant Negro was not repudiated by the election. Rather, "it was simply an indication that the Negro does not yet know how to use his vote. He doesn't know how to vote for the best pay-back . . . and then last week, Negroes were frightened, almost desperate."

[4] The Common Council was the name used for the city council until 1974.

(*Michigan Chronicle*, December 5, 1964). Tired of arguing (i.e., fatigued), Cleage left.

In the vacuum remaining after Albert's departure, Milton Henry was brought in to lead the party as state chairperson, but it was all to no avail, because the FNP soon faded into history.[5] Regardless of the specifics concerning the political organization, the general lesson had been learned by the Henrys and those working with them:

You don't get power with votes ... What you have to have is power to get the votes and that's a distinctly important lesson to learn ... You can't get a vote when you're in the man's system, you know, and get power gaining it just because you do have the votes. You got to get the votes counted ... Politics with a third party injected [wouldn't work because the] black independent party would still not have the money or capacity to make its votes count. You can keep the machines running. They jammed up the machines on us and all that kind of stuff. (Henry 1970, 12)

Experiment attempted, alternatives exhausted, and now somewhat alienated from the Cleages, the Henrys and their associates pushed in a different direction – Malcolm X's. The timing here was opportune in many respects. After his departure from the NOI, Malcolm interacted with the Henrys quite frequently, giving speeches at events and discussing what should be done. Milton even traveled with Malcolm to Africa for the Afro-American Broadcasting Corporation to cover Malcolm's visit to the second annual summit of the Organization for African Unity (OAU). Malcolm had traveled to the OAU to make Africans aware of the African American's plight and to acquire their support for the black struggle, financial as well as political, and specifically for taking the African American case to the United Nations.

One of the major reasons for moving toward Malcolm was that his assessment of the horrific conditions involved and the intractability of dealing with American racism, especially in the context of the urban North, seemed to be correct (trust was built through effective evaluation after all). There had been much discussion, activism, court rulings, and legislation concerning African

---

[5] Some questioned the viability of the institution from the beginning. One of the most astute critics (Cruse 1967, 415) noted that

Organizationally, the Freedom Now Party movement presented a new opportunity for the entire Negro movement to have a thoroughly independent rallying point. But it had to be a truly all-black movement in order to safeguard its independent quality. Yet this movement started off with an *interracial* organizing committee.

He then posed the question, "How is it possible to organize an *All-Black* political party with an *interracial* committee creating its policy?" He continued, "The downfall of the Freedom Now Party movement was its inability to create a program that the organizers were prepared to fight for and to implement. This committee did not understand, or care to grasp, the differences between a *political party* and a *movement*" (415). There may have also been an issue about competition within the organization between its Detroit and New York chapters.

Americans in the United States during the early to mid-1960s. Michigan in general and Detroit in particular appeared to lead the nation in many respects in their attempts to acknowledge, explore, and bring about change in the political, economic, and social conditions of blacks. These efforts were largely unsuccessful, however, in remedying the problems that beset the black community. Being on the most optimistic side, Fine (2000, 335) argued that

> there had been significant civil rights gains in Michigan with regard to access to public accommodations, government contracting, and the membership of the state civil service, [but] lesser gains in the areas of private employment, housing, education, law enforcement, and sex and age discrimination.

Other studies, however, were much less generous about the failures of Michigan in general and Detroit in particular (e.g., Sugrue 1996; Farley et al. 2000).

Additionally, the increasing departure of whites from Detroit and increasing arguments against the many activities being undertaken on behalf of the black community (e.g., Grant 1970) seemed to reveal what whites thought about the idea of living within an integrated city. Richard Henry well summarized the sentiment in a very sobering reflection:

> The trouble was that we [blacks] as a people... live among a majority population, the whites, who have an exceedingly strong sense of being a people and an exceedingly great pride in themselves as a race. They see nothing now – and they saw nothing then: during the 25 years of our pursuit of integration – that they can gain from joining with us in a fusing of races and a leveling of racial esteem. Indeed, whites had, in fact, something very distinct and valuable which they could lose in the process: their sense of racial superiority...
>
> It was this – racism: all pervading and ubiquitous – which made integration impossible from the beginning. For if the majority did not want it (and they did not), and if the clinging of whites to their belief in white supremacy were too strong a force for the minority of blacks to overcome (and it is), then integration of the races in America was clearly impossible. The result is a set of intriguing choices for black people.
>
> We can ignore the reality – that integration not only does not, but could not, exist – and we can bring destruction upon ourselves, literally, as a result of actions based on our refusal to recognize and accept reality. Next, we can accept the reality but cling to the goal anyway. Finally, we can accept the reality and then work out a strategy for our own best interests, based on a recognition of the reality. (Obadele 1970c, 132)

What should they do? Well, Malcolm X advocated the third option. Exactly what he suggested about the problems confronting African Americans was somewhat vague as well as complex, but at the time, he had acquired the trust of the burgeoning black nationalist community, and they were willing to follow.[6] Malcolm's approach was fourfold.

---

[6] This said, it is worthwhile to reflect on what was going on at the time, for in many respects, it is forgotten that Malcolm X was really just getting started during this period. He had only been free from the Nation of Islam to pursue as well as develop his ideas for about eleven months, and six of those months had been spent in Africa, trying to raise awareness of the black situation as

First, as when he was with the NOI, he maintained that separation between blacks and whites was necessary. The reason for this changed along with his status. When he was with the NOI, Malcolm X argued that blacks should be separate from whites because the latter were going to be destroyed by Allah for, generally, how they acted in the world and, more specifically, for how they treated African Americans. After his departure from the NOI, however, separation seemed more an issue of political effectiveness and, as noted earlier, an acceptance of reality. Blacks needed to organize themselves to be more effective as a collective group. As he states in his "Ballot or the Bullet" speech in 1964,[7]

The political philosophy of black nationalism means that the black man should control the politics and the politicians in his own community. The black man in the black community has to be re-educated into the science of politics so he will know what politics is supposed to bring him in return.

The economic philosophy of black nationalism is pure and simple. It only means that we should control the economy of our community. Why should white people be running all the stores in our community? Why should white people be running the banks of our community? Why should the economy of our community be in the hands of the white man? Why? If a black man can't move his store into a white community, you tell me why a white man should move his store into a black community. The philosophy of black nationalism involves a re-education program in the black community in regards to economics. Our people have to be made to see that any time you take your dollar out of your community and spend it in a community where you don't live, the community where you live will get poorer and poorer, and the community where you spend your money will get richer and richer . . .

So the economic philosophy of black nationalism means in every church, in every civic organization, in every fraternal order, it's time now for our people to become conscious of the importance of controlling the economy of our community. If we own the stores, if we operate the businesses, if we try and establish some industry in our own community, then we're developing to the position where we are creating employment for our own kind. Once you gain control of the economy of your own community, then you don't have to picket and boycott and beg some cracker downtown for a job in his business.

The social philosophy of black nationalism only means that we have to get together and remove the evils, the vices, alcoholism, drug addiction, and other evils that are destroying the moral fiber of our community. We ourselves have to lift the level of our community, the standard of our community to a higher level, make our own society beautiful so that we will be satisfied in our own social circles and won't be running

well as gain financial support for the creation of diverse African American institutions. Much of what we and others knew about what Malcolm X was attempting to do politically was thus in process and discussed only within speeches, conversations, interviews, and an article or two. At no point in time did he lay out in detail what he imagined the solution to the African American situation to be. He did, however, outline a variety of directions that needed to be pursued, and this is what the individuals interested in following his advice had to use.

7 See http://www.hartford-hwp.com/archives/45a/065.html.

around here trying to knock our way into a social circle where we're not wanted. So I say, in spreading a gospel such as black nationalism, it is not designed to make the black man re-evaluate the white man – you know him already – but to make the black man re-evaluate himself. Don't change the white man's mind – you can't change his mind, and that whole thing about appealing to the moral conscience of America – America's conscience is bankrupt. She lost all conscience a long time ago. Uncle Sam has no conscience. (X 1964)

Clearly drawing on the issues of self-determination and sovereignty, he continued,

A segregated district or community is a community in which people live, but outsiders control the politics and the economy of that community. They never refer to the white section as a segregated community. It's the all-Negro section that's a segregated community. Why? The white man controls his own school, his own bank, his own economy, his own politics, his own everything, his own community; but he also controls yours. When you're under someone else's control, you're segregated. They'll always give you the lowest or the worst that there is to offer, but it doesn't mean you're segregated just because you have your own. You've got to control your own. Just like the white man has control of his, you need to control yours. (X 1964)

Second, Malcolm X still maintained that African Americans needed to engage in armed self-defense as a way to offset the violence that was being directed against them. This response would assist blacks in not only saving their lives but also realizing their humanity. On this point, invoking Hobbes, Malcolm X (1964) is emphatically clear:

In areas where the government has proven itself either unwilling or unable to defend the lives and the property of Negroes, it's time for Negroes to defend themselves. Article number two of the constitutional amendments provides you and me the right to own a rifle or a shotgun. It is constitutionally legal to own a shotgun or a rifle. This doesn't mean you're going to get a rifle and form battalions and go out looking for white folks, although you'd be within your rights – I mean, you'd be justified; but that would be illegal and we don't do anything illegal. If the white man doesn't want the black man buying rifles and shotguns, then let the government do its job...

If he's not going to do his job in running the government and providing you and me with the protection that our taxes are supposed to be for, since he spends all those billions for his defense budget, he certainly can't begrudge you and me spending $12 or $15 for a single-shot, or double-action. I hope you understand. Don't go out shooting people, but any time – brothers and sisters, and especially the men in this audience; some of you wearing Congressional Medals of Honor, with shoulders this wide, chests this big, muscles that big – any time you and I sit around and read where they bomb a church and murder in cold blood, not some grownups, but four little girls while they were praying to the same God the white man taught them to pray to, and you and I see the government go down and can't find who did it [then it's time for action].

Third, Malcolm argued that African Americans needed to stop discussing their problems and their solutions in the context of civil rights, which were under the jurisdiction of the United States – the same entity that has engaged in and/or facilitated the same oppressive conditions that prompted activism in the first place. Instead, he maintained (as mentioned earlier) that African Americans needed to start discussing their problems and solutions in the context of human rights, which were under the jurisdiction of the international community where people of color were in the majority. Indeed, he increasingly saw the black struggle as being part of a larger struggle against violence and oppression. This was the fourth and final part of his emerging approach to black liberation: internationalization.

While some of this sounds reminiscent of the Malcolm X of the NOI, there were important differences. For example, Malcolm no longer saw all whites as evil or viewed them collectively as devils. Indeed, he was willing to interact with anyone who was interested in working to resolve the situation, but he acknowledged that whites could not join the movement directly because psychologically this was something that blacks needed to do for themselves. Others could work in their own communities on behalf of African Americans. Most importantly, Malcolm no longer sought to avoid engaging with the world as he had done as a minister of the NOI. Instead, he tried to "join" the civil rights movement, but only in an effort to radicalize it and make it more relevant to poor blacks in American cities. He even made overtures to work with Martin Luther King. These efforts were not reciprocated in large part because Malcolm X was not able to shake his earlier image as a violent militant, something that King could not associate with if he wanted to maintain his support base.

Despite the immediacy of Malcolm X's rhetoric and discussions of impending explosions within the inner cities of America, the Henrys and their associates moved slowly as the strategy was being developed by Malcolm X. For example, in 1964, to address self-defense needs, they created the Medgar Evers Rifle Club, named after the civil rights leader who was killed in 1963. Another, the Fox and Wolf Hunting Club, was created in 1965, probably in response to one of Malcolm's older famous quotations. They knew more was needed, but considering all that they had attempted before and intermittently interacting with Malcolm about what should be done next and how to do it, they were not quite sure of what to do. They knew they were past GOAL and that the FNP was at an end. The next step, however, was unclear, and in this space, they did not move quickly, and understandably so – the stakes as well as the risks were extremely high.

All of this deliberation and slowness changed when Malcolm was assassinated on February 25, 1965, in New York City. After he was gone, those who had looked to him for guidance seemed lost, especially Milton Henry, his dear friend and a pallbearer at his funeral. Through grief, however, the Henry brothers, Albert Cleage,[8] and those associated with them found their way back to Malcolm as well as to each other. As before, Milton (who had changed his

---

[8] Cleage had transformed his church from a mainstream Christian church into a Pan-African Orthodox Christian church as part of the Black Christian Nationalist movement.

"slave" name to Gaidi Obadele, his "free" name, to reflect his new African consciousness) took the lead as the national chairperson. This time, however, Richard (now Imari Obadele) played a greater role.

In 1966, embodying the spirit of the new movement, Imari wrote a small book titled *War in America: The Malcolm X Doctrine* (Obadele 1968). The book would not be published until 1968, but it had some readers prior to publication. Drawing on Malcolm X explicitly, *War in America* outlined the path that Imari believed would have been advocated by Malcolm had he lived. Indeed, he said that the book was for the followers of Malcolm, referred to as the "Malcolmites." It was not clear who these individuals were, how many of them existed, or where they were,[9] but it was rumored that after reading *War in America*, numerous individuals from around the United States agreed to its basic principles and would do what they could to bring its vision to light; not in an overt, aggressive manner but in secret, from the underground, like the RAM. This group called itself the Malcolm X Society. This was a small, semi-underground organization composed of individuals in Detroit and a few other cities around the United States (Obadele 1970c, 152).

The approach advocated by this group was simple. As conceived, the Malcolmites would work within the governmental framework and state structure of the United States, winning black people, first in Mississippi (a place with a large number of African Americans), to the cause of independent land and power, follow[ing] this with election victories (the Sheriff's offices, particularly) within the US federal system and, finally, take the black state out of the US federal union at the moment when white power could no longer be successfully resisted or neutralized in its efforts to prevent the creation of a new society in the black state. (Obadele 1968, 1)

In many respects, the arguments put forth in *War in America* were quite similar to what Malcolm X had been discussing in the last few months of his life. Drawing on these arguments, Imari discussed the fact that Africans in America had been engaged in struggle since the founding of the United States. He discussed the growing militancy of young blacks in the North,[10] where they seemed no longer willing to tolerate the frequently described "horrific" conditions under which they were forced to live, that is, poor education, inadequate housing, chronic un- or underemployment, and police brutality. These were not the end but the beginning, however, for *War in America* as well as Malcolm X viewed such efforts as largely disorganized expressions of dissatisfaction, disappointment, anger, hopelessness, and hopefulness, adding up to little but revealing the potential of what could be.

---

[9] Some of the usual suspects could be found: Imari and Octavia Obadele, Gaidi Obadele, Charles Enoch, Raymond Willis, James Dawkins, Abdullah Muhammed, Masepo and Shamba Bolongongo, Umbasi Mfalme Adefomi, and others.

[10] This includes Harlem, Rochester, and Philadelphia in 1964; Watts in 1965; and Omaha, Chicago, and Cleveland in 1966.

Clearly the Malcolm X Society generated attention from existing authorities. The name, the objective, and the rhetoric used all resonated with those monitoring African American radical political behavior. At the same time, the secretive nature of the organization as well as the fact that there appeared to be no overt activities undertaken by its members would have rendered repression largely covert, if there was any at all. I say this because anti–Malcolm X Society behavior during this time is not really identifiable in available records beyond a few isolated instances of surveillance. This was to change, however, and change quickly.

Perceiving no answers coming from existing African American organizations regarding the plight of black America as well as no interest in their problem from the larger white society,[11] African American urban youth set ablaze a mass flare on what were frequently referred to by whites as "riots" or by radical blacks as "rebellions"/uprisings (a practice I maintain later). What had been missing was a political harnessing of the unrest, a focusing of energy toward some sort of unified objective and program. The opportunity presented itself in Detroit.

In 1967, the uprising/riot in this city represented nothing less than a watershed in local-level challenges to public order. By most accounts, it was the "worst civil disorder experienced by an American city in the twentieth century" (Fine 2007, 291). Beginning on July 23, 1967, following a police raid of an illegal drinking establishment in the heart of the black community and continuing for eight days, the event resulted in damage that was extensive by any measure. During the uprising, forty-three individuals were killed, hundreds more were wounded, and there was millions of dollars' worth of property damage. As discussed by the most definitive account,

the damage caused by the riot (uprising) took various forms: the numerous stores that were looted or burned; the homes that were damaged or destroyed by fire; the loss of wages for workers and of sales for businesses; the additional costs incurred by the city, state and federal governments; the injuries sustained by civilians and law enforcement personnel; and, above all, the lives that were lost.

The most conspicuous form of riot/rebellious damage was the looted and/or burned store. According to the American Insurance Association, 2,509 stores were looted, burned, or destroyed by the riot, well above the less than 1,000 buildings suffering a similar fate in the Watts riot. The damaged or destroyed Detroit establishments, nearly all of them looted, included 611 supermarkets, food, and grocery stores; 537 cleaners and laundries; 326 clothing, department and fur stores; 285 liquor stores, bars and lounges; 240 drug stores; and 198 furniture stores. (Fine 2000, 291)

The response to the event was equally as severe. Essentially, the city was occupied as thousands of state police, National Guard, and U.S. Army personnel were called in. In addition to this, numerous curfews and other restrictions on

---

[11] Indeed, if anything, they perceived a revulsion toward them and a certain degree of hostility through the media and police.

civil liberties were imposed for weeks after the event,[12] involving 7,200 individuals who were arrested in the period that followed (with 539 being convicted of illegal activity).

Most relevant to the current research is the fact that amid the sea of violence, disorder, conflict, rebellion, and opportunism, the Malcolm X Society chose this exact moment to come aboveground. On the second day of the uprising/rioting, at 8:54 in the morning, Gaidi Obadele sent a Western Union telegram to the mayor of the city (Jerome Cavanaugh), which was as brief as it was bold (Radical Information Project 2010):

Regarding insurrection in Detroit, speaking for Malcolm X Society
We will ask for cessation of all hostilities by insurrectionists
By seven PM today provided following eight points are accepted

1. Withdraw all troops
2. Release all prisoners
3. Give amnesty to all insurrectionists
4. Set up district police commissioners
5. Agree to urban renewal veto by residents
6. Divide city council and school board by districts
7. Provide funds and community owned businesses
8. Institute compensatory and compulsory equal employment enforcement.

As for a response to this telegram, the relevant authorities did not believe that the Malcolm X Society (or any organization for that matter) had the power to control what they viewed as a mass, disorganized outpouring of emotions and violence, and they consequently ignored the message.

There was a fundamental misunderstanding, however, between the Malcolm X Society and the relevant government officials that was crucial. When the Malcolm X Society spoke of the "insurrectionists," they were not speaking of the random black looters or arsonists. They were discussing those individuals associated with the black underground, the individuals engaged in the systematic procurement of weapons, ammunition, gas, and other valued resources or engaged in sniping that pinned down police officers within their stations of designated areas of the city. The Malcolm X Society meant negotiation with these individuals. Unable or unwilling to differentiate between distinct types of activities taking place and actors undertaking them, however, the police believed that the society was speaking about talking to as well as reasoning with the average black looter or arsonist, which they felt was not possible.

Regardless of the accuracy of the Malcolm X Society's proposition and disbelief by authorities about its ability to speak for aggrieved blacks, the

---

[12] By comparison, the riot in Los Angeles (Watts) lasted seven days (from August 11 to 18, 1965), killing 34 people, with nearly a thousand injuries. There were 3,332 arrests (with 2,038 convictions) and much less property damage. Again, state police and the national guard were called in to reestablish order.

sheer boldness and timing of the declaration guaranteed that the organization and all affiliated with it would be monitored quite closely in the future. The surveillance of the group thus continued, but this activity was now infused with a certain immediacy. The target was no longer some small civil rights organization that was trying to change some textbooks. The target was now a small black nationalist organization that drew its inspiration from one of the most controversial black leaders in U.S. history and that may or may not have had connections with one of the most destructive episodes of violence in recent memory.

After the flames had died down and the federal and state troops had left Detroit, the Malcolm X Society saw another opportunity to mobilize the black masses that had stepped forward in rebellion. In this context, the Henrys once again teamed up with Albert Cleage. Specifically, they held a press conference to raise awareness of the society as well as the ripeness of the situation for action and change. They also began the business of preparing for the next steps.

During this period, Albert's role was especially important. Through his publication, the *Illustrated News*, his sermons, and other actions, he established himself and those associated with him as central to the burgeoning radical consciousness emerging in Detroit. As a result,

into the church flocked literally hundreds of black men and women – longtime militants, recently black blacks, and not-quite-black-yet-blacks.[13] They were men like Poppa Wells, an 82-year-old atheist, numerous agnostics, some Muslims, and some others who had a great disdain for religion in general and Christianity in particular because of the role of Christianity in enslaving and then de-culturizing and de-humanizing our people. They came together in Central Church (Cleage's church) because the murderous, brutal actions of the police and National Guard had taught us not just unity but brotherhood. (Obadele 1970c, 157)

This solidarity between the Obadeles/Henrys and Cleages was not to persist, however. As Imari Obadele/Richard Henry (Obadele 1970c, 158) suggested,

the trouble lay . . . in Cleage's concept of nation. As the weeks wore on and each Sunday he baptized more people into the black nation, it became clearer and clearer that he did not really view political independence as an immediate objective, that he did, instead, believe that a sort of apprenticeship was necessary, a logical progression from our position as colonized people to a position as controllers of our local communities within the US federal system (as mayors and businessmen), to a position – only later – as citizens of our own independent black political nation. This called for a degree of participation in – and expectation of – the American political and economic systems which the Malcolmites and other nationalists had already written off.

---

[13] This referred to the length of time that diverse African Americans were perceived as being committed to the cause of political-economic transformation.

Albert also did not look favorably on the creation of rifle clubs in his domain. Despite his advocacy for armed self-defense, this was simply further than he was willing to go. This tactical difference would come to a head as the Malcolmites came to associate with another black radical, Robert F. Williams, who is discussed subsequently.

Robert F. Williams Joins the Republic (Kind of)

After the telegram in the wake of the Detroit riot/rebellion, it was another eight months until the Malcolm X Society emerged again in an open, high-profile manner. When they did, the event would be historical. Joined by a variety of black nationalists from around the United States (with a strong Detroit component), on March 31, 1968, in the Derby Room of the black-owned Twenty Thousand Hotel, the Declaration of Independence for the RNA was put forth, national leaders were elected, and local consulates were established in the various cities represented at the meeting.[14]

---

[14] Coincidentally, three days before the Detroit riot/uprising, an unrelated national conference on black power was held in Newark, New Jersey. A Newark riot/uprising had only taken place a few days before that event, on July 12, revealing a similar dynamic of organizational responsiveness to mass action.

Although it was not clear that members of the Malcolm X Society were in attendance at the earlier meeting, given the wide variety of attendees, this would not be completely out of the question. As Woodard (1999, 87) noted,

Writing for the *New York Times*, Thomas A. Johnson reported that the delegates included "representatives of the National Urban League, the Southern Christian Leadership Conference, the National Association for the Advancement of Colored People, the Congress of Racial Equality (CORE) and the Student Nonviolent Coordinating Committee" and that other groups included "such black nationalist organizations as US, from Watts, and Harlem's Mau Mau and the Organization for African American Unity, which was founded by Malcolm X." Furthermore, Johnson observed, "Black Muslims, teachers, laborers, civil servants and two New York City police inspectors are attending the all-Negro meeting."

In one confidential report of the U.S. Department of Justice (compiled by the FBI) regarding the RNA (June 13, 1968), it is noted that "the Malcolm X Society, prior to its dissolution and incorporation into the RNA maintained no headquarters, had no formal membership as such and did not hold any meetings" (U.S. Department of Justice 1968, 2). Communicating the tenor of the event, three resolutions were passed at the July 12 event: (1) complete release of all those jailed during the Newark riot/uprising, (2) support for the right of blacks to revolt when necessary, and (3) a request for the United Nations to investigate the conditions of blacks in Newark.

The context of the event was especially important. There was clearly a national phenomenon of uprisings and riots under way. Prior to the Detroit riot/uprising, there were ten others: Hartford, Connecticut (July 12–15), New York City (July 14–20), Fresno, California (July 15–17), Plainfield, New Jersey (July 16–20), Greensboro, North Carolina (July 17–20), Patterson, New Jersey (July 17–21), Erie, Pennsylvania (July 18–20), Minneapolis, Minnesota (July 19–20), Englewood, New Jersey (July 21–25), and Hattiesburg, Mississippi (July 22). Interestingly, on the same day as the Detroit riot/uprising, there were also events in eight other cities: Birmingham, Alabama; Lima, Ohio; New Britain, Connecticut; New York City; Phoenix, Arizona;

Expanding beyond the usual suspects from the past few organizations that were created (discussed earlier), within this meeting there was a veritable who's who of black nationalists from around the United States. Indeed, as configured, it was clearly one of the most diverse, broad-based groups of the period. In keeping with the tenor of the event, many took this opportunity to announce new names, casting off their "slave names" for "free" ones. Although exiled in Peking, China, Robert F. Williams was selected as president (he did not change his name); Milton, now Gaidi Obadele in Pontiac, Michigan, was selected as first vice president; (Bahiyah) Betty Shabazz, the wife of Malcolm X, from New York City, was selected as second vice president; Edmond Bradley, now Obaboa Olowo of Los Angeles, California, was selected as treasurer; Richard Henry, now Imari Obadele from Detroit, Michigan, was minister of the interior; Imiri Baraka, formerly Leroi Jones, from Newark, New Jersey, and Maulana Karenga, formerly Ronie McKinley, of the U.S. organization from Los Angeles, California, and Baba Oserjeman Adefunmi, formerly Serge King, of New York City, were selected as ministers of culture; attorney Joan Franklin was selected as minister of justice; Queen Mother (Audrey) Moore, from New York City (former Garveyite and Communist Party member), was selected as minister of health and welfare; H. Rap Brown, formerly Hubert Brown, of Washington, D.C., from the Black Panthers, was selected as one of the ministers of defense along with Mwesi Chui, formerly John Taylor; Charles Howard was selected minister of state and foreign affairs; Henry ("Papa") Wells was selected as the vice speaker of the National Council of Representatives; and Max Stanford of the RAM was selected as special ambassador.

While many of the individuals involved in the RNA have been the subject of scholarship in their own right, perhaps no other individual was as noteworthy as the president-in-exile, Robert F. Williams. Next to Malcolm X, perhaps no other single individual embodied the newest phase of the African American struggle than Williams. The two men were similar in many respects but very different in others.

For example, like Malcolm X, Robert F. Williams was initially involved with an organization viewed as a mainstay within the black community. Different from Malcolm X's organization, however, Williams's NAACP was much more conservative in nature.[15] Also, different from Malcolm X, Williams was a

Rochester, New York; Toledo, Ohio; and Kalamazoo, Michigan. New York City and several cities in Michigan exploded in the days that followed (e.g., Pontiac and Flint). Set within this situation, the founding of the black nation was extremely noteworthy.

[15] Of course, the NAACP was a very diverse organization in many respects. As Tyson (1999, 110) notes,

From the earliest days of the postwar freedom movement, some Southern black NAACP leaders wanted to move faster than the national office. This created uneasiness and antagonism between the Northern-based national office and its nearly all-black Southern branches. The national office, though distant from the South, regarded itself as perfectly qualified to dictate political tactics and disregard local problems. Though it soon became commonplace to describe firm believer in the U.S. constitution; he simply believed that white Americans ignored the document when it came to black folk. Indeed, although Williams would later be associated with what would become "black power," he viewed himself as essentially an "integrationist" and patriot at heart. As Tyson (1999, 206) argues,

Neither a nationalist, a Marxist, nor a liberal, exactly, the NAACP leader from Monroe reached out to potential allies in all camps while remaining committed to equal rights for all under the US constitution.

Finally, unlike Malcolm X, Robert F. Williams had spent most of his life in the deep South. For a time, he had lived in Detroit, in particular during the race riot of 1943, but this was for only a brief period (Tyson 1999, 40–42).

Despite these significant differences, through a relatively complex series of events, by the mid-1960s, Williams emerged as a hero of the African American struggle. With Malcolm X dead, it was easy to view Williams as the heir apparent to lead the increasingly radicalized black struggle. As Tyson (1999, 300) reports,

in an internal memorandum dated August 28, 1969, agents [of the U.S. government] observed, "Williams has been a powerful and influential, if behind-the-scenes, figure in the most powerful of the black militant groups in this country; and it would seem that he may well be emerging as the over-all acknowledged Black Militant leader of the future." The report made careful review of the political landscape in the Black Power movement. "Recent months have witnessed an apparent diminution in the leadership of Stokely Carmichael, H. Rap Brown, Eldridge Cleaver and other black leaders," CIA analysts noted, "and one wonders if Williams may be about to claim the center of the Black power stage, with the aid of his 'inside' helpers."

Clearly the RNA was aware of this popularity when they approached him about being president of their organization. As Imari Obadele (1970c, 170) says,

in retrospect the idea of nominating and electing Robert should have been obvious: He was, after all, the foremost living black nationalist, from America, in the world. But the actual idea came from the brain of Brother Agbo (Charles Enoch), who, at one of the preparatory meetings of the Malcolm X Society excitedly broached the idea, pointing out, among other things, that Robert was the only person with stature enough to unite all black nationalists in America, that he was, in addition, a tried revolutionary and a consistent black nationalist. Robert's international standing was also important, as was the fact of his residence in China. There was no thought from that point on but that we should nominate Robert.

the NAACP as an overly cautious, politically conservative organization, it is important to distinguish between the local branches, which were the wellspring of many grassroots insurgencies, and somewhat staid national office.

Williams and his chapter exemplified this division.

Williams's path to his involvement with the RNA was important. When first approached, he was not immediately willing to side with the black nationalists. Like many, including the Obadeles, Williams initially attempted to work within the existing U.S. system, seeking protection from the violence of whites as well as access to a decent job, food, and housing generally controlled by them. While the latter was important (e.g., jobs), it was the former (protection) that proved to be the more problematic issue. The latter would invariably be covered by African American hard work and ingenuity, which was generally in line with American culture and laws; the former, however, would require blacks to significantly challenge American culture as well as several laws at the same time. As blacks pressed for change, whites attempted to terrorize the black community to scare them off. This Williams and others did not allow.

When threatened with potential as well as actual white violence, he and others who had served in the U.S. military were unwilling to accept the fact, after serving their country and the larger cause of democracy abroad, that upon returning to America, things would simply go back to the way that they were before with regard to tolerating racism. Accordingly, they used their training to stay together, gather information about their opponents, and put forth a determined but measured amount of largely preventative force. As such, they engaged in firing practice as well as other military drills, they protected the perimeter of any place where they met, and they kept surveillance on the broader black community, all with a preparedness to escalate the conflict if deemed necessary. In short, if a fight came, they were ready for it. That was essentially all that Williams did. Of course, given the context of the South in the late 1950s and early 1960s as well as some of the aftereffects of this position, these activities were not simple at all, and that is the reason why he was so important for the RNA.

Inevitably, Williams broke with the national office of the NAACP (in 1959), which tried to rein him in, stop his rhetoric and his highly publicized uses of armed self-defense, and deny him the legitimacy of an affiliation with the historical civil rights organization. As a somewhat independent political actor, however, he became even more ambitious, traveling the United States and the world, engaging in various activities. He had unprecedented and now legendary meetings with radicals from all over the country as well as foreign visitors to America (most notably one with Fidel Castro after the Cuban revolution). Williams also attempted to directly counter the NAACP's interpretation of the black struggle as articulated in the *Crisis* by presenting his own, more radical publication called the *Crusader*. Within this newsletter, he discussed not only the importance of armed self-reliance but also "black economic advancement, black pride, black culture, independent political action" (Tyson 1999, 191), and also the importance of internationalizing the African American struggle, looking around the globe for solutions and useful methodologies of investigation. Like Malcolm X toward the end, Williams tried to find friends, associates, supporters, and allies wherever he could, and like Malcolm X, he did fairly well in this regard.

Isolated and somewhat vulnerable, however, in August 1961, after several days of escalating black-white confrontations in Monroe, North Carolina, a caravan of local, state, and federal authorities was traveling to apprehend Robert for his role in the emerging conflict as well as in an alleged case of "kidnapping" (Tyson 1999, Chapter 10). This prompted him to flee with his family first from Monroe (which added a charge of "interstate flight") and later from the country (which added yet another charge). After their successful and highly publicized escape, the Williams family first traveled to Cuba, one of the key revolutionary regimes of the time as well as one of potential high interest to the international media. It was from here that Robert aired his radio program called "Radio Free Dixie," which was heard in selected parts of the United States and on which he continued his critique of the United States, his discussion of the black struggle, and further built his reputation as a leader and voice of the oppressed.

While Cuba provided an opportunity for him to complete his famous book, *Negroes with Guns* (1962), the country also began to turn him against the communist world as well as the life of the exile. Later, he would travel to North Vietnam during the Vietnam War and to China during the Cultural Revolution, both countries providing him access to important revolutionary leaders as well as prompting continued interest from the international media, but again both countries soured him on communism/socialism and made him miss the United States. Later still, he moved to Tanzania, which is where the RNA met up with him.

By the time Gaidi and Imari Obadele approached Robert F. Williams in 1968, he was very much interested in trying to figure out exactly how he could get back to the United States.[16] Robert was no fool. He was well aware that

---

[16] The backstory for the recruitment was somewhat complex. In fact, initially, the RNA organizing committee did not believe that Williams would say yes:

> Worse than her own refusal to serve in the government (she later recanted and the next day signed the Declaration of Independence), Mae Rose told the delegates that we should not nominate Robert, for he would not want to accept the leadership of the government and would, she suggested, be inclined to view its establishment with something less than favor. We know this last to be untrue, of course, because we had sent Robert some information on the Conference and he had cabled Gaidi: "The eyes of the world are upon you. Use this moment well." Yet the fact was we had not asked Robert specifically if he would accept the Presidency, and so we really did not know if somehow Mae knew something we didn't, but we pushed ahead, knowing, at the least, that Robert would approve the formation of the government. As it turned out, four months later, as Gaidi and I walked along a dusty road with Robert in Dar es Salaam, Tanzania, with Mae along, Mae would raise the subject (we had at that time virtually forgotten the incident and had no plan to raise it), telling Robert she had moved against his being President, and Robert would tell her simply: "Mae, you were wrong." He said the formation of the government could hardly have occurred at a better time. (Obadele 1970, 171)

the RNA needed him about as much as, if not more than, he needed them. Accordingly, Robert requested that the RNA generate some resources for his return as well as legal assistance in addressing his problems there. He also suggested that they try to arrange some type of exchange with individuals in Tanzania, sending books and medicine for the development of a hospital. Of course, the legal assistance was not a problem as the RNA had Gaidi Obadele. The resources for Williams and Tanzania, however, were something of a problem because the funding for the RNA was supposed to come from the members, and it was not quite clear yet how well that was going to work.[17]

Regardless of the difficulties, on September 12, 1969, Robert F. Williams returned to the United States with Gaidi Obadele on a specially chartered flight, with only the two of them as passengers. Once back, however, the RNA didn't quite have their leader. Seemingly fearful of what would happen next, Robert basically kept quiet and was reluctant to put himself into the spotlight with the RNA. Interestingly, while he was quiet with the new organization he supposedly led, he assisted the U.S. government in better understanding China, providing briefings to individuals in the Office of Asian Communist Affairs (Tyson 1999, 303). Needless to say, the juxtaposition of these two activities (nonaction in the RNA and complicity with the U.S. government) did not pass without some discussion within the Republic of New Africa.

Although Robert allowed the RNA to cash in on his notoriety and he was central to the launching of their group, the bulk of the organization's program still stayed centered around Malcolm X. Invoking his ideas, as modified by Imari Obadele and a few others, the primary objective of the RNA was to establish African American independence from the U.S. government. Specifically, it sought to

1. Establish a government for Africans in America;
2. Obtain land for the establishment of an independent country in the deep South: Alabama, Georgia, Louisiana, Mississippi, and South Carolina;[18]
3. Hold a plebiscite among Blacks in order to determine the "national status" of the "New Afrikan population in North America"; and,

---

[17] According to the confidential Department of Justice report mentioned earlier, Williams's attitude toward the RNA was a bit of concern for those in attendance at the meeting where the Henrys' visit was discussed. At this meeting, it was revealed that Williams said he "did not intend to make any statement regarding the Republic of New Africa or do anything in behalf of the RNA" (U.S. Department of Justice 1968, 5). He also went on to mention that he had no resources to provide for the RNA. Some sources suggest that the RNA believed that Williams might contact China and/or Cuba on their behalf and obtain resources from them. When this did not come to pass, they had to look to their members and citizens for taxes (a 3 percent income tax).

[18] It is occasionally maintained that the RNA was also seeking an island from which they would petition for a seat at the United Nations. With this position, they would then push the issues of black nationhood and reparations for slavery as well as discrimination.

4. Obtain reparations for the treatment of Blacks as slaves[19] (Republic of New Africa 1968a)

The establishment of a government was deemed especially important because it completed the list of international requirements for a nation: (1) having a people with a common history and culture (in this case, the descendants of African slaves in America), (2) having a people with a common territory (in this case, the areas of highest African American concentration in the United States over the longest amount of time), and (3) having a government (in this case, the RNA).

Different from the earlier organizational efforts (from GOAL to the FNP to the Malcolm X Society) undertaken to pursue shifting objectives, the activities here involved pursuit of the core objectives identified previously in such a way as to reduce the likelihood of successful repressive action from the government. Indeed, reflecting a high degree of what I earlier referred to as "reappraisal," the reasons for the creation of the new organization and tactical shift were simple:

It was to remove the Malcolmites and the other black nationalist revolutionaries in America from a position where the United States might with impunity destroy them to a position where attacks upon us by the United States become international matters, threatening world peace, and thereby within reach of the United Nations, thereby within reach of our friends in Africa and Asia who would help us. We could not entertain hope of help in our struggle from international sources so long as we conducted our struggle within the United States federal union and as if we were citizens of the United States... The Republic was brought about, when it was, to frustrate hostile action of the United States against the seekers of land and power for blacks on this continent, and to create proper safeguards for ultimate success. (Obadele 1968, 3)

In this view, no longer could the repression of blacks be kept a domestic policing issue within the confines of the United States. Land was important, for it served as part of the definition of nationhood, and it would thus provide an essential component for the RNA's objective. More importantly, the land would provide the actual physical space that African Americans could occupy and at some point govern.

A base in the South was deemed especially important for several reasons. Most prominently, it was believed by RNA leadership that as far as any ancestral home could be identified, the South was as close as African Americans could get. Most blacks came from or at least through there, viewed historically. There was a connection to both the African and the American past through its culture (e.g., food and language), economy, societal relations, and political heritage, especially in the shining example of rebellious spirit shown during the civil rights period. Differing from Marcus Garvey, RNA leadership did not see

---

[19] Accordingly, one would always hear RNA members declare, "Land, Independence, and Self-Determination," "The Struggle Is for Land," or "Free the Land."

Africa as the ultimate destination for their efforts. Very clearly, it was felt that America was their home, or at least the place where African Americans had toiled and suffered the longest, rendering it the place that they would have to carve out as their own. In addition, there were tactical reasons for choosing the South as well. For one, the North was viewed as essentially indefensible, leaving African Americans easily surrounded by authorities, without access to important resources (water and the land necessary to grow food) and geographically fragmented from one another. In this context, African Americans were essentially trapped. However, in the South, blacks could make up the majority, depending on where one was, and the land was bountiful. The terrain was spacious and, if properly configured, could be defensible by layering defenses, spreading out troops, and such. Additionally, certain locales provided access to water, which was important because this could be used for travel, commerce, and defense.

As for other aspects of the RNA's plan, the plebiscite was necessary for two reasons. First, African Americans would need to be made aware that their "nation" and government existed. Second, the plebiscite would provide the formal proof necessary to identify blacks as a nation with the RNA as its representative.

Finally, reparations would compensate blacks for the wrongs that were done to them during slavery and afterward ($200–400 billion) – allowing them to try and catch up or at least hold their ground. In addition to this, these funds would be used to offset the costs of transporting African Americans to their new nation (whenever it could be located) as well as its subsequent development.

How would the new nation be brought about? What would initiate the process? Several strategies were put forth. First, there was the movement organization of the RNA itself. Second, a Declaration of the RNA would be provided to U.S. authorities, and if they complied, then no further action would be necessary. If, however, the United States did not capitulate to RNA demands,[20] the strategy was straightforward, albeit far-reaching. For example, the RNA would have to convince African Americans that they were a nation and that selected counties in the South as well as select cities in the North (those with predominant black populations) were theirs (Republic of New Africa 1968b). Under RNA influence, African Americans would then need to take advantage of the numerical concentration of blacks in specific voting jurisdictions and get various public officials elected who were supportive of the RNA. Once in power, these individuals would appoint sympathizers to the black nationalist cause. They would also appoint members of the Black Legion, the military wing of the RNA, to the police force to protect and serve the African American nation, essentially deputizing the African American army. Following a technique of "electoral secessionism" and a variant of "domino theory," the

---

[20] These were provided to the office of secretary of state Dean Rusk on May 29, 1968 (*Ujamaa Newsletter*, June 15, 1968).

RNA would start with one state, county by county (Mississippi was the most logical starting point given the size of the black population), and then they would move progressively through the other relevant states. If at any point the U.S. government attempted to block any of these efforts, then the RNA would threaten to employ guerilla warfare in inner cities throughout the United States where the black underground existed until the RNA was granted what they desired. Here the RNA was attempting to harness the fear of the destructive power revealed during the Detroit riot/rebellion.

Differing from most secessionist groups and some black nationalists (e.g., the RAM), however, the RNA did not try to hide their strategy. Rather, their objectives and plans were communicated via RNA press releases and publications as well as through interviews on radio, on television, and in popular magazines like *Esquire*.[21]

Despite the significant change in orientation, in certain ways, the group's tactics did not change much from the GOAL. For example, the organization would still engage in many legal forms of protest: rallies, petitions, political education courses, food drives, lectures, conferences, and the publication of "independent" newsletters and newspapers as well as other activities long developed in black communities, including armed "self-defense" programs like shooting practice. In other ways, however, the organization changed dramatically. For example, though the strategies were the same, the content of these activities were significantly radicalized. The group engaged in efforts to legally separate parts of the United States, it had begun to try to figure out how land could be purchased in Mississippi to serve as the capital of the new nation, it elected a government, and it attempted to develop a security force or army. Additionally, members of the RNA engaged in assorted violent and occasionally illegal activities, for example, stockpiling weapons (mostly handguns and rifles), running military drills (various formations, collective firing practice, and hand-to-hand combat), engaging in shootouts with police, and in one instance even hijacking a plane.[22]

[21] In the January 1969 edition of *Esquire*, a multipage section was dedicated to the organization, including such titles as "We Want Georgia, South Carolina, Louisiana, Mississippi and Alabama – Right Away," "...We Also Want Four Hundred Billion Dollars Back Pay: Separatism Command" by Sherrill (1968a), "Meet the President: He's Robert F. Williams, of the Not So Illusive Republic of New Africa," "Milton Henry, First Vice-President, Talks about the Republic of New Africa," "...And the Cabinet: The Ten Ministers, Including the Venerable Queen Mother Moore," "Whitey's Reaction: From a Grudging Yes to an Oh, No, No, No to the Usual Confusion" by Sherrill (1968b), and "Eeny, Meeny, Miney, Mo...A New Nation Is Empowered to Choose Who Stays within Its Borders."

[22] These activities resulted in the organization being categorized as a terrorist organization by the National Memorial Institute for the Prevention of Terrorism Knowledge Base (http://www.tkb.org/Group.jsp?groupID=4226). This point is not without some controversy. It is not completely clear that the individuals who engaged in the relevant activity were RNA members at the time.

Viewed in context, the tactical shift of the RNA was not unique for the period. In fact, it reflected broader changes that took place within black resistance. As Haines (1984, 130) identifies,

from the closing years of the last century through the 1960s, the guiding philosophy of Black liberation has evolved from (a) gradual assimilation through the acceptance of segregation, to (b) more immediate assimilation through the aggressive pursuit of racial integration, to (c) the preservation of racial integrity through the acquisition of political and economic power. Not all Black organizations have proceeded from the first of these to the last, to be sure, but the long sweep of history has seen the sequential rise and fall of each of these positions.

A similar process has occurred in the realm of tactics. This century has witnessed the waxing and waning of several tactical repertoires, beginning with (a) Black self-help; followed by (b) legalism; (c) nonviolent protest ranging from peaceful, nondisruptive demonstrations through intentionally disruptive actions; (d) violent self-defense; and, among a few groups, (e) urban guerilla skirmishes. All but the last two have enjoyed a degree of hegemony for a time.

Not all of these institutions were alike. For example, the strategy undertaken by the RNA was noticeably different from strategies undertaken by other black power organizations such as the Black Panther Party (BPP). Although several discussed a black nation, none had actually attempted to openly select a location, develop a plan on how to get it, and engage in efforts to put this plan in motion. On this point, the differences from the BPP were especially clear.

In part, the approach to black power adopted by the RNA reflected black life in Detroit. For example, the RNA position on segregation and biracial collaborations emerged from Detroit's history of strained race relations. Within this city, there were high degrees of segregation and isolation of blacks from whites, significantly different from the situation found in the Bay Area, which moderated the position of the BPP. Set within this context, Detroit represented one of the most contentious black-white situations in the United States, experiencing race riots in 1833, 1863, 1943, and 1967.

Additionally, although there had been some biracial collaborations earlier in Detroit, this was generally a rare situation by the time of GOAL and definitely by the time of the RNA. During this period, blacks and whites were living divided lives politically, economically, and culturally. Equally important, perhaps the most visible attempt at such a collaboration resulted in what would kindly be referred to as an immense failure (Farley et al. 2000, 42). This situation is very different from the multi-ethnic collaboration one would see in the Bay Area before, after and during the same period relevant to the Black Panthers.

There were also important demographic and economic forces at play. Within Detroit, there was the third largest black population in the United States as well as a highly employed, concentrated, and radicalized black working population. Additionally, there was an African American community that had been relatively stable over a long period of time, developing strong churches as well as advocacy organizations (Farley et al. 2000). Indeed, although many have historically referred to Brooklyn as the "mecca" for blacks because of the large number of African Americans there, Detroit could be thought of in the same way but on a somewhat smaller scale.

It was in this context that the RNA was born.

Clearly, the timing for such an effort seemed perfect, and this increased the perception of threat by those in authority. As noted in an article by Robert Sherrill (1968a, 72),

> inside the loosely knit community of 23,000,000 Negroes in this country, the recently revived proposal for the creation of a separate black nation from a portion of the United States has probably more support than whites would like to think.[23]

These are, of course, nonrandom insights about selected parts of the black population. More rigorously collected information, however, lends support to the basic point as well. For example,

> Robert Hutchins, director of the Center for the Study of Democratic Institutions in Santa Barbara, says ghettologists estimate that about thirty percent of the black slum-dwellers are advocates of separatism, at least in the Los Angeles area; inasmuch as fifty-seven percent of Los Angeles' blacks live at slum level, this means only about one-sixth of the Negro total, if these experts know what they're talking about, would like to leave this country and set up one of their own. But even one-sixth, if applicable to slums everywhere, comes to a million or so Negroes eager to make the break and who are – according to the timetable of New Africa's politicians-in-exile – ready right now to get this started with guns. A Columbia Broadcasting System poll last year found only six percent of the blacks ready to carve out a portion of this country or go abroad; but even that amount comes to 1,380,000, and the CBS poll was pretty middle-class. (Sherrill 1968a, 72)

Detroit-specific surveys revealed further support for the generally favorable development of the RNA. Concerned with the causes and aftereffect of the July riots in 1967, in August of the same year, the *Detroit Free Press* (DFP) undertook a random probability sample survey of African American attitudes with the support of the Detroit Urban League (1967). A follow-up study was

---

[23] He continues (Sherrill 1968a, 72),

> The nation was officially alerted in 1967 to how restless the natives of Harlem and Samtown and Bootville really are when the Conference of Black Power met in Newark, New Jersey, and passed with tumultuous cheers a resolution calling for "a national dialogue on the desirability of partitioning the U.S. into two separate and independent nations," one black, one white. Most newspapers reacted with either shock or outrage, especially when the Black Power conferees illustrated what they had in mind by physically ejecting white newsmen in a rather rough style.
>
> In the South, of course, where black militancy moves much more slowly, one will find few Negroes who are even aware of the proposal: but in the black neighborhoods in Northern and West Coast cities, the dream is dreamed quite regularly; and among the black intelligentsia, it is considered a legitimate topic for cocktail-party debates; as often as not the argument turns not around the desirability of separation but about the means to achieve it and the geographic area to be demanded of whitey.

conducted in October 1968, where the same study was repeated (*Detroit Free Press* 1968). As the RNA was created in March 31, 1968, this takes place right in between the two surveys.

Regarding the examination of these studies, one finds some support for the general argument regarding the favorable context for the RNA, but generally the overall context was not facilitative of such an effort. For example, the DFP shows that from August 1967 to October 1968, blacks generally felt that they had more to lose by engaging in violent action (from 53 to 63 percent) and that if war broke out, the United States was worth fighting for (from 67 to 77 percent). This does not bode well for secession. This said, there is a clear finding within the DFP that a specific subset of African Americans was especially relevant for the potential RNA threat. For example, the research disclosed that among "rioters" in 1967 (10 to 12 percent of all respondents), nonreligious individuals and the young were more likely to support black nationalism, measured as accepting a "militant" position, avoiding whites socially, fighting with other Negroes for rights, and building a separate black society apart from whites in the United States or Africa. This does not bode well for the separatist agenda.

The authors of the study suggested that there was a potential for growth in this category of respondents, moving in the direction of the RNA's position. This would be especially likely in a "repressive atmosphere" (*Detroit Free Press* 1968, 12), which they did not believe existed, but nevertheless it was identified as being potentially explosive with regard to influencing black public opinion. This is where I differ with the interpretation of the data. Though there are no explicit measures of repression in the survey, the authors do note a precipitous increase from 57 to 71 percent in the number of respondents who identify police brutality as a problem that could lead to another riot or rebellion. These results present an interesting paradox but something broadly consistent with existing research: repression may be necessary to close the window on additional radicalism, as it could help eliminate the challengers, but the use of this behavior could also be associated with opening up the window further by provoking the disengaged.

Summary

Within this chapter, I discussed how the founding of the RNA was intricately connected with the involvement of two individuals, Malcolm X and Robert F. Williams, and the organization that was created before the RNA (i.e., the Malcolm X Society). Each in its own way influenced the individuals in the RNA, what they believed as well as how they would attempt to do what they did. Understanding these influences is crucial, for it reveals the logic behind the path taken as well as the ones avoided.

PART IV

EXAMINATION

7

Birth of a Black Nation

To examine what repression and dynamics within challenging organizations contribute to the demise of social movement organizations (i.e., demobilization), one has to identify and monitor the individuals, ideas, institutions, and interventions of the relevant SMO over time as they are subject to varying levels of repressive behavior and internal dynamics. Additionally, one must also identify and monitor the efforts undertaken by the dissidents to *sustain* individuals, ideas, institutions, and interventions, despite the efforts authorities undertake to undermine them.

As will be seen, the founding of the Republic of New Africa set in place many elements that would both help and hinder the organization in the future. Clearly the beginning phase was a difficult period for the group of black nationalists that joined the new organization. The RNA was attempting to create a government essentially from scratch (e.g., obtaining members, identifying supporters, drafting documents, laying out the structure, and assigning activities to different sectors of the organization) as well as inform the public of what was going on through a variety of strategies (e.g., press conferences, articles, and rallies). Unfortunately, the results of all these efforts were limited as members and the resources they brought with them barely trickled in.

Despite these "birthing" pains, the beginning of the organization was largely tension-free from an overt repression perspective – the type of repression they most feared. There were some controversies, which was to be expected, but generally there was nothing obviously hostile directed at the organization from political authorities. This was quite amazing, given that the secessionist movement was being started under the watchful eye of the U.S. government, who were seemingly ever-present at meetings and events alike. During the period of the founding, however, the overt repressive actions of the authorities were minimal. Indeed, most of what transpired at the time could be attributed to the movement alone. This said, repression is not completely absent from the period (the records were in part generated from covert activity after all); repression is just missing in the form that existing literature, common data sources, and the RNA generally focus on. The challengers were not aware of what was being done to them, however, and thus repression is not really part of the story – at least, not at this point. As I suggest, though, that previous repressive behavior directed against individuals in other, earlier movement organizations and/or the fear of being subject to government coercion is present. Such an effect resides more in the minds of activists at the time, for (as noted) it is not actually occurring – something to which my argument was not sensitive. As such, there were largely no intersections between external and internal factors to speak of – at least not in the way originally conceived.

In this chapter, I first discuss the initial characteristics at the founding of the RNA (i.e., individuals, ideas, and so forth). I then consider how these changed over time and the roles that dissident-organization dynamics and state repression played in these changes.

In the Beginning

Following a black nationalist conference in New Jersey during 1967, the plan to create the African American nation[1] had been made by the Malcolm X Society. The call on March 3, 1968, was simple and actually rather plain, given the content. In line with Malcolm X's desire to bring together a broad range of black institutions, a message was sent to different organizations around the United States:

As you may have heard, the Malcolm X Society is holding a National Convention in Detroit at the end of the month (Saturday and Sunday, March 30 and 31) to set up a separate Black government. This letter is to invite you and members of your group to participate in this historic conference. (DPD-SIB, March 27, 1968)

It continued,

By way of background I should point out that it is our irreversible intention to create for black people who wish it a fully functioning government, separate from and independent of the jurisdiction of the United States and to acquire land for that government, through negotiations, if possible, from what is now the continental United States (The Malcolm X Society proposes Mississippi, Louisiana, Alabama, Georgia, and South Carolina).

All sessions will be held at the Shrine of the Black Madonna (formerly the Central United Church of Christ), 7625 Linwood Avenue, in Detroit. The all-day working sessions will deal with key problems associated with a move of this character and magnitude . . . Please let us know if you will attend.

---

[1] This refers to the entity that the social movement organization the RNA would turn into after African Americans arose and accepted their governance.

Individuals

In preparation for the convention, the Malcolm X Society quickly moved to action: buses were chartered, accommodations were secured (i.e., the homes of institutional members as well as the homes of friends), an agenda was developed, background papers were written, and speakers were selected. As stated by one of those involved, to make the event happen,

a small group of Malcolmites worked many long and intense hours. Our idea was to do as much advanced planning and detailed reasoning as we could, in order to assure that we would be able to emerge from the two-day conference with a black government created. We did not underestimate the task. We were mindful of the many days that were spent by whites in Philadelphia in 1776 to spin out their declaration of independence; we know that the creation of the formal stated fact of independence for any people was a thing which clearly required more than two days. But two days was what we had. We were determined to cut our cloth to fit that pattern. (Obadele 1970c, 160–61)

The division of labor was clear, largely divided among several Detroiters who had been involved in one way or another across the different organizations discussed earlier:

Among [the group of organizers] were Charles Enoch (free name: Brother Agbo), whose ideas and friendship we relied upon so much and who served as Conference Coordinator; Ray Willis, without whose brilliant and determined work as Discussion Chairman, we could not have accomplished what we did accomplish in two days; my close friend Thomas Lockett, who would be responsible for security; Shamba Bolongongo (slave name: William Kuhn), who would work with Enoch as Assistant Conference Coordinator; Umgaji Mfalme Adefunmi (slave name: Henry King), who would serve as Press Chief; Kwame (slave name: Bill Hill), who would be in charge of Research and Reproduction; Ronald Pugh, in charge of credentials; Rita White, in charge of housing; Mary Kuhn and Clara Lockett, (also) in charge of credentials, and Bolanile Obadele and Verlyn Thomas and James and Jesse Wallace, James Dawkins and my wife Octavia. (Obadele 1970c, 161)

Central, as always, were the Obadeles and Cleages. Gaidi Obadele was national chairperson of the Malcolm X Society, the hosting institution; Imari Omadele was one of the platform participants, an invited speaker during one of the numerous plenary sessions; and Albert Cleage[2] was supposed to host several events at what would become his Shrine of the Black Madonna church. Although several things were the same as they had been (i.e., the locales and the people), others were very different (i.e., the roles played, the names, and the objectives).

The response to the call was not as significant in number as many expected, but on the relevant date, between one hundred and two hundred individuals arrived. On March 29, 1968, black nationalists from different parts of the United States began to roll into Detroit, ready to begin. Broadly interested in

---

[2] Around this time, he changed his name to Jaramogi Abebe Agyeman.

the idea of black separation, the participants seemed to be there for different reasons – some came out of desperation, some came out of fear, some came out of anger, some came out of an acceptance of the inevitability of such an action, some came out of pride, and some came out of hope. Most were critical of the civil rights movement and all that it had and had not achieved. Most were also critical of the U.S. government's repressive action taken against African Americans engaged in trying to improve their lives. Of course, this is not repression of the RNA, for it did not exist yet, but behavior directed against earlier movements (discussed later).

In this context, many of the believers in black nationalism came together, not to struggle within the United States as citizens in a civil rights approach but to acknowledge officially their "separateness" as a distinct nation and to seek nationhood from that unique position in a black nationalist approach.

As attendees arrived for the first session, on the morning of March 30, they were asked in which capacity they wished to enter. Some came as "delegates" (those ready for immediate separation), some came as "technical advisors" (those who had specific areas of expertise regarding assorted topics but had not yet committed to separating), and some simply came as "observers" (those who were interested but not quite ready to accept separation and all that it entailed). The designations were important. All attendees were given badges signifying their status, but only delegates could participate in the discussion and vote on the various issues that arose. In the morning, there were approximately sixty-four delegates. As individuals arrived from different parts of the country, heard about what was taking place, and participated in different ways, the number increased. By the end of the first day's event, the number of delegates had risen to approximately two hundred. Directly in line with the argument discussed earlier, this would have been the first concrete steps taken toward trust building: demarcating oneself from "others" and beginning the "we."

The diversity of participants was noteworthy. For example, there was

Baba Oserjeman Adefunmi, with his strictly authentic formal Yoruban dress, beautiful long robes and beads, his wives, his entourage, his pomp and circumstance; the portly, goateed, dignified Obabos Alowo, business manager for a black Los Angeles tool shop, bring[ing] with him the wisdom of many years in the struggle, including 20 years as a black nationalist in the Communist Party, and many years matching wits with and winning against the white man; the strong yet softly beautiful, darkly lovely widow of Malcolm X, Betty...; the indomitable Queen Mother Moore, of New York City and the freedom struggle all over America, 73-years-old, as active and alert and as full of a sense of humor as one half her age, a veritable institution of our struggle, who with her sister, Virginia Collins of New Orleans... and other women had worked for reparations at a moment when most of us could not spell the word, whose entire life is an example of personal commitment to, personal sacrifice for freedom for our people, and justice for individuals... and Henry "Poppa" Wells of Detroit, almost as old as Queen Mother, quite as clear in his mental processes, him too with the precious ability to laugh at himself, and at the world, a one-time Muslim who studied years ago under

Mr. Farrard [mentor to Elijah Muhammad – the founder of the Nation of Islam] but now a vocal and inveterate atheist who could not believe in a God who would permit the things which have happened to black people during the last 300 years. (Obadele 1970c, 168–69)

Ideas

With a reasonable crowd present, at approximately 9:00 A.M., Ray Willis (the discussion chairperson) opened the event and introduced the delegates. Immediately, a call was made from the floor to change the black power "conference" into a "convention" so that the actions of the participants could be directed toward black nationhood. This quickly passed. Imari (Obadele) then made some remarks before Ray led the discussion as well as the vote on the objectives of the convention and on the agenda items to be addressed. The first series of items to be dealt with during the morning sessions (going from 9:00 to 11:00) included the "question of sovereignty," "approaches to citizenship," "the Declaration of Independence," the name of the (new)[3] nation and "the creation of the new government."

From 11:00 to 12:00, there was a brief session with the media, subject to convention approval. Here the basic outline of the proceedings was laid out, admittedly not much by that time but enough to be deemed worthy of news coverage later. A few newspapers showed up. From 12:00 to 1:00, lunch was served, and there was seemingly a growing sense of excitement about what was transpiring, observable from the different ways that people described what they saw, heard, and felt. From 1:00 to 2:00, elections were held and officials selected, and from 2:00 to 4:00, basic guidelines were given regarding reparations and diplomatic relations with other organizations and other countries. Each of these sessions went over time, and after the last one ended at 5:00 P.M. (an hour past the schedule), it was another three hours before the group reconvened to address the last two items: guerillas and guerilla warfare and defending blacks from U.S. military service. The first discussion concerned the most effective strategy for dealing with bringing about change in the United States (viewed over the past few decades of experience) as well as leveraging what was believed to be an African American strength (their presence in U.S. cities). The second addressed a longer-term problem within the black community: the fact that a great many would-be revolutionaries were being sent to fight for someone else's nation.

What was astounding about the whole meeting was not only the ambitiousness of the agenda and the thorough nature of the coverage of the different topics but also the degree of control exhibited by the conveners (i.e., the rigidity of the event). Indeed, aside from the explosion of colorful clothes and occasionally impassioned invocations of black self-determination, the convention seemed more like a formal business meeting guided by *Roberts Rules of*

---

[3] Some argued that it already existed and that all that was being undertaken was a formalization.

Order – or perhaps *Malcolm's Rules of Revolution* would be more appropriate – than it did a gathering of often vitriolic and passionate social movement activists (a common character of black power advocates at the time).

Interestingly and likely relevant to the last point, most subjects discussed at the convention did not garner much discussion or debate. For example, on the issue of citizenship in the new nation, without exception, all argued that whites should be excluded from citizenship. Although they could not be citizens, however, it was maintained that they could live in the Republic, once completed. Citizenship would be withheld to prevent the re-creation of the largely negative influence on black life that they exerted within the existing United States.

Exactly which African Americans should be considered "citizens" did create a little discussion. On this point, some suggested that all descendants of slaves should be considered. Others suggested that only those who were "conscious" of the black nation should be considered citizens. In the end, the group leaned toward the side of inclusiveness, leaving the RNA open to all blacks in America, regardless of awareness concerning their shared identity.

Similarly, the Declaration of Independence was passed relatively easily and with little discussion. By any measure, it was an ambitious statement, broadly summarizing the experiences and aspirations of those engaged in struggle throughout the United States to improve the conditions for African Americans. It began by immediately distinguishing itself from the U.S. document:

We, the Black People in America, in consequence of arriving at a knowledge of ourselves as a people with dignity, long deprived of that knowledge as a consequence of revolting with every decimal of our collective and individual beings against the oppression that for three hundred years has destroyed and broken and warped the bodies and minds and spirits of our people in America, in consequence of our raging desire to be free of this oppression, to destroy this oppression wherever it assaults mankind in the world, and in consequence of our inextinquishable determination to go a different way, to build a new and better society in a new and better world do hereby declare ourselves forever free and independent of the jurisdiction of the United States of America and the obligations which that country's unilateral decision to make our ancestors and ourselves paper-citizens placed upon us.

We claim no rights from the United States of America other than those rights belonging to human beings anywhere in the world, and these include the right to damages, reparations, due us for the grievous injuries sustained by our ancestors and ourselves by reason of United States lawlessness.

Ours is a revolution against oppression – our own oppression and that of all people in the world. And it is a revolution for a better life, a better station for mankind, a surer harmony with the forces of life in the universe. (Republic of New Africa 1968a)

Perhaps no section was as important as the "Aims of the Revolution," which would largely serve as the guiding objectives for the organization for most (if not all) of its existence. There were fourteen in total:

1. To free black people in America from oppression;
2. To support and wage the world revolution until all people everywhere are so free;
3. To build a new Society that is better than what we now know and as perfect as man can make it;
4. To assure all people in the New Society maximum opportunity and equal access to that maximum;
5. To promote industriousness, responsibility, scholarship, and service;
6. To create conditions in which freedom of religion abounds and man's pursuit of God and/or the destiny, place, and purpose of man in the Universe will be without hindrance;
7. To build a black independent nation where no sect or religious creed subverts or impedes the building of the New Society, the New State Government, or the achievement of the aims of the Revolution as set forth in this Declaration;
8. To end exploitation of man by man or his environment;
9. To assure equality of rights for the sexes;
10. To end color and class discrimination, while not abolishing salubrious diversity, and to promote self respect and mutual respect among all people in the Society;
11. To protect and promote the personal dignity and integrity of the individual, and his natural rights;
12. To assure justice for all;
13. To place the major means of production and trade in the trust of the State to assure the benefits of this earth and man's genius and labor to society and all its members; and,
14. To encourage and reward the individual for hard work and initiative and insight and devotion to the revolution. (Republic of New Africa 1968a)

The core of the effort was a somewhat radical reflection on the Duboisian paradox of African American double-consciousness. The RNA simply suggested that blacks should consider the treatment they had received from whites since they had arrived in the country and, in particular, since they had started efforts to change their situation through the civil rights movement. With these events in mind, they asked blacks to choose what comes next (as Malcolm X, Albert Cleage as well as Gaidi and Imari Obadele had articulated in some manner previously). For the RNA, the answer was clear: whites didn't want blacks in the United States – at least, not as equals. They never have. They never would. More than that the U.S. government and many whites had allowed blacks to be treated violently. As the authorities were unable to protect blacks, as Hobbes would support, they had the legal and moral right to seek an authority that would. In response, the RNA suggested (in not only the "Aims of the

Revolution" but in the other literature as well) that African Americans should leave the United States and make a better world.

By adopting this position, many viewed the RNA as idealist, utopian, or dystopian – depending on one's view of this (re)imagined community. But in certain respects, the RNA was probably one of the more realistic of the many groups that emerged during the period. In fact, the RNA's realism is seen in their sober analysis of the situation. Clearly invoking Malcolm X, their realism emerged from viewing American society not as *it should or could be* but as they believed *it was*: segregated, unequal, and quite violent at times – at least that experienced by the majority of blacks and especially those who were the poorest in the city. As they stated in one publication (Republic of New Africa 1968a, 4),

(blacks) have never been part of the American Nation. Though our people have struggled for 100 years to change the American Nation and become a part of it, we have failed to become a part of it – we still live separately, go to school and church separately, socialize separately, and act and react separately (as well as differently). And there is no real hope now that we can change America, because white people, who are in the majority, do not really *want* America changed. For our part, black people could not become a part of America unless she did change, for there is too much racism, inequality and oppression of everyone who is not white.[4] (emphasis original)

The Declaration ended with as much forthrightness as it opened:

In mutual *trust* and great expectation, we the undersigned, for ourselves and for those who look to us but who are unable personally to fix their signatures hereto, do join in this solemn Declaration of Independence. And to support this Declaration and to assure the success of our revolution we pledge without reservation ourselves, our talents, and all our worldly goods. (Republic of New Africa 1968a; emphasis added)

What was the RNA trying to do? One of the clearest statements on this belongs to Imari Obadele, who increasingly came to be seen as *the* major theoretician and archivist for the new nation, producing much of the written material as well as leading the way in instruction at the time. As conceived, the RNA (a much weaker and smaller nation) was trying to move the United States (an admittedly stronger and larger nation) into a situation where it would make some settlement, some deal with African Americans through their government, the Republic. Harking back to the attempt of the Malcolm X Society to negotiate with the occupiers of Detroit, the RNA concluded that

such a settlement must result, obviously, from a trafficking in the issues at stake (i.e., paying attention and discussing the topics that mattered to African Americans). Where the big country chooses not to traffic, even indirectly or by third parties, all hope for negotiated settlement – indeed, all hope for freedom, save by some miracle or catastrophe befalling the big country – is gone. (Obadele 1970c, 174–75)

---

[4] Interestingly, this is similar in some ways to what Albert Cleage was writing in his series "Message to the Black Nation" within the *Michigan Chronicle* during 1967 and 1968.

This underscored that the objective of the RNA as "a fundamental policy, from the time of the founding convention on, [was] to create situations designed to force the United States to negotiate with [the RNA] and settle justly the issues of land, sovereignty and reparations" (Obadele 1970c, 175). Exactly what "situations" needed to be created to compel the government was not clear. Indeed, over time, it was revealed that there were different opinions about what this entailed, but largely it involved squashing the imagination of black Americans about who they were and what was possible as well as necessary. This would come later, however. At the beginning, though, it was enough simply to state the point.

What was clear was that the "situations" created would largely prompt some overt repressive action from the U.S. government, who were not expected to give anything up without a fight. To be successful, the RNA would need to be prepared for what the government would do (reappraisal had to thus be significantly developed and consistently highlighted). This followed from everyone's experiences and observations of how the civil rights movement was responded to but also to the activities of Malcolm X, Robert F. Williams, the Deacons for Defense, and several other black organizations at the time – the history of which was generally covered by the diverse members of the organization.

Institutions

As for the structure of the Republic, paradoxically, the RNA adopted a U.S.-like model where a great deal of power largely resided in the national government, including the president, first and second vice presidents, ministers, and ambassadors – similar to many SMOs. There was essentially no attention given to what local consulates, consuls, or chapters would do which would serve as a part of contention later. The executive branch held important powers (Republic of New Africa 1968b). For example, it appointed ministers, ambassadors, deputies, and others; it carried out legislation and directions of the National Council of Representatives; it carried out the "aims of the revolution"; it prepared and submitted national budgets; and it served as commander in chief of the military. The top-down model was the predominate African American institution during the civil rights movement and into the black power movement. One could also argue that this followed the general pattern through this time in the United States. Although unique in aspirations, therefore, the means toward this end were highly consistent with prior history.

The ministers were especially important for the RNA because they dealt with nine key problems:

1. treasury (i.e., receiving and releasing funds as well as managing budgets)
2. finance (i.e., generating funds)
3. justice (i.e., safeguarding the black community against "adverse" legal processes and developing legal defense for revolutionaries)

4. defense (i.e., defending the lives of black people, territory, and property; developing a black army; and influencing all existing black military and paramilitary groups)
5. education (i.e., creating a black school system and promoting an African American–oriented curriculum)
6. culture (i.e., promoting creativity within the black community)
7. state and foreign affairs (i.e., establishing relations with other nations and promoting African American interests both nationally and internationally)
8. information (i.e., informing black people about all RNA-related business as well as motivating African Americans to support the aims of the Republic)
9. interior (i.e., developing and guiding various components of the RNA)[5]

In the design put forward by the RNA, the National Council of Representatives, or NCR (i.e., the legislature), had numerous powers: they would levy taxes, approve budgets, and allocate approved funds; they set revolutionary policy relevant to all areas of life; they approved all presidential appointees; they ratified treaties; they held sole power to declare war; and they audited all government operations. In the beginning, however, there seemed to be no funds, which would return as a recurrent problem for the organization, but there were numerous policies that the group initiated rather quickly.

The judicial branch (i.e., court) was composed of three judges, chosen by the NCR. This entity held the power to rule on the constitutionality of government actions and actors, something that would become especially important later. It also held "jurisdiction in all civil, criminal and maritime matters" (Republic of New Africa 1968b, 4). The Constitutional Commission (also appointed by the NCR) hired all lower-level personnel.

More local-level government entities, such as individual city chapters (i.e., "consulates"), were essentially reduced to "representing" the national government within the smaller-scale jurisdictions and implementing the various

---

[5] Although the actual structure of the government did not garner much attention or discussion among the members, there was some discussion about what the different positions should be called. Indeed,

for a long while it looked as if the offices of the government would bear those names used for old (West African) political positions. Indeed, we prepared a complete list of such Yoruban names. This was done under leadership of Baba Oserjeman Adefunmi, chief of the Yoruba nation in North America, a priest, and North America's foremost missionary in the Yoruban religion and teacher of Yoruban culture … The move to use African titles was borne along by a strong anti-white, anti-west feeling, which many of the delegates shared … In the end the move for African titles did not prevail, largely because most delegates seemed to feel that they were too complicated and too alien for the average person in our bastardized race to relate to; they seemed to feel that the use of the African titles would create just another – and major – obstacle in our communicating with our brainwashed people. (Obadele 1970c, 167) nationally determined policies. Consulates were organized to be mini-governments with distinct sections mirroring different ministries.

The issue of jurisdiction was especially problematic for the RNA. As both its land (the counties in the South and cities in the North where blacks were predominant) and its government were held in "captivity," it was essential for them to establish clear lines of communication as well as hierarchies of control and leadership.

After deliberating about objectives, structure, institutions, and labels,[6] discussion moved to who would occupy the different positions; in short, it became time to select the leaders of the black nation. At the time of the elections, three things were revealed by the slate of candidates put forward. First, there were a large number of positions in the RNA. As a result, there were eleven separate votes administered and two other categories discussed. In the following, I identify the different positions as well as nominees selected for each position, noting non-Detroit origins and/or other institutional affiliations where applicable:

1. Attorney General: Robert Rocky, Gaidi Obadele, and Samuel Pearson
2. Minister of Defense: Robert F. Williams (in exile), Gaidi Obadele, and Daniel Aldridge
3. President: Robert F. Williams (in exile), Gaidi Obadele, and Max Stanford (from New York/RAM)
4. Vice President: Max Stanford (from New York/RAM), H. Rap Brown (from the Black Panther Party), and Gaidi Obadele
5. Treasurer: Robert Brock and Huey Newton (of the Black Panther Party)
6. Minister of Culture: John Breeze, Betty Shabazz (from New York), and Queen Mother Moore (from New York)
7. Secretary of War: Robert F. Williams (in exile), Jihad Milak, and Chaka
8. Minister of Information: H. Rap Brown (from the Black Panther Party), Alfred Hicks, Daniel Watts, Daniel Aldridge, and Imari Obadele
9. Minister of Foreign Affairs: Thomas Lockett, Gaidi Obadele, and Ray Willis
10. Minister for Foreign Affairs: Nelson Fullerton
11. Ambassador to East Africa: Betty Shabazz, Majile Adefunmi, and George Martin
12. Ambassador to Far East (China): Robert F. Williams (in exile), Mae Mallory (from New York), and Henry "Papa" Wells
13. Some kind of ambassador: John Grayson, John Braie (Los Angeles), and Mae Mallory (from New York)

Second, as different names appeared, drawn from different parts of the country and different organizational affiliates, there was some diversity revealed in

---

[6] Interestingly, what was not discussed was the approach that would be taken to address the repression most feared.

each position, but not a tremendous amount. There was also a strong Detroit bias to the candidates. Although candidates from different cities and organizations were advanced, the largest number came from the local community. Third, it was clear that the Obadeles, especially Gaidi, and Robert F. Williams were clearly favored as their names were identified in more categories than any other individuals.

While everything generally moved smoothly with regard to the identification of candidates for each position and the tallying of votes, some controversy emerged about whether people could or should be nominated who were not in attendance.[7] For example, Robert F. Williams, who was currently in exile, was not brought up in this context; indeed, as president, he was to be the organization's "ace in the hole." But the possibilities of Albert Cleage, Glanton Dowell, and Edward Vaughn, a local bookstore owner and important leader in the community with previous connections to the college NAACP chapter, were questioned; none were present at the event, but all were being considered to serve in some capacity. Two attendees argued strongly against this practice: Betty Shabazz and Mae Mallory. Specifically, they maintained that if these individuals could not bother to attend such an important meeting, then they likely could not serve the new nation. Albert Cleage's absence had not been quite as deafening as his silence was at that moment.

Robert F. Williams's candidacy was discussed, but not with regard to whether he should be nominated or elected (he was clearly identified as acceptable) but rather with regard to whether he would serve, if elected, and what impact, if any, his absentee role would play in the organization. The possibility of his not accepting the position was explicitly raised by Mae Mallory (Robert's former colleague in struggle from Monroe, North Carolina). With this as her second major objection, she was quickly becoming viewed as something of a problem. Although the Obadeles had not broached the topic explicitly with Williams at their recent meeting in Tanzania, they believed that he would be supportive, and thus his nomination was sustained.

As efficiently as everything else, the election was held and there were no real surprises with the victors. Williams took the presidency, but as he was in exile, Gaidi Obadele (as first vice president) assumed power as the executor in charge of daily operations. Betty Shabazz (Malcolm X's widow) was elected second vice president, which meant that if something happened to Gaidi Obadele and Robert F. Williams, she would step in as de facto leader. William Ellis was selected minister of finance; Joan Franklin was elected minister of justice; Baba Oseijeman Adefunmi, Leroi Jones/Imiri Baraka, and Ron Karenga were

---

7 Only one other tension was revealed during the day (Detroit Police Department, Special Investigation Bureau, April 3, 1968). During the break when convention participants addressed the media, at one point, Imari Obadele mentioned that the new nation had an army in Cuba as well as diverse militants across the United States ready to use violence if necessary (i.e., "arsonists" and "looters"). To this, Gaidi Obadele simply looked at his brother and told him to "shut up."

elected ministers of culture; Chaka was selected secretary of war.[8] After being overlooked in the initial nomination process, Queen Mother Moore was also elected minister of health as well as minister of welfare, and Imari Obadele was elected minister of information.[9]

Out of the afternoon session on reparations and diplomatic relations, there emerged an RNA policy that quickly passed. In effect, the organization identified that African Americans were owed reparations because the fruits of the labor of their forefathers were being enjoyed by the descendants of those who enslaved them. In the form of land, gold, or some acceptable alternative, these were to be pursued "vigorously," along with United Nations recognition of this situation and African American separation. Toward this end, the ministers of state and foreign affairs were directed to conduct elections wherever the RNA maintained consulates to ascertain how blacks felt about pursuing reparations. This was to be accomplished by October 30, 1968.

Interventions

Establishing the government was only part of the plan for the first day. As the RNA claimed to speak for all African Americans, it was crucial for them to get this message out to their "constituency." Without the black community, there would be no mandate to govern and thus no legitimacy for the government.[10] By taking action, the RNA revealed its uniqueness. In one fell swoop, they had reversed the historical pattern generally followed up to that time: they first declared the government and then sought to generate support from the nation it sought to govern. This was one of the reasons for their holding a follow-up convention in May and pushing for an October revisitation of the whole government. It was hoped that by that time they would have reached more black people and with that increased participation, there would likely be different preferences with regard to the leadership of the nation.

As conceived, there were numerous strategies for reaching out: press conferences, rallies, conferences, and demonstrations. However, as in the civil rights

[8] There was some controversy with these outcomes:

Neither Rap Brown, nor Stokely Carmichael, nor the venerated journalist Charles P. Howard, Sr., whose health had finally failed him was there. From the beginning it was clear Stokely was not ready for the creation of the government (not only his statements made this clear but he, like Karenga, was in the area but chose not to appear at the Convention); but it would be clear finally that Rap was not ready and when, some seven months after the Convention, and a few months before his death Mr. Howard would return to work at this U.N. office, he would confess to us that he did not think the plan workable on the surface and had not read WAR IN AMERICA or our other materials, or studied it. (Obadele 1970c, 173)

[9] By the time of the hearing, Betty Shabazz had left the organization because she did not think it wise to constantly divulge RNA plans before the members had an opportunity to work on a topic (e.g., revealing the five states that they would attempt to acquire to build the new nation).

[10] The minister of state and foreign affairs was also directed to identify, establish, and cultivate diplomatic ties with "friendly" nations and to determine ways to "support" all efforts at national liberation and the right of self-determination.

movement, getting media attention was deemed especially important for the RNA. This was not hard to do. Given the objective of the dissidents, it should come as no surprise that even before the convention, they quickly captured the media's attention. Indeed, prior to its emergence, it had received coverage in the black-owned *Michigan Chronicle* (e.g., *Michigan Chronicle* 1968a, 1968b) as well as the black-owned *Detroit Courier* (1968). The stories here were not only that a black government was going to be created but that reparations and five states in the deep South would be pursued. It was also generally noted that Robert Clark of the Mississippi Freedom Democratic Party (the first black elected to the Mississippi House of Representatives since Reconstruction) would be attending, along with nationalists from around the country.

Even the *New York Times* covered the upcoming meeting with their article "Militants Seek Black Government" (March 28, 1968), addressing the same general points. Interestingly, the follow-up coverage in the *Times* on the Tuesday after the first day of deliberations had a very different tone to it ("Negro Group Asks End of Ties to US," March 31, 1968). This article repeated the basic storyline, but it also mentioned that the media was excluded from the proceedings, and the article itself was peppered with extremely aggressive quotations from Gaidi Obadele, who was simply referred to as "Milton Henry" in the article. For example, Gaidi is quoted in the *New York Times* as saying, "We want out." He then goes on to characterize the United States as a "dirty pot" and a "vicious, corrupt, parasitic system." Finally, he notes that "independence would keep Negroes from supporting President Johnson and the Vietnam war, keep them out of military service and keep them from paying income taxes."

Though a partially accurate depiction of the RNA, it was not nearly as complete as they would have liked. Indeed, one does not come away from the article or any of the national media coverage with the sense of the RNA's meticulousness, thoughtfulness, and concern for law and governance or with a reasonable assessment of why some blacks came to the decision that they did regarding independence and secession. On April 1, the *Times* focused on Robert F. Williams, his travels in Cuba and China, his possible return, and his telegram of support for the "emerging black nation" ("Negro Now in China Chosen as President by Black Nation").

Coverage was a bit more comprehensive in the regional media. On April 1, 1968, in the Cleveland *Plain Dealer* (a paper with the largest circulation in Ohio and one of the largest in the nation), the article "Black Nation Draft Constitution" gave some context to the black nationalists' claims-making effort. It stated, "'Life is meaningless for black people in these United States,' Milton Henry is quoted as saying" (the name Gaidi again being ignored). Aside from this single sentence, however, the rest of the article focused on the five states, the questionable nature of black citizenship, and the tribal dress of some of the participants. The *Michigan Chronicle* on April 6 ("Black Separatists Set Up Government") focused on the actions of the RNA government pursuing litigation for reparations, maintaining "false" citizenship in the United States, and presenting the list of elected officials.

Even more important than the media attention, however, was getting the RNA house in order. This involved a large number of meetings and discussions far away from outsiders, very different from the civil rights movement where a great many of their activities were taken in and for the public.

Of significance in this period of the RNA are the frequent references to "oppression," including the systemic inequalities in the economic and political system, and to "repression," including systematic attempts by political authorities to undermine challenges made against them. These references make sense as the principal motivation for black independence was the fact that as society was structured at the time, most African Americans could not generally acquire and sustain even a reasonable quality of life. These references are important for understanding how repressive behavior influenced what took place – both at the point of the founding and later on.

Perhaps the clearest influence of government coercive action (as a concept, not as an actual practice [yet]) can be found in the particular approach the RNA adopted. The earlier repressiveness of U.S. political authorities against previous African American SMOs made blacks think about leaving the United States and create their own government in the first place. In one respect, the idea for separation itself was nothing less than an aftereffect of state repression. The government and many whites had consistently proven themselves incapable of or disinterested in with making sure that African Americans were not treated in a violent and/or discriminatory manner. In particular, it was the viciousness of police responses to black protest that proved especially salient in the minds of the RNA. Blacks did not want to be caught off-guard or helpless. Additionally, it was the consistent disregard for the value of African American life that provided one of the most compelling reasons for a more international orientation for the organization (i.e., appealing to the global community with human rights) as opposed to an exclusively domestic one (which was more the orientation of the civil rights movement). Drawing on Malcolm X, it was believed that only through internationalization could African Americans be protected. Repression was only one of the influences here, however. It was the earlier attempts at black advancement and reflection on the objectives as well as the methods used toward these goals that also prompted the blacks involved in the RNA to create the Republic. Trying and failing caused African Americans to rethink their approach to improving the situation.

Changing Characteristics and Assessing Causes

Individuals

Though the founding of the RNA included members from all over the United States, in the months that followed, the records from both the U.S. government and the RNA itself focused exclusively on the activists in the Detroit caucus or chapter, the original headquarters of the RNA and the place that accounted for the largest number of its members.

The list of the core membership included a reasonably sized group of approximately twenty-three consistently present individuals: Gaidi Obadele and his wife, Imari Obadele and his wife, Ron Pugh, Ray Willis, William Hall, Lavis Simmons, Andrew Hayes, Anderson Howard, Clara and Thomas Lockett, Jesse Wallace, Sandra and David Mundy, Elizabeth King, Selina Howard, Warren Galloway, Tyrone Travis, Sam Pearson, Mary Bolonglono, Sam Davis, and Brenda Ralston. Needless to say, this changed over time. Although the participation of the individuals identified earlier was fairly stable over the initial period of interest, there was one important absence (Robert F. Williams) as well as one important departure (Albert Cleage). The reasons for both clearly point to dynamics within the movement (i.e., they were internally oriented) and not state repression as the explanation for (de)mobilization at this stage (i.e., they were not externally oriented). I say this because during the period, overt repressive action was essentially nonexistent. For example, according to the available material, there were no raids, arrests, instances of harassment, or any of the other forms of overt activity during this period.

Regarding covert activity, few officers were assigned and few police-hours were logged for surveillance. Indeed, according to the database, the police did not start logging hours until late April or early May – a full month after the founding convention (see later). Despite the limited overt behavior, however, we know from the records that domestic spying was extensive in the beginning as the police attempted to figure out who was who and what was what (through the large number of informant reports and police reports concerning the history of the RNA).

Regardless of any effort that was extended, the RNA expressed few concerns about infiltration and informants, suggesting that the Republic was largely oblivious of these efforts and that neither overt nor covert repressive action played any role in their deliberations about what to do and how. During the period in question, the issue of possible infiltration was only raised once, and that was by Betty Shabazz at the founding convention (i.e., the first official meeting of the group). This interest and sensitivity were likely attributed to her late husband's experience toward the end of his life.[11] Regardless, there was no follow-up discussion of this topic with any other member during RNA events, and thus the concern could not have been that significant – despite the source.

Given his orientation toward the U.S. government, Imari Obadele would have been more than willing to mention the opposite case. Accordingly, I view his statements concerning the issue of low-level repression after the founding to be quite telling. He states,

---

[11] Toward the end of his life, Malcolm X (El Hajj Malik El Shabazz) became convinced that he was under constant surveillance from different U.S. intelligence and police organizations.

It was true that the Detroit Police Department engaged in some surveillance of key New Africans, and in information gathering. It is also true that Army Intelligence, mainly because of my working as a Technical Editor for the U.S. Army for nearly seven months after the founding, evinced more than a fleeting interest in us. The FBI displayed an intense and abiding concern, and they, together with the Detroit police, stooped on occasion to send out bogus mailings, on our letterhead and over my and other signatures, designed to confuse and demoralize our citizens. But the official attitude in Detroit was that if they ignored us, we would simply go away. The attitude of the federal government was much the same. (Obadele 1970c, 214)

Interestingly, the data as well as the RNA's own perceptions fly in the face of most opinions about the period. Recall for example the comments of Goldstein (1978) about the high degree of repressive behavior during this time as well as the pressure from federal, state, and local authorities to keep a lid on any dissident behavior, especially that of blacks and/or radicals. Michigan- and Detroit-specific narratives would also suggest a different approach.

What accounts for this discrepancy between reality and mass as well as expert perceptions? I think a large part of the explanation resides in the fact that we are discussing a political democracy and one that had recently (e.g., Voting Rights Act of 1965) taken steps to acknowledge its limitations with the treatment of its black citizens as well as to implement some laws to address these limitations. This is relevant to the "domestic democratic peace" (Davenport 2007). Additionally, the explanation resides in the objectives and tactics being pursued by the RNA. As designed, they were not engaging the police in an overtly hostile manner like the Black Panthers or trying to take on specific political-economic institutions like the students engaged in sit-ins who attempted to directly integrate Woolworths through nonviolent direct action. The RNA was engaging in a wholly distinct approach. In particular, influenced by the government responses to the civil rights activists (i.e., previous repressive behavior), members of the RNA were trying to separate, using nonviolent direct action with the potential for violence (only if their activities were interfered with or frustrated by the lack of progress). Even with the rather contentious nature of the time period, the U.S. government did not seem to feel that it could or perhaps should engage the RNA in a more aggressive manner – at least, not until they did something to deserve it. Indeed, in a sense, the authorities appeared to treat the movement as something of a potentially dangerous joke that had not yet risen to the point of actually being dangerous. The government seemed to look on the African Americans associated with the movement in the same way they had viewed the Malcolm X Society during the riots and rebellion of 1967; as Tilly would suggest, they were acceptable behaviorally but unacceptable ideologically and organizationally.[12]

---

[12] This is speculative given the spotty nature of the documentation on the internal workings of the relevant government agents, but it does seem to be a reasonable conclusion.

As expected, with little repression, there were few expressions of anger or fear regarding the authorities seen in the RNA during this time period and few attempts to counteract any perceived negative situations. Indeed, the framings that were employed at this time tended to be of a positive variety, suggesting that the organization was oriented toward action and did not perceive any resistance.

This brings us to the issue of the within-RNA dynamics. Here there are three points to make.

First, regarding the absence of Robert F. Williams mentioned previously, it is important to remember that in the Tanzania meeting with the Obadele brothers, he had made it clear that he "officially" wanted nothing to do with the organization, at least nothing that would require his time. Indeed, Williams was trying to secure some support for an initiative in Tanzania (Mississippi State Police – Complaint Report, June 9, 1968). He was to be president of the Republic in name only.

Why was he like this? Interestingly, Robert F. Williams's position could be associated with potential repression related to his earlier activities when he was politically active in North Carolina. Essentially, he did not wish to run afoul of the law – again. Williams was already wanted on a kidnapping charge, and his return to the United States as well as a continuation with radical activity would have threatened his participation in the Republic and his freedom in the United States. In the parlance of the earlier discussion, Williams was exhausted, but not seemingly in a general sense. He was specifically exhausted regarding his concern with being persecuted by U.S. political authorities. Williams's reluctance to associate himself with the RNA may also be attributed to a difference of opinion between him and the Republic about what should be done in the African American struggle. By most accounts (e.g., Tyson 1999), Williams was a patriot and believed that the United States, warts and all, was worthy of support and allegiance.[13] At no point does it appear that Gaidi or Imari Obadele tried to talk Williams out of his position, however, bringing him in line with the RNA, rectifying the breach, and overcoming the likely disappointment felt by the membership when the difference became more apparent. In a sense, the RNA gambled on Williams and his international connections – connections that simply did not bear fruit. The RNA was tolerating a potential situation of divisiveness and factionalization on the chance that greater connections would facilitate their survival.

The second point concerns the departure of Albert Cleage – one of the earliest activists involved in the RNA. Over the course of several discussions, it became clear to Gaidi Obadele that Albert Cleage had to be removed from the RNA. Initially, Obadele had concluded that Cleage did not want his churchgoers

---

[13] It was not his support for the United States that got him back in the country but the separatist RNA with their legal assistance, the inflated status that being RNA president provided him, and his awareness of China.

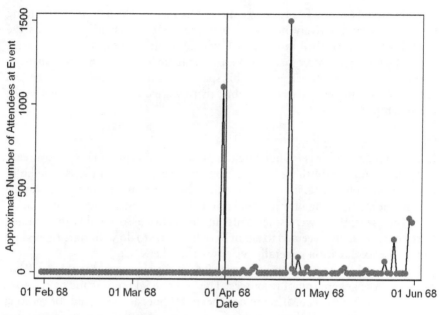

FIGURE 7.1. Attendees of RNA events around the founding.

to associate with the Republic and that he made explicit statements to this effect. Revealing a degree of lost commitment, Cleage never seemed to mention selected events when he had the opportunity to do so (e.g., during sermons), and he did not encourage interaction. As Cleage was viewed as a spokesperson for the organization, one of the main initial supporters and a major presence in Detroit radical circles, this was extremely problematic. Later, Obadele became particularly disenchanted with Cleage's treatment of the RNA in his church. For example, he noted that Cleage charged the RNA rent and another member mentioned that he had locked up the PA system, forcing the RNA to bring its own. At one meeting, several members got upset with Cleage's advocating exclusive use of nonviolence. As noted, the RNA also generally advocated this practice, but not exclusively. When threatened, they felt that blacks had the right to protect themselves. By April 25, Obadele had concluded that Cleage had "failed in his mission" to bring the church to the RNA and that, in fact, he had driven them away from it – not fostering divisiveness within the Republic. In this context, he was no longer considered a spokesperson, and all associations were "officially" broken – a solution that was deemed mutually satisfactory.

There is yet another way to look at individuals in the organization, and that concerns the number of attendees at RNA events (Figure 7.1). Considering this indicator, it is clear that the estimated number of attendees during the relevant period was generally small, with fewer than fifty to one hundred people attending most events. The two exceptions here include the day of the founding itself, which cumulatively involved more than one thousand, as well as the Black Unity Day Festival in late April, which involved about fifteen hundred. The inclusion of the latter is somewhat problematic because it involves an event largely centered around Cleage and his specific call to action. Although he had not officially left the RNA at that time, there were clearly some strains in the relationship.[14]

Ideas

As the organization was founded on the principles of beginning a government, recognizing and establishing black nationhood, seeking reparations, and holding a national plebiscite, it makes sense that there were no major changes in the organization's thinking in the period immediately following the event in question. That said, there were some shifts in the tactics associated with attaining these ends, shifts that seemed to again have had little to do with state repression and whose explanation generally resides within the RNA.

For example, one of the most immediate and pressing needs for the RNA concerned the generation of resources. This is a crucial point made by resource mobilization literature. SMOs are not cheap: rent needs to be paid for meeting locales; letterheads and flyers need to be designed, printed, and mailed so that internal communication can take place; the organizational message needs to be distributed externally; uniforms need to be purchased so that the officials look official; and gas and bus or plane tickets need to be acquired as different members of the group need to travel. Indeed, the amount of resources required by the group increased with the ambitiousness of the RNA's objectives.

This put the organization in something of a bind from the outset. By design, the RNA was trying to address the needs of the neglected and discriminated-against black community, and it was attempting what many black organizations at the time attempted: to provide the services that the U.S. government and civil society were unable and/or unwilling to provide (e.g., protection, education, employment). The key strategy for accomplishing this objective was an ambitious bond project. Not wanting to rely on the same white patronage that had undermined and co-opted earlier black civil rights activists, the RNA decided to rely on African Americans, their primary constituents, to support them (a strategy of black self-help). The plan was to have each African American purchase a $100 bond in the Republic, which would give each some stake in the venture, some expected redeemability and some return on investment.[15]

---

[14] Carefully looking at the attendee list, it also seems clear that individuals known to be associated with the RNA were not present.

[15] With median family income for African Americans in Detroit at approximately $19,095 in 1950 and $25,800 in 1990 (as but one part of the black community), the amount requested in addition to periodic "taxation" was not insignificant. In contrast, white median family income over the same period was $26,456 and $54,180, respectively (Farley et al. 2000, 50).

The figures being discussed at the time were crucial to understanding what they were trying to do:

[The RNA] estimated that of 30 million black people in America, three million (one in ten) were ready to set up a separate nation – to become New Africans – if [the RNA] were simply to provide them a minimal explanation of the concepts involved and then provide them an *opportunity* for becoming New African citizens. [Additionally, they] estimated that another seven million black people would become New Africans if they received detailed information on the Republic *and* were provided an opportunity. (Obadele 1970c, 175; emphasis original)

If each of the original 3 million purchased a $100 bond, then the Republic would have $300 million. Of course, in the beginning, there were fewer than three hundred persons with citizenship. In this context, their work was cut out for them.

Ironically, the problem with this approach was that it was likely illegal for a separatist movement to sell bonds for its new nation within the sovereign territory of an already established nation. Nobody seemed to know the specifics about this, but the RNA's minister of justice (Joan Franklin) busily set about trying to figure this out, causing a bit of confusion within the organization because bonds were to be the main source of start-up capital and this could not yet be initiated. Equally as interesting was the lack of concern with the potential illegality in domestic U.S. law with separating from the United States, which was largely not discussed.

Adapting to this situation and acknowledging the legal problem, the RNA moved from bonds to "certificates of recognition" for support of the RNA, which were simply official IOUs for monetary gifts. While appropriate for navigating the short-term problem of U.S. illegality, this did not address the issue of exactly what individuals were "gifting." "Donations" of members started shortly after this in an effort to assist the Republic in meeting its financial needs. Magnanimous ideas were thus out there, but the realities of what the RNA was and how it would pursue its objectives were not yet clear. This was understandable, given what was being attempted, but it didn't make mobilization any easier.

What is worthy of mention here explicitly is the lack of discussion about China and Tanzania being potential sources of support, which was something floated when Robert F. Williams was first mentioned. Additionally, there was no discussion about illegal ways of obtaining money. In the literature and in the popular culture, organizations such as the RNA have frequently been associated with bank robberies, drug dealing, and other illicit activities, but at the founding (across all sources), there was no discussion of this at all. This becomes relevant later on, as does explicit action taken by the U.S. government to block resource acquisition (a different method of influence beyond the scope of the current investigation but one followed infrequently, according to the available records).

Institutions

The structure of the Republic was largely set after the founding of the organization for at least a few months. As discussed earlier, diverse aspects of the
RNA government were viewed as temporary. With more African Americans
becoming aware of and, it was hoped, more involved in the RNA, it was
assumed that candidates as well as maybe even some policies and/or practices
would change over time. These were all to be revealed and discussed during a
meeting in Chicago in May. This would directly tend to enhance trust among
the new recruits and the original members, for it would establish a sense of
accountability and responsivity within the organization.

The only real modification that occurred in the month or so following the
founding involved the development of local consuls. As noted earlier, exactly
what local chapters were supposed to do was unclear. Perhaps going back to
the days of GOAL, the RNA seemed more interested in setting a path or starting
a conversation and letting others follow than in micro-managing the day-to-
day activities of a broad-based institution. In the RNA case, however, the
vanguard approach would not be acceptable. People needed to have something
to do in the new nation or they would become disinterested and not join or
participate. Adjusting to the situation, the RNA changed the position of "bond
chairperson," which existed in the different places with consulates, to "caucus
chairperson." The job of this individual was to meet, take roll call and collect
information about members, get the RNA message to all those in attendance
and to the local community, prepare for the plebiscite, and collect donations.
Additionally, consuls were also to prepare proposals for what they would like
to see changed in the RNA, suggestions that were to be presented at the May
meeting in Chicago.

Although this seemed straightforward, the tasks to be undertaken by each
consulate were not always understood, transparent, or equitable, which would
make trust building difficult. For example, getting the message out normally
meant getting the information from the Detroit caucus out to the other consulates. Exactly where individuals would meet was left to each consul to figure
out. There was thus a reliance on local networks within the different locales
to get things done but a large dependence on RNA headquarters to set policy
and objectives. Such inequity would be a sore point later. Indeed, without a
more distributed sense of accountability, this left trust building and trust itself
as something exclusively determined by the leaders of the RNA.

Again, I do not attribute these changes to repression. Quite the contrary,
these shifts reflected decisions made by RNA leaders to address issues of recruitment, retention, and resource acquisition, distinct from the concerns about
what the U.S. government would do to them. To the extent that political
authorities were thought about at all, such concerns involved the parameters
of the existing legal system and the RNA's ability to navigate around or through
them.

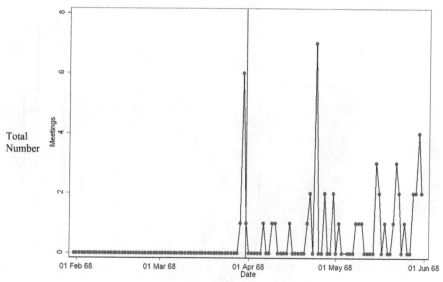

FIGURE 7.2. RNA meetings around the founding.

Interventions

In the weeks following the founding, the RNA undertook a small amount of activity. In line with the argument outlined earlier, I do not attribute this low level of activity to the repressive behavior of the U.S. government. Rather, I again attribute it to the condition of the RNA, which was largely focused on getting itself together (i.e., picking leaders, establishing the government's structure, allocating tasks, and generating start-up funds). However, this is not to say that there were no activities being taken during this time.

For example, there were a number of meetings where the members were brought together, directly enhancing trust in the organization (Figure 7.2). This was logical given the fact that the RNA had to discuss and determine what needed to be done for the new nation to be created. One can especially see the activity surrounding the founding itself (with six individual meetings being reported on a single day) as well as the Detroit Area caucus meetings of April 24, 1968 (with seven individual meetings). Before and after the latter event, there was slightly more activity. In line with Republic directives, the basic structure of the meetings was fairly consistent, continuing the largely formal nature of the founding. The meetings began with a roll call, there was a presentation made by local officers regarding what was taking place throughout the RNA, and there was a more or less open discussion regarding new business that largely concerned local issues.

Awareness of the relatively low number of meetings and of the limited participation was somewhat high within the organization. Indeed, rather quickly,

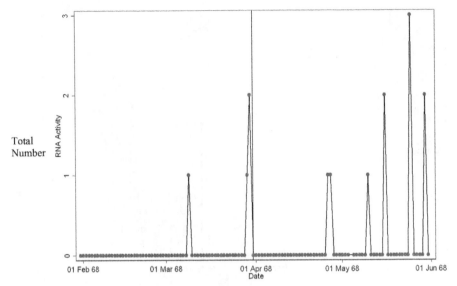

FIGURE 7.3. RNA activity around the founding.

there began a steady stream of notes to this effect, coming from assorted members of the RNA. For example, the minister of information sent out a memo on May 14, 1968, that read,

Dear Member of the Detroit Caucus

The last line of the Declaration of Independence, which *you* signed, reads as follows:

"And to support this Declaration and to assure the success of our Revolution we pledge without reservation ourselves, our talents and all our worldly goods."

This was a pledge not only to yourselves and your fellow signers, but to the Revolution itself. Since then, many of you have come to no meeting or any other function; you have not given to the Caucus or to the government the benefit of your talent or your money. We call on you now to live up to your pledge.

Your participation at Chicago is, as the other enclosed letter points out, vital. It is also important that you sell at least ten tickets for the "Theatrical Cabaret" which the Caucus is having on Saturday, May 25th. We think that you will be quite pleasantly surprised by the Theatre presentation: it is a drama with dance (The Chavou Afro Mod Dance Group), produced by our Caucus, and with a revolutionary theme. We count on you to help make this a success.

At the beginning, there were also very few overt manifestations of collective action directed outward (e.g., speeches, social events, demonstrations and marches; see Figure 7.3). Given the objectives of the organization at this point, the lack of activity was understandable and, in a sense, was called for. The last thing the RNA were prepared to do was engage in traditional forms of contentious politics (i.e., a protest demonstration), further challenging the government beyond the already bold and contentious challenge they had already put forth simply by existing.

The disinterest in and rarity of dissident behavior after the founding is informative, however, for it suggests that SMOs, even or especially those involving highly contentious activities, are not constantly engaged in dissent. Accordingly, if one was focused on trying to ascertain the influence of government repression on challengers and challenges, they must first make the case that challengers were interested in as well as capable of engaging in relevant behavior. Those of us concerned with SMOs and state repressive action sometimes forget this, but SMOs are not all about gun battles with the police on the streets or mountainsides, smuggling explosives, dramatic confrontations with judges in court rooms, or fiery speeches in city parks. There are long periods of discussion and planning, and a great deal of that is just not outwardly oriented. To paraphrase Poletta (2002), sometimes the struggle is an endless series of meetings and discussions. This may especially be the case when the ambitiousness of the objective is significant and the way forward is unclear.

Summary

Within this chapter, I have discussed the beginning of the RNA and attempted to identify the degree to which repression and/or internal dynamics of the organization influenced the individuals, ideas, institutions, and interventions at the RNA's origin. From the existing data, it was clear that repressive action did have an influence on the RNA, but not in the way researchers typically discussed or even in the way I described earlier. For example, there was no concern with contemporaneous values of repression. In the beginning there were no members getting harassed, beaten, arrested, or shot. Rather, there was concern with repressive action that had been historically directed against the African American challengers in general, the possibility of repression (i.e., previous and imagined repressive activity). The internal dynamics took these historical experiences and filtered them into a new political institution, a new set of objectives, and a repertoire for such action as well as a new identity. With this foundation established, the internal workings of the RNA generally carried the greatest impact. From this origin, however, the dynamic exchange between the U.S. government and the black nationalist challenger was established.

8

To Ocean Hill–Brownsville and B(l)ack

On taking office in 1966, Mayor John Lindsay of New York unveiled an ambitious plan for school decentralization as part of his design to fix the city's school system. Several districts in predominantly African American and Puerto Rican communities were chosen for pilots of the decentralization plan. Among the selected communities was the Ocean Hill–Brownsville (OH-B) school district in Brooklyn. On May 9, 1968, after some serious deliberation and in line with the powers provided by the mayor, the OH-B school district governing board dismissed ten teachers on charges that they were unable to control their pupils and did not support decentralization. To protest this action, hundreds of teachers in the district, who were union members, went on strike during the latter half of May and the entire month of June, shutting down numerous schools throughout the city. The impact of the strike was devastating (indeed, one author refers to this as *The Strike That Changed New York*; Podair 2002). In response to these actions, the OH-B governing board refused to reinstate the teachers and banned all who protested the governing board's actions from returning to their posts in the fall. After an investigation, the ten teachers who were dismissed were cleared of the charges by a trial examiner, but the OH-B governing board still refused to reinstate them.

This led to an extremely explosive situation. On one hand, with the planned expansion of decentralization, the teacher's union feared that it would lose its hard-won city-wide bargaining rights and would have to negotiate separately with more than thirty local governing boards. On the other hand, the OH-B governing board felt that it was asserting the right of community control over school operations and hiring that it had been promised by the mayor's plan. Adding to the degree of hostility, the conflict broke down along racial lines, with the predominately white and Jewish teacher's union as well as the city board of education on one side pitted against the predominantly African American and Puerto Rican district governing board as well as various community leaders on the other. Attempting to resolve the crisis, Mayor Lindsay ordered the teachers back into the OH-B schools. After some initial resistance, the teachers were put back in place. Although an important aspect of the conflict was over, though, the difficult issues brought up by the conflict simmered for quite some time.

This was not a topic with a limited audience. Indeed, because it was New York, the events received attention around the United States and around the globe. One of the most interested observers of the OH-B situation was the RNA, then seven months into its existence. Seeing the importance of the conflict for the emerging African American nationalist struggle, the idea of local community control or sovereignty, and the immense news coverage given to the topic and locale, the RNA decided to intervene. As conceived, the RNA would go to Brooklyn and help the community separate from the United States, bearing the flag of the new republic but without their overt military component so as to reduce the overt response of U.S. political authorities (something of a reversal of policy regarding never purposely making oneself vulnerable). This decision to go to Brooklyn had important implications for the social movement, prompting extensive discussion about who they were, what they were actually capable of doing, and what they should do as well as where. Directly related to the topic of interest to this book, the decision to engage with OH-B was clearly determined by several key members inside the organization, and that decision created the beginning of some significant tensions within the RNA. These acts were largely independent of any efforts actually being undertaken by the U.S. government. Here dynamics were very much driven by internal factors, with external factors hardly being present at all – at least as conventionally conceived. Nevertheless, the ghost of repression was still apparent; it was just not central to what was taking place.

Prior to Ocean Hill–Brownsville

In the two months before October 15, 1968, when the RNA decided to go into Brooklyn,[1] things were moving at a snail's pace within the organization. As Imari Obadele recalled,

through that first summer, the summer of 1968, recruitment moved slowly; few new consulates were started, and our increase [in membership] was largely in the already established consulates. Even recruitment here was hampered by a lack of funds, which resulted in an inability of top national officers to visit the local organizations and in a dearth of printed material. We were also hampered, of course, by being largely salesmen of an idea that as yet was unconnected to a gut-issue and testing-ground as, say, the non-violence of Doctor Martin Luther King had been connected to Montgomery and the bus boycott. (Obadele 1970c, 181)

---

[1] It is hard to affix the exact date of entry, but this is the estimate provided from reading the relevant documents in the Red Squad file.

The tasks that the RNA had set for itself were not easy ones, and as the rubber met the road, the nation began to take its first steps. In so doing, the organization started to get a better feel for how difficult their path was going to be. Again, this was reflected in the ideas and institutions developed, the individuals engaged, and the interventions undertaken by the group. Each is discussed in what follows.

Ideas

During the pre-OH-B period, the RNA was advocating for and trying to get others interested in reparations, nationhood, and a national plebiscite. In this respect, the organization was stable; the fundamental beliefs of the movement did not change. This made sense because the organization did not really have the need, nor did it have the opportunity, to shift. A large part of what took place after the founding of the RNA was fathoming a way to achieve their goals and put their ideas in motion. That said, in late May, two changes were instituted within the organization to help it reach its goals. These would influence what occurred later, both inside and outside the group. Of the two changes implemented, both concerned exactly how the RNA would address some of its fundamental problems, and both concerned how the Republic was structured (discussed later).

Institutions

The first change implemented within the organization was the adoption of the Income Tax Act. Acknowledging that the organization had limited financial capacity but needed to pay for a variety of items as well as activities, on May 31, at 40 North Ashland Avenue in Chicago, Illinois, approximately thirty members of the RNA attempted to address what was probably the biggest weakness within the organization. To remedy the situation, Ray Willis (the minister of finance) proposed a flat tax rate on all citizens with one deduction per dependent of $100.[2] This passed relatively quickly. After some discussion, the RNA enacted the following; it

> levied and imposed a tax of 3% upon the taxable income of every individual who is a citizen of the Republic of New Africa, and upon every corporation either doing business in the Republic of New Africa or whose stock is controlled by citizens of the Republic of New Africa. (Republic of New Africa, 1968a)

The outcome of this effort was mixed. On one hand, the policy changed the profile of the organization, as it rectified a major limitation in its structure – at least theoretically. On the other hand, the change made the organization much weaker as it institutionalized an organizational squeeze on the existing

---

[2] Utilizing a program called Dollartimes that factors in inflation (http://www.dollartimes .com/inflation/inflation.php?amount=100&year=1968), this is approximately $687.46 in 2014 dollars.

membership as well as on potential recruits in a way that made the RNA an increasing burden on the very lives of those whom it was trying to assist.

The second change within the organization was the legislative act that established the Black Legion, the RNA's military. Similar to the income tax, the creation of this body was supposed to resolve another perceived problem – this time not just for the RNA but for the larger African American community as well. Specifically, the RNA tried to address the heightened security threats to the black community by the overt behavior of racist police as well as other members of the white community. This addressed a longer historical problem as well.

The creation of the Black Legion was also tied to the greatest repressive fear of the organization: being directly hit by an overt, aggressive assault like that waged nonviolent civil rights activists (from whites in general and the police in particular). The RNA vowed that it would never be hit in such a direct manner without preparation. Two reasons existed for this. On one hand, the RNA vowed never put themselves in a position where they were vulnerable to this type of attack (i.e., being out in the open, unarmed and unprepared). Instead, the RNA would try to build themselves in the minds of black folk and then step forward to claim the nation en masse. On the other hand, the RNA would prepare to defend themselves by creating an armed wing, trained in shooting, hand-to-hand combat, and diverse survival skills. This was the essence of the organization's reappraisal – armed self-defense from overt general assault, both immediately after the attack and a "second strike," which would be delayed after the initial attack as retribution. The plans for the former were pretty straightforward, whereas the plans for the latter were never quite clear, seemingly on purpose. For example, there was always reference to people being "underground" but nothing concrete – across source material.

As conceived, the Black Legion would be composed of selected citizens between the ages of sixteen and fifty, the men and women being in separate units for reasons that were not provided in detail. All were to engage in two hours of training per week, and once a month there would be practice on a field training site. In addition to this, all male citizens between the ages of sixteen and fifty and all female citizens between the ages of sixteen and thirty (without young children) were mandated to join the Universal Military Training Force. Similar to the state of Israel, in an effort to have as many soldiers as citizens, this force involved at least two hours of military training a month, when individuals would learn how to shoot, dress wounds, and otherwise take care of themselves in a conflict situation. Finally, to prepare RNA members as soon as possible and engage the whole family, there was to be a Junior Black Legion composed of all children between the ages of nine and fifteen. In these units, youths would undergo a less rigorous but largely similar program.

Comparable to the results of the income tax initiative, the outcome of this effort was mixed. On one hand, in line with the reappraisal concept, the creation of the Black Legion addressed one of the core problems confronting African

Americans and one of the main motivations for starting the RNA: the lack of protection that blacks received from the government, especially when it came to pursuing their civil and human rights amid significant and/or violent white resistance. Drawing on the inspiration of and representing the logical continuation of the thinking of Malcolm X, Robert F. Williams, the Deacons for Defense, and the RAM (the last of which accounted for a good number of the organization's recruits), this action simultaneously allowed the individuals associated with the RNA to fulfill one of their most long-standing aspirations, and it gave the organization something concrete on which to focus. Regarding the last point, the creation of the army was much less abstract than nationhood or sovereignty, and it was more immediate than the acquisition of reparations or the five states being pursued for the nation.

On the other hand, the creation of the military put the RNA into a particular category of black nationalist organization – one viewed as aggressive, dangerous, and worthy of state repression beyond surveillance and note taking. Indeed, because of the degree of formalization involved, the creation of the black army made the RNA seem more threatening than the Black Panthers, who, although armed, never went to the extreme of calling their members "soldiers" or their structure an "army." Things got even more complex because the RNA went further than claiming to have an established "aboveground" army. It also claimed to have an "underground" one like that used during the Detroit riot/rebellion, which was prepared to use guerilla tactics throughout the United States, if necessary, burning American cities to the ground (i.e., their second-strike capability). This was connected to the earlier discussion at the founding.

What were the motivations for these actions, and how do they relate back to the subject of social movement (de)mobilization? It is relatively straightforward that the move for RNA taxation had nothing to do with actual state repression that was directed against the dissident organization – again, at least not directly. The need for resources was simply an internal matter exacerbated by an inhospitable but not yet overtly hostile external political environment. It is equally clear that the move to build the Black Legion was directly related to state repression and the inability/unwillingness of U.S. political authorities to protect African Americans from violence emerging from its agents or those within the society who frequently worked on their behalf. This said, it is clear that the creation of this army did not reference anything specifically targeting the RNA. Rather, it referenced the impetus for armed self-defense that came from the longer and broader experience of African Americans with coercive activities directed against them over time as well as the perceived likelihood that something would be directed against them in the future. In so doing, RNA behavior sought to increase trust not only within the organization, showing that it could meet member needs (i.e., life), but also indirectly, demonstrating that it would attempt to serve the needs of the broader black community, which could potentially be drawn to the relevant organization by such an effort.

Interestingly, the formation of the Black Legion did not immediately result in increased overt repressive activity, as one might expect from existing literature. Upon hearing that the RNA would start an army, according to the records, there was no increase in the number of searches or the level of harassment or arrest for raids. There was an increase in the number of police monitoring the RNA, however, and these individuals started logging longer hours. Overt behavior was thus not yet deemed necessary, but covert activity was. The increase in the latter was not observed or perceived by the RNA – at least not from the government or RNA records. Their subsequent nonresponse thus makes sense.

Individuals

The changes within the organization had some interesting implications for the core membership. Actually, many of the dynamics within the institution are revealed in a typical meeting of the period. For example, on June 9, 1968, there was a meeting of the RNA at Imari Obadele's house on Muirland Street, right near the heart of the black community. The usual group members were in attendance, along with some of the important notables from out of town: Imari and Gaidi Obadele, Ray Willis, Ed Bradley, Obaboa Awalo, Queen Mother Moore, Wilbur Gratten, Willie Thomas and his wife, Leroy O'Caster, Lana Mitchell, Brenda Ralston, Lavis Simmons, Elizabeth King, Mae Mallory, Warren Galloway, and Henry "Papa" Wells.

The meeting began with Gaidi Obadele discussing Robert F. Williams and his unwillingness to make a formal statement about his role in the new government. Williams was to send something to this effect soon, but most were not expecting much, if anything, by that point.[3] Although several were disappointed with this news, Queen Mother Moore was especially upset because she argued that this would hurt their chances of securing external support for the RNA. Most of the people whom she had contacted regarding their contributions to the RNA were willing to do so in part because Williams was involved. If they took him out of the picture, it was not clear what would happen, and this caused her much frustration and a few harsh words for Williams.

Continuing to discuss the exiled president, Imari Obadele reiterated Williams's request for resources to be distributed to Tanzania and then discussed an attempt made to get the Tanzanian government to bring forth a resolution to the United Nations regarding the plight of African Americans. The responses were noteworthy. The issue of the Tanzanian initiative was met with skeptical remarks, attendees noting that their own needs could barely be met, let alone doing something for people in another country. The issue of Tanzanian advocacy on behalf of the RNA did not receive any response at all, because it was quickly mentioned that the Tanzanians had not said anything regarding the proposal. It seemed to be lost on everyone that neither the

---

[3] Williams ended up sending something that they could distribute, but it was a general point about the need for the nation, not anything specific about him and his role.

Tanzanians nor the RNA were really in a position to assist the other and that the resource-poor helping the resource-poorer was a pretty sad predicament in which to be.

After a while, conversation moved to what actions the RNA could take to improve their situation. On this topic, there was some discussion about buying one hundred acres of land at Fort Shelby, Mississippi, to start a city and a steel company. Presumably, this would be done to employ members of the RNA while building the city as well as using the steel produced to generate some much-needed cash. While citizens of the RNA would inevitably serve as labor for the company, more immediately, the labor could be procured from students at nearby historically black colleges and universities (HBCUs). It was suggested that the equipment for the factory might come from China or Tanzania, but given the lack of responsiveness from these countries to other RNA outreach efforts, this seemed unlikely.

Thinking out loud about what could be done, the ever-animated Mae Mallory (Robert F. Williams's old colleague) started discussing the idea of setting up African shops all over the country to trade goods to and from "the continent" (i.e., Africa). Imari Obadele, seeking to draw on his writing background and interest in publishing, mentioned that he wanted to start a magazine to assist in getting the RNA's message out more efficiently. Seemingly having heard enough, however, Gaidi Obadele quickly shot all these down, noting that the new nation could not possibly afford such a thing. Chiming in directly on this issue of funding or the lack thereof, Joan Franklin reported that bonds could not be pursued in support of the new nation and that there were a number of problems with going in this direction, including being arrested and charged with fraud. At this point, somewhat disconnected from the rest of the meeting, Betty Shabazz mentioned that insofar as it related to the financial side of the RNA, she was against a welfare state (i.e., the idea that governments would attempt to take care of their citizens as some form of safety net or providing free services). Instead, Shabazz wanted to inspire creativity and productivity in the new nation, not laziness and dependence.

Quiet until this time, Ray Willis returned to the tax bill and highlighted some problems in addition to the ones that Joan Franklin had mentioned. Specifically, he noted that the tax would be a burden on the people because they wouldn't pay taxes to two governments at the same time. Besides that, he continued, the RNA wasn't even established yet to any real degree. Given this context, and the fact that the RNA wanted an army – aboveground and below – as well as other far-reaching objectives, he thought that this presented an impossible situation and believed it best if he resigned from his position.

What is important for the current book is that up to that time, Willis's decision, as well as all the conversation and proposals, clearly had nothing to do with repression. Rather, they reflected the complex perceptions, which were largely negative, of the tactics used by the RNA and the likelihood that using them would not get them where they wanted to go.

With this, the meeting was adjourned, and individuals got into their cars, drove over to Canada (which was minutes away), and had a small social gathering, where the evening continued. Representative of the period, the event ended with a reasonable amount of participation and initiative, but at the same time, it ended with more questions raised than answered as well as more problems put forward than solutions.

Also present during this period was an increasing tension between the two brothers Gaidi and Imari Obadele. Indeed, barely half a year into the new organization, as more issues came up, it seemed that the Obadele brothers more frequently held different opinions. For example, although on the same page with regard to taxation (although Gaidi was a bit more fiscally conservative than his brother), on the issue of the Black Legion, Imari was more favorably disposed than Gaidi. The difference here might simply be one of life experience. Whereas Gaidi already had some interaction with the military and the potential for combat situations, Imari had not. Indeed, Imari noted his longtime commitment to this issue when he wrote,

Octavia [his wife] would remind me that as long as she had known me I had dreamed of a black army to take the South. But the fact was I did understand that to make a nation here – whatever else we might achieve in efforts at preliminary negotiations and diplomacy we would ultimately have to win our land by fighting for it and taking it. (Obadele 1970c, 179)

In contrast, Gaidi Obadele viewed the army and the inevitably of violent conflict in a much different light. As Imari recalled,

Gaidi, as a lawyer, well recognized that the U.S. constitution gave sole power to raise an army in this land to the U.S. Congress, and he cautioned [Legion] officers to stay free of all involvements which in the first year might land [them] in prison or saddle [them] with malicious un-productive prosecution.[4] (Obadele 1970c, 180)

If this was Gaidi's belief at the time of the Black Legion's creation, as one of the leaders of the organization (and de facto president during the relevant period), one wonders how the military policy got headway. One explanation is offered by Gaidi Obadele himself when he maintains that at a crucial point in the organization, the members were influenced by the Cuban example; the writing of the French intellectual and revolutionary Regis Debray; and the military backgrounds of many in the RNA at the time (Obadele 1970c, 20). Indeed, Gaidi seemed to suggest a logic comparable to "if one has a hammer, everything starts looking like a nail" with regard to the approach the RNA selected. His was the superior position (he thought) especially because "the mass of people, even the average worker . . . isn't going to get out here and join some military thing where he might lose his job tomorrow. He might want to.

[4] Other records confirm this as well.

I'm not even too sure how many would want to, but he's not going to do it" (Obadele 1970c, 21–22).

Although the preceding statement is clear and unequivocal, Gaidi's position was not always straightforward. For example, the de facto leader of the RNA felt that he could not influence the direction of the organization if the majority of the membership was predisposed toward a particular type of strategy. Additionally, on the TV show *Firing Line* with William F. Buckley, which took place on November 18, 1968, at one notable moment, Gaidi responded to an inquiry about what could and should be done with white people who wanted to assist his cause by saying that they could die. Although he denounced the more militaristic aspects of the RNA when he reflected about it, he tended to downplay his own participation in such declarations and activities at the time. This is common in retrospective research.

Interventions

The new plans of the RNA had some direct influence on what they actually did.

First, the RNA had to let it be known that they would be engaging in tax collection. Accordingly, memos were sent out to all citizens indicating the intricacies of the new taxation system. This included discussions of payment schedules, mailing addresses, exemptions, and moral and legal responsibilities.

Second, the RNA attempted to raise its army. In many respects, this effort was extremely limited. Part of the issue dealt with whom to recruit. Initially, members of the underground army had lobbied to be placed aboveground via informal discussions and meetings so that they could continue in their duties to defend the black nation. This was not deemed wise by the RNA leadership, however, because of their primary method of training and operation: short-term engagements, concealment, and evasive action and mobility. Additionally, because of their methods (i.e., clandestine-style organization and hit-and-run tactics), the underground army was necessarily small. Such a configuration was not an appropriate method of operation for an aboveground operation necessary for defending individuals from a frontal, military-like assault or wanton viciousness of the kind seen unleashed against fleeing protestors during the civil rights movement, nor was it believed that the conversion from one could be easily made to the other.

With these considerations, it was reasoned that the Black Legion should begin anew. Developing the right training protocols and finding the available recruits, however, was a rather arduous task, and this moved extremely slowly. Another issue dealt with growing awareness of and resistance to the Vietnam War (especially the perception of African American casualty rates) and the increasing discomfort within the black community with the idea of military service regardless of the government for which they would be fighting. In a sense, the last thing an African American probably wanted was yet another military organization seeking war participation – even one that was presumably more closely linked with their interests. By the time the RNA went to OH-B in Brooklyn, therefore, there were a variety of dynamics already at play, which compelled some modifications to the way the dissident organization did things, hurt the organization's morale, limited its actions, and led to a strain that would become evident later. Again, however, none of these issues involved repressive behavior explicitly being directed against the RNA, and thus they were largely driven by internal factors.

Changing Characteristics and Assessing Causes

While OH-B represented a call to action, exactly who was called and what was called for was not especially clear. The RNA had developed a plan though. Essentially, the RNA wanted to engage in what was called "expanding sovereignty." This meant two things: (1) that a position needed to be taken to "avoid or delay, insofar as possible, a military contest in Ocean Hill–Brownsville to decide the question of sovereignty" and (2) that a position needed to be taken where sovereignty would be exercised by the RNA in OH-B "along those limited lines that are most readily available to [the RNA] and to gradually expand this exercise until it is total" (Obadele and Carson 1969, 4). Accordingly, the OH-B effort was viewed as an "independence project" comparable to what the RNA was planning to do in the South, specifically in Mississippi and Alabama. Some even suggested that it should supersede other efforts for at least two years.

Accordingly, at a conference in Detroit on January 18–19, 1968, the RNA met to try to put together some plan of action for OH-B. From this effort, a great many ideas emerged (Obadele and Carson 1969). This included the following:

1. *Defense.* Declaring an "open" city with no arms and no defensive troops, initiating a Domestic Tranquility Patrol to protect the citizenry, and instituting a "top-rate counter espionage section," which would provide information about what was taking place and by whom (Obadele and Carson 1969)
2. *Welfare and communication.* Instituting health and day care facilities and a hospital for residents, a radio station, a TV station, and a newspaper
3. *Politics.* Distributing and flying the flag of the RNA, inviting foreign governments to tour, requesting admission to the United Nations, and organizing foreign aid to assist with the development of the independence project
4. *Economics.* Opening a job referral service, opening a manufacturing and assembling facility, and opening a film and TV production studio and a printing and/or recording facility
5. *Education.* Opening a public school system and an after-school system

There was also some attention given to what might need to be done, for example, defending the open city from "an invasion of paratroopers," "attacks from US forces on RNA installations or citizens," "attacks by white civilian military forces," or an "assault by US [forces] on local government officials, through legal attacks and propaganda." Notice that all forms of repression believed to be relevant are still overt in nature and fairly aggressive, reflecting the dominant approach to reappraisal adopted at the time. Despite the uniqueness of the effort being contemplated, the engagements of the "last war" loomed heavily.

To counter these activities, the RNA, in conjunction with the OH-B black community, would engage in "appropriate self defense measures" and "intense non-cooperation of [the local] population," pressing for a "UN Cease Fire Team" and some coordinated mechanism of communication within OH-B and the outside world. Clearly the nonviolent and defensive approach reflected the Black Legion's underdevelopment and acceptance of the military situation within which the organization found itself. The Black Legion was not ready, and likely never would be ready, to take on U.S. forces directly – as most insurgent efforts. It was questionable that they would be able to consistently and/or effectively patrol as well as protect designated territorial zones of interest. Additionally, there was little to no discussion of the so-called second-strike capability either – admittedly a provocative concept and one that might draw a coercive response.

However, if the RNA were not ready for something they had discussed and something for which they had attempted to prepare, then how would they address all of the other issues on their agenda? As the approach to reappraisal appeared deficient, albeit untested, this also raised some trust issues both within and outside of the organization about what they were actually ready to do (repeatedly among the RNA as well as between the RNA and the Brooklyn community).

Acknowledging the difficulty of pulling off what had been discussed (in terms of cost and human resources), the RNA attempted to develop different ways to get around this. Perhaps one of the most innovative was the "Freedom Corps,"[5] "which [was] the vehicle through which persons of all ages [would give] their services to the various independence projects of the Republic of New Africa" (Republic of New Africa 1969). The basic idea was to use students from HBCUs as the workers to help establish and sustain the OH-B initiative. The RNA had cultivated a relationship of this nature through a series of student conferences sponsored by the RNA's Ministry of the Interior on December 7–8, 1968, in Brooklyn and January 18–19, 1969, in Detroit. The Freedom

---

[5] In 2002, President George Bush created the USA Freedom Corps to coordinate volunteer efforts throughout the United States. He strangely made no reference to the effort put forward by the RNA several decades earlier.

Corps emerged from these discussions with several dozen student groups from different schools ready to volunteer.

As could readily be discerned, the needs were great in OH-B. Accordingly, the RNA advertised for receptionists, office "leg men" (i.e., gophers), typists, stenographers, linguists, writers, artists, math tutors, teacher's aides, custodians, nurse's aides, helpers, maintenance men, seamstresses, teachers, carpenters, plumbers, electricians, doctors, lawyers, dentists, chauffeurs, scientists, nurses, interviewers, clerks, engineers, and cooks (Republic of New Africa 1969). Notably, there was no mention of the need for police officers, military personnel, or individuals who specialized in intelligence gathering or analysis. The RNA was careful not to further incite or unduly provoke U.S. authorities, who, up to that point, had not taken any overt steps to hinder the organization or its efforts. The organization was generally optimistic that with the eyes of the world on OH-B, as long as they stayed within certain parameters of engagement, the U.S. government would do the same – a paradoxical evaluation given their reading of American history but one generally consistent with their idea of going global. They were not making their case directly; however, they expected the media to do this, which they never did – at least not the way they anticipated.

Understanding its institutional weaknesses, the RNA was clearly not trying to accomplish everything on its own. There were even areas where they attempted to collaborate with existing political authorities to advance their objectives, which was paradoxical given the objective of secession and a source of some tension inside the secessionist organization. For example, in another effort resulting from the Detroit conference (within the Education Committee meeting), the RNA tried to partner with existing public schools to get space for an after-school program and offer RNA citizens work as teachers in existing schools. Clearly the RNA benefited from this because through their engagement, they could attend and monitor governing board meetings, use existing schools to hold RNA events, and distribute materials in school mailboxes and/or over the intercom during regular working hours. Several of these efforts turned out to be successful. For example, Junior High School 271 agreed to let the RNA run a program in its school and for one of their citizens to teach a "Nation-Building" class. The OH-B school district governing board also agreed to let the RNA-led Yoruba Academy hold sessions in two of its schools from 3:00 to 5:00 P.M., on a daily basis.

Now, it might seem that seeking collaboration with the existing government was antithetical to the RNA and its objectives as well as potentially threatening to building support within the black community and among members. But the RNA reasoned that they were not yet in a position to challenge U.S. authorities outright and decided to gain access to the relevant population as well as subvert the establishment from within. Once in the "establishment," however, the very government being challenged began to look more legitimate, a point raised on more than one occasion.

Questions aside, one can immediately see the appeal of such an approach and campaign. The educational effort in particular would engage a group of African Americans highly sensitized to the RNA's message. The OH-B effort in general would allow the organization to pitch its ideas to a northern audience in front of the world. In effect, OH-B would be the RNA's "Selma" (i.e., a critical rallying point for African Americans in their struggle), where thought met action and ideas met reality.

The group could definitely use a positive dose of momentum. As noted earlier, things within the RNA were actually starting to get a bit depressing in the organization, as revealed in the preceding meeting, and the excitement established at the founding was somehow being lost in the long meetings, discussion groups and seminars on citizenship and international law, and debates about what is and is not a nation. Something was needed.

Despite some of the positive aspects of OH-B, however, one could also see the negatives of such a campaign (e.g., as exhaustion and some lost commitment began to rear their heads), and this was immediately brought out in the group discussions. These negative concerns are addressed in the following.

Ideas

Once the RNA got involved in the OH-B initiative, it was quickly noted that Brooklyn was not Mississippi (the main target of the RNA). And, the argument continued, if Mississippi and the other four states of the Deep South were the popularly conceived focus of the organization, then it could appear that the RNA was somehow betraying its mission and was erratic or disorganized in its decision making.[6] This position was muted and largely overrun by the Obadeles, especially the increasingly more aggressive Imari. Indeed, the latter had convinced his brother and many of the other members of the governing body that OH-B was the right thing to do and the right time to do it – a perfect agency frame.

As a result of these discussions, some serious shifts occurred in the RNA's approach to its objectives; indeed, in certain respects, it changed them significantly. For example, up until that time, most of the discussion and planning regarding the black nation was focused on the South, albeit almost exclusively undertaken in Detroit and the other consulates. Recall that in *War in America*, the North was viewed as an indefensible, cramped, isolated, and resource-poor location where African Americans were essentially trapped. In this context, the North was largely seen as a departure point where blacks would be initially contacted and later transported to the new nation in the more defendable, expansive, and resource-rich South, where African Americans could live life abundantly. Note here the use of the military-like references, which clearly identified that the RNA was concerned with how (if needed) it would engage

---

[6] I suppose the proper analogy would be the Southern Christian Leadership Conference's taking as its first major initiative a boycott of Woolworths in Harlem or some other city in the North because of employment discrimination.

with U.S. political authorities contentiously. Again, there were interests with repressive action but not that explicitly deployed against the organization at the time.

The crisis in OH-B was not viewed as distinct from the RNA's overall program but as an accelerator to it. Differing from most of the South and even people in places where the RNA was located, the argument went, the residents of OH-B had already revealed themselves to be interested in local black control over a specific territorial jurisdiction controlled by the United States. As one RNA member articulated in the *Michigan Chronicle* in 1969,

Ocean Hill-Brownsville residents insist that local control is essential to end the victimization of their children... and Lindsay's police occupation, which represents the larger white community walking in and overturning local black control whenever it chooses to, proves that real local control by blacks within the U.S. federal system is impossible.

The member continued, "If people in Ocean Hill-Brownsville and anywhere else really want local control, as they insisted they do, the only way to achieve it is outside of the U.S. federal system and as a part of the Republic of New Africa" (23). From this perspective, the residents just needed to be pushed a bit further on the issue of separation and nationhood. If this could be done, this would represent an immense success for the RNA and one that would take place under the gaze of the world's media (Malcolm's dream).

Was the OH-B decision influenced by repression at all? I find no evidence for the argument that repressive behavior employed at the time had anything to do with the shift in organizational focus (i.e., the move to OH-B), at least not in any manner directly involving the RNA. Clearly the heavy-handed police effort of the Lindsay administration to impose a policy on a group of African Americans in Brooklyn factored into the RNA's deliberations, but the coercion was not directed against the dissident organization as explicitly as existing literature would posit.[7] Accordingly, I think it is reasonable to conclude that this decision was largely made independently of repressive action. Equally as important, this decision was also largely independent of those closest to the events involved. At the time, the RNA was located in Manhattan, not Brooklyn. They had no initiatives under way in this part of New York, and none of their members were engaged in the OH-B effort at the outset of the conflict. Indeed, the Manhattan RNA office was largely against the OH-B initiative, viewing it as a distraction from the largely southern-oriented nature of the RNA program.

All this said, there was some repressive activity being directed against the organization, and there was a cluster of activities, a few instances of harassment and arrests, immediately preceding the October decision to go to Brooklyn (Figure 8.1). Additionally, there is some evidence that this repression had an impact on the organization locally in Detroit and not on the OH-B decision,

---

[7] Challengers are not motivated by attacks on those outside of the challenging institution in this work.

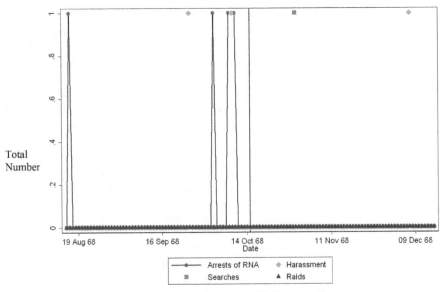

FIGURE 8.1. Repressive behavior around Ocean Hill–Brownsville.

which was viewed as a national RNA project. The complexities of the situation are illustrated in the following example.

On October 9 or 10, 1968, Warren Galloway, Selina Howard, Dorothy Saunders, and Leroy Wilds were traveling from Detroit to New York to assist in the burgeoning OH-B campaign. The four were stopped and arrested en route. At the time, they had numerous weapons concealed in the car. After their arrest, on the next day, members of the RNA Consul in Detroit became convinced that somehow the police were getting information about them, but they were not clear exactly how (i.e., suspicions were aroused and thus covert action was identified). The concern prompted the RNA to search members before organizational meetings, which I maintain diminished trust. After it was discussed that only a few individuals knew about the travel plans of those arrested, one of those identified as being aware of the action (Timothy Chambers) noted that the FBI had come to him and asked if he knew anything about the four RNA members. He did not tell the FBI anything and referred them to his attorney (Gaidi Obadele – as he was instructed to do). Later, on October 21, in response to the earlier repressive activity, the RNA decided that to prevent the disruption of the organization from another stop and arrest of several people at once, members would not travel as a group, or if they did, one member was to be designated as the spokesperson, leaving the rest silent. These activities would further diminish trust as well as complicate mobilization.

This was not the end of the affair. For almost two weeks straight, the organization discussed the arrest at a variety of organizational functions. Differing

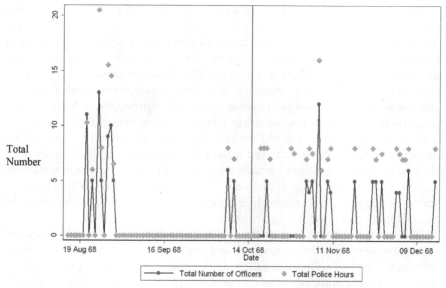

FIGURE 8.2. Additional repressive behavior around Ocean Hill–Brownsville.

from the literature, these discussions were without expressions of fear or anger, but the group nevertheless modified their behavior in various ways because of it. However, and this is an important point, the RNA only modified certain activities regarding organizational security and not their engagement in activism writ large. This is very different from the views in existing literature of the causal process whereby repression is believed to directly influence all of the contentious behavior undertaken by an SMO. In this period (in line with what I earlier identified as "reappraisal"), the group tried to change their methods and to inform the members of this in an effort to offset the perceived negative aftereffects of repressive behavior. No other part of the organization was affected.

What is fascinating about this period is the difference between the subjective perceptions of repression within the organization (i.e., "the feds are out to get us") and the objective reality of actual hours put into observing, monitoring, or disrupting the organization by the authorities – at all levels. For example, while the number of officers on duty was quite variable for most of the pre-OH-B period, right before and for several months after the decision to go to Brooklyn, the trend stabilizes with approximately five officers pulling eight-hour shifts (Figure 8.2). This suggests that the degree of seriousness with which the RNA was monitored had increased and that the structure of the repressive apparatus had also stabilized. Revealing a greater concern with infiltration, although only a couple of references had been made in late October, by December, the topic was raised more consistently in the RNA, although still at a relatively low magnitude and frequency.

As suggested earlier, there were some expressions of fear as well as some expressions of anger immediately preceding the decision to go into Brooklyn. These do not reference repressive behavior specifically; rather, they represent vague, potential threats to members of the RNA (indeed, in one meeting, it was announced that all members traveling on RNA business needed to be escorted by a member of the Black Legion for their protection, just in case). Revealing that the RNA was responsive to these emotional expressions, at least in some minimal sense, there is one situation where it was maintained that by trying some activity, something could be lost. As expected, this was countered by discussing what could be achieved if the RNA tried to do something. Prior to this, there was an "urgency" frame, which noted that the time was fortuitous for the RNA to try to do something. This did not respond to a "negative" frame, as suggested by existing literature, but it does fit the context given the impending decision to go into Brooklyn.

Following the institution of the OH-B campaign, overt manifestations of repression were rare. Only one search and one instance of harassment in Detroit were noted in the two months following the initialization of the project. There was some lagged influence of an earlier event, revealed not in the coding but in the reading of meeting notes. For example, at an RNA meeting on October 30, 1968, at the YMCA Fischer Branch, located at Dexter Avenue and West Grand Boulevard in Detroit, approximately forty people entered after being searched by respective female and male security teams. The meeting opened with the chair, Lavis Simmons, warning everyone not to accuse any other members before they have spoken and heard what they had to say, clearly signaling that there was some tension in the group. He then took the names of those who wanted to speak.

The floor was first turned over to Imari Obadele, who had just returned from Brooklyn. He began with telling everyone that things in OH-B were heating up and that he wanted to go there and stay for an extended period of time, a request that had already been made to the cabinet and appeared to have been approved. The Detroit Consul was already aware of Imari's absence as they had not seen him for some time and they were aware of his being in OH-B, but they did not seem to know of his arrangement with the Cabinet to go there for a longer time. Following some brief discussion, Imari outlined what was going on in OH-B and noted that the New York Consul was going to try to grow. Toward this end, there was the (by now) commonplace solicitation for funds.

Imari then switched gears, noting that an upcoming fashion show, scheduled for November 17, would be pushed back a week, and he then requested some assistance with housing out-of-town guests who were coming to Detroit for a meeting. Returning to less local RNA business and a topic of earlier discussion, he mentioned that he had sent literature to unspecified Tanzanians and that they appeared to be interested in the organization, suggesting that someone would come to visit in early 1969. Standing up in the middle of Imari's presentation, Lavis Simmons made a heartfelt request that additional funds be collected for taxes at about $2.00 a week more "for the good of the country." Another small collection was made.

There were then some random personal issues brought up, which had emerged as an interesting practice. Next to speak was Selina Howard, who informed the group that because of a nervous condition she had recently developed, she would need to leave the RNA. Her activities in the organization would have to be delegated to others. Timothy Chambers, earlier accused of being an informant by Daniel Aldridge, said that he was looking for Daniel to get a formal apology and retraction. He also mentioned that he would beat him up when he saw him. The group was informed via some member that Mrs. Thomas Lockett was in need of some funds as well. She had asked some of the "sisters" for some help but as yet had not heard anything from anyone. Another small collection was made.

At this point, the meeting ended, and immediately Imari asked Timothy Chambers to chat for a minute, motioning to Brother Calvin (an RNA security guard) to accompany them. Once together, Imari asked Timothy where the receipts were for the land purchases that had been made for the RNA. Timothy said that he had one but had lost the other, walking away slowly. Anderson Howard, who had come over after Timothy left, told Imari that this was not true and that he had seen them when he was over at Timothy's house the other day. Upon hearing this, Imari called Timothy over and told him to produce both the receipts. Timothy then "rushed from the building." A few days later, in the presence of several Black Legion members, Imari gave Timothy until November 8, 1968, to address the retraction of the Daniel Aldridge accusation issue as well as to produce the land receipts. This was not followed up in the records.

In line with the contentious nature of the decision to go to OH-B and continued local difficulties, after resources and personnel were moved toward Brooklyn, there were numerous emotions expressed within organizational meetings. Directly related to the book's argument, these expressions generally concerned local-level vulnerabilities within the organization or personal squabbles and not state repression – again, at least, not directly. There were also a few expressions of fear, but these concerned the organization's capacity to engage in the efforts with which it was involved.

As expected, a few times, framing efforts were put forward to negatively spin the situation. For example, within a week of the OH-B decision, someone argued that the RNA was just getting started and that shifting focus at this early date might hinder development in other areas. This was immediately followed, not by an "urgency" frame, as suggested by the literature, where the importance of taking action was put forward, but by an "agency" frame, in which it was maintained that OH-B was viewed as the perfect opportunity for the RNA to press its interests forward and, in fact, that the RNA was the perfect organization to do this. This opportunity was not believed to exist indefinitely, however. In December, there was another use of an agency frame, which largely mirrored the earlier one regarding the appropriateness of the RNA taking. Following this, there were two negative frames employed within the group: perverse-effects (i.e., that anything done would likely make the situation worse) and futility (i.e., it does not matter what we do, it will not likely work). This emerged from having attempted to engage in a campaign (OH-B) but not being able to do so in a thorough and appropriate manner.

Institutions and Individuals

Following these dynamics, it should come as no surprise that over time, the OH-B independence project proved to be something of a strain for the RNA and became a situation of divisiveness for the core members of the organization as well as for the broader membership. For instance, the impetus of the project largely came from Imari Obadele, with some initial support from Gaidi and some support from other RNA members in different parts of the country. For many, however (largely based in the Manhattan Consulate), this effort represented the last straw in a series of poor decisions that prompted them to depart, be forced out of the Republic, or decrease their involvement.

At the beginning of the RNA's OH-B initiative, the organization established a National Steering Committee for the Freedom Corps, responsible directly to its president and the cabinet. The committee was divided into five components, each with its own elected leader:

1. The Council for Political Policy and Action under the leadership of philosophy professor Albert Mosley of Howard University as chairman and Rochelle Kendricks of New York
2. The Council for Welfare and Communications Policy and Action under the leadership of Kwame Lateef (formerly Richard Northcross) of Pontiac, Michigan, along with Neville Parker (Cornell University) and Amani Lateef (formerly Sheryl Northcross) of Pontiac as co–vice chairpersons
3. The Council for Economic Policy and Action under the leadership of John David of Toledo, Ohio, as chairman and Mjuzi Mweusi (formerly John Soaries) of Brooklyn as vice chairman and Dzaona Yaa Asantewa (formerly Barbara Hampton) of Howard University as recorder
4. The Council for Economic Policy and Action under the leadership of Dafina Sheshe (formerly Rosemary Minyard) of New York University as chairperson, Sister Bolade Adezbalola (formerly Denise Harbour) of Brooklyn as vice chairperson, and Mareia Adams, also of New York University, as recorder

The fifth component, the Council for Defense Policy and Action, did not immediately choose members, and there was no follow-up in the archival material consulted for this research.

Despite the structure identified previously, it is clear that, in practice, there was a lack of general awareness regarding what was being done in different parts of the RNA. For example, on October 15, 1968, Selina Howard and another member named Tombura returned from New York to Detroit and had a meeting with Elizabeth King, Lavis Simmons, Dorothy Saunders, Hazel Gibbs, Brenda Ralston, and someone named Kenyatta. As noted, those in attendance were completely shocked by what Selina and Tombura had seen in OH-B: inflammatory literature written by Imari Obadele, seemingly endorsed by the RNA but actually all new to them. Specifically, there were four pamphlets: one maintaining that the United Nations, Africans, and African Americans agreed to help the RNA in OH-B; one declaring that OH-B was the first "liberated territory" for the Republic; one declaring the seriousness of the endeavor; and another declaring that the Black Legion would drive out the police. None of the individuals at the meeting was sure what to make of what she had heard, but Charles Moore, who was head of the New York Consulate, said "he was through" and "didn't want anything more to do with any of them in the RNA" (Michigan State Police 1968, 2).

Upon learning what was taking place, Gaidi Obadele "blew his top." Clearly revealing that this represented a significant deviation from the strategy put forward to avoid U.S. persecution, Gaidi asked Imari if he had "lost his mind" and why he had used his name to sign the letter instead of his own. When confronted with this, all Imari said was that he did not think that what he wrote was inflammatory, except the part about throwing out the police. He went on to say that he was needed in New York and that Lito Durley would replace him as minister of information for the RNA so that Imari would be freed up to focus full-time on OH-B. Additionally, undisturbed by the discovery and discussion, Imari then made a plea for financial support (noting that the office cost $200), and also seemingly undisturbed by the day's events, a small collection was again taken up. Shortly after the request, the meeting ended, and there was no further discussion.

About a week later, on October 23, things came to a head once more when Imari maintained that he was too far from the "scene" in Detroit and wanted to set up an RNA office in New York permanently. When asked about how this could be afforded, he said that "every member could be assessed so much every month to pay for said office" (Michigan State Police 1968). At this point, there was some serious disagreement. Several of the members asked if the "small group (in Detroit) were being taxed too much." Henry "Papa" Wells pointedly told Obadele that he was not right to do what he was trying to do and went on to argue that most of them were poor and "could not afford any more taxation." Imari's response was emphatic but persistent. He said that while times were tough, "now is the fertile time" for New York (another agency frame). To Obadele, OH-B was ready for separation, and if the RNA failed there, then they could just "wrap it up because no one would touch them with a ten foot pole" (Detroit Police Department 1968). He went on to say that OH-B would not be a Detroit-only operation and that the other consuls would be asked to support the effort, but he wanted to know from Detroit first. Yielding somewhat and calming down from the earlier, heated interaction, the Detroit

Consulate inevitably said that they would support the project to the best of their abilities. However, Gaidi Obadele was not present, indicating that the action had not received all of the support from the powers that be.

Although the OH-B project survived this early test, its implementation still provoked problems for the RNA and moved to even greater divisiveness. For example, the Council of Political Policy and Action met in February to evaluate the OH-B project. Shortly thereafter, they sent a letter to the national office (specifically to Gaidi and Imari Obadele as well as to Sonny Carson, one of the local activists in Brooklyn most committed to the effort). The letter itself was quite critical of what was being done or rather not being done. As they stated,

the Council of Political Policy and Action, composed of Bros. Gratton, Mosley, Harris and Sister Kendrick met in New York on February 22, 1969 . . . The Council . . . questions the national priority which has been set up by the government body because we feel the Republic of New Africa has not developed resources to achieve them. We feel there should be a re-orientation of our efforts in order to create the kinds of bases that we need in order to achieve national objectives. Re-orientation should specifically deal with the creation of strong consulates. We believe that it is the lack of strong consulates that is the cause of our not realizing our national objectives [in] Ocean Hill-Brownsville. A further reason for the non-attainment of the national priorities is due to non-functioning of certain national cabinet members in carrying out their duties. The Council of Political Policy feels the national priority as set forth in terms of the separatist vote, the concept of limited sovereignty and all the attendant proposals stemming therefrom are premature when compared with the level of development in the community and the consulates to which they apply . . . The limited functioning of a national Freedom Corps as a first line cadre, the deterioration or failure to build a functioning Black Legion to support the Independence Project in Ocean Hill-Brownsville, the wide gap between the coordination between cabinet level and consulate level activities, and the lack of financial support for Ocean Hill-Brownsville Independence Project have all contributed to the lack of progress of the project. This failure in key areas leads us to the point to question the concept of prisoner exchange between the Liberation Front of Viet Nam and the Republic of New Africa and to consider it merely another unreality. (Republic of New Africa – Council of Political Policy and Action 1969)

Sensing the seriousness of the critique and the urgency of the situation, the five-page response to the letter from none other than Imari Obadele was made within a week. This response was no less detailed or critical than the letter received, and as Imari was one of the leading proponents (if not the leading proponent) of the effort, the content was quite protective of the general effort as well. He begins,

I am greatly disappointed to have received a letter of this sort which is so grossly deficient in constructive specifics and which indicates that an entire special meeting of leading Freedom Corps personnel, attended by a National Minister was spent in so fruitless an activity when the rest of the Government is depending on the Council for Political Policy and Action to accomplish certain tasks. (Republic of New Africa 1969, 4)

In the letter, Imari clarified the structure of the council, noting that all council members were not present at the meeting discussed in the letter and that Brother Grattan as a national minister had a "superior position" over all others. Obadele clarified what the role of the council was supposed to be, noting that the council was not to criticize the government but to come up with the tasks necessary to make OH-B a success. As he continued, complaints could have been lodged, but not in the council's submission. He identified which councils were functioning properly in his opinion, that is, the Council for Defense Policy and Action under the leadership of Brother Odinga and the Council for Welfare mentioned earlier. Imari not only discussed matters of which the council was readily aware but also some of which it was not, for example, the progress of recruitment into the Freedom Corps and the replacement of the chairperson of the Council for Economics (Dafina Sheshe was going to replace Fred Chandler, who was going to study at the University of Pennsylvania). He explained that the description of the activity of other ministers, whom he mostly defended, as "non-functioning" was inaccurate because they were active but just not in ways obvious to the council. As for the activity of the consulates relevant to the nationalist objective, Imari went on to clarify the structure of the government:

With respect to the Consulates it must be understood that no Consulate in the Republic of New Africa has any reason for existing at this point [except] to promote and achieve national objectives. At this point that is the law. The primary national objective of the government is to free the subjugated territory of the Republic of New Africa. Thus, the major purpose of every Consulate does so in order to support the Independence Projects (i.e., OH-B and Mississippi). Therefore a Consul must understand and well perform a two-sided program: he or she must do those things that are necessary to win citizens and strengthen those who are already in the fold but he or she must also use his or her ingenuity to bring the maximum resources of the Consulate to the services of the Independence Projects.[8] (Obadele 1969, 4)

Part of the forcefulness of Imari's response was due to the fact that the council identified the lack of support that the RNA was receiving as something of a sore point. On January 28 (a month before the submission of the council's report), Imari himself had indicated in a letter to the general membership that as of that date,

most surprisingly, only three Consulates – Washington, D.C., Cleveland and Chicago – have forwarded their tax money (Detroit had already contributed $100.00 to the Ocean Hill-Brownsville project). Worse, *no* Consulate had, as of this writing, forwarded its land money (Detroit had put up over five hundred dollars earlier, which has already been used in the Mississippi Land Project).

---

[8] He then fired the leaders of the council (Mosley and Kendrick) and hoped that they understood that this was best for the RNA. He also expressed his hope that they would stay on as regular members of the council in a nonleadership position. It is unclear if they did, but it was unlikely.

This letter is to urge you to make every effort to forward both the tax and land money by Friday if Possible, but no later than Sunday. There are details of the Mississippi Independence Project which cannot be revealed at this time; but it is crucial to the Republic's success that we have several thousand dollars cash right away. *Later* is not good enough! We are calling on you and the citizens in your Consulate to make a sacrificial effort now if you are really devoted to Revolution. Please let Obaboa know exactly what he may expect from you and when... I can only repeat that the need for this money – particularly, the land money – is immediate and *crucial*.

For Success of the Revolution,
Brother Imari
Minister of the Interior

Imari and the other leaders of the government were well aware of how poorly the RNA project was being supported and that there were quite a few free-riders at the time, for all of its projects were suffering a similar fate. It probably only made it more frustrating to have others raise the issue. The lack of openness to criticism, however, did nothing to shore up trustworthiness within the organization. Indeed, it began to have the opposite effect.

Interventions

With most of the focus and energy of the RNA moving toward Brooklyn, exactly what the RNA in Detroit did on a day-to-day basis changed. For example, as noted later, the sheer number of meetings decreased after the OH-B decision. Interestingly, however, the sheer number of attendees (Figure 8.3) and topics per meeting (Figure 8.4) increased significantly as the group attempted to work through everything that was happening to and among them at the same time. With fewer meetings, more business was addressed in each meeting and more individuals showed up to see what was taking place. There were still some collective actions put forth (e.g., in early November, as can be seen in Figure 8.5), but these were fewer than what had been seen during the period before the OH-B decision.

What is also noteworthy during the post-OH-B period is that there was a shift in internal security. With Imari Obadele in Brooklyn, Gaidi Obadele increasingly absent, and no one else yet stepping into the vacuum, perceptions of organizational vulnerabilities among the remaining members seemingly increased and trust seemed to diminish. This manifested itself in numerous ways. For example, security for the consul had been changed from Harold Jackson to Donald Jackson to Andrew Hayes over the course of months, as the need for improvements and availability of the members shifted. During one RNA meeting toward the end of the period under investigation here, Mwesi Chui was going to conduct a study of present security measures throughout the RNA in general but in Detroit in particular.[9]

---

[9] Chui never got to this because of other duties and needs arising, but it is informative that he saw the necessity for such a thing.

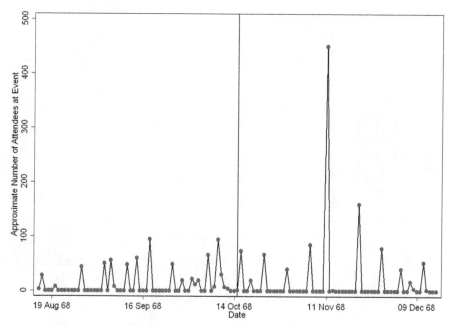

FIGURE 8.3. Attendees of RNA events around Ocean Hill–Brownsville.

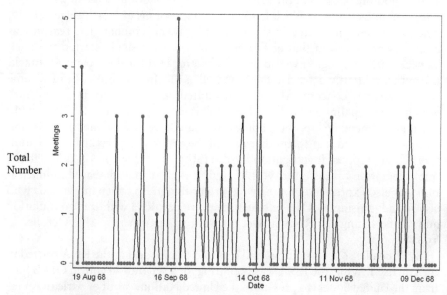

FIGURE 8.4. RNA meetings around Ocean Hill–Brownsville.

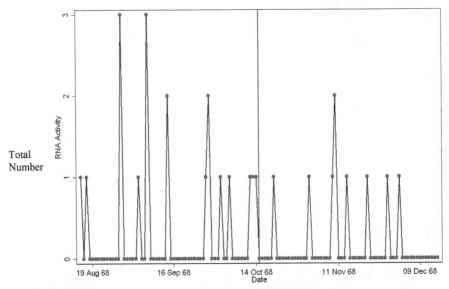

FIGURE 8.5. RNA activity around Ocean Hill–Brownsville.

At the same time, there was also increased discussion of Black Legion preparation or the lack thereof. This normally involved a plea to have individuals
attend shooting sessions at the Frederick Douglass Shooting Club at 2217 Puritan Street in Detroit and Black Legion training sessions at Northwestern Field,
where they were instructed in shooting and physical combat. The reason was
clear. It was perceived that as the organization increasingly started to "stick
its neck out," the Legion would need to be prepared for the inevitable attack.
In another militarily defensive move as well as an effort to crowd-source some
of their security concerns, the RNA instituted an "Inner-City Defense Unit"
with district captains and defined zones. This was done so that the RNA could
defend the "membership, their homes, and families – in case the Black Legion
was mobilized and sent to another part of the country to partake in some military action" (Special Investigation Bureau [SIB], August 6, 1968). Although the
implementation of this effort was limited, it is clear that increased militariza-
tion was also expressed in a somewhat interesting move, when individuals who
secured advertising in RNA publications were provided with free ammunition
and a rifle (citing the RNA in Detroit Police Department – SIB, October 4,
1968).

By December 6, 1968, things had changed a great deal as the RNA started to
turn on itself. While the RNA was preparing for a separation vote in OH-B (i.e.,
from the United States) to present to the United Nations proof of African American dissatisfaction (the effort was officially cancelled the following summer),
the Detroit Consul was also preparing for a "People's Trial" for Elizabeth King,
who was suspected of "passing information" to the police, the culmination

of rising concerns about infiltration. Mildred Kohlmeyer had just recently been cleared of similar charges. While the national effort pushed forward, the local effort in Detroit began to feel the strain of sustained mobilization, frustration with absent leadership, and seemingly no progress on the organization's main objectives, leading to exhaustion, lost commitment, and some departing members.

What was especially interesting about this situation was that this took place on the heels of perhaps the biggest media coverage that the organization had received up until that time. On November 18, 1968, Gaidi Obadele (with guards at either side in full Black Legion regalia) was interviewed by William F. Buckley on his TV show *Firing Line*. In certain respects, the event was a success. Gaidi had made it onto one of the most successful shows of the period and had discussed the objectives of the RNA on national television. In other respects, however, the event did not go well. When confronted about his plans, Gaidi barely responded, which although probably the right thing to do tactically so as not to reveal too much was not the right thing to do on a prime-time television program, leaving the leader of the black nation sitting there speechless. Signifying the continuing difference of opinion between Gaidi and Imari Obadele, despite the high-profile venue, there was absolutely no mention of OH-B or the efforts being undertaken there. Needless to say, this did not reflect well on the RNA, its objectives, or its tactics. Indeed, it well represented the difficulties the RNA faced in this period, when even potentially good things turned sour.

Summary

Within this chapter, I have examined the RNA's first major campaign: their effort to convince as well as facilitate the secession of Ocean Hill–Brownsville, Brooklyn, after a dispute emerged about local political control over the educational system. I have attempted to gauge the reason for the effort as well as the aftereffects of this decision on the individuals associated with the organization, on the structure of the RNA, on the ideas espoused within the SMO, and on the interventions applied by them to reach the desired goal. As found, the decision to go to Brooklyn can be exclusively laid at the feet of the RNA. Several members within the organization, led by Imari Obadele, saw the developments in OH-B as an extremely important opportunity for the RNA to advance its agenda. Prior to the campaign, there was little to no overt repressive behavior, and suspicion of infiltration and surveillance was limited.

After the decision to go had been made, engaging with OH-B led to some important tensions within the RNA (setting the seeds for divisiveness and factionalization at different levels and in different ways). For example, those geographically proximate to the activities in question (i.e., those in the Manhattan Consulate) felt that the effort was premature and potentially foolish. In addition, those in Detroit felt increasing pressure to support the effort as it became clear that they served as the financial backbone of the organization. Finally, some individuals throughout the RNA began to criticize the effort and to reflect about whether the emphasis on the northern city detracted from the RNA's general message and southern orientation. All of this tended to diminish trust in the organizational vision and the tactics selected to get there. Indeed, at a few moments, the disagreements got somewhat heated, putting two of the more important leaders of the organization (Imari and Gaidi Obadele) increasingly on opposite sides. Reappraisal was not believed to be an issue at this time, as most discussion and preparation had involved overt confrontation with U.S. political authorities, which, in the OH-B case, was downplayed and explicitly avoided. Problems with reappraisal began to reveal themselves, however, because it was becoming apparent that although overt repressive action was a focal point for the dissident challenger, there was growing concern about covert activity.

9

New Bethel and the End of the Beginning

As the RNA approached its first year of existence (March 29–31, 1969), members attempted to celebrate their achievements as well as deal with some administrative business at the second National Legislative Convention.[1] The event was to be held at New Bethel Baptist Church in Detroit, the church of C. L. Franklin, who had opened his doors to his old associates. As you may recall, New Bethel Baptist had earlier served as an important locale for the individuals associated with the RNA as well as the place where the opening ceremony of the Republic was held. There had not been much connection since that time.

In preparation for the scheduled events, there was much to be done, and distinct agendas were brought to the meeting by the different attendees as they attempted to repair and strengthen the struggling SMO. For example, there was still tension about what to do with the Ocean Hill–Brownsville initiative, which had largely fallen to the pressures discussed in the last chapter. In addition, however, other issues were emerging (e.g., how the RNA could continually fund itself, how African Americans could be better informed about the RNA, and what should be done in the South).

Despite the importance of these issues, everything would be overshadowed by what became known as the New Bethel Incident: a hostile and violent exchange between the Detroit Police Department and RNA members at Franklin's church during the anniversary, where a deadly shootout and subsequent raid, mass arrest, and interrogation of all attendees occurred. The event influenced the RNA members who were in the church, but it also had reverberations that were felt nationwide throughout the organization, impacting ideas and activities pursued by the RNA and some of the aspirations and activities of those unaffiliated with the dissidents. In a clear instance of "backlash,"

[1] Recall that the first was held at the founding.

with overt repression leading to more, not fewer, individuals rallying to the RNA, the New Bethel Incident brought together assorted individuals throughout Detroit and the United States to focus on the RNA for a while and even to support them in numerous cases, but for very different reasons and at varying levels of engagement. With this incident, the RNA finally had its "Selma" (its dramatic and catalytic event that would serve as a focus for mobilization), but the event was not quite what members thought it would be; in part, this was because the event exacerbated some internal tensions that existed within the organization. Although strengthened in several ways from the incident, overall the SMO was severely damaged in terms of its general approach to reappraisal and decreased trust, beginning a downward spiral from which it would not be able to return.

Prior to New Bethel

Survival and continued existence are definitely a measure of success in social movements. In early 1968, a group of African Americans had boldly stated that they wished to separate from the United States of America, and toward this end, they went about drafting a constitution, electing officials, setting up a government, holding meetings, giving speeches, hosting conferences and workshops, establishing and training a military, and trying to purchase land as well as distributing food, clothing, and an alternative view of political life in the United States. This said, as the first year of the organization came to a close, it became clearer for those in the RNA that the organization was beset with a number of problems mostly of their own design and generally not related to repression (as typically concerned), but this would soon change.

The previous year diminished trust in the RNA because not only had there been no significant movement made toward the originally stated objectives of the organization but it appeared that they were moving in a different direction entirely, one not desired by many of the members. Related to this, there were issues regarding who was selected to lead the RNA as opposed to who actually seemed to lead the organization, and there were issues on what the major emphasis of the group should be, which pulled the RNA in different directions. The period before the New Bethel Incident thus presented numerous troubles for the RNA, and they attempted to deal with them to the best of their abilities. As earlier, we discuss different aspects of the SMO in turn.

Ideas

Part of the difficulty with the RNA during this period was that it became a victim of its own ambitiousness. Established at the first National Legislative Convention in May 1968, it was determined that by October 30, the RNA should have accomplished a great deal (Republic of New Africa 1968a). This deadline, however, was repeatedly pushed back because the institution was behind and they were trying to catch up.

Specifically, there were five broad areas in which the RNA was supposed to make progress. In "Finance and Commercial Industrial Development," the Republic wanted to establish book-, record-, and clothing-producing facilities; collect income taxes from approximately four thousand citizens; issue stamps; and manage a $500,000 certificate program. The RNA had only collected taxes from a fraction of the desired population (approximately several hundred were on the citizenship rolls). In "Culture," the RNA leadership wished to establish a magazine as well as a theatrical group. The former was printed inconsistently and the latter did not yet exist. Regarding "Information," the RNA wished to open a printing office in Los Angeles, where they had a connection, and put forward enough literature regarding recruitment to support such efforts. Neither was successful, but the latter had progressed a great deal, with at least some flyers and announcements being distributed to consulates throughout the United States. In the area of "Justice," the RNA wanted to be able to defend its citizens and establish local "tribunals" to deal with "enemies" of the black state and/or its citizens. Neither was fully functional. Finally, regarding the category of "Defense" (related to the last item), the RNA wanted to establish and maintain a full-time army for adults and youth. The plan was to involve the full citizenry (of the RNA) in a Universal Military Training program, which could serve as a reserve for the new nation. The adult army had been established, but it was small and training was inconsistent; the junior army was in development; and the Universal program was far behind the desired stage of development.

In addition to these five general areas, of the four original pillars of the RNA, none had been significantly developed: (1) establishing a government, (2) obtaining reparations, (3) holding a plebiscite, and (4) obtaining land for the nation. For example, a national government existed, but it was viewed as "provisional," that is, temporary, until a greater number of African Americans participated. A plebiscite was held, but only a small one in Ocean Hill–Brownsville on March 21, after approximately two weeks' notification and with some limited interference from the police that resulted in low turnout (with several hundred). Exact totals from this effort were unclear, but with this act, ten representatives were sent to the Second National Legislative meeting from this community, and it was believed that there was a relatively clear mandate among their constituents that separation from the United States was desired. This was a far cry from a national plebiscite or even a plebiscite within the cities that had RNA consuls, but it was something. Finally, although there was some small land purchased by the RNA in Mississippi, it was not clear to most members exactly where this land was, how much there was, and when citizens could move there.

All of this caused some serious doubt within the organization about the path selected, and it seems reasonable to conclude in this situation that trust began to waiver. One saw this repeatedly in the questions and comments emerging at RNA functions.

Institutions

During the two-month period before New Bethel, the most important issue confronting the RNA was the acquisition of resources. At almost every meeting, there was a discussion about what needed to be done and how nothing could be achieved without some assistance from the citizens of the Republic. The discussion is interesting because increasingly, there was less conversation about the black community writ large, and the focus was squarely on those already in the SMO. In addition, the response to everything that arose (e.g., requests for rent money, a plane ticket, or paper) inevitably seemed to result in a request to raise tax money from the citizenry, initially from the people present at RNA events and consistently from those in Detroit.

For example, on December 19, 1968, after a long discussion of who was *not* in attendance and why, Imari Obadele began talking about the Ocean Hill–Brownsville petition drive and how important it was (again). This effort was to make the community specifically aware of the initiative to pull Ocean Hill–Brownsville out of the United States, generally aware of the RNA effort to secede as well as get some sense of existing support for such actions. Related to this, Imari started talking about how the nature of the conflict between the United States and the RNA was all encompassing, noting that citizens had to sacrifice for the struggle. In fact, in one somewhat flip and sexist comment, he maintained that all the female members should donate their diamonds. When the women laughed at what they believed to be an obvious joke, Imari became angry and chastised them for not being serious revolutionaries. This resulted in several rounds of back and forth as each side attempted to reveal their commitment to the struggle.

On February 6, 1969, right after Dorothy Saunders started the meeting and Brenda Ralston read the minutes from the last one, John Saulsberry (the meeting chair) asked for a tax collection and payment of dues, rent, and so forth. This request was followed by Wesley Steele (of the Finance Committee) mentioning that the organization only had $54 in the bank and that Imari Obadele (not at the meeting) had last week requested every member pay $250 for their land certificates. The dramatic difference between desire and actuality was not discussed. On February 13, it was revealed that John Davis paid $150 for a flight to Ocean Hill–Brownsville on his credit card. The group present at the meeting determined that this should be reimbursed, and although they suggested that the amount should come out of the RNA bank account, they still needed some more money, and thus a collection was taken (yielding $6); this would be repeated every week until Davis was paid back. In a telling moment, Davis stood up and mentioned that he was not really concerned with the $150 but was concerned with the ability of the RNA to pay off the next trip as well as the one after that. This question went unanswered.

Finally, on March 13, 1969, John Saulsberry (again serving as meeting chairperson) noted that the Masonic Hall for the first anniversary convention was going to cost $275 for three days and they had not yet put down a deposit (the event was two weeks away). As with everything else, a collection was initiated for the hall, dues, rent, Black Legion travel, and the RNA paper. The venue was later changed when the money could not be raised and C. L. Franklin offered the RNA a bargain for old times' sake.

Over time, the willingness of the members to acquiesce to repeated demands for financial support diminished. For example, on January 22, 1969, Kwame Lateef (slave name Richard Northcross) noted that there was a February 21 program at the Olympia Stadium for Malcolm X Day and that he wanted some ideas about what should be on the program as well as how it could be paid for. There were no suggestions and no response. Later in the meeting, Lito Durley talked about the printing of the *New African* paper, noting that it was moving along. He then asked about financing of the printing costs. Again, there was no response. A third solicitation within the same meeting arose after it was reported that the Louisiana Consul was stranded in Detroit when the car they were using broke down. At this point, there was a collection, which generated $27.50, to assist the counsel with getting home.

A slightly more contentious situation emerged on January 16, 1968. At this meeting, the minutes were read from the previous week and a collection of $28 was taken up. John Saulsberry (chairperson) then inquired about contributions to the Malcolm X land certificates. This caused something of an uproar as many of those in attendance asked why they should invest in another certificate when they had not received the first, which had been promised for months. Saulsberry then proceeded to lecture the group on how important the land was, but to no avail: the membership had seemingly had enough.

After this point, the tax extraction issue began to be raised more directly and more consistently. For example, some members openly began to speculate that it was not fair to keep asking the individuals who showed up at the meetings for more money. Essentially, the small cohort in Detroit, who seemed to be attending meetings the most consistently of any in the RNA, repeatedly became responsible for subsidizing all other parts of the government. While committed to the RNA and what it was trying to do, it was not believed that the burden of the new nation should be concentrated on such a small group of people.

This discussion is especially interesting given my concerns. Clearly I do not attribute any of these difficulties to state repression, again not directly. It is revealed in some of the records that U.S. political authorities contacted banks, employers, and utility companies in an attempt to interfere with the livelihoods and lives of RNA members by getting them to raise fees, fire them, or withdraw leases (indeed there is some evidence of this within the records). I do not find anyone complaining about how expensive things had become (i.e., as in rates had changed), however, and I do not hear of people arguing that they lost their jobs (in mass numbers) or that they could not find work. Yes, many members of the RNA maintained regular jobs as they were attempting to secede. This is part of where the complexity enters. I do not find anyone whom the government was hindering financially. What I do find, however, are people complaining that they had unpaid expenses (i.e., rent, airline tickets, and doctor bills), presumably because of what they felt they gave over to the RNA. Here the cost of doing (revolutionary) business had turned into the business of surviving the costs of doing (revolutionary) business under seemingly overt neglect by the RNA and covert surveillance by the United States.[2]

At the same time, there was the issue of the relative importance of how the RNA should be structured, that is, the issue of local consuls versus the RNA's national government – another point of divisiveness and exhaustion. In the pre–New Bethel Incident period, nothing revealed this more than the Ocean Hill–Brownsville effort. For example, preparing for a meeting in late March 1968, members of the Manhattan Consul (i.e., Stephen Brown, Elvira Dirton, Bill Fitch, Donald Gulston, Calvin Henderson, Willard Kelly, Rochel Kendrick, Diana Nilaja, Khadeja Nilaja, Alfred Thompson, Thomas Turner, and Mercedes Edwards) discussed among themselves and Minister of Justice Joan Franklin what they thought about the Ocean Hill–Brownsville initiative. At this meeting, openly breaking with the official RNA position and the dominant position within the cabinet, Franklin was quite critical, stating that the effort "was a project that was gone into without a lot of thought on the National level" (Radical Information Project 1969).

She went on to say that the effort never really was on the agenda. In fact, She maintained that Imari Obadele was supposed to go to Ocean Hill–Brownsville and investigate the situation, seeing if it was something that the RNA should get involved with. What emerged from this effort, however, was Imari taking it upon himself to start working with another RNA member (minister of education Herman Ferguson) without any consultation with the rest of the leadership. Imari then went on to convince the others of what he thought should be done. Joan noted that "as far as she's concerned Ocean Hill Brownsville doesn't make any [difference] one way or the other, but [the RNA] could be doing something worthwhile" (Radical Information Project 1969). This was a major criticism from one of the core members of the RNA, and it was a major limitation that the nearest RNA consulate to Ocean Hill–Brownsville did not share enthusiasm about or engagement with the project. Indeed, they were actually quite critical as well.

---

[2] Of course, being aware of government action that results in bill collectors being called, extension of credit being denied, and related matters (revealed in some of the records but inconsistently) is different from such actors being undertaken and some actors suffering from them. Finances were being extended, and thus this has nothing to do with repression. Rent had to be paid, bus tickets purchased, and so on. One's ability to pay for these items is subject to government influence. Given available records, I am hesitant to evaluate these relationships. I do not mean to suggest that government interference of the type mentioned here did not play a role in SMO survival. I simply suggest that I am not able to evaluate this claim as rigorously as I can others. This is clearly a limitation but one of which I am aware.

Later, on the same day as the Joan Franklin conversation, the Manhattan Consulate busily tried to work the backrooms prior to the anniversary meeting in Detroit, hoping to "figure out a way [they] could show the people that the Ocean Hill-Brownsville project was a [waste] of time" (Radical Information Project 1969). Ultimately convinced that they could not be effective at swaying opinion, they didn't attend specific sessions of the meeting prior to New Bethel, feeling they would involve yet more one-sided conversations about what Imari Obadele and Herman Ferguson wanted to do in New York (a relatively clear indication of perceived organizational rigidity – another internal problem confronting the RNA).

As discussed earlier, it makes sense that the tensions within the RNA around Ocean Hill–Brownsville would fall along geographic lines. Given the lack of authority as well as independence of local consuls built into the organization, it is logical that if some initiative were to be taken within one's domain by the RNA national government, the relevant local members would feel ignored and possibly offended by the imposition from the top. Anyone looking at the structure of the RNA would have clearly seen the bias toward the national government and that the existing structure favored the policy the national government had chosen. As conceived in the founding documents, local consulates were to be supportive of the national government in every manner. The irony of the whole situation was clearly missed, however. The RNA attempted to capitalize on the local initiatives within Brooklyn by stifling the initiatives of the Manhattan Consulate as well as neglecting the local difficulties in the Detroit Consulate.

Again, I do not attribute any of these interpersonal and structural difficulties to repression. Rather, it seems clear that they emerged from distinct opinions maintained by individuals in the RNA about what should be done and by whom. Strong-willed individuals put on a path were inevitably going to butt up against one another. The history of GOAL, the Freedom Now Party, and the Malcolm X Society revealed that much. Additionally, the departure of the Cleages and Franklins spoke to this point quite clearly.

Individuals

From the records, there is an indication of personal tensions within the organization, again largely not connected with overt or covert repressive action but regarding differences in opinion concerning RNA-related matters. For example, some in the RNA seemed to have problems with Imari Obadele and his behavior within the organization. On more than one occasion, he is identified as being "heavy-handed" and "dictatorial" – clearly this is related to what I discussed earlier as organizational rigidity. There was always a sense of immediacy to Imari's actions that was tolerated and perhaps admired by the membership, but there was also an unwillingness by him to explain the reason behind relevant action or a willingness to have suggestions countered. Thus, on January 19, 1969, at a "steering committee" meeting at the Twenty

Grand Motel at 14th Street and Warren Avenue, Imari broke every one into workgroups but then reassembled various preestablished working groups so that they could hear his proposal on the open city in Ocean Hill–Brownsville. Somewhat differing from his generally pro-militaristic position and even from some of the things that he would later write himself, he suggested that there be no soldiers in the project and that the members assist the community in policing themselves. The other members rejected this approach, and it was suggested that this was precisely what the Black Legion was for. Confronted with this, Imari disagreed, at which point Jay Akri from Cleveland stated that he could not "run every Ministry in the nation" and that it was the collective that would determine what was best for the RNA, not him. To this, Imari again said simply, "No."

Imari was not the only Obadele who was presenting issues for the RNA, but the nature of Gaidi's difficulties were quite different from his brother's. Whereas Imari's issues concerned the way he interacted with the other members, Gaidi's issues were that he rarely interacted at all. As the first-year anniversary approached, Gaidi rarely attended regular RNA meetings, despite the fact that important topics were seemingly brought up all the time. He did attend more higher-profile meetings (i.e., those with outsiders and/or the press). Now, it makes sense that as the vice president and with Robert F. Williams in exile, the de facto president of the RNA need not attend every meeting. But a group as small as the RNA and one with important deliberations taking place almost daily could have used a bit more attention. This absence led to some distrust among not only the leadership but the broader membership, because there began to be rumblings of questionable management.

Importantly for the current discussion, neither Obadele brother's behavior with regard to the other members seemed attributable to repressive behavior, which was still largely absent (at the overt level) or unacknowledged (at the covert level). Imari seemed to respond to perceived mobilization opportunities such as that found in Ocean Hill–Brownsville, ready to push and pull the organization to the means and/or ends that revealed themselves. Gaidi's motivations were less clear. On one hand, he was not really engaged with most RNA business. As mentioned earlier, he rarely attended meetings, and when he did attend, he spoke very briefly. On the other hand, Gaidi seemed to be consistently involved with all legal matters of the organization as well as those involving the media; the former (the law) obviously fell within his area of expertise. One example of the latter (the media) was perhaps the second best exposure that the organization had received. In January 1969, the RNA was featured in a detailed story in the popular men's magazine *Esquire*. Within the detailed eight-page layout, the article addressed what the RNA wanted, who its elected officials were, how whites responded to the black nation, and what the group was doing to reach their objectives. The message emerging from the text seemed generally in line with what was emerging in the meetings he did not attend, suggesting some connection. Interestingly, Robert F. Williams was identified as the president without much discussion that he had not actually done anything (at least not yet).

While Gaidi's involvement in the RNA was odd at times, the strength of his commitment was seemingly never in doubt. Consistent with his earlier struggles against the military and the state of Michigan, one could say that one thing he did continuously and seemingly joyously was the practice of law. As to what mattered most for Gaidi, this was revealed when he confronted a judge who attempted to bar him from some legal proceeding because he had renounced U.S. citizenship. To this, Gaidi simply responded that until he had the rights due to him, he was not a citizen, at which point his participation in the case was disallowed. This was clearly not the thing that someone disconnected to or disinterested in the cause would say. Indeed, from the action, it is clear that Gaidi's ability to practice law was consistently in jeopardy, as his standing in the court seemed to vary with the judge's discretion and tolerance.[3]

Now, although neither Obadele brother's relationship with the RNA was easily attributed to state repression, I would argue that their relationship to one another and therefore indirectly their relationship with the RNA was influenced by coercive government action. For example, the FBI had attempted to feed internal dissension between the two brothers by writing letters to Gaidi that questioned the activities of Imari. In one specific letter, allegedly written by a disaffected member of the RNA but actually penned by an FBI agent, Gaidi was asked what Imari had done with all the money he was given over time (the letter was apparently shared with a few other leaders). One could imagine the impact of such a letter after the repeated requests for tax dollars and after being told that Imari had once again returned to Brooklyn to advance the Ocean Hill–Brownsville cause, looking at office space or paying for some other expense. This must have had some influence on trust not just with Gaidi but also within the general leadership. At the time under investigation, though, such a position was not revealed in the available information. This does, however, explain actions taken later.

Interventions

When the RNA approached the one-year anniversary, numerous activities seemed to take up most of their time.

First and foremost, they were still engaging in the controversial Ocean Hill–Brownsville effort, that is, running a school; trying to make black residents aware of the RNA through distributing pamphlets and conducting lectures, workshops, and conferences; and attempting to successfully complete the vote for separation. As discussed earlier, these activities were not attributable

---

[3] In the case mentioned, the judge allowed him to continue.

to government repression specifically directed against the RNA (i.e., selected behavior). But one could argue that such activities were the result of coercive action being directed against blacks in general (i.e., indiscriminate, nonpolitical behavior) or, equally as important, oppressive action (i.e., economic discrimination that deleteriously affected African Americans but not because of what they believed or were trying to do politically).

Second, during the period in question, the RNA was trying to purchase as well as cultivate land in Mississippi. They allegedly acquired a small plot in Jackson and were busily trying to secure more as well as move a handful of people onto the property to get things going. The Mississippi connection with repression was complex. The territorial base was pursued in the first place to escape white violence and control, specifically anti-change-related activism enacted to provide the RNA with a base from which they could push discussion of their persecution with an international audience. Once established as a nation (in part determined by land), the dissident organization thought it would have access to the international platform of all nations to address their grievances. With this platform, they would have the opportunity to state their cause, get assistance, establish alliances, keep the U.S. government at bay, and begin negotiations. At the same time, the history of antiblack violence was fairly extensive, and this was countered by what was believed to be an equally long history of black resistance to this violence. Repression was thus considered in the selection of the tactic as well as the locale itself, but so was resistance. Land was further sought because it allowed the RNA to realize one of its most important end objectives: nationhood.

Third, the RNA trained the Black Legion and increasingly refined the security situation of the RNA with organizational sweeps and searches as well as increased concern about what everyone in the group was and was not doing (a different form of organizational rigidity whereby all movement participants were increasingly put under scrutiny). Specifically, the Black Legion seemed more directly connected to the idea of state repression and more generally to anticipate white violence. The unit was viewed as a deterrent and preventative ("defensive") measure that could protect the broader organization and its members. Indeed, the active preparation for the possibility of repressive behavior and/or white violence took up increasingly more of the organization's time, but this only involved a subset of the membership in its implementation. There always seemed to be fewer than ten individuals at any one Black Legion meeting (a few leaders but the majority being a subset of the rank and file). In all honesty, however, it is hard to make any determinations here because there was also a black underground that one was never really clear about, and members of the underground were seemingly engaged in various activities that would be mentioned every now and then (e.g., an attack on a police station or a police officer somewhere in the country). Although the Black Legion was viewed as a defensive measure, therefore, it was possible that it could be viewed as a provocation for or to state repression (i.e., that it could be viewed "offensively"). This perspective would soon emerge more prominently.

Changing Characteristics and Assessing Causes

To this day, the New Bethel Incident stands as perhaps the event with the most notoriety concerning the RNA. This is the event that placed them securely on the national as well as international news and under the enhanced scrutiny of U.S. state and federal authorities. Clearly the creation and unveiling of the RNA was noteworthy and OH-B garnered some major attention, but the events involved did not garner as much consistent attention as the New Bethel Incident for as long a period. Despite the notoriety of the events in question, however, many of the facts involved with the New Bethel Incident are still unknown. The basic, uncontested elements were discussed in hundreds of articles throughout the period and were the subject of much discussion as well as disagreement both inside and outside the RNA, within the black nationalist movement, in diverse government committees and around the country.

Very much like the year before at the founding, on March 28, 1969, black nationalists from all around the United States converged on Detroit – coming by car, bus, train, and airplane to the corner of Linwood Street and Euclid Avenue. The event was near the epicenter of the riot/rebellion of 1967, approximately three blocks away. As not all accommodations had been worked out ahead of time (because it was not clear exactly who could be coming), the housing issue occupied a tremendous amount of time. The local consul thus worked very hard to find places for people to stay as they arrived. While these logistical issues were being worked out, those coming rested in their cars, on floors, and in chairs, any place where they could catch a few moments before everything began.

As expected, the agenda was full, and there was much to do, especially since the first day was basically lost with the travel-related matters. There were officials to be elected (e.g., Supreme Court justices). There were proposals and resolutions to be evaluated (e.g., ones concerning the "Judiciary Act to establish Review Boards" [lower courts] for misdemeanors, public health, and slander; the appointment of a Supreme Court of Justice for issues like subversion, sabotage, treason, and libel; and the creation of the People's Supreme Arbiter Act, which gave citizens the right to overturn court decisions dealing with specific topics). There were organizational initiatives to be discussed (e.g., the Ocean Hill–Brownsville Independence Project). And there were updates to be provided (e.g., what was going on with President Robert F. Williams, exactly how poorly was Ocean Hill–Brownsville progressing, and what was to be done with the financial situation of the RNA).

The discussion of these issues would be started but not resolved. At the end of this first day, there was an altercation. As the meeting was coming to an end, several members of the RNA stood outside on the street, having just escorted

Gaidi Obadele and other RNA ministers out of the building into a car and out of the vicinity.[4] At this point, two officers (Michael Czapski and Richard Worobec) exited their car and approached. They were patrolling in the area. Before getting out of their car, they informed the dispatcher that they had seen several African American males in the alley behind New Bethel Baptist Church with rifles filing into vehicles.

It is not definitively known exactly what happened here with regard to what (if anything) was said or who shot first, but within minutes, Officer Czapski was killed (almost immediately), and Officer Worobec was shot several times before getting to his car, calling for backup, and driving away, shortly thereafter crashing his car into a pole. Now stuck, the officer fired several shots, but this seemed more as a way to signal other officers, who quickly arrived at the scene as opposed to targeting the RNA members. Remarkably, none of the RNA standing outside were injured.

Fearful that the conflagration could potentially escalate into a riot/rebellion like in 1967, when the police had underresponded, this time the authorities erred in the opposite direction. Within minutes (so quickly, in fact, that it appeared they were already near the location or even on the scene),[5] dozens of police officers from diverse precincts arrived. Perceiving the large and aggressive show of force, the RNA members who were outside moved into the church.

What happened next is similarly shrouded in controversy. For example, either the RNA members entered the church, took position behind pews and the front altar, and fired on officers as they came in (the police version), or the RNA members ran into the church, informed the others that the police were outside, and proceeded to hide throughout the church but mainly in the basement, unsure about what was going to happen next, when the police began firing (the RNA version). Important in the latter version is the point that the RNA did not shoot at the police first. In the former version, the police were shot at immediately and frequently until they were able to subdue the RNA gathering with approximately fifty officers and the discharge of several hundred rounds. The last point about the amount of ammunition used is something that both sides could agree on as well as being supported by independent investigations after the event.

After the exchange of bullets, within twenty minutes (around midnight), all occupants in the church were in custody. Only four RNA members were injured by gunshots. One had a leg broken either on purpose (the RNA version) or by accident (the police version), as authorities aggressively entered the building. Shot at, a little damaged, and seemingly somewhat traumatized,

---

[4] As one of the primary functions of the Black Legion was to protect the RNA leadership, Gaidi Obadele was the de facto president of the republic, and the meeting attendees were about to leave the building, the large contingent made sense.

[5] This is not an unreasonable assumption because it is clear that the authorities knew the event was going to take place and, at least, surveillance of this type of event would have been standard.

approximately 142 African Americans were then hauled off to a nearby police station. At the station, all were processed (had a file opened) and most were questioned regarding their identity, profession, who they knew in the RNA, and what they did in the organization. Several were examined with a nitrate test, which revealed whether they had recently fired a gun. All this started around 12:30 A.M.

Quickly, the news of the events at New Bethel spread throughout the black community. Reverend C. L. Franklin was not in attendance at the event, but he was told what had happened to his church and to the event attendees. As noted earlier, the devastation to the building was quite significant as several hundred rounds of ammunition were shot into the structure, doors were busted, benches were thrown over, and glass was broken all over the place. Upset by what transpired, numerous blacks (some in but mostly out of the RNA) contacted Democratic representative James Del Rio, an African American, who arrived at the police station around 12:40 A.M. to see what was going on. After several hours and not believing that what was taking place was legal or appropriate, at 4:35 A.M., Del Rio went to get Judge George W. Crockett Jr., who was something of a controversial African American legal figure, as he had recently received attention for his (legally allowable) discretion in dealing with blacks who came before his court. In the meantime, the police continued to process and interrogate their prisoners without giving them access to legal counsel, phone calls, or any idea of the charges under which they were being held.

Joined by Reverend Franklin and Del Rio, Crockett assessed the situation, and they uniformly determined around 5:00 A.M. that what was taking place was not right and definitely not legal. In an effort to eliminate the long internment, Crockett set up a makeshift court in the police station along with the Wayne County prosecutor, William Calahan (who was white). At approximately 6:00 A.M., they began to process the thirty-nine African Americans remaining in the police station, most of the others having been released by then.

One by one, each individual was brought before the makeshift "court" and, in this setting, it was determined what the RNA member was accused of (if anything). After this, the judge determined what should be done with the person, the prosecutor gave his opinion, and a judgment was rendered. On the vast majority of the cases, there was no disagreement between Crockett and Calahan, resulting in most being released. Things came to a head, however, when Crockett wanted to release a prisoner whom Calahan wanted to retain for further examination. Crockett said that the person should be released, but the prosecutor objected. It is not clear what the motivation was, but Crockett argued that the prosecutor had acted inappropriately and was potentially in contempt of court for his behavior. With that, the impromptu court session was terminated, the prosecutor was informed that he had to present information to the court to show that he should not be held in contempt, and both individuals left.

After this (around 2:30 P.M.), all hell broke loose. The media discussed the shooting, the secessionists, what they were doing in Detroit in general and at New Bethel in particular. Diving right in, the media examined what the RNA believed, what they wanted, what they were doing, and what they thought about whites and America. Across dozens of articles, they talked about the efforts of the police to counter the "militant" threat and to stem the potentially riotous situation before it got out of hand, as it did in 1967.

Despite both events (the pre-1967 riot/rebellion and New Bethel) involving contentious interactions between the police and African Americans, however, the major differences between this event and the prior one were not discussed, but they were clear to observers of the time. For example, in the pre-riot/rebellion situation of 1967, the police activities were directed against blacks held in high esteem (former soldiers) and not members of a highly politicized and relatively unknown radical African American organization. It was the distinguished nature of the previous victims that facilitated the mass outpouring of emotion and support as the treatment of this particular group seemed completely unjustified, and many individuals could imagine themselves as being caught up in a similar situation (recall the ever-widening history of police harassment); this is directly in line with existing theory. Mistreatment of blacks in the service of their nation seemed to violate all that was deemed appropriate. African Americans were off fighting for their country only to come back and be dealt with aggressively and disrespectfully. "Just let the brothers drink" seemed to be the message at the time, regardless of the legality of the establishment and the potential aggressiveness of the soldiers being pulled out of it during the raid. In contrast, the context surrounding New Bethel was very different. Here the African Americans were not as immediately recognizable or deemed worthy of sympathy to whites or to blacks. These African Americans were not coming home to America from fighting abroad; in fact, they were trying to separate from America and were fighting at home to do it.

Of course, the RNA was trying to separate because of the harsh treatment that blacks had received from whites, which they had just received. In this light, the black nationalists did not initiate the conflict. Rather, they defended themselves as Malcolm X, Robert F. Williams, the Deacons for Defense, the RAM, and the Black Panthers before them had advocated. More than that, they had defended themselves "successfully" against the police as those who would do them harm had been killed or injured in line with the organizational model of reappraisal. Given that the event was exactly the type of event predicted by the RNA and one for which they had prepared repeatedly, this would not have affected the members of the RNA in a deleterious fashion as expected in existing literature, leading to anger and fear or retaliation and flight, respectively. Quite the contrary, RNA members knew this day would come and had acted more or less exactly as they were supposed to under the circumstances. Such an occurrence and response would have also bolstered trust within the organization – at least, with regard to this particular element of the RNA's overall program.

In other ways, the context of the New Bethel Incident was similar to that of the African American experience in Detroit and around the United States in general. For instance, in attacking the black church, a sacred space for the African American community had once again been targeted by white aggression, and this would prove to be an extremely important issue. One can imagine that if the RNA had met in a warehouse or some other locale with less importance to blacks (as well as the broader white community), the violent nature of the interaction might not have been viewed in the same way, because in these other spaces, it was not expected that restraint should be exercised. But, in the case of the church, especially a black church with its historical significance regarding safety and sense of community as well as when it was revealed that other means could have been used to deal with the situation (e.g., bullhorns and tear gas), what happened was viewed as highly inappropriate by the black community and numerous whites as well, revealed by the strange bedfellows who stepped forward to speak up on behalf of the RNA following the event.

Within this situation – the unclear initiation of the violence, the highly aggressive and violent nature of the police response to what took place in a sacred African American locale, and the potential illegality of the police with regard to the mass arrest and processing of black prisoners – the attention and support of the black community was significant. Individuals and organizations who were previously not giving the RNA any attention or saying anything on its behalf were now defending its right to exist. Indeed, many within the black media, mainstream black clergy, and local and national black politicians rallied to the RNA. In doing this, they still made sure to keep an arm's length from the RNA's message of secession, but nevertheless they were supportive of the institution in the abstract.

For example, when asked if he would again rent to the black separatists, C. L. Franklin said definitively yes. He quickly added, though, that he would ask them to keep their guns at home. He went further to say that he and the RNA both believed in the same thing; they just pursued it in different ways. For a while, it did not seem to matter that the RNA wanted to separate from the United States and that they actually might represent a threat to the integrity of the United States. For a while, they were just a group of aggrieved black folk who rented some space in a church (as many did and would) and who got shot at and injured as well as arrested for coming together in that effort (again, as many had and would).

Interestingly, Ralph Abernathy of the Southern Christian Leadership Conference, or SCLC (Martin Luther King's second in command but now the leader of the institution), got involved in the investigation of what took place at the church. This was paradoxical, because four of the individuals in attendance at the RNA meeting (minister of education Herman Ferguson, Arthur

Harris, Mandels McPherson, and George Samuels), who were arrested, tried, convicted, and released on bond, had been earlier arrested and convicted of trying to murder someone with similarities to Abernathy on October 3, 1968 (i.e., Roy Wilkins of the NAACP and Whitney Young of the National Urban League). That Abernathy ended up engaged with the cause that in some way supported the RNA was an important turn of events, to say the least.

Given the initial positive rallying call around the members of the RNA as victims of illegitimate state repression, individuals and organizations in opposition to such a view were soon compelled to voice their disagreement, clearly establishing where they stood (lest they be associated with supporting the group and its message). For example, the police and their supporters as well as some blacks began to speak out against the RNA. In the *Detroit News* (1969a), one African American wrote,

Rarely has Detroit been more shocked and angry, or more moved to express its shock and anger. By telephone calls, letters and picketing, citizens are telling public officials and the press what they think about the amazing affair last weekend at the New Bethel Church and the even more amazing affair in the court of Recorder's Judge George Crockett Jr.

These expressions of public feeling, by the way, come from blacks as well as whites. There is a common revulsion for the character and conduct of the militant group involved in the disturbance at the church, for the slaying of a police officer, and for the unseemly haste with which Judge Crockett let arrested persons go free.

[The citizens referenced in the letter – the "silent"] feel no kinship with Robert F. Williams, the organization's President, a fugitive believed to be hiding out in Red China, or with Rap Brown. Nor does the *responsible* Negro community share the Republic of New Africa's naïve view that the way to solve the racial problem is to secede from the union. (emphasis added)

More direct black denunciation of the RNA emerged as well. After a couple of weeks had passed (on April 18, 1969), Reverend Ray Shoulders, coordinator of the Michigan Human Rights Council and a political moderate, issued the following:

We decided to make a statement of our position because there is the impression that all black people embrace [RNA] separatist philosophy, which we don't... It has seemed to us that since the RNA episode at the New Bethel Baptist Church that black people have been afraid to speak out against them. We thought it was about time somebody took a position on this. (*Detroit News* 1969a, 3)

In its statement, the council denounced "the concept of the RNA as being misleading and detrimental to the best interest of the black people of America" (*Detroit News* 1969a, 3). The council reaffirmed its faith in an integrated American society, although it acknowledged "the frustration of blacks who feel that the gap between the dream and reality is so great." The statement continued,

We feel that separatist efforts are self-destructive. The American black, despite the persistence of much discrimination, is still more inside the total American society than he is outside of it. We cannot isolate ourselves from the benefits of American advanced technology and revert to a semicolonial position of a satellite nation. (*Detroit News* 1969a, 3)

Hundreds of more sentiments like this appeared in feature articles, in letters to the editor, and on radio and television broadcasts throughout the media of the day.

However, at the same time, others began to push back on this pushback, revealing a wide variety of opinions about the RNA as well as the police action taken against them. The mix of opinions is well illustrated in the *Detroit Free Press* (1969) editorial titled "Efforts to Understand Separatists." It began,

My great concern is for the society which produced the group of separatists. These men must have been so brutalized during the period of development, in American ghettos, they lost hope in the "American Dream." The society caused them to experience more brutality than they could endure. The sensitivity of these men has been worn to the bone – Rosetta H. Sadler

MR. HENRY of the Republic of New Africa asked the question. "What about those black women and children who were assaulted in a Christian church?" I for one would never take my wife and children to church knowing my fellow parishioners were armed – Terrence Nagle

IN YOUR EDITORIAL "Keep Isolated Incident Within Narrow Limits" you joined the mayor, police commissioner and all too many others in assuming that Police Officer Czapski "died because of the irrational act of an irrational extremist group." No one who saw the shooting has substantiated that assumption. Let us consider the other possibility. I quote the lead paragraph of a front page article that appeared in your paper on Feb. 23 of this year: "An extraordinary psychological study of the Detroit police force has concluded that most white police officers are at best unsympathetic, and at worst, hostile to Detroit Negroes" – Alan Douglas

I FAIL to understand just why the Republic of New Africa found it necessary to be armed at their meeting unless they were looking for trouble. It's natural that police would investigate armed men pouring out into the street from a building. It's also likely that these same men would be in a rather belligerent mood and ready to shoot. Incidents such as these and also Crockett's type of justice give whites second thoughts at complete integration and only tighten the noose around the black ghettos – L. Drolet

THE UNFORTUNATE shooting incident on Linwood last Saturday night proves once again that the Detroit Police Department persists in assuming the strange right to forcibly break up, or otherwise harass, any black meeting held anywhere and for whatever purpose – Anonymous.[6]

---

[6] Invoking what has become commonplace today in the area of pundits, some began to voice an opinion about the opinions being put forward. For example, on April 29, there was a protest of the ad hoc action group Citizens of Detroit to identify their dissatisfaction with news that they

The federal government held one of the more interesting opinions about the RNA revealed at the time. The opinion, however, was somewhat divided.

On one hand, according to federal politicians, during a Senate investigation conducted at the same period, the RNA was not viewed seriously. One government official referred to the organization as "crackpotish," and another viewed them as "quite insignificant." They continued, "If I thought they had any real following, I might be alarmed but the type of program they are advocating, while it might well run afoul of the law, has negligible approach" (*Detroit News* 1969b). Regardless, the shooting, mass arrest, and flurry of debate around these events was enough to prompt an open debate regarding the RNA as well as the conclusion that this was a matter for intelligence and law enforcement. The RNA took exception to this latter view: if they were so "insignificant," then why were they receiving such attention from the authorities?

On the other hand, the RNA had been deemed worthy of observation and evaluation by local, state, and federal police. From the available records, local and state law enforcement in particular, but some federal police as well, had already been on the case. The group had been constantly monitored, and most of those involved in monitoring knew that the first-year anniversary was coming. Indeed, according to available material, members were increasingly being observed at meeting places, in their homes, with their visitors, regarding their travel habits, and even in workplaces. Outing themselves as well as what they were up to, all three levels of government testified at the Senate Government Operations Permanent Investigation Subcommittee. This suggested that not only was the group under surveillance but also that it had been infiltrated. In this context, the RNA was viewed as a serious threat. For example, a Detroit detective portrayed the group as one prepared to do whatever was necessary to bring about the desired end (*Detroit News* 1969b). The organization's aims were clearly identified, as were its means. For example, it was noted that the RNA's goal was to have a "militia of 22 million trigger fingers" ready to take action (*Detroit News* 1969b, 18). Those testifying also were well aware of who was in the organization and how some members overlapped with other black nationalists, most notably the RAM, the Black Panthers, and the SNCC. Additionally, following the recent arrests, it was suggested that the police had even more information about who were and what was involved. This suggested that people talked: "rats" were among the RNA's membership.

viewed as having "a foundation in [white] racism." They continued, "We accuse the Detroit News of forming and reinforcing racial hysteria and ignorance to a point worthy of a fascist state. Regardless of motivation, we hold the Detroit News responsible for the continuing polarization of our community." In perhaps the most poignant criticism, the group charged that "the Detroit News has a policy that shockingly differs from its coverage of crimes committed by whites against blacks." Similar but more thoroughly analyzed as well as more detailed criticisms about the media's role in the conflict were presented in "Mass Media a Racist Institution: Coverage of the New Bethel Incident by the Detroit News and the Detroit Free Press" by the Detroit Area People against Racism (1969).

It should come as no surprise that after the New Bethel Incident, a great deal changed within the RNA. Many changes were directly attributed to the repressive activity that occurred at New Bethel but also to government behavior that followed the shooting. Additionally, some activity seems attributed to dynamics within the organization not connected to government coercion. Still other changes were connected to an interaction between external repression and internal organizational dynamics.

Individuals

Perhaps one of the most notable modifications within the RNA concerned the membership. Immediately following the shooting and mass arrest, some individuals simply stopped showing up (repression prompted exit), and some showed up but no longer seemed to be engaged (repression prompted silence/trauma). At RNA events, new people started showing up who were undoubtedly undeterred by the enhanced repressive activity, which suggested a completely different type of person from the risk- or cost-averse individuals normally discussed in social science literature (e.g., Gilda Zwerman's work). In this highly fluid and contentious situation, RNA events were filled with emotion, mostly fear (but also some anger), as some individuals within the organization came together, as some began to turn on one another (repression prompting factionalization). Imari Obadele (1970c, 260–61) discusses the difficulties of this period in the following passage:

Ray Willis was gone, because without the active support of those abroad who professed to be our friends, it seemed to him our course would prove too long, prohibitively costly and, therefore, not apt to lead to success. Malcolm's wife Betty was gone, moving away quietly just after we entered Ocean Hill-Brownsville, because she had cautioned us that we should not identify our land mass or reveal so much of our strategy (as we appeared to be doing in Ocean Hill-Brownsville as well as in *Esquire* magazine) and we had rejected her counsel. Rap Brown had never come on board, telling Herman (Ferguson) during a hurried aside at a mass rally that he didn't understand what we were doing and that we could use his name if we wished – but never taking the time to find out what we were doing. And Charles Howard, the aged but distinguished black U.N. journalist, named the first Minister of State and Foreign Affairs, telling us in the handsome lobby of the United Nations office building in November 1968, not long before his death, that he did not think we had a breath of a chance of liberating five states or any territory now in the continental US. Ron Karenga was suspended, while Amiri Baraka interpreted his "operational unity" with respect to the Republic to mean that he need not attend a single meeting or put anything directly into the national bloodstream. And now Joan [Franklin] was gone.

In a little while Gaidi too would be gone..., as we moved through May and June and July, the brilliant, nerve-teasing court examinations of Alfred 2-X and Brother Chaka and, finally, Viera, all the brothers bound over for trial [who were accused of shooting the police officer outside New Bethel], largely on the testimony of a weak and venal "brother" from Los Angeles named David Brown, Jr., who only recently had come into the Consulate there, but bound over on lesser strengths than the prosecution had wished, and all free on relatively modest bond to await trial, because of the legal application and genius of Gaidi and Lee Molette and Kenneth Cockrell.

After a while, things stabilized within the membership and emotions calmed, but not in an especially good way for the RNA. For example, at one unscheduled meeting on April 3, 1969, at 2595 Puritan Street, RNA members met presumably to talk about the unfinished business of the recent New Bethel convention, but most of the time was actually spent talking about the shooting as well as the arrests that followed, a general pattern that persisted for quite some time (repression prompted discussion of repression). Indeed, this is how it would be for months after the event. During the meeting itself, nothing special happened, aside from a thorough retelling of what had been seen and experienced. Without affirmative tactics being discussed, New Bethel was in line with the existing approach to reappraisal because it involved an overt assault on a nonviolent RNA event, but it was also different from the reappraisal put forward, which had important implications. Having prepared members for a raid and arrest but not the severity of violence involved, magnitude of arrest (overwhelming) or legal as well as political aftermath (outwitting), the RNA had to work on reestablishing the willingness of members to put their fates into others' hands – again. Trust was thus bolstered in some ways but diminished in others.

Immediately following the meeting, there was another one held at Imari Obadele's house with a subset of the first group. Here different people were "interviewed" one at a time about what they had seen, and some time was spent discussing changes that needed to take place in the RNA. At this meeting, individuals were instructed not to talk to the police and, if they were detained, to refer the officer to Gaidi, the RNA's lawyer. This reappraisal attempted to prepare the members to respond appropriately when subjected to specific forms of overt repressive activity, which was still the focus of the organization. Unfortunately, this information was not immediately given to everyone in the organization, and thus they were somewhat left to their own devices, which would inevitably decrease trust in the organization.

As when individuals were arrested traveling to Ocean Hill–Brownsville from Detroit and the RNA reflected on who might have information about the route, numerous changes in the organization were directly attributed to countering state repression. During the post–New Bethel Incident period, after it was reported that the organization was subject to varied surveillance efforts (leaked during government inquiries and into newspaper coverage), the RNA began to fear covert repressive action in general as well as infiltration in particular and wanted to counter any efforts by the authorities to pick apart the organization through harassment, interrogation, or questioning/turning of its members. Additionally, it is interesting that the shooting, the injury of the four RNA members, the raid of the church, and the mass arrest of individuals affiliated

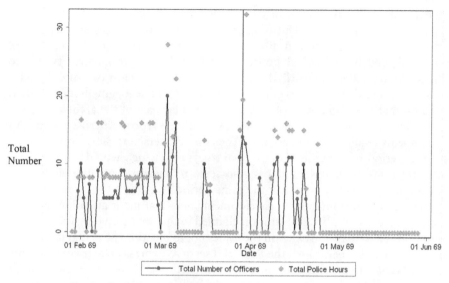

FIGURE 9.1. Repressive behavior around New Bethel.

with the RNA, in other words, the happenings of the New Bethel Incident, were basically the only things that occurred overtly during the period. There were a few isolated repressive events following NBI (a raid in mid-May, two arrests in late May, and another arrest in mid-June), but that is all, and these were nowhere near the scale of New Bethel. This is not to trivialize the events that occurred. Indeed, the resonance of the related repressive activity is highly significant. Rather, it shows the *importance that a single repressive event can have for a social movement organization*. This is largely ignored in existing literature, which tends to consider the impact of all events contemporaneously, ignoring the resonance through a social movement in its discussions, thoughts, and actions of a single event (for an exception here, see Davenport 1996; Loyle et al. 2013).

One reason for the low level of subsequent repressive activity could be that the perpetrators of the raid, mass arrest, and interrogation (Detroit Police Department) were not uniformly treated well in the media, which must have curbed their willingness to proceed overtly (similar to that argued by Koopmans and Statham 1999). In fact, because the events took place in a black church, the police actually seemed to take quite a bit of heat for their actions, especially in the African American community but in other communities as well. This likely prompted the police to withdraw from taking further overt action and increase their covert activities, which evidence does reveal.

Regardless of the explanation, with this tactical shift, one can observe an increase in the number of officers assigned to the RNA (Figure 9.1). Indeed, for about a month, records indicate that it was common for there to be at least ten to fifteen officers on duty specifically dealing with the dissident organization at any one point in time. This is almost twice as many as were on duty before then (on average). One can also see that, again on average, the number of hours logged by individual police officers rose to approximately twelve to fifteen hours. After late April, there are no reports for almost two months. This is not because there were no police assigned and no one logging hours. Rather, I think that in the chaos of period, this particular part of the archive was not retained for some reason. Interestingly, very little is reported across the various documents available in the archive. The conflict seemed to slow down and go into a period of lower-level activity or abeyance, which would tend to leave less trace material. RNA records also seem to suggest that the police–RNA intervention wound down over the same period.

There are some interesting developments here that merit attention. Following the revelations about infiltration claimed in the Senate investigation as well as various newspaper articles on the topic (not to mention the actual increase in covert repressive behavior), the RNA did seem to express greater concern with covert action in general and infiltration in particular, revealing that domestic spying was effective at producing the desired impact of refocusing the challenging organization on itself: membership and trust. Of course, the RNA's response represents a relatively complex one because the covert action under discussion by the group was *not actually real but imagined*; the RNA was not aware of the existing informants and only believed that they existed.[7] As the organization began to look for the individuals who seemed to be providing information about them, the group went from suspicion to paranoia. Things became even more tense in the organization as they attempted to specifically identify the informants and agents provocateurs with a series of investigations conducted within the various consulates: in New York (which gave up the names of the New Bethel Incident shooters) and in Detroit (the organization's home base).

Interestingly, the dynamics involved with informants and with infiltration were occasionally counterintuitive. For example, Imari Obadele speculated that one reason why there was no massacre at New Bethel was "because present at this convention was a number of informers and agents whose identities were not all known to Detroit police" (Obadele 1970c, 254). If they killed one of these individuals, it could be considered an accident, but it might terminate their recruitment of blacks into their ranks for years to come. This was not idle speculation. Rather, all it took was a casual glance at the newspapers. For example, in the *Michigan Chronicle* on April 19, 1969, in an article titled "Informants May Have Seen All," it is stated that the RNA-sponsored meeting was attended by agents or informers from at least three organizations: the CIA,

---

[7] Though the number of discrete discussions seems small given the earlier discussion, this is largely attributed to the fact that I coded individual references to the initial point of possible infiltration and not all subsequent references to the same.

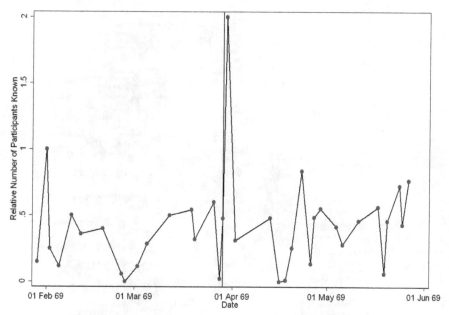

FIGURE 9.2. The effectiveness of covert action around New Bethel.

the FBI, and the Detroit Police Department's own "subversive squad." Indeed, the article goes on to blame law enforcement not only for the death of the police officer, which could have been stopped, but also for the escape and non-identification of the shooter.

One can see how well covert activity was working in the dramatic improvement in the ability of the informants to identify those in attendance at RNA functions relative to all individuals present, identified and unidentified (Figure 9.2). Prior to the New Bethel Incident, the relative number of known and identified attendees was quite variable (anywhere from 0 to about 100 percent, increasing as the anniversary approached). At New Bethel, there was actually an overidentification of individuals known to informants relative to the total number estimated to be there.[8] After NBI, however, the authorities at first experienced decreased awareness with an influx of new faces and departure of the old. However, shortly afterward (toward the end of April), there was a steady increase; this was so much in fact that by the end of the relevant period, all attendees were basically known. In large part, I attribute this to the increased intelligence gained from the arrest and interrogation of arrestees. With this information, the police were able to get a better sense of the overall organization, who was involved, and how the different people related to

---

[8] In part, this was a function of the fact that many individuals identified as being at or near the event did not attend all activities and were not caught in the mass arrest.

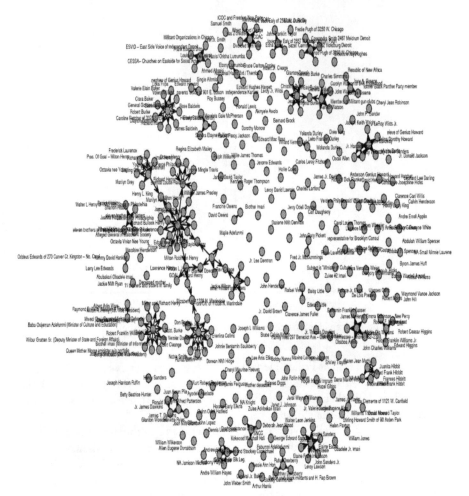

FIGURE 9.3. Complete network diagram of RNA.

one another as well as where people lived and congregated. I have provided a
network diagram of relevant connections in Figure 9.3.[9]

---

[9] These images were derived from the compiled police files of individuals arrested after the RNA
meeting on March 30, 1969, in the New Bethel Baptist Church. The police records indicate
the name and address of the individuals, their known associates and family members, occupa-
tions, and presumed roles in the RNA. The records also include the prior case file numbers of
these individuals with relevant police agencies, for example, the Detroit Criminal Investigations
Bureau, the overall Detroit Police Department, the FBI, and the New York and Chicago police
departments.

Steve Wendel extracted three forms of information from these police files: the names of
individuals, the names of their associates and family members, and their prior police records.
The files are inconsistent in the spelling and presentation of the names of individuals, and we

What is important about the diagram is that one can see certain clusters of association between individuals identified as being known to others when questioned by the police. With this information, the authorities would be able to focus on those clusters with the greatest number of connections (i.e., people who were frequently identified as being connected or known to others). Then they would have a reasonable understanding of who was related to whom as well as how, reducing the amount of guesswork about who to monitor, harass, and eliminate. Under the microscope before, after the New Bethel Incident, the RNA was now under an even more efficient gaze.[10]

Following the NBI, as predicted in existing literature but differing from their earlier responses, the members of the RNA engaged in a series of fearful utterances about what happened to them and about what could happen to them again. Some anger was expressed around June, but for most of the post–New Bethel period, the dominant emotion was fear: fear of investigation, fear of additional shootings, and fear of infiltration. For example, when asked during a meeting on April 4, 1969, what was going on, members were told that "top members" of the Black Legion Army had gone underground and would undergo a change in uniform so as to prevent detection in the future (Detroit Police Department – SIB 1969, 10). Members of the army were being especially targeted, it was concluded, because of their military training and the connection with armed engagement.

Differing from existing literature, these expressions did not result in the expected responses. For example, there was a jeopardy frame used in late May acknowledging that what was being done could be at risk, and there was a futility frame around the same time, when it was mentioned that the group might not succeed in its endeavors. However, the amount of negative framing did not seem to match the severity of the situation. Additionally, continuing to refute existing literature, positive framing was seemingly not employed to

---

used both automated name matching and manual standardization to connect each individual's list of relationships with other individuals in the files. Numerous individuals have multiple entries in the files, which were matched automatically and then manually verified. The resulting processed file includes a single entry for each individual, with standardized lists of relationships with other individuals and of prior police records. The processed file was then verified against the original files and evaluated with standard social network statistics.

For the purposes of this book, we have displayed this relational information with the standard Fruchterman-Reingold layout algorithm. For visual clarity, isolates are not displayed. Similarly, the names of individuals are only displayed when the individual has two or more relationships. We indicate the existence of prior case files with each police agency by coloring the nodes, as described in the text.

We processed the data in the statistical package R (version 2.5.1) and generated the network diagrams using the Social Network Analysis package for R developed by Carter T. Butts (version 1.5).

[10] I am not suggesting that, in the late 1960s, police used the same techniques to discern connections that I apply, but given the information collected, it makes sense that authorities would apply a similar type of logic – resulting in a similar conclusion about clusters and targets.

specifically counter negative frames. Rather, positive framing appeared to be directed toward sustaining an overall level of morale, cohesion, and trust within the organization, amid increased fear of what was taking place around them as well as distrust of one another. This was observed in early May (a possibility frame, where it was mentioned that the RNA could achieve what they set out to do), mid-May (an agency frame, where they had to respond at the time or else fail), mid-June (again an agency frame), and late June (another possibility frame).

In opposition to my conclusions in earlier chapters, I maintain here that the activities of the organization relevant to demobilization are largely attributable to state repression – at least initially (i.e., they are explained by forces outside of the organization), attributed to both overt and covert activity. However, demobilizing activity was sustained and worsened by the social movement itself, thus representing an important interaction. In a sense, following New Bethel, each member of the RNA became an embodiment of and a physical carrier for state repressive action – the U.S. government could be represented by anyone at an RNA function who would put forward suspicion or a memory of earlier repression. Existing literature (especially the quantitative research) has largely ignored this. In some qualitative work (Poletta 2002), some attention has been given to the resonance of diverse events within the minds of activists, but these utterances and remembrances are not as easily and systematically identified or examined as the records employed in the current study. Additionally, the RNA study even raises the question of who is and is not an activist and/or state agent when challengers end up "doing the work" of government repressive action.

Seeing these debilitating dynamics, however, the leaders of the RNA tried to counteract the deleterious influences of this process, attempting to improve reappraisal and trust. I discuss these efforts in the following.

Institutions

While the overall structure of the RNA was not really influenced by the New Bethel Incident, after the event, it was clear that things began to shift in the organization in terms of how business was conducted. For instance, Gaidi Obadele increased his participation and streamlined the organization by appointing new regional vice presidents: Obaboa in the West, Hekima for the East, Dara Abubakari for the South, and Imari Obadele for the Midwest. Some were up for reelection, but the New Bethel Incident had interfered with the selection process, which was to be undertaken on the day following the mass raid, arrest, and interrogation. In the situation of heightened security, the role and importance of the Black Legion (the military arm of the RNA) was increased significantly. Nowhere was this clearer than with regard to the soon-to-be all-encompassing search for informants.

Following the New Bethel Incident, discussions within the organization about what happened as well as within the media regarding what was known about the RNA led many in the organization to conclude (correctly) that there were informants in their midst. As noted earlier, this was not new, but this time the belief was more widely diffused throughout the organization. Regardless of the situation, however, the RNA had previously tolerated the possibility of infiltration almost as if this was the cost of engaging in dissent. Earlier, there had been no extensive search for infiltrators. The only way they had attempted to counter the situation was through establishing and convening subcommittees. Specifically, this was an effort to limit the number of individuals involved in any one meeting to those who were believed to be trusted. Generally, however, this did not work. In a crisis period (i.e., one where the organization took major "hits"), during which the organization had to do something to counter the government or at least appear to do so for morale, the informant situation could no longer be tolerated. Even if these individuals could not be found, to reestablish some trust in the organization, the RNA had to search for them – even if only superficially. This represented a major shift in the organization because up to this point (as noted numerous times), reappraisal had been focused on overt confrontations with political authorities.

The organization chosen for rooting out informants was (unsurprisingly) the Black Legion. With a relatively rapid and largely undiscussed shift in mandate, new uniforms were created and organizational leaders were placed underground so that they would be less likely to be identified and captured as well as unfortunately less able to attend meetings and familiarize themselves with other members. The Legion stepped into action quickly, but not in a fashion making the whole organization privy to its activities, which might have revealed to authorities what was taking place. Rather, the Black Legion dealt with individual RNA members, one at a time. For example, on April 3, 1969, it was maintained that a "committee" of Black Legionnaires would meet with David Mundy because he was believed to be passing information to the police. There was no other reason for this conclusion other than that he had been seen talking to the police as the RNA were being placed on the bus after the New Bethel Incident. After evaluation (the contents of which were never disclosed), it was determined that David was not an informant. Numerous other members of the Detroit Consulate were examined in a similar manner. In all cases, it was discovered that the person interviewed was not an informant. Paradoxically, the organization continued to look for traitors while diligently having their efforts documented by the very individuals they were trying to identify.

The Legion was not only responsible for assuring that individuals within the movement organization were not *working for* the U.S. government, they were also responsible for keeping individuals from *talking to* the U.S. government, a different component of reappraisal. For example, on April 13, an incident similar to the David Mundy situation arose when it was mentioned in a meeting that an RNA member who saw the shooting at New Bethel had been "talking it all over town." She was "approached," seemingly by the same "committee" that talked to Mundy, and told to "shut up or else"; this revealed a degree of coercion that had not previously been identified but had begun to appear more consistently. The woman was subsequently kicked out of the RNA. The record here is partial in that there was no determination made about involvement in any anti-RNA activity, and in fact, the woman was never mentioned again. Institutionally, however, this was an important example, because more responsibility, power, and independence were given to the Black Legion, and it began to engage in more activity. It is hard to argue that trust in the Black Legion specifically or in the RNA generally was increased by these activities, because no informants were ever discovered, and there were no open discussions about what the Legion was doing. Indeed, the Black Legion disrupted the RNA as it began to develop its own protocols for all meetings as well as how other events would be conducted (e.g., establishing arrival times, searches, locale selection).

In response to these shifts, the U.S. government also stepped into action (revealing the connection between intelligence and government behavior), covertly trying to exacerbate the tensions within the organization by "overwhelming" it. Knowing the RNA to be fearful of some infiltration, the government attempted to make it fearful of all its members. For example, right after "shutting up" the talkative sister, in the middle of a meeting, it was noted (by an informant turned provocateur) that three members (i.e., Leroy Wilds, Ernest 2-L, and Andrew Hayes) were not present. The provocateur mentioned that this was "bizarre," because the three never missed a meeting. Individuals began to talk about this as being suspicious, which is exactly what the government probably wanted them to do. Perhaps sensing this influence, however, the provocateur was told by the meeting chairperson (not an informant) to "stay cool" (obviously referencing a spate of "uncool" behavior that had been taking place) and to say that they were "on tour" for the RNA (i.e., on assignment). The U.S. government thus tried to provoke distrust within the RNA through internal discussions about insecurity and fear, which would further compel efforts to be taken within the organization to shore up its vulnerability, but paradoxically, it would also serve as a mechanism to disrupt the organization and distract it from other objectives.

Interventions

Following the New Bethel Incident, the RNA engaged in a vast array of activities, some to address perceived vulnerabilities in the organization and some to sustain the organization and advance it further. Each is discussed in the following.

Perhaps most important, the RNA revealed that it needed to limit its reach, and thus it had to reduce the amount of attention as well as resources being allocated to Ocean Hill–Brownsville. As Imari Obadele lamented,

it was important that leaders should be possessed by the moment and by the realization of what we could accomplish in the moment, through daring and application and perseverance. I was possessed by it. And Herman [Ferguson]. And Arthur [Harris].

And Obaboa [Olowo]. I thought Gaidi was, but he wasn't, and that was nearly fatal. I thought John Davis was, but he was at work to destroy the Republic. I hoped [Mwesi] Chui would come to be possessed. I hoped Wilbur Brattan – who finally proved to be a socialist first and black nationalist second – would. I did not know then that Leito Durley, who became Information Minister when I became Interior Minister, had something else on his mind. Ray Willis needed now only a courteous moment to leave us, his friends, because he deeply felt that OH-B was the wrong project at the wrong time. Ron Karenga and Amiri Baraka were busy with personal projects and uninvolved; Betty Shabazz, affrighted by such an early, specific challenge to U.S. authority; Joan Franklin, pragmatic, legalistic, and cold to all vision. And these were the leaders, the national cabinet (except for Arthur and John Davis).

It was important that they should be possessed of the vision. But I thought we would be enough – me and Obaboa and Herman and Arthur, with Gaidi, the actual head of the government, whom virtually all the nationalists in the county loved and respected, and whose charisma now – save for Rap Brown and Stokely Carmichael, in a different way – was without peer. For, I knew that most other people are lighted and filled by the leaders, that the true insights of people are usually not trusted in and of themselves by the people in whom these insights appear – until the leaders verify these insights with the passion and glow of their own same insights. I knew the people, the rank and file New Africans, would follow us – for we had first told them that now was the time for nationhood, confirming their own half-believed insight, and they had followed, and it would be so in Ocean Hill-Brownsville if we but shared with them our light and our passion.

But I helped to conjure up a mirage. I mistook my passion for Gaidi's, and I led a nation of black people to believe a vision and a passion existed where it did not, at least not in an enduring form. (Obadele 1970c, 255)

Feeling the stress of the post–New Bethel context, the leadership attempted to rein the organization in and control it from a small core, even smaller than it had been previously. This change would make the organization less susceptible to government penetration as well as attack. Paradoxically, it would make it less comprehensible to the members and somewhat less trusted. Much of this involved changing how meetings (the cornerstone of RNA mobilization) were conducted.

For example, on April 13, it was determined that meetings would be held on different days of the week (see Figure 9.4). There would no longer be standard, established periods. John Saulsberry also mentioned that "some meetings will be cut abruptly . . . and everyone [would] be [put] out of the building, and out of the area, in approximately one and a half minutes." If that wasn't enough, before all meetings, RNA members were to search for listening devices in the room where the meeting was to take place on either side of the relevant room as well as above it.

Different from much of what was discussed earlier, these actions were direct responses to state repression. The presumed effectiveness of the RNA's counterapproach, however, would be determined by how well the organization had already been penetrated. If the government was not well entrenched and deep

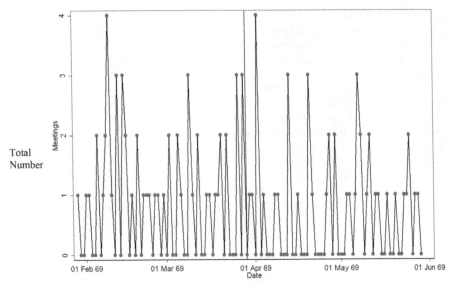

FIGURE 9.4. RNA meetings around New Bethel.

inside the RNA, then these activities might be effective at preventing further penetration, but if the organization was already well penetrated (which they were by this time), then they might just confuse, frustrate, and potentially scare off the members or potential members (which they tended to do). The sequential and interactive influences were thus crucial for understanding what happened.

Meetings were changed not only in terms of how they were run but also in terms of how they were structured. Specifically, there were an increasing number of short meetings held, at different times during the day, with increasingly smaller subsets of people in them. This allowed the RNA to restrict its communication to individuals whom it felt were true members of the organization and not informants. Accordingly, we see a larger number of meetings being held and fewer individual speakers relative to before the New Bethel Incident. Unfortunately, these changes also made it hard for the different members to understand what was happening, decreasing the overall comprehension of the institutions, objectives, tactics, successes, and failures. Put into a vacuum, increasingly reconfigured into a shifting maze of subcommittees, the members of the RNA were largely being isolated from one another. In this context, the very community of the RNA was being structurally revised and removed – diminishing communication, awareness, and, I would argue, trust.

In terms of sustaining the organization, the RNA tried to take advantage of the new media environment offered to them after the New Bethel Incident to get part of their message out. Of course, the interest in the organization was severely divided between a largely hostile white audience, a curious as well as part-skeptical black and white population, and a largely supportive radical black constituency. The two brothers (Gaidi and Imari Obadele) attempted to navigate between them all. For example, different brothers would address different audiences and pepper their rhetoric appropriately with whatever nationalistic, legalistic, and/or moralistic flavor was required for the occasion. I do not mean to suggest that they were being disingenuous. Rather, I mean to suggest that they were trying to be strategic enough to discuss the parts of their message that were most appropriate for particular settings.

As an interesting outgrowth of the New Bethel Incident, rhetoric emerging from the RNA acknowledged that they were increasingly isolated from other black organizations. Once allowing them to occupy a distinct niche, their isolation now left them vulnerable and much less able to appeal to an African American population that seemed to be confronted with an ever-increasing number of black organizations, many associated with no police persecution, arrests, court battles, or violence. Although the initial RNA effort attempted to bridge these differences by drawing on black nationalists from throughout the United States, as the different activists and dissident organizations attempted to survive in their own local and hostile environments, such as Newark (Woodard 1999) and Los Angeles (Brown 2003), it became harder for the RNA to attract and interact with organizations in other cities. In short, repression pushed the challengers into greater localism. To counter this, at least in Detroit, the RNA attempted to increase its formal allegiances with other organizations. One such effort was the black "United Front." Unfortunately, as with many of the efforts at the time, there was no front to be established, as the various potential partners were doing their best to keep alive as well, caught in their own series of antiblack nationalist activities (e.g., Goldstein 1978). Here is where repression of a social movement family becomes relevant to understanding the fate of individual SMOs.

Summary

Within this chapter, I have examined the RNA's first major experience with overt repressive action: a shooting, mass raid, arrest, and interrogation known as the New Bethel Incident. I attempted to gauge the aftereffects of this event on the individuals associated with the organization, the structure of the RNA, the ideas espoused within the SMO, and the interventions applied by them to reach the desired goal through a comparison to the period preceding it.

As found, the New Bethel Incident significantly affected the RNA, but in ways that were somewhat unexpected. For example, though the New Bethel Incident was something for which the organization had prepared and during which it performed well (losing no members and killing two police officers), the overall experience was not a positive one for the organization, as my argument of reappraisal would have suggested. This is because, while the New Bethel Incident was generally within the realm of expectation, the sheer largesse of the event (where everyone in the relevant meeting, including many of the leaders of the RNA, were taken) was much more than what was expected – they became what I referred to earlier as "overwhelmed." Additionally, the group was quickly engulfed in a long-term legal battle for which many of them were generally not prepared as well as a relatively newfound presence of or interest in covert repressive behavior, of which they became increasingly aware following the New Bethel Incident. This led the RNA to be what I referred to as "outwitted," as they attempted to adapt to a form of repressive action for which they were not ready. While the group attempted to adjust to the new circumstances prompted by repression, the government continued to try to disrupt the organization, and the RNA continued to discuss what had happened.[11]

Now, it should be clear. I do not believe that repressive behavior accounted for all aspects of demobilization during the post–New Bethel Incident period (i.e., reducing members, changed organizational structure and tactics, and modifications in the ideas of the RNA). Rather, repression appeared to interact with earlier developments in the RNA (e.g., the inability of the organization to advance assorted pillars of their objectives and a growing rift and vacuum in organizational leadership). These within-RNA dynamics weakened trust in the organization, which in turn made them vulnerable to the repressive action that was directed against them. Finally, the members of the RNA internalized government coerciveness as they discussed possible subversion and kept reliving the earlier repression in their search for traitors among them.

---

[11] Given Gaidi Obadele's legal background and the long-term legal battles of the civil rights movement, one would have expected that this would be part of any black SMO's strategy of reappraisal, but this was not the case. Part of the reason for this is a lack of sexiness. Preparing for legal battles is not very exciting for the black masses, who cannot largely follow, nor do they have much interest in, the intricacies of the American legal system.

10

When Separatists Separate

The aftermath of the New Bethel Incident was mixed for the RNA. On one hand, the overt repressive activity exerted at the anniversary and that experienced afterward galvanized the black community around the dissident organization as a group of African Americans trying to improve their situation had been treated coercively by the U.S. government – something that blacks in Detroit (and throughout the United States) were quite familiar with by that time. At a level not previously experienced, this situation brought all types of individuals and organizations to speak on the RNA's behalf, including C. L. Franklin (the pastor of the church that hosted the ill-treated RNA meeting) and even the NAACP (although there was clearly no love lost between the two organizations). As the white police department and their supporters slandered and seriously questioned the black judge Crockett, who had participated in freeing New Bethel attendees arrested after the raid, the black community was brought closer to the RNA, if only in an awkward moment of mutual hostility toward anglos with guns.

On the other hand, the overt and covert repressive activity of and following the event led to a series of problems for the RNA. For example, there was a national search for the killer of one police officer and the shooter of another within the organization, which increased government scrutiny and harassment of members. According to newspaper articles and government committee testimony, the RNA was subject to a wide variety of domestic spying, including physical surveillance and informants. Later, there was a series of trials for those allegedly involved in the shootings, that is, Alfred Hibbitt (or Alfred 2x; slave name: Sam Love, an RNA member from Detroit), Rafael Viera (an RNA member from New York), and Clarence Fuller (an RNA member from Detroit). As if this were not enough, on the heels of these events, Robert F. Williams (the exiled president of the RNA) finally came back to Detroit on

September 7, 1969. Although it was believed by many that his return would assist the RNA, shoring up its connections with other black organizations and compelling greater coherence around one of, if not the most prominent, black nationalist leaders in the United States, his return was actually highly disappointing and a bit divisive as he became consumed with the details of his potential extradition to North Carolina on an earlier kidnapping charge. With the realization that Williams would not lead the RNA, a series of events occurred that would significantly cripple the dissident organization, leading to Imari Obadele's suspension as well as the development of a faction dividing the RNA between the two Obadele brothers, who differed in their approaches regarding what should be done.

I argue that both repression and internal dynamics were responsible for the situation outlined earlier, although again not always in ways generally expected but generally consistent with my theoretical explanation. Additionally, there seemed to be nothing that the organization could have done to decrease the impact of this costly intersection (modifying neither their reappraisal nor their level of trust – which they both tried), except to try to start anew (which just simply could not be done). Again, we begin with a discussion of the two-month period before the faction and move to a discussion of the organizational fissure itself as well as the two-month period following it.

Prior to Separation

Leading up to the RNA's factionalization, the challengers underwent something of a reactive period. The dominant leaders within the RNA decided to scale back its earlier ambitiousness and focus on a few selected projects and objectives. Most notably, this involved securing the safe transportation and freedom of the organization's president (Robert F. Williams), which compelled the RNA to have month-long legal discussions between RNA members on one hand (most notably Gaidi Obadele as legal counsel) and the British and U.S. governments on the other. Additionally, there was the security of the rest of the cabinet, which had been left completely vulnerable at New Bethel. Indeed, the image of the RNA's leadership cowering under the pews of the church and hiding in the basement during the police assault had quite an impact on many within the organization. How could they create a new nation when they couldn't protect a large number of their leadership, all concentrated in the same locale, from assault?

Confronting limited morale in the Detroit base of operations, a concerted effort was made to bring to the city some of what had been lost during the earlier period of the organization's existence. This involved trying to connect with other black nationalist organizations such as the Black Panther Party, which was growing significantly throughout the United States and which had started one of its earliest chapters in Detroit in 1967. This also involved trying to prepare the community in Detroit for a "freedom vote" (a small plebiscite on what they would like to do with their American citizenship) as well as trying to recruit more African American youths into the organization. These were tied to at least two of the four pillars of the RNA articulated earlier: establishing a government and holding a plebiscite. Under stress, the organization returned to its origins.

With the organization beset by numerous problems, however, none of these efforts would come to pass – at least, not as completely as desired. Because of these shortcomings, trust in the organization diminished as the RNA was not able to deliver the goods. Moreover, the power struggle that ensued over the black nation turned many off from the internal politics of the RNA (leading to exhaustion and departure). It is in this context that substantial demobilization occurred.

Institutions

Organizationally, the RNA attempted to tighten its belt, instituting even more rigidity into an already legalistic institution. Addressing the security situation as well as the rather decentralized, consulate-specific orientation of the organization, which was basically allowing individual chapters to do as they wished until some federal policy was established, in a rare act, Gaidi Obadele issued an executive order on August 28, 1969, stipulating that all citizens of the RNA were to work with and be subordinate to the newly approved regional vice presidents. He also outlawed "secret operations" – most likely a stab at his brother's independent spirit. Within the same memo, Gaidi Obadele noted that all military appointments needed to be approved by regional vice presidents as well as the president, he ordered the post–Ocean Hill–Brownsville, Brooklyn, and older (but largely disgruntled) Manhattan consulates to work together, and he appointed a new national public relations officer (Charles Moore). The last move obviously was an effort to get the RNA seen in a better light after the series of bad press surrounding New Bethel.

Following Gaidi Obadele's lead, similar orders began to emerge from the (re)activated core of the RNA. For example, on September 19, 1969, a memo was issued from the deputy Black Legion commander indicating that anyone disobeying orders within the Legion would receive an immediate court-martial. This memo also went on to outline the RNA chain of command, which was something that had not been as clearly stated earlier. Notably missing from the discussion was the role of the cabinet, regional vice presidents, or, essentially, anyone not directly in the Legion itself. The memo appeared to articulate that the Legion was to be self-contained and have direct connections only to the leader of the RNA and no one else. This represented a clear example of organizational rigidity but also consolidation.

In fact, things became so tightly run by the RNA leadership during this time that by November 12, 1969, Gaidi Obadele had officially begun to shut things down entirely, and as one, but an important, example, he issued an executive order that canceled the upcoming legislative convention. Because of the New

Bethel trial of Alfred Hibbitt for assault, intent to commit murder and Robert F. Williams's potential extradition to North Carolina, it was deemed by the RNA leader too complex for the organization to engage in yet another activity. That both events taking all the attention of the RNA were legal in nature, the specific domain of interest to Gaidi Obadele, should come as no surprise. Essentially, this suggested that with Gaidi's attention focused on the two cases exclusively, all other business had to come to a halt. This was also his comfort zone, and thus focusing on these activities made sense – at least from his perspective.

Given the existing structure of the RNA, no one could counter the directives put forward by the president. As mentioned earlier, although Robert F. Williams technically outranked Gaidi Obadele, up until that time, he had not played a role. The regional vice presidents could take some action, but there were other things that they were precluded from doing. Finally, the cabinet was in something of a disarray. Of the original eleven cabinet members, only seven remained, their roles and activities were highly variable, and without any conventions or presidential/vice presidential initiative, there was no opportunity to replace them.

In this context and across domains, the RNA either floundered or failed. Indeed, in the records, one can see repeated pleas for participation in movement events and the ever-present calls for the collection of taxes. Fewer dollars were coming in, however, and at one point a local newspaper covered the story of an RNA phone being cut off (*Detroit News* 1969b). It turned out that the suspension of phone service was simply related to the fact that the RNA was moving to a cheaper locale, but the story nevertheless served as a reflection of the difficulties believed to have hit the RNA.

During this time of organizational crisis, nonexistent resources, and personal difficulties, the RNA reached out to the Black Panther Party in Detroit. In a way, it made more sense to try to ally with another besieged black nationalist institution than to try and go it alone, and with this realization, the two attempted to collaborate more consistently. The effort never went anywhere beyond conversations (i.e., nothing concrete emerged), however, in part because the Detroit Black Panthers were under even more duress than the RNA. The record here is less clear than with the RNA, but there appears to have been significant overt as well as covert activity directed against the challengers (like that directed against them nationally; Davenport 2010). That effort was extended in this direction did reveal a concern in the organization.

Interventions

Insofar as the preceding issues influenced RNA behavior, the pattern is clear. During the prefaction/separation period, more resources and attention were consumed by the trials and legal problems of Robert F. Williams, and the implications of dealing with them proved readily apparent. As a result of the shooting of Officers Czapski and Worobec, there had been an intense search by the police for the shooter throughout Detroit as well as in the other locales where RNA attendees at New Bethel had traveled. In addition to federal, state, and local investigations, the RNA conducted their own, adding more strain to the organization.

Quite rapidly, three RNA members were accused of shooting the officers (Clarence Fuller, Alfred Hibbitt, and Rafael Viera), and once arrest warrants were issued, each of them came forward to turn himself in (with consultation with the RNA leadership). Only one of the accused, the one involved with the killing of the police officer (Rafael), was significantly delayed in coming forward. This individual received a great deal of attention.

By any measure, Rafael was an interesting character. He was a Puerto Rican, former navy man, injured Vietnam vet, Ocean Hill–Brownsville tutor, and over-all "journeyman" through assorted black and Latino struggles of the period. In Ocean Hill–Brownsville, he had come across the RNA. While Clarence Fuller's and Alfred Hibbitt's cases moved rather quickly to court, Rafael's was delayed as the RNA dealt with extradition from New York to Detroit as well as the negotiation of his surrender. Even the relatively smooth cases were highly con-tentious, as Gaidi Obadele was repeatedly found in contempt of court (e.g., on May 6, 1969 [*Detroit News*], on May 10, 1969 [*Detroit Free Press*], and on August 1, 1969 [*Detroit News*]).

It is in this context (right on the heels of a break between a hearing and Rafael's trial) that Robert F. Williams came back into the lives of the RNA. On August 16, 1969, after months of silence, Mabel (Robert's wife) returned to Detroit, noting that her husband would soon follow. With this news, the RNA began to prepare and vigorously discuss the topic. At an RNA convention in Washington, D.C., from August 22 to 24, Robert's return became something of a major point of contention. At this event, which represented an important gathering of RNA consuls from around the country, it was commonly main-tained that Robert could not be arrested and that there would not be "another" March 29 (referencing the overt assault on the black nation at New Bethel). Some believed that the U.S. government might create some trouble with his return, and the RNA began to work on contingency plans. For instance, it was argued that if there were any problems at Detroit airport when Robert returned, members could jump the fence. Contingency plans were also made to sneak RNA leadership into New York, into Mississippi, and out of the country into Canada, if Robert and the rest of the government were targeted in an attempt to eliminate the RNA in one fell swoop. Accordingly, Black Legion preparations were increased, and taking it upon himself to prepare for the worst, Imari Obadele engaged in some highly aggressive posturing, arguing at one point that if the airlines and the British were to hold Robert, then they would have to suffer the consequences. This deviated from the Legion's prior stature of nonaggressiveness and decreased visibility (pre–New Bethel) but was more in line with their changed orientation (post–New Bethel).

Despite the preparation and discussion, however, there were no problems when Williams returned. He exited the plane with Gaidi Obadele (they had been flying by themselves on an empty plane) and was immediately taken into custody by the FBI. He was later released in Detroit and, the leadership had presumed, to the RNA. This was not to be the case.

Individuals

Regarding Robert F. Williams coming into the fold of the dissident organization, I say "presumed" because the organization had consistently expressed high hopes (across sources) that he would come into the RNA and help repair it, restoring the trust and hope that had been lost. It was assumed that as *the* black nationalist leader of the time, he would provide the guidance and inspiration that seemed so desperately needed for the African American institution clearly at the front of the revolution. Imari Obadele's hope was visible as he stated, "I was confident that Robert, once home, would provide the strong, on target, decisive leadership we lacked. Now, [he] is coming at last certain and imminent, a matter of days, I worry less about the leadership and turn my mind to shoring up the citizens" (Obadele 1970c, 266).

Initially, it looked like Imari was on the right track. When Robert first returned, he appeared to engage with the RNA – partially at least. On several occasions, he showed up at RNA functions (e.g., on October 4 for a regular RNA meeting), and while in attendance, he made some remarks about providing assistance for different RNA initiatives. Interestingly, these are among the most militant meetings in the compiled database, for they represent the relatively unique instances when the RNA discussed buying guns (five thousand of them, to be exact), moving to a swamp to train under guidelines drawn up by Robert, and purchasing dynamite. Interestingly, Williams did not make or respond to any of these suggestions. Additionally, after these few isolated statements (or perhaps because of them), Robert was not seen at another meeting, and the discussion of weapons was never as obvious, exclusive in focus, or suggested in such a large quantity again. On those rare occasions that Robert did reengage during this period, he aggressively questioned what was being done to raise his legal fees or complained about his extradition to North Carolina, Klan country – a place to which he said he would never return.

As a result of these exchanges and experiences, Imari Obadele (1970c, 269) changed his opinion about the black leader, saying that

Robert F. Williams... now in America, proved to be such an unbelievable disappointment that scores of us wondered at various times if this were the same individual who had written those flaming, unequivocal *Crusaders* [newsletters distributed by Williams], the same man with whom Gaidi and I had met and talked with in Dar es Salaam, the same man who had met the East African press corps with us as President of the Republic. In the weeks immediately following Robert's arrival I called at his home several times, inquiring when he wanted me to bring records and brief him on the nation, particularly the consulates... Once I simply left the series of documents for Robert's perusal at his leisure. Then, finally, Mabel [Williams's wife] met my persistence by telling me that Robert did not want to know any details about the Republic because he had been subpoenaed to appear before [a] Senate investigating committee and he wanted to be able to tell them truthfully he did not know anything. I was astounded.

This opinion seemed widely shared throughout the RNA.

Robert, however, was not the only one absent. Increasingly, with the president of the RNA returned, Gaidi Obadele (its vice president) was not around. He attended to movement legal business with consistency, competence, and keen insight. For example, in newspaper articles, he was described as making motions, denouncing rulings and the criminal justice system. However, with regard to the RNA, he seemed to withdraw from the day-to-day activities. Increasingly, the mundane, day-to-day fell to his brother, Imari, and other senior members of the RNA (a form of internal exit perhaps).

In contrast to Gaidi Obadele, Imari attended more meetings, assisted in establishing new initiatives like collecting clothes for the needy, and planning a national convention in Philadelphia on November 27. Imari's presence and role as part of the inner core of the government structure was not uniformly viewed positively (revealing additional divisiveness). On one occasion, he was confronted by Sister Okura (formerly Selina Howard), who belabored the fact that her rent was due, her gas was off, and the RNA not only had not helped but had repeatedly asked for taxes (Detroit Police Department 1969).[1] It is not clear from the records if these problems were addressed. In the same meeting, it is discussed that Imari had largely ignored the membership by double-booking the organization to two distinct activities on the same day, an action that was taken as an indication that he was disorganized as well as inconsiderate.

It follows from this sentiment that on October 27 and November 3, there were meetings where there was explicit discussion about ousting Imari Obadele from the RNA or at a minimum reducing his power in the organization because of accusations of repeatedly failing initiatives, changing plans, and redirecting or potentially misusing funds. Gaidi was not in attendance for these discussions. Imari's absence at these meetings was telling as well, because it was during this period that he also appeared to withdraw from the RNA, not attending educational classes (on October 20), rallies (on November 7 and 9), or meetings (on October 17 and 20 and November 6 and 9), which he would normally have attended given the historical record.

The absenteeism became problematic because with neither brother present (a form of departure), the RNA was being run by others – seemingly for the first time. For example, at the October 20 meeting, Charles Thornton began by discussing that the RNA should set up an educational class at St. Joseph's Episcopal Church on 31 King Street that would teach black history, revolution, and RNA history. Charles noted that a nation-building class was just starting on Monday, Wednesday, and Friday from 7:00 to 9:00 P.M. at the bookstore on Linwood and Monterey Streets. He continued, noting that on October 18,

---

[1] This is a revisitation of a specific issue brought up earlier on October 11.

Alfred Hibbitt spoke at Spain Junior High School at 3700 Beaubien Street at 7:00 P.M., speaking out against the closing of Detroit General Hospital. He mentioned that a follow-up meeting would be held on October 25 to address the same issue. Continuing with a discussion of future events, Charles noted that Imari Obadele said there would be a national convention of the RNA in Pittsburgh, Pennsylvania, on Thanksgiving Day. Selina Howard spoke up immediately, noting that there seemed to be a lack of communication between members. As she stated, Imari seemed to be making decisions, and nobody knew about them until after they had been made. In line with this, Cleam Peoples stated that he had just talked to Gaidi Obadele, who said nothing about the convention being held in Pittsburgh. Indeed, he understood that the national convention was to be held in the latter part of December in Baltimore, Maryland. Attempting to table the issue, Elaine Eason mentioned that some of these issues would be addressed at the justice meeting on Friday, October 24. The meeting ended with a talk about a benefit show to be held at the Roy Auditorium at Wayne State University on November 8, with proceeds going to the president of RNA for his fight against extradition. As conversation continued, there were some grumblings about the purpose of trying to save someone who seemed to have no interest in them. On this point, no one had an answer.

Ideas

During the prefactional period, the ideas of the RNA were essentially static. At this time, there was barely enough time to pay rent and keep from arguing with one another to reflect on what the RNA was supposed to be, let alone how it would get there. Indeed, with Robert F. Williams's disappointing return, it seemed as though the original idea of the nation began to wither. Very telling was the fact that the four pillars of the RNA were barely discussed. Indeed, to the extent that there was an idea of the Republic, what was being contemplated was not *one* vision of what it could be but two.

Unlike earlier chapters, attributing what was taking place in this period to either repression and/or internal RNA dynamics is difficult. On one hand, many in the RNA would be quick to point to state repressive behavior, especially its covert form, to explain the current situation in which it found itself. The initial search for subversion within the organization post–New Bethel, the subsequent lack of discussion of the topic, the constant subdivisions of fewer individuals across meetings to establish some noninfiltrated communication, and the paring down as well as restricting of the organization could all be attributed to the efforts of the U.S. government to destroy it and to the organization's attempts to counter this behavior. Once seemingly immune to fear of what the U.S. government would do (Tyson 1999), even Robert F. Williams appeared to finally succumb to its repressive machinations, becoming an apparent shadow of the man who had survived decades of struggle and exile. On the other hand, some called attention to members and not spies or mass arrests. These individuals discussed being overwhelmed by the enormity of what was involved in taking on the U.S. government. Imari Obadele clearly thought this of his brother, Gaidi, who (in turn) seemed to think that of his brother as well. Each just dealt with his awareness of the situation in different ways: Gaidi withdrew, Imari immersed. The idea of the nation seemingly dwindling in the parting of their ways.

Changing Characteristics and Assessing Causes

As for the events surrounding the development of a faction within the RNA, again the situation seems awash in conflicting and contrasting facts as well as perceptions. What is readily acknowledged across source material, however, is that at some point, Robert F. Williams resigned as president of the RNA, creating a power vacuum as well as a legitimacy problem within the organization. The obvious heirs apparent, the two brothers, Gaidi and Imari Obadele, developed different perspectives on how the RNA should proceed, and this partially divided those within the institution as different factions emerged around varied political agendas.

From the source furthest from the RNA in many respects comes the most widely distributed information about what took place. On November 16, 1969, it was announced in a *Detroit News* article that the "Henry Brothers split" (again note the use of their legal/slave names). In this piece, Gaidi Obadele announced that Imari had been suspended. Imari ignored his suspension and blamed internal subversion within the RNA for the current difficulties within the dissident organization and simultaneously downplayed its magnitude. Indicating that there was some merit to the comments made by Imari, the article went on to discuss exactly who and what was involved in the RNA, noting that there were approximately two hundred hard-core members in the organization and that two thousand had attended meetings. There was then a brief but informative discussion of how many individuals were viewed as being members in each of the major cities around the United States. Here it was discussed that Detroit had the most members with fifty; Dayton and New Orleans followed second with twenty each; Brooklyn and Phoenix each had fifteen; New York, Boston, and Washington, D.C., had ten apiece; and Cincinnati and Chicago each had eight. Looking at membership logs and attendance in Detroit from informant reports and internal documents, this estimate was not that far off, which suggested some surveillance information must have been leaked (further increasing suspicions within the organization). In an article within the *Free Press* on November 20, the split was more explicitly denied by Imari Obadele, but in the same article it was noted that Gaidi had suspended his brother because of his repeated advocacy of violence, highlighting a significant tactical difference between the two.

Informant reports from the Detroit Police Department revealed a somewhat different dynamic. For example, prior to Imari Obadele's suspension, things seemed more or less as they had been, except for the fact that neither Imari nor Gaidi was attending functions. For example, neither was in attendance for a November 7 rally to support Alfred Hibbitt regarding his murder trial. The event was not inconsequential. At this meeting, an announcement was made that the Black Panther Party and other black radicals would join the RNA at its Pittsburgh convention. In his speech, Alfred mentioned that such unity would be a good thing. Also at the rally, black lawyers identified the need for "houses of sanctuary" throughout the black community so that individuals could have places to go when they were trying to hide. Additionally, neither brother was to be found at either of the two meetings on November 9 or at the rally in support of Robert, who made a rare appearance, on that same day. Again, the events were not inconsequential for the RNA. For example, in one of the November 9 meetings, it was announced that a new consulate would be started in Jamaica, New York. The lack of copresence indicated that something was going on, or rather not going on, between the two brothers, but it was not clear exactly what.

The records go on to identify that on November 16, with both brothers present, Gaidi Obadele suspended Imari from two of his three positions: regional vice president for the Midwest region and minister of the interior. Imari was allowed to stay as speaker of the House, a position from which he could not be removed by Gaidi given the current structure of the organization. At this event, it was also identified that the Pittsburgh convention was canceled, that money was being sought for Robert F. Williams's legal battle, and that all committees of the RNA were suspended until Robert and Alfred finished their court cases. The last confirmed Gaidi's position that the RNA could only deal with so many things at once and that the tasks that should be undertaken were legal in nature. Toward this end, Gaidi began to hold meetings at his house with a select group of individuals from the RNA, continuing his solidification of control over the organization.

Internal correspondence within the RNA generally confirms much of what had been identified previously, but again the sequence as well as the content of the discussions are slightly different. Leading up to Imari's suspension, there was discussion of executive orders being issued and memos from deputy Legion commanders, establishing a particular prioritization within the RNA leadership. In one of the documents, Imari Obadele was suspended on November 22, 1969. In a later one, Saulsberry terminated tenancy in the office generally used for RNA functions and opened a new office in a nearby YMCA because it was affordable. Something was clearly going on, but toward what end?

Perhaps some of the most useful information emerges from the two brothers themselves. In Imari Obadele's unpublished manuscript describing the period, he identified that during the time being discussed, he felt that he had lost his brother to intrigue (Obadele 1970c, 273):

Unknown to me then, agents from the Detroit espionage ring – including a woman informer who had been early identified for Gaidi – now surrounded Gaidi, and Robert

[Williams], and began to push Chui's anti-civilian line, with the added emphasis that Herman [Ferguson], Dara [Abubakari], and Imari (three of the four Vice Presidents, and the top officials most active in the Government!) were not only "interfering" with the military but generally preventing the government from operating. Odinga told Robert a version of my threat to carry out a military reprisal against Great Britain ("Imari declared war on England"),[2] and Robert quickly agreed that that was a mad man's act. John Davis, more covert in his destructive work, accomplished his ends mainly by encouraging Gaidi in his tantrums and along nonsense lines of reasoning whenever Gaidi would, through emotion and haste, get started on some illogical track.

Direct contact did not help things get any better. When the two brothers did actually meet, interactions were brief and dismissive. At these meetings, Gaidi was generally formal and quite short, whereas Imari was essentially quiet and reserved, something that he generally was not. Despite all this, however, Imari still seemed to love and admire his brother, which was most likely a big part of his difficulty. Note that while Gaidi's "heart and mind" seemed clear, Imari felt Gaidi had been distorted by the people around him. As he admits (Obadele 1970c, 280),

I felt sorry for Gaidi. I knew, in part, what the trouble was. He was perpetually tired and tensed up. His personality gathered people to him, and when they had legal problems and engaged him, as they often did, he latched on to those problems with great emotional output. He took on too much. Felt for too many people. He ended up short-tempered and angry-voiced at those he loved. And now Odinga and Chui and John Davis were working on him. Now at least two of the people in the circle closest to him as the crisis unfolded were enemy agents, including the female informer, long ago identified, who now also had made herself the closest of friends with Chui, and now Gaidi had to know the agents were there because someone in the small group who had helped him prepare and mail the letters of suspension and cancellation, mis-judging when the mail would be delivered, had given a copy of both letters to the press before me or anyone else had received delivery on them.

Although the RNA had tried to develop some way of searching for internal subversive elements (i.e., informants),[3] they had not quite figured out how to do it or how to eliminate the pernicious effects that suspicion and doubt would have on the organization. Indeed, the earlier RNA position of allowing infiltration because of the difficulties in identifying and eliminating it while trying to establish a consensual, open environment for citizens essentially ate away at the core of the RNA as it could later not tell friend from foe (trusted from untrusted). The dissident organization was doomed to poor reappraisal if the government was able to infiltrate, acquire useful information, and adapt to all changes.

---

[2] Essentially, it was believed that if Britain would not release the black leader, African Americans would have to free him through force, if deemed necessary. Although several appeared to support this position, the view was clearly in the minority.

[3] Unfortunately, we have less information from government operatives of this period.

The lack of preparedness for covert repression was also reflected in the fact that the RNA spent most of its time preparing for overt repressive action. Indeed, they had created a whole military unit for this objective. Accordingly, there was no Black Legion countersubversive unit to deal with domestic spying, and if there had been one, it is not clear what they would have done. It is said that military units fight the last war or perhaps the last battle; this appeared to be the same for SMOs – they fight the last campaign, the last conflict cycle (as it were). As most of the RNA had cut their teeth on the activism of the civil rights movement and developed their opinions about what should be done in that context, this limitation made sense.

As for Gaidi Obadele's activities, Imari's preceding characterization provides some useful insights. For example, at the cabinet meeting the Saturday before Thanksgiving, when Imari was suspended, his departure reduced the cabinet to six individuals, all deemed relatively trustworthy and loyal to Gaidi. After being prompted, Gaidi explained why he had suspended Imari. He accused him of "causing Betty [Shabazz, the widow of Malcolm] and Joan [Franklin, former minister of justice] to resign and of calling the convention" without consulting anyone else (Obadele 1970c, 280). Perhaps the bigger problem concerned the fact that Robert F. Williams had not tendered his resignation on his own but that he had been asked for it by Gaidi and the reduced cabinet. Although this immediately caused a major stir in the organization, it raised a larger question: how could someone get rid of the most popular black power activist of the time and cut off one of the principal sources of legitimacy for the organization? To address this issue, a group (including Imari) was immediately put together to talk with Robert and gauge his true disinterest.

The outcome was relatively fast but definitive. After conversing with Robert, it was agreed that his withdrawal was reasonable, especially because it seemed that he did not have any interest in being affiliated with the RNA and he was going to be a cooperating witness in an upcoming Senate investigation. No one thought that the president of the RNA should be assuming such a position. Believe it or not, this was not the worst part of the meeting. At one point, the biggest problem of all was dropped when Herman Ferguson and the New York delegation argued that the "entire [RNA] government [should] be swept away and an interim committee be empowered to run things until an election" (Republic of New Africa 1970, 281). This announcement put everything into an uproar, and the magnitude and intensity of the subsequent conversation was beyond everything experienced to that point.

The RNA survived this debate, which embroiled everyone throughout the organization. Out of these deliberations, the "nation" continued, and it was determined that a legislative convention should be held on January 25 in Detroit, where a new government would be elected, and that Imari and Gaidi would send out the announcement together. This was the plan at least. It did not work out this way. Gaidi cancelled the event (again) and, confused, some would listen to his notification while others listened to Imari, Herman, and others, who showed up at the convention, trying to figure out what to do. No one was quite sure what was going on, and in response, individuals were forced to choose between the two sides, their approaches and supporters.

Individuals and Institutions

Factionalization is generally characterized as a very emotional and highly personalized affair. The activities of the RNA were no different. Given the hierarchical structure of the RNA from its inception and the increasing tendency in this direction after the New Bethel Incident, when the leaders were involved (as they were in this case), there was essentially no distinction that could be made between individuals and institutions. Again, what happened varies somewhat from source to source, but by and large the story is a clear one.

Amid news stories of internal divisiveness, on December 3, 1969, it was announced in the local media that Robert F. Williams had resigned as president of the RNA. The next day it was reported that Gaidi Obadele (still referred to in the media as Milton Henry) had taken over as chief executive, a position that he had essentially held since the founding but an important acknowledgment nevertheless. As correctly predicted by Gaidi, however, there was little time to deal with transferring leadership, as other matters pressed the organization. For example, on December 4, 1969, Alfred Hibbitt's trial was under way, involving testimony from a California RNA member serving as the state's main witness. Alfred was later found innocent. On January 5, 1970, Clarence Fuller's trial was delayed, and ten days later, his case and Rafael Viera's were combined.

After the reported organizational split, RNA business was consistently in the news. For example, on January 26, 1970, it was noted in the *Detroit News* that the "Richard Henry faction" of the RNA (again ignoring his free name) had picked its chairman as well as a new name, the new "Provisional Government of the RNA." The name was "provisional" because (as earlier discussed) it was to stay in place until the larger black population participated and elected their government. To this, Gaidi, head of the "Milton Henry Faction," responded that any and all activity undertaken by the other group was illegal and a clear distinction was made between the two organizations when he stated that his organization was interested in "exchange, talent, respect and love," whereas his brother's was simplistically characterized as a "dictatorship." In a *Detroit News* article of January 24, 1970, Imari claimed that there was no split at all but rather identified that there was "in-fighting" within the organization, a position that he maintained consistently, arguing that differences in opinion were natural – especially within a dissident organization. On January 29, 1970, again there were still mixed opinions about the faction issue. Gaidi maintained that there were opposing factions, and again his brother classified the conflict as one of dueling, strong-willed personalities.

Informant reports provided a different vantage point from which to observe what was taking place. At one meeting, on November 30, 1969, Gaidi (through

John Davis) removed John Saulsberry, who had served as meeting chairperson for quite some time, and who was someone who had worked with his brother, noting that under his watch, funds had "come up short too often." Gaidi also took the bold move of suspending all cabinet members pending reorganization of the RNA. As the government elected at the beginning of the RNA was due to expire in January 1, 1970, this move was especially dramatic. As if things were not complex enough, during this time, informant reports revealed that RNA members had been informed that Robert F. Williams had officially resigned as president, noting that his affiliation with the RNA potentially hampered his extradition fight. This was reported within the media four days later.

The November 30 meeting was particularly interesting because there was more than one informant at the meeting,[4] and the second revealed slightly more disagreement as well as confusion than the first (something that was generally not found). For example, with Henry "Papa" Wells as chairperson, a letter from Gaidi (who, along with his brother Imari, was not in attendance) was read. In it, he suspended Saulsberry because of financial irregularities and improper control of meetings. Reference was made that rent had not been paid for the RNA office, at which point Saulsberry disagreed. Clearly siding with Gaidi, John Davis began to argue with Saulsberry about this issue, the two standing, moving toward one another, and almost coming to blows. Gaidi was not the only one sending messages to be read. Another citizen (Edward Littell) had a letter from Imari requesting that he be given all "national dollars," handing them over to be used as he saw fit. Selina Howard and Mildred Kohlmeyer immediately said no, and another round of disagreements began. Things continued in this manner until, in an effort to overcome differences, those in attendance at the meeting temporarily supported Gaidi's appointment of Davis to replace John Saulsberry as deputy minister of the interior pending further investigation of the claims made, and a smaller meeting was set to address various consulate issues. From this accommodation, it was clear that although the leaders had gone their separate ways, the members in Detroit had not yet followed suit, revealing perhaps trust among the membership but not necessarily from member to leader. Indeed, this parsing would never quite be complete (differing from conventional conceptions of a faction), but there would be attempts.

For example, a December 5 meeting was extremely telling about the condition of the RNA. On that occasion, it was revealed that one faction associated with Gaidi Obadele supported John Davis in his new role, while another faction associated with Imari supported John Saulsberry. Things were not allowed to get out of hand, however. To some degree, the process of evaluation that was initiated to investigate John Saulsberry's alleged improprieties ended up clearing him, allowing him to be reinstated as chair. Although Saulsberry was

---

[4] A relatively rare occurrence but something that did happen approximately ten times.

cleared (he would quit in February for "health reasons"), however, problems persisted in the RNA as certain members did not either inform others of changes in meeting locations or, after being informed, refused to attend (a form of internal exit). On occasion, events became so contentious that individual members began to fear congregating because it was not clear whether the other faction might cause trouble for them (verbal harassment, physical fighting, or perhaps worse).

On December 12, there was something of a truce put forward, and an RNA meeting was held that involved individuals from both "factions" (without Imari but Gaidi) being present. This was done not only to attempt to repair the breach between the two sides but also to discuss the recent police shooting of the Black Panther leader Fred Hampton in Chicago, Illinois. While representing a potential opportunity for unity, the meeting collapsed into yet another moment of difference, as some members did not wish the whites in the room who were lawyers for Rafael Viera to be at the meeting. Politely but sternly, some RNA members requested that they leave, and they waited until they did so. Disagreeing with this position, perhaps because of the magnitude of the slight to a fellow lawyer working hard for the struggle, Gaidi Obadele and his wife left. Arguments continued after their departure among individuals from both sides. In this context, the meeting came to an end.

Contrary to newspaper accounts, police records indicate that on December 14, both brothers did attend a meeting together, something that was not believed to occur. At this time, Gaidi issued something of a "pep talk" to the citizens of Detroit, while Imari (again) denied having a falling out with his brother. Imari repeated this at the February 22 and March 1 meetings as well (the first again with his brother present). Other attempts were made to overcome the breach, but more serious problems began to reveal themselves. For example, in a meeting on March 3, the creation of a citizen-wide letter was discussed to encourage attendance at the upcoming RNA convention. At this request, Imari gave up seventy names and addresses, but John Davis, again speaking for Gaidi, refused to give up his list to be included with the others. About the same time, there was discussion about creating a committee to "investigate applicants, eliminate troublemakers and informants."

Trust was not the only thing diminishing during this time. For example, Gaidi Obadele again moved to remove John Saulsberry, replacing him with the newly freed Alfred Hibbitt (who literally owed his freedom to Gaidi), but others disagreed with this move, arguing that Gaidi did not have the authority to make such changes. Gaidi, communicated through John Davis, disagreed. He thought that this was completely in the domain of his position. In these respects, the division was less clear, as RNA citizens still convened collaboratively, fighting proxy wars on behalf of the leader they preferred. What was clear, however, consistent with the newspapers, was that there was a grab for power being made by the new executive officer, and not all agreed with supporting this move.

Internal RNA documents reveal a less personalized confrontation within the RNA. For example, on December 28, 1969, it was judged by the Supreme Court of the RNA that a constitutional convention should take place on January 21–25, 1970. The convention was deemed necessary to (1) decide which laws would continue and which were needed, (2) revise and update the unfinished constitution, (3) authorize a new government structure, and (4) elect officers for that structure. There was some debate about exactly who would be allowed to participate. Gaidi wanted to increase participation to anyone who would attend (latent citizens), but Imari wanted to restrict it to those individuals who had accepted citizenship in the RNA ("conscious" citizens or "citizens of record").

This seemed to contradict the earlier difference between the two, with Imari advocating fast advancement and Gaidi advocating moving slowly. However, in actuality, it revealed the different levels of their awareness. Having greater contact with members, Imari likely believed that the key to success for the black nation lay in dealing with those who were almost truly committed and very active. In contrast, having had less contact with the core membership but realizing that some new blood seemed important, Gaidi felt that the key to success lay in reaching out to more individuals, not simply the committed.

Confronted with this dilemma, the Supreme Court of the RNA ruled that all citizens were encouraged to attend the convention (including all African Americans like at the founding) but noted that if 40 percent of all citizens were not in attendance from a specific community, then voting could be done by delegates selected for each area. In addition to this, it was ruled that each existing consulate should submit proposals for consideration about what should be done in the future, and a tax pledge would be written up and distributed for all citizens to remind them of their obligation.

Essentially, the convention was established not only to assist the RNA in surviving until the more detailed convention could take place on the second anniversary in March 1970, but it was also intended to move the organization in a direction less prone to the limitations of the current one. For example, it was argued by some (Chokwe Lumumba – a newer but increasingly vocal member – and the Detroit citizens in attendance) that the existing government was too complex, and that while three functions of government must be carried out (executive, legislative, and judicial), these need not be divided across different institutions, because in the context of a captured "Third World people," this was potentially inefficient and slow. Under the code of Ujamaa (appropriately meaning "people together"), different aspects and levels of government could be unified into one national body. This would overcome the weakness of local councils handling local affairs with no awareness of or interest in national policy. Rather than the rigidity, therefore, the RNA attempted additional change to the organization facilitating greater democracy and participation.

Not all accepted this. It was argued by others (e.g., Brother John of Philadelphia) that a different vision should perhaps be taken. These members maintained that

we must at this time, get off our ego trip and decide whether we're going to continue the merry-go-round of Ministers, constitutions, proposals, etc. or we going to realize that the revolution is here and now and it was taken off of the theoretical drawing boards and into the experimental laboratories at the field. (Anderson 1970, 7)

They continued,

Constitutions and declarations of independence and such, are totally meaningless to the struggle of black people at this present time and serve no purpose other than to inflate egos and keep us away from the real revolution...the Philadelphia Consulate are opposed to the present structure of the Republic of New Africa. What is needed is a simple revolutionary structure. Such ranks as President, Vice President, Minister, ambassadors should be abolished. We propose that the leadership of the Republic of New Africa begin to move to the public land in the south. Also that the Legion be abolished and instead, a People's militia be formed to defend our territory...we've confused ourselves long enough for this massive administrative paperwork machine called a republic. We must come out of this convention with a program that is moving citizens into the area we call our nation, we must now dissolve this "paper tiger." (7–8)

Although the basic sentiment of simplification was supported by all in attendance (e.g., delegates from Boston, Detroit, Philadelphia, Washington, D.C., Delaware, Erie, Milwaukee, and Grand Rapids), it would take another three days for the details to be painstakingly worked out. Somewhat drowned out by the other voices and the general sentiment, Imari was perhaps the only person who did not blame the structure, but indeed he pointed his finger at "the people," blacks in general and citizens in particular, for the RNA's unstable existence.

In addition to the broad strokes discussed at the convention, there was debate over several other items, for example, the African-oriented versus American-oriented names for the positions (revisiting a topic brought up at the founding); reemphasizing and establishing a better connection with the South; articulating the most reasonable concept of the broadened electorate; and attempting to deal with the local development of the Black Legion, departing from the more centralized structure that existed.

Although, for the most part, the discussion moved along well under the cloud of divisiveness, things were not always smooth. At different points during the event, there was discussion of grievances. For example, at one point, there was a detailed recounting of the news article in which Gaidi had again identified that there were two factions in the organization. It was also noted that Gaidi had illegally attempted to cancel the convention. Individuals chimed in to put forward questions for the two brothers to address, but with only Imari in attendance, this was not possible. With Gaidi and those affiliated with him absent (boycotting the event and departing from the part of the organization with which they disagreed), the activities came off as something of an electoral coup. This did not go without discussion, either.

Intermittently, there was mention of those not there with some regretting that the convention was not quite the same without them. Others maintained that their presence was not needed for the RNA to exist. Indeed, at one point, someone mentioned that Gaidi and Imari as well as those affiliated with them *"were not the whole Republic of New Africa."* This represented a defining jump from the earlier concept of the institution, which was believed to be intricately connected with the brothers and the small cadre of people around them. Seemingly a tense moment, all tension was defused when Imari agreed. In fact, he suggested that both he and his brother should appear before the convention and be held accountable for what they had done. Again, however, Gaidi was not there and not likely to come. It is not clear what would have happened had he been present though. Not all were in favor of Gaidi's presence at all. For example, Sister Jeanette went so far as to say that she questioned the logic of involving Gaidi in what was taking place, given what he had done to and what he had not done for the RNA thus far (Anderson 1970, 15). This comment passed without response from Imari, who obviously had mixed feelings throughout the whole affair.

Following this event, the RNA continued, but in a very different form. By this time, the second trial of Clarence Fuller and Rafael Viera was in session. Collective meetings continued with occasional disagreements about who was and who should be in charge and where the RNA was going.

By the time of the next convention, the shift in the RNA was complete:

The elections in March of 1970 occurred by process of three regional conventions and the polling effort in the National Territory conducted by Dara Abubakari. All persons who participated were conscious citizens or citizens of record of the Republic of New Africa. No effort was made to include any beyond the conscious citizenry. Imari Obadele was elected as President by this process. The initial selection of the draft of the code of the Umoja was also made by this process. The final version of the code of the Umoja in 1970 was approved by representatives to an April, 1970 Peoples Center Council meeting in Ithaca, New York. (Republic of New Africa 1970, 3)

As for the actions of the RNA, it is hard to attribute much of what took place to any explicit consideration of state repression, but it is possible. On one hand, there was internal development and reflection undertaken by the citizens about where they were and where they thought they should go. Much of what the convention revealed concerned a realization that the movement had moved too quickly for its own good. The rapid divergence of goals in part brought to a head by the New Bethel Incident, which added another point of divergence about state-challenger interactions (but clearly present before this time), had diminished trust within the organization. On the other hand, repression was not completely absent. For example, the convention included an extensive discussion regarding how the existing structure of the RNA rendered it vulnerable to specific forms of repressive action. Here the adoption of a wholly inappropriate technique of reappraisal with its emphasis on countering overt government action was acknowledged. The attendees of the convention set themselves toward righting these wrongs.

Clearly these ideas emerged within a context where federal, state, and local authorities were attempting to disrupt and in certain respects destroy the RNA. The group had been infiltrated and the realization of the situation (revealed in the media and ongoing legal actions) prompted the members to act accordingly. Given the priorities of the RNA with regard to the potential for an overt confrontation with local authorities and those associated with them (articulated from the beginning), the RNA was not ready for what political authorities would do to them or, in part influenced by this, what they would do to one another. As a result, the reality of repressive action was quite significant as the organization was still attempting to deal with a repressive event that had taken place eight months earlier (fighting the last attack as it were – modifying an old war phrase).

Covert repressive action also took a toll on the organization, but only indirectly, as the group was never actually aware, at least in any detail, of what was being done to them. In this context, the devil was not in the details; the devil resided in the lack thereof. Here the problem for mobilization and the key to demobilization resided in the imagined influence of a ghost in the dissident machine. In this world, behind every conversation, behind every action, behind every thought lay the possibility that all was not what it seemed. Indeed, in this world, with fears of infiltrators and agents provocateurs, the government came to have a power that it never actually had in reality. Stuck in this context, the RNA was caught between a rock, a hard place, and a shadow.

In terms of concrete changes implemented,

the new government [the Second Provisional Government largely affiliated with the individuals connected with Imari Obadele] was designed to be a unity government, a government of reconciliation. In a surprise move the convention had declined to name any of the old national officers to the new government. Instead, a five-member Ujamaa Committee – headed by Hekima Ana [formerly Tom Norton] of Milwaukee and with four Regional Vice Chairmen – was named. [The other chairpersons named were Ronald Jimmerson of Grand Rapids, Michigan, for the Midwest; Asekia Omoile, of Philadelphia, Pennsylvania, for the East; Olatunji Oluya, of New Orleans, for the South; and Sister Shurli Grant, of Los Angeles, for the West.] The main job of the Ujamaa Committee was to organize four Regional Conventions in which all citizens who attended would have equal vote (no delegates) and at which a new constitution would be adopted and a permanent government elected. The date set was 28–30 March 1970. (Republic of New Africa 1970, 8)

The influence of overt repressive behavior, such as arrests, raids, trials, and physical harassment, on the internal divisiveness and changes within the organization is difficult to establish here, because there were hardly any such

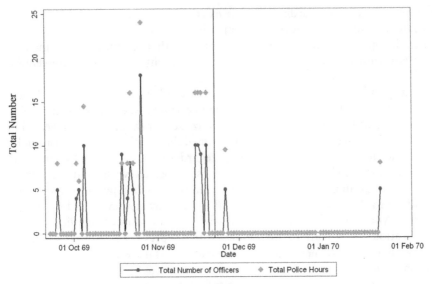

FIGURE 10.1. Repressive behavior around RNA separation.

activities discussed within the source material at the time (a major limitation from the perspective of the study).[5] According to the database, there were only a few repressive acts that took place prior to the eruption of the factionalization issues, and there was no mention of other government action. If any coercive acts were discussed, it was those that took place months before at New Bethel and those directly related to the on-again/off-again trials of the organization members.

Despite the lower number of overt behaviors, the police appeared to be intermittently busy with covert action during the period in question. For example, there was a burst of activity in late September and early October and then no recorded activity to late October, when several days' worth of hours were logged before another gap appears (Figure 10.1). This is quite different from the period of activity prior to New Bethel. After the internal divisiveness occurred (noted by the solid line in the figure), there was a brief period of police activity reported and then another few months before anything again took place.

Regardless of the significance given to the topic, there are very few discrete instances where the RNA discussed individual events of infiltration, and those instances that did take place occurred after internal battles, revealing that once the wound was opened, it was hard to close, and indeed was subject to new infections. Here external and internal factors interact, but in a staggered fashion, with first shock and later reverberations.

[5] Other government actions were not mentioned at all during this time.

Viewing emotional expressions made within the organization provides insight into the RNA. Leading up to the internal divisiveness, there were numerous instances where anger was expressed. For example, on October 22, Selina Howard fumed about being unable to pay her bills, being promised assistance from the RNA and then not hearing a word about the issue later. Indeed, Selina's rant was so severe that it closed the meeting down early. As one can see, in line with the general sentiment of this chapter, the anger concerned internal issues of the RNA, not what was being done to them by external authorities.

Following the factionalization, the expressions of anger are not necessarily lower, but those that do occur take place with greater amounts of time between them and, moreover, they're separated by numerous expressions of fear. For example, on December 14, at an RNA meeting, an aborted attempt at a disruption of Reverend Charles Williams's church on Woodrow Wilson Street was discussed. The RNA had planned on taking over the church if they were denied an opportunity to address the convocation, but the action was called off because of the large police presence at the event, which could have resulted in arrest or worse. As a result, the RNA members left the church as soon as they could. Here the fear explicitly concerned state repressive action. On December 23, there was a discussion of having three meeting places to bring "about the greatest amount of protection and security" for the members in attendance.

Again, these expressions did not lead to negative framing. In fact, a "jeopardy" frame (i.e., one where it was maintained that by trying some activity, something could be lost) emerged during a period when anger was expressed. With no negative frames being put forward, it makes sense that there were no positive frames put forward to counter them. None of this really fits with the explanations within existing literature regarding framing.

Ideas

Regarding the ideas being expressed at the time of factionalization, it is perhaps here that the differences developing in the organization were most clear. As for why the two brothers parted ways and how they differed, according to Gaidi, the RNA developed momentum in the wrong direction because it had two problems in a row that brought those interested in a "military" solution into prominence (i.e., one directly concerned with overt repressive behavior [New Bethel] and one involving the capacity of the RNA to protect Robert F. Williams). This was problematic, he maintained, because

you can't make that damn revolution with that gun. Our emphasis should have been political and it should have been designed like the Jews did, like [Chaim] Weizmann and that group, the Zionists did, because our aims are highly moral and we should never let them [whites] put us [in] the position of being the criminals. We are the people who've been wronged and therefore they on a political basis have to deal with us. And don't deal with us on the basis of their criminal law because some idiots running around this country talking about we're gonna tear you down, blow you up and so forth ... [No, we] want you to deal with the problems and this country has enough wealth to be able to deal with the problem and eliminate all these other side effects – the illiteracy, the ignorance, the bad housing, the bad food and all the rest. (Henry 1970, 20)

This was different from Imari's understanding of the situation. He believed that the military considerations were more important and that strength came from a "carbine," aggressive posturing and an ambitious plan, harking back to the catalyst perspective adopted by GOAL years before. Such a position would not be acceptable to the average person in the RNA or black community, reasoned Gaidi. As he noted,

the average guy working in the post office isn't going to get out here and join some military thing where he might lose his job (and potentially get shot) tomorrow. He might want to. I'm not even too sure how many would want to, but he's not going to do it. And the reason he can't afford to do it [is] because he might be fired and he's got a family and it's more important to take care of his family and try to take care of and hold the family unit important and instill something in it because if we can preserve our family units, then, then, this race might be able to survive. (Henry 1970, 22)

This speaks to the core of the difference between Gaidi and Imari Obadele, an unresolved division represented by juxtaposing the organization's two influences: Malcolm X and Robert F. Williams. As Gaidi (*Detroit News* 1971, 12) states, "the thing that's at the heart of our problem between myself and my brother, the different wings, [was the] preeminence in the thinking that Imari has [regarding] the military." Imari railed against such concerns, but not directly at his brother. At a legislative convention in Washington, D.C., in August 1969, Imari (Obadele 1970, 268)

reminded [the audience] of the small reasons that we, though revolutionaries, too often "cop out," leaving the Movement the poorer: because everyone else is jive; because you have to get your individual "thing" together and keep up with the Roosevelt Joneses. I said, "we admire the resolute and victorious Vietnamese, but we seem not so sure that freedom and an uncertain future are better than well fed, indolent, two-car slavery. A people like that deserve no freedom. What is more, they will get no freedom." I said, however, the children deserve it.

Clearly it was not that Gaidi was afraid of taking a more aggressive posture. He was after all the brother who had been ready to enter World War II more than ready to fight. In contrast, he was convinced that the "nation" was not ready for such an engagement and thus should step away from such a position. As he stated,

Robert [Williams] is afraid of the military emphasis and I think he'll tell you that ... one of the tendencies that military people [have] ... [is] their ignorance about certain things. Not the military at the top ... [the leaders are] politically astute. But when you go to [the lower level actor] and you start getting individual lieutenants and these little corporals and so forth [they are not ready for what is necessary]. (Henry 1970, 15)

In short, there was an imbalance in the RNA perceived by Gaidi, that the organization was geared toward one part of the struggle (the gun as well as the aggressive posturing that came with it incorporated into their increasingly important approach to reappraisal) but that they missed the other, more important part (building support within the masses). Unfortunately, it was probably lost on both brothers and was not brought up in the records consulted that the tension between the two aspects of struggle, which was pulling the RNA apart, had never been dealt with by Malcolm X himself. On these matters, his thinking was evolving and not yet definitive by the time of his death. In a sense, and both brothers would probably readily acknowledge this, the difference was less one of tactics than one of timing.

On one hand, Imari and those associated with his view wanted to push ahead immediately with an aggressive, militarily-oriented approach built on strategic use of coercion, intimidation, and international law. He wanted to move forward with the RNA agenda of moving to the South and advancing the plebiscite as well as black nationhood. It was also at this time that Imari laid out the plan for developing a capital in Mississippi on seven hundred acres as well as creating new African model communities on farms relying in part on African American college students in what he referred to as the "Freedom Corps." On the other hand, Gaidi did not wish to push ahead, instead advocating gradual political preparation and a version of moral suasion. He wanted to move forward with the RNA agenda of developing support in the North and holding a plebiscite for black nationhood. In short, Imari thought that the people were ready. Gaidi disagreed. Distinct in opinion with differential interest, awareness, and sensitivity regarding the inner workings of the movement, the two brothers parted, and with Robert F. Williams out of the picture (the one figure after Malcolm X who could and did for a time unify them along with the others in the RNA), there was little to prevent their parting. This forced the "nation" and its members to choose sides – which they did.

Interventions

With regard to the activities undertaken by the RNA following the divisiveness, the group generally moved from external engagement to internal maintenance but with diminished frequency. As one can see in Figures 10.2–10.4, there is a little more activity prior to the division, but not much. What is different is the frequency of meetings across days. Prior to the internal problems, the RNA was meeting consistently with few if any gaps in between. After the internal problems, however, the organization stopped meeting as frequently, and one can see gaps in between meetings becoming larger.

The activities undertaken after the internal divisiveness erupted revealed that the most important concern was the continuation of the RNA itself. The

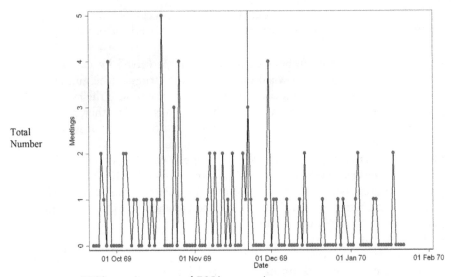

FIGURE 10.2. RNA meetings around RNA separation.

leadership of the organization was in crisis because at the founding, the election of the leadership was viewed as being a preliminary first-step effort. The leaders were merely to be in office until January 1, 1970, by which time it was believed that a larger number of African Americans would be participating in voting and would be electing a new government with a broader constituency. Unfortunately, however, following the internal rift, this deadline approached

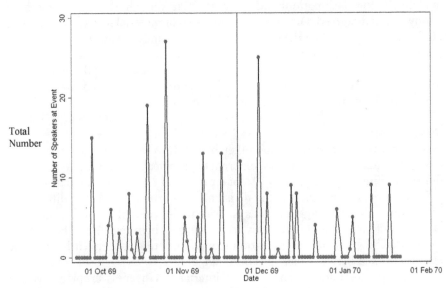

FIGURE 10.3. Speakers at RNA events around RNA separation.

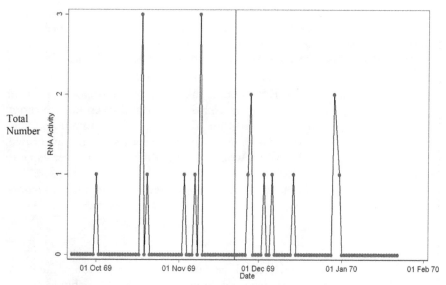

FIGURE 10.4. RNA activity around RNA separation.

very quickly. Indeed, while Gaidi and Imari (among others) disagreed on larger objectives, they also disagreed on next steps. For example, an internal document from the RNA from 1980 titled "statement in support of present leadership of Provisional Government, Dara Abubakari President" (Lumumba 1980, 1–2) lays out the dilemma quite well:

A constitutional crisis arose in 1969 prior to the elections of new provisional government officers. The Constitutional commission either never functioned or was never established. In either case no Constitution was approved before the end of 1969. Moreover, a conflict arose between chief executive Gaidi Obadele and Imari Obadele, Chairman of the legislature, as to how the elections for new officer should proceed. This matter was brought before Chokwe Lumumba at the RNA Supreme Court by Gaidi Obadele's representative John Davis. Gaidi Obadele informed the court that his brother Imari was preparing to conduct elections for new officers. Gaidi Obadele challenged the process by which the elections were to be held. The process calls for the old legislature to elect the new provisional government. Gaidi Obadele proposed election by process of convention. According to Gaidi's plan all-new Africans attending the convention will be allowed to participate and vote. According to the alternate plan proposed by Gaidi Obadele the election will be extended to all new Africans of record via mail.

Imari Obadele objected to the court's exercise of jurisdiction over the matter. Imari Obadele contended that the Supreme Court could not exercise jurisdiction over the legislature.

The court held that the Supreme Court had jurisdiction over any provisional government body in matters of constitutional interpretation or interpretation of founding conference guidelines. The court moreover held that the old legislature could not elect new officers.

The court held however that if less than 40% of new African citizens of record were in attendance at the convention called to elect new officials the elections could be by delegates representing areas where conscious citizens resided. In late January 1970 the provisional government constitutional and election convention was held.

From notes taken by a non-RNA citizen submitted to the organization later (Anderson 1970), we know that the constitutional and election convention itself was a roller-coaster ride of an affair with long sessions, ambitious plans, second-guessing, speculation, last-minute details, a repeatedly growing crowd, and the constant belief that Gaidi would join the event, which never came to pass.

At the end of the event, the RNA stood divided against itself, and the factions were clearly in place.

Summary

Within this chapter, I have described the development of a faction in the RNA. Although it is easy to argue that external subversion of the RNA should be held accountable for the internal rift, this would be too simplistic and not altogether accurate. Instead, it is more appropriate to argue that the faction emerged from substantive differences within the leadership about how to deal with diverse problems confronted by the organization present since the founding of the RNA, including but not exclusive to state repressive action. Unfortunately, the relatively top-heavy and rigid social movement organization in terms of developing objectives and general campaigns could not accommodate various opinions. Following the departure of the president (Robert F. Williams), the two dominant figures in the RNA (Gaidi and Imari Obadele) differed about what should be done next and at what pace action should be taken. With regard to overt repression and the RNA's course, Gaidi advocated stepping away from the more aggressive and radical positions that would invite government sanction (i.e., decreasing militarism, working on petitions and consciousness raising in the North). In contrast, Imari advocated stepping toward a more aggressive and radical position that would invite more government sanctions (i.e., increasing militarism, working on moving to the South, and pursuing reparations). With regard to covert repression, Gaidi seemed to suggest that deradicalization would reduce this problem. On this point, Imari seemed to be hell-bent on identifying traitors and bringing them to justice. Neither approach served as effective reappraisal, and in this context, along with the poor performance of the organization in reaching its goals, trust was diminished and divisiveness grew. The only way to reestablish trust was for members to go with the faction that they felt best had their interests at heart. The affiliation seemed to come with a ticking clock as members waited to see something for their loyalty.

Now, this said, it is obvious from the records that informants in the RNA provided tremendous amounts of information regarding all aspects of the RNA:

meeting locales, topics, attendees, absences, disagreements, common points, alliances, planned events, actual events, and important reflections. These could be and seemingly were used as the substance for counterintelligence activity such as false letters and propaganda distributed via the media. These efforts no doubt cultivated further mistrust in the RNA. What is clear, however, is that repression did not function as most have argued in the literature on social movement demobilization. Both the type of repressive action highlighted by individuals within the movement (overt as opposed to covert) and its timing (contemporaneous as opposed to delayed) were misleading. Repressive behavior resonates throughout a social movement, and it corrupts all that it touches directly (through increasing suspicion) and indirectly (through increasing internal sweeps). Both diminish trust and, indeed, accelerate distrust as well as more broadly hindering mobilization, perhaps better conceptualized as an unraveling process. Once the fabric of a SMO begins to come apart, it is a race to put it back together, as prior disagreements in conjunction with government efforts to push the unraveling forward battle against one another to determine the fate of the institution. In this context, the U.S. government decided to push the RNA again and, in so doing, pull the final straw.

II

Mississippi

The Last Stand(off)

In the wake of the Gaidi-Imari Obadele controversy, the RNA went through a period of instability, uncertainty, and change. While two separate organizations began to form around each of the Obadele brothers, a third organization came into existence where members from both attempted to come or stay together. Not quite able to accept the death of the original vision, this "third way" tried to find a path toward reconciliation without either of the brothers being present. This relatively tempestuous period often resulted in disagreement as issues regarding personnel (e.g., which faction was the meeting chair affiliated with) and guiding orientation (e.g., which faction advocated a particular issue) kept emerging. The situation eventually became intolerable, and two factions essentially killed the third way, leaving only the two smaller factions. First, there was increased tension within organizational meetings about the general state of the RNA and where things should go in the future that on more than one occasion erupted into explosive arguments. Second, dueling conventions were held in late March 1970 (Imari Obadele's being held in Grand Rapids, Michigan, while Gaidi Obadele's was held in Atlantic City, New Jersey), with each meeting barely bringing a few dozen.

Over time, the Gaidi Obadele faction dissolved, but it did not do so quickly. Indeed, the organization limped along for months with few attendees, no real program of action, and few activities. For instance, several of the meetings involved playing a tape of a speech or watching a film and then discussing it. In contrast, the Imari Obadele faction did persist, but on a smaller scale than the original RNA. This version of the organization also changed in many ways. For example, responding to the now pervasive concern with covert repression, there was an increased interest in investigating all new applicants as well as rooting out and eliminating troublemakers/informants (which significantly slowed growth as a backlog of unprocessed individuals quickly developed).

This version of the original organization also attempted to return to the RNA's core – thereby attempting to reestablish the trust of the membership. For one, there was an effort made to address the founding objectives of the RNA as much as possible, first moving the capital to New Orleans to be closer to the South and then to Jackson, Mississippi, to begin the land base for the nation.

All the while, the Detroit chapter of the organization kept the RNA alive with meetings, discussions, and diminishing financial contributions. This situation created its own difficulties as a new cohort emerged, including individuals such as Chokwe Lumumba (slave name Edwin Taliafero) who increasingly came to play an important role in the organization and did not believe that the RNA was effective with regard to the objectives pursued or tactics employed.

With a raid directed against the new headquarters based in Jackson, Mississippi, everything would change still further. During this event, eleven RNA members were arrested, including the president of the organization (Imari Obadele) and one of the vice presidents (Hekima Ana). In the aftermath, the organization went into a tailspin from which it did emerge but far from where it had been in terms of the individuals affiliated, the size and robustness of the institution and the types of its activities. Interestingly, during this time, the group did clarify its ideas as well as objectives, but it still differed on exactly how to get where it wanted to go.

Clearly repression of an overt fashion (e.g., a raid, shootout, and mass arrest) assisted in driving the organization to its eventual demise but only by exacerbating preexisting divisions that were partially related to government coercion – earlier and contemporaneously. This event revealed the inadequacy of the RNA's approach to reappraisal and significantly reduced the trust of the membership. Covert repression played less of a role at this stage of the RNA because prior purges, mass flight of citizens, factionalization, and reduced interest had significantly decreased the number of activists to a highly trusted but numerical small cohort. The group was still infiltrated, but discussion of infiltration had all but disappeared.

Perhaps the most important factor leading to the RNA's demobilization had little to do with government repression but a lot to do with Imari Obadele's inability to relinquish power over the organization and an ensuing power struggle that emerged with Chokwe Lumumba for control of the RNA leadership. Unable to step down or aside, Imari attempted to hold on to the reins of the still top-heavy SMO, and paradoxically, this pushed the RNA closest to its primary objectives right before the repressive event that helped to cripple the challengers. I say "helped" because the government did only some of the damage. Again, the RNA did the rest, and in this light, they stood for the last time as they were. What existed after the raid, shooting, and arrest was not the same, and thus I mark this as the end of the 1968 version of the RNA.

Following the pattern established earlier, in this chapter, I discuss the period before the Mississippi raid, address the particularities of what happened during the raid itself, and then proceed to discuss the period that followed. This allows us to ascertain what was and was not related to state repression, internal dynamics, and the intersection between the two.

Prior to the Raid in Mississippi

Once the dust had settled after the resolution of the factional issues, those affiliated with Imari Obadele's group moved pretty quickly on a number of fronts. They had a revolution to save as well as a nation to build, after all, and they had lost some time with this internal strife. This was seen in several ways.

Ideas and Interventions

Perhaps the most significant issue that emerged during the period in question was an attempt by the RNA to return to one of its original pillars: to set up a government in the South. This idea was born from the argument that the RNA had lost its way, distracted by Ocean Hill–Brownsville, raids, arrests, trials, subversion, and personal infighting about seemingly all of this.

Toward this end, during the relevant period, there were more trips to Mississippi that were taken as well as several fund-raising efforts to generate cash for the acquisition of between four and twenty acres of land. As early as January 1970, there was discussion regarding 150 RNA members being needed to move to New Orleans (where the new headquarters and the new president were to be located) in preparation for the subsequent official inauguration of the nation in Mississippi. All the while, activities continued in Detroit, the place where the largest number of members was still concentrated.

In many respects, New Orleans was ideal for the RNA. It was new, taking them out of the rut that was Detroit, and it was considerably closer to the goal set by the organization but not quite there. Essentially, it would serve as an important springboard for the new nation as well as a step in the direction of the eventual southern migration. No longer would the RNA be based in the Midwest and North, just talking about the South. This was deemed crucial by the RNA's leadership for rejuvenating trust in the organization and increasing the recruitment of new members.

The plans for what would be done on the land were also in discussion by the new group of leaders. Shortly after the March convention of 1970, a new economic code was established outlining what the RNA would do and how. In *New African Ujamaa: The Economics of the Republic of New Africa* (Republic of New Africa 1970, 1), it was stated,

The fundamental objective of our national economic activity (is) 1) to provide for every individual in the society five essentials of decent human life: food, housing, clothing, health services, and education, has six essential – defense, and 2) to provide for the nation as a whole sufficient surplus wealth to achieve our world freedom commitment and, afterwards, the full-blown pursuit of exploration, research, and inquiry.

How would this be achieved? Essentially through education, housing, and land, earnings and disposable income – all collected as well as distributed by the central government.

Additionally, the RNA leadership began to make plans for the next stage of the RNA. This is clearly articulated in one publication, *Come to the Land* (Obadele 1970b, 26–27; capitalization original), where they state,

In a few short weeks, on a site of land in Mississippi less than 50 acres in size, the first model community of the Republic of New Africa will begin a building. The flag of the Republic will fly high over the site, and the first capitol of the Republic (the Republic's President is now headquartered in New Orleans) will be erected there.

But it will not yet be liberated land. There will be, of course, the same kind of control and privacy – the same kind of "sovereignty" – that General Motors or Corning Glassware exercises over their various acreages in America, where, like countless other plants in America, they erect fences and use electronic devices and armed guards to keep alien bodies out. But it will not be true political sovereignty. Like General Motors and Corning Glassware, the New African Model Community will still be technically under the sovereignty of the state of Mississippi and the United States of America.

Nevertheless this move to the land must mark a hard won and important landmark in the struggle of Africans in North America for freedom, justice and a good, meaningful life. Not since the Maroons – the brothers and sisters who, during slavery, used to burn plantations and slit the throats of their masters and escaped to the woods and set up communities that succeeded in surviving for various periods – not since these men have Africans in North America laid claim to land in undertaking to wrench it from the grasp of white American controllers. It is both an end and a beginning, this move to the land. It marks the end of the theorizing about the partitioning of America and the creation of a separate black nation here – see arising that goes back past the century to the Civil War, deep into the days of the Maroons. And it marks the beginning of the true Black nationalist revolution, which, being a NATIONALIST revolution, is a revolution for LAND (since without LAND there is no NATION).

On March 31, 1971, the first land celebration took place, following the acquisition of numerous acres in Jackson, Mississippi. A limited number of members from Detroit and New Orleans traveled to Mississippi for the occasion in a caravan of cars, food, music, and the like. Regardless of the absolute size of the affair, however, the symbolic importance of the establishment of "El Malik" (after Malcolm X, who, before his death, took the name El Hajj Malik El Shabazz) was not lost on either the RNA or the authorities, who viewed everything carefully.

The issue of land was especially important for the RNA because it was the second of the four pillars of the organization: a common history, *a common land mass*, a common government, and compensation for slavery and discrimination. While it might be the case that African Americans have a history, a government (the RNA), and some land (a few acres), the issue of how commonly known these were among African Americans (i.e., how aware blacks were of their common existence and exactly how widely such opinions were held) was an issue that the RNA never quite resolved. Additionally, reparations were not likely: they weren't even on the agenda for most African Americans at the time, let alone the U.S. government. In line with this, the RNA continued to engage the Detroit population with meetings, seminars, and nation-building classes as well as a few other locales throughout the country. Additionally, they engaged in an ambitious effort to involve the Jackson, Mississippi, community in their nation building, especially the local youth at Jackson State University (like during Ocean Hill–Brownsville, with numerous discussions, lecturing, teach-ins/outs, and pamphleting).

Now, black opinion about the land and the need for acquiring it was one thing. Paying for it was something else altogether, and this sent the RNA back to the task of generating resources – yet again. Given the earlier problems with relying on the Detroit Consul, the new RNA leadership began trying to find a different way, one that would be less strenuous on the membership. Imari Obadele's solution was both creative as well as somewhat far-fetched, and at the same time, it returned to one of the core RNA pillars. Imari figured that the U.S. government should pay for black migration. For example, in February 26, 1971, the RNA approached the Detroit city council for $200,000 to help five hundred black families move to Mississippi (*Detroit News* 1971) with the relevant program serving as a something of a pilot. Interestingly, the motion to grant the hearing was undertaken by a former NAACP official (Robert Tindal), who said that he wanted to hear what the RNA had to say. This did not work out well for the group, although they did get an opportunity to put forward their argument: the request was denied by council on the grounds that city funds must be spent for the city jurisdiction alone and not for private individuals. Undeterred, the RNA moved to get the state of Michigan to pay approximately $7.5 million for the black exodus. This request was also denied, leaving the RNA (again) to try to raise funds on their own, something that they had not been able to do since the founding.

By June, the financial crunch of the RNA came to a head when a farmer who had sold some land to the RNA (Lofton Mason) claimed that the black nationalists still owed a significant amount of money on the property ($25,000) and that he would have the dissident organization removed for trespassing if they did not pay what was due (several had moved in, and the black nationalist flag hung high on the property). Opinions vary on the source of this problem.

The farmer and U.S. government maintained that the claim emerged simply as a result of the money owed. In stark contrast, the RNA claimed that this situation arose after prompts and threats by authorities against Mr. Mason. Evidence exists that supports both claims (money was owed and Lofton was approached by the U.S. government about the sale),[1] but the resolution of the dispute is not relevant for the current research. The sequence of subsequent

---

[1] It was not clear what he was told when he was approached.

events is relevant. For example, to address the dispute, the state attorney general for Mississippi issued warrants for trespassing in mid-May 1971. According to varied public statements, the attorney general was already upset about the lack of federal action on the RNA issue, noting that individuals should not just be able to come into a state and declare a separate nation without something being done to stop them emerging from federal authorities.[2] Interestingly, the federal attorney general did not respond to any calls for assistance, viewing the RNA's activity in Mississippi as a state issue.[3]

The problem with the farmer became sufficiently important to the RNA that at the meeting of the national convention on June 3 in Washington, D.C. (then called the People's Center Council, or PCC), a significant amount of time was devoted to its discussion. As a result of this deliberation, the RNA decided to hold a "people's court" session the following month to assess the legitimacy of the Mason's claim and determine (as a nation) what should be done. At these proceedings, which had lawyers for the defense as well as prosecution, evidence was presented, topics were deliberated (without Mason being present despite an invitation), and it was decided that the farmer was guilty of fraud because he had failed to continue with the agreed-on land deal (*Detroit Free Press* 1971). As for the farmer's claim, the RNA said that it had paid $1,000 out of $2,000 for the property (not $25,000, as argued by the farmer) and had made $3,000 worth of improvements.

Unfortunately, not only did the RNA's court hold no standing in areas still under U.S. territory, but the broader context militated against the organizational program. For example, while the largest number of African Americans was still concentrated in the geographic area where they suggested the black nation be built, this region was experiencing a historical outmigration extending back to the 1940s, commonly known as "the second great migration." During this period, a couple of million African Americans left the "black belt" for the Northeast and Midwest (including Chicago and Detroit – interestingly). This was especially important for the RNA because it was the better-educated individuals with greater skills who tended to migrate. This is why, in part, the RNA targeted the local black colleges. Here they could find the skills that they needed as well as individuals that they thought would be sympathetic to what the RNA was saying.

As for the new geographic focus of the organization, the reorientation of the RNA toward the South can be attributed to both external and internal factors. Externally, the RNA had taken some serious hits that influenced its objectives and tactics. There was the denial of support from the Detroit City

---

[2] This, of course, missed the hypocrisy behind the state of Mississippi allowing white supremacists to engage in similar subversion of existing political authority around the same historical period without any such claims.

[3] Though the organization base in Detroit and later New Orleans should have identified the RNA as a federal problem, this was never raised.

Council for the movement of five hundred families to the South. There was the increased hostility from Mason regarding his land. There were a few arrests of lower-level RNA personnel. There was also the arrest of Imari Obadele himself, on August 7, for assaulting a newspaper reporter who refused to stand when he, as president of the RNA, entered a room for a press briefing. There were further attempts at developing alliances with different organizations such as the Pan African Congress, different factions of the Black Panther Party (which had largely been ignored), and the Black Conscious Library, among others.

Internally, the group was largely engaged in trying to account for expenses (e.g., guns, auto repairs, and office equipment), sending individuals to Mississippi from Detroit as well as New Orleans (e.g., one hundred planned to go in March and several went on August 7 to help Imari with his recent arrest), and trying to figure out how to assist others interested in going South (e.g., paying travel expenses for individuals such as Yusef Kenyatta, who wanted to go to Jackson but could not afford it).

At this time, feeling the pinch of financial desperation, there was greater discussion within the organization about illegal activity than at any other period in the organization's history.[4] For example, there was talk about "knocking off" "narco joints" (i.e., places where drug dealers held cash and drugs) on July 15 as well as August 8, and even a jewelry store (as noted in various FBI documents). Financially strapped, some members of the RNA started looking for solutions.

There was even discussion of stealing a movie projector from Wayne State University on August 7 and ambushing police on August 8.[5] The records do not reveal that any of these actions were taken, but their mention alone, as well as the historically unprecedented nature of the discussion, reveals some important changes in the condition of the RNA.

Individuals and Institutions

With the shift in power within the RNA from Gaidi to Imari Obadele and also the strategic shift and geographic focus from the North to the South, two individuals emerged within the organization to exert influences and play especially important roles on the RNA: one familiar (Imari) and one new (Chokwe Lumumba).

Finally free from being under the shadows of his older brother as well as of Robert F. Williams and with a mandate for leadership provided by the national election (by admittedly a limited number of voters), Imari emerged as an important if not the predominant driving force in the newest manifestation

---

[4] This appeared across distinct sources and document types.

[5] Although one might question the sources here, it should be noted that such utterances were not recorded earlier, and now they appeared in a variety of different sources at a time when such behavior would be viewed as organizationally necessary as well as legitimate from the RNA's view. Something, or rather someone, had changed.

of the RNA. Acknowledging that the organization had strayed away from its core objectives, he quickly took it upon himself to help initiate a return to these goals, thereby attempting to recapture the trust of the nation's constituency and potentially build it.

Part of this involved trying to reinvigorate the sense of purpose within the RNA. For example, at the People's Center Council meeting in Washington, D.C., in June 3, 1971, it was determined that citizens needed to be "pure of heart," accepting what was called "Nguzo Seba" (the seven principles) of Umoja (unity), Kujichgulia (self-determination), Ujima (collective work and responsibility), Ujamaa (cooperative economics), Nia (purpose), Kuumba (creativity), and Imani (faith). In Detroit, such beliefs were infused into the nation-building classes offered by the RNA and in the mission of a RNA school discussed on July 6. At the same meeting, another core element of the RNA was emphasized: getting people interested in demanding reparations and land, which up to that moment they had admittedly done rather poorly.

Another part of this initiative involved moving the organizational head-quarters closer to the South (in New Orleans) and beginning the acquisition of property within the "subjugated territory," especially in Mississippi (an inter-action, but one intricately connected with specific individuals). Of course, as discussed earlier, one could not view the New Orleans move as simply fulfilling RNA objectives. By 1971, there were a great many disappointments that those involved in the organization now associated with the city of Detroit. It is here that the RNA lost touch with a former associate (Albert Cleage/Jaramogi), Imari's brother (Gaidi), and many of the individuals originally associated with the organization (e.g., Betty Shabazz, Queen Mother Moore, Ron Karenga, Amiri Baraka, and numerous others); and it is here that the RNA was hit with the New Bethel Incident as well as the problem of factionalization. Detroit was also somewhat bittersweet because it was where so many had become politically mature and furthered their path to nationalism. For the RNA to grow, however, it may have been necessary to move. The change from the histor-ical base of the RNA and the center of the largest number of RNA citizens (major changes, mind you) was only possible with the presence of someone believed to be capable of sustaining and potentially even increasing the solidar-ity and activity in the main consulate. This is where Chokwe Lumumba becomes relevant.

Chokwe initially emerged in the RNA amid the strife of the factionalized and reconstituting RNA. A trained and educated lawyer (like Gaidi Obadele), he was appointed to the RNA's supreme court, becoming the lead counsel in adjudicating the constitutional irregularities at the time that national elections were due (pursued by Imari and those affiliated with him) but were being held back (by Gaidi and those affiliated with him). During this phase, Chokwe frequently ruled in the direction favored by Imari. He also sided with Imari by voting with his feet, attending the meetings associated with this faction. Later, when Imari began to travel a great deal, Chokwe assumed the position of RNA spokesperson and Detroit Consul, a position that had not previously existed but which acknowledged the significance of the Detroit members to the organization. Leading up to the Mississippi raid, shooting, and arrest, however, Chokwe yet again decided to vote with his feet and decided to move to Mississippi, grooming Anderson Howard to take over the Detroit operation.

Now, this is not to say that there were no other individuals involved with the RNA but rather to acknowledge the key roles played by a selective few, continuing the trend established earlier and revealing the continued rigidity top-heaviness of the organization. Indeed, one can see from looking at meeting records of attendees from informants and/or at the roster of the People's Center Council that there were still many individuals associated with the RNA; not as many as at the beginning but still slightly more than a dozen who consistently participated. There was some serious turnover (i.e., departing members). From the founding government, only three individuals were left: Imari (president), Amiri Baraka (still minister of culture although hardly ever attending), and Herman Ferguson (still minister of education). All others (including Chokwe) were new. For example, Hekima Ana was midwestern vice president, Dara Abubakari was southern vice president, Alajo Adegbalola and later Asekia Omosli were eastern vice presidents, Ife Ajaniku Abubakari was western vice president, and Chokwe Lumumba was Detroit counsel. There were also new ministers of economic development (Joe Brooks), information (Sundiata/Stu House), defense (Alajo Adegbalola), finance (Rachi Hekima), state and foreign affairs (Aneb Kgotsile/Gloria House), interior (Agadja), student affairs (Bokeba Wantu Ejuenti), another one for education (Akbar Lee), captain of Uhuru House (Halisi), vice consul, and another minister of finance (Kwesi Tambuzi) and deputy minister of information (Aisha Ishtar Salim).[6]

Interestingly, unlike the founding documents, which listed everyone in the government, letterhead during this later period listed only five names: Imari Obadele (as president), Hekima Ana (as midwestern vice president), Dara Abubakari (as southern vice president), Asekia Omosli (as eastern vice president), and Chokwe Lumumba (as Detroit counsel). Perhaps, by this time, the RNA had learned not to provide too much information on organizational materials. Regardless of the reason, however, the letterhead actually revealed a great deal about its top-heavy nature and how the new RNA functioned.

Insofar as one can understand why the RNA took the actions that they did prior to the raid, shooting, and arrest, the explanation is again complex but, by now, familiar. For example, the return to one of the organization's original objectives – land – was seemingly done to address a glaring limitation in the RNA's legitimacy. Essentially, there had been no significant movement

---

[6] Note that I do not provide slave/legal names because records were not clear on this, indicating that informants were not really sure who these people were and physical surveillance did not prove to be helpful.

toward achieving the goal. This was particularly crucial because movement had been made on the other two pillars of the RNA: a common history was being acknowledged and a government had been established. The land was the only thing that was missing for the establishment of the nation. Indeed, with this they would be able to have a base from which they could propose their plebiscite (another key objective), have a local community that would physically reflect what the RNA was talking about, and pursue the reparations needed to build it (the last key goal).

There are other reasons for the move to the land. In certain respects, the organization was not only pulled to the South but pushed out of Detroit and the Midwest. The internal dynamics of the organization that resulted in the split between Imari and Gaidi Obadele made for an uncomfortable situation, and their presence in Detroit must have been a constant reminder of what had transpired. As a handful of the members left to create the land base for the new nation, however, the majority stayed in Detroit. According to the records, some stayed out of fear of what Mississippi might involve. Some stayed to continue what they started. Some stayed to maintain a connection with the people most likely to populate the territory: the beleaguered, somewhat shell-shocked and wavering members and potential members of the Detroit consulate. Mississippi would prove the RNA worthy to those who believed, buying legitimacy for the process and perhaps gaining some new blood as they were finally delivering the goods. In one fell swoop, the RNA went from theory to practice (reality) – on a smaller scale than initially discussed, but an important step nonetheless.

At the same time, without adequate resources for such activity, one can view the move to Mississippi as a desperate attempt to follow through with what the organization had said it would do at the very beginning. From this view, the RNA's actions were rash and unwise. Rather than expanding and shifting direction, some thought they should reflect about what had happened and better prepare for the next stage.

Repression was clearly involved at this point, but again in a different way than anticipated. As far as the RNA knew, it was highly infiltrated with informants and under constant surveillance. The problem was that they did not know exactly how bad the covert repression was, as they attempted to freeze membership or at least slow it down until they could get a better fix on how best to investigate those entering as well as those who had been present for some time – a very different reappraisal from the one adopted earlier. Unfortunately, the RNA could not stop the departure of older members, and thus the overall number of attendees in meetings and other RNA events went down.

Absent from the records are more overt manifestations of repressive action such as arrests, questioning, harassment, and car stops with shootouts like those found with the Black Panther Party. Indeed, in many respects, an overt hands-off approach seemed to be employed (yet again), at least within Detroit. Perhaps with informants, agents provocateurs, and a belief of rampant infiltration, nothing else was needed. Perhaps overt repression in a political democracy is simply not deemed acceptable even under very specific types of political threats. Mississippi was another matter altogether. Upon moving to the South, the RNA expected and confronted overt activity in Jackson, which was told back to Detroit. Moving directly into the "belly of the beast," this was anticipated, and efforts at reappraisal within the newest RNA reflected it; perhaps a holdover from the earlier approach. Again, the RNA received much less repression than imagined ("underwhelming" in the language employed earlier, which might best be viewed as a different form of outwitting).

For example, on March 9, 1971, several individuals in Detroit were arrested for drugs and running a red light. On another occasion, on March 25, 1971, members of the RNA had weapons confiscated. By the time of the land celebration, the RNA was ready for some more government action of this sort. At the celebration, amid the crowd of approximately 150 with a large contingent from Detroit, there were several uniformed, well-armed members of the newly constituted military wing, the Young Lions (which replaced the Black Legion). The Young Lions seemingly held the police and white observers at a distance, but it also increased the degree of attention that the group received and set the tone for the rest of their interaction with Mississippi. Indeed, after the celebration, the Mississippi attorney general issued another plea to the U.S. attorney general for some assistance in dealing with the black nationalists.

In essence, the Mississippi attorney general asked, "How can we just let some revolutionaries come to our state and attempt to carve part of it all for themselves and still be a government?" Federal political authorities still had no answer, but through the FBI – the long-term nemesis of the RNA, whose mandate pushed it to follow the organization to Mississippi and initiate greater activity – increased coordination was undertaken with local and state authorities (at a level not previously seen). Detroit police were consulted as well to provide background information, but they had no direct involvement in what would transpire.

Changing Characteristics and Assessing Causes

Regarding the particulars of the Jackson, Mississippi, raid, shooting, and arrest on August 18, 1971, there is a high degree of convergence across observers about what took place. As identified earlier, however, there is some divergence, but in a way that makes sense.

As for the noncontroversial part, at approximately 6:30 A.M., thirty officers – fifteen from the FBI and fifteen from Jackson Police Department – along with an armed vehicle, went to 1148 Lewis Street to serve a fugitive warrant. The warrant was for Jerry Steiner, a fugitive from nearby Battle Creek, who was wanted for allegedly robbing and slaying a seventeen-year-old attendant, which had occurred the previous June. It had not been determined if the subject of the warrant was affiliated with the RNA, but it was rumored (from an undisclosed source) that he was with them.[7]

Once surrounded, the occupants of one building (out of two on the property) were told via a loudspeaker to exit the premises. After the RNA did not emerge, gas was fired into the building, which in turn led to an exchange of gunfire. At this time, one officer was killed (Detective Louis Skinner) and two more were injured (Patrolmen Billy Crowell, who lost an arm, and FBI agent William Stringer, who was wounded in the leg). Again, none of the RNA were injured, but after several hundred rounds were exchanged, largely from the police side because of their superior firepower, seven members of the RNA surrendered and emerged. Four other RNA members were arrested in a second, nearby building (1320 Lynch Street) without incident.

All told, the impact on the RNA was almost immediately devastating. Among the arrested were Imari Obadele (the president of the RNA), Hekima Ana (the first vice president, slave name Thomas Norton), Tamu Sana Ana (Hekima's wife), Addis Ababa (slave name Dennis Shillingford), Offogga Quddus (slave name Wayne Maurice James), Njeri Quddus (Offogga's wife), Chumaimairi Fela Askadi (slave name Charles Stalling), Karim Njabafudi, Tawwab Nkrumah, Aisha Salim, and Brother Spade de Mau Mau. All individuals taken from both raids were charged with assault and battery with intent to kill, with no bail offered, as well as federal charges of assaulting a federal officer with bail set at $25,000.

Following the arrests, both houses as well as the surrounding area were thoroughly searched. This resulted in the reported retrieval of two bombs, various booby traps, a "Vietcong type" bunker system, and a tunnel. There were also some guns found, some relating back to criminal events in other parts of the country. For example, although later dismissed, it was suggested that one of the weapons might have been stolen from a Detroit armory along with a bazooka, gas masks, and bayonets. Another gun was initially tied to a murder. After the search, the members of the RNA were taken to the Jackson jail, where the now infamous picture was taken of them, walking chained, shirtless, disheveled, and barefoot through the streets of Jackson, Mississippi (shown on the right within the flyer in Figure 11.1).

Given the circumstances of the exchange and the actors involved, differences in accounts of the episode are not surprising. For example, the police maintained that a legitimate tip led them to the RNA. The RNA argued that the police were there to destroy the organization, knowing full well they would find no one engaged in any criminal activity. The police argued that they allowed plenty of time for individuals to come out of the building in question before they did anything, but they noted that the RNA did not comply, compelling

---

[7] Despite what the police tip has indicated, Jerry was not found in the RNA facility, but this was the designated justification for a search nevertheless.

THE BLACK MISSISSIPPIAN

JUSTICE 1916 ?   JUSTICE 1971 ?

Violence and injustice against Black people in Mississippi is a long established pattern. If We do not die at the hands of racist whites, We become victims of a white racist system of justice. Untold hundreds of our sisters and brothers have rotted in Mississippi's prisons. They were robbed of the opportunity to lead productive and useful lives.

How can We forget Medgar Evers, Emmett Till, Vernon Dahmer, Jo Etha Collier, Andrew Goodman, Michael Schwerner, James Chaney, Phillip Gibbs, James Earl Green and Ben Brown.

The governor of Mississippi, a few weeks ago approved sentence suspension for Charles Wilson one of the convicted murderers in the fire bomb death of Vernon Dahmer, so he can operate his business. Others convicted for same murder have had a number of sentence suspensions in the past year.

Yet, Gibbs and Green were murdered in the Jackson State College massacre and no criminal charges have been brought against their murderers.

The injustice of the Mississippi court system continues today in the prosecution of eleven citizens of the Republic of New Africa (RNA), four of whom were not even in the vicinity when Jackson police and the F.B.I. made their sneak, pre-dawn attack on the Government Center of the RNA on August 18, 1971.

Although they were defending themselves against a sneak attack by gunfire and tear gas, RNA citizens have been charged with murder, conspiracy and treason. Our Brother Hekima Ana has already been sentenced to life imprisonment in Parchman Penitentiary on weak, conflicting testimony from the police themselves.

Mississippi justice is oppressing the RNA -11 just as it oppresses all Black People regardless of their personal beliefs or philosophies.

On July 17, 1972, Offagga Quaduss goes on trial for murder at the Hinds County Courthouse. Your support for our Black Brother is needed.

FIGURE 11.1. RNA flyer following Mississippi raid.

additional action. In contrast, the RNA maintained that they hardly had any time at all to come out before the police began their attack. U.S. authorities maintained that they were fired upon and only returned fire. The RNA argued that almost immediately after being told to come out, police opened fire, and in an attempt to protect themselves, they returned fire.

Individuals and Institutions

The impact of these events on the RNA was as immediate as it was severe. With the arrest of the president and first vice president, the leadership of the RNA automatically shifted to Alajo Adegbalola (the second vice president). Despite the shift in power to facilitate the continued functioning of the RNA, however, the organization remained focused on their colleagues, who became known as "the RNA 11." This makes sense as Directive Number 00006 (Republic of New Africa 1971), issued by the minister of defense and eastern regional vice president (Adegbalola) on June 28, noted that it was the duty of new African security forces to secure "the President first. Children (0 to eight years old). The first Vice President. The second Vice President. The third Vice President. The fourth Vice President. In that order." In this regard, the RNA failed; their two leaders lay in prison. They also failed in being able to ward off a raid, although (again) they did manage to kill one of the government officials and wound some others – a partial victory of sorts, given the approach to reappraisal identified earlier.

As for the others who were arrested, their fates varied. For example, in October 1971, attorneys John Britain, Fred Banks, and William Miller quickly secured the release of Njeri Quddus so that she could have her baby (at the time she was six months' pregnant). Charges of murder, waging war against the state of Mississippi, and assault were dropped against Aisha Salim, Brother Spade de Mau Mau, and Brother Tawwab, who were released on personal bonds. The remaining eight were retained in custody. In November, nine of the RNA 11 were charged with state capital crimes and federal conspiracy. Legal proceedings continued for quite some time. In May 1972, Hakima Ana went to trial and was convicted of murder, resulting in life imprisonment. Not all accepted this without complaint: the ruling was objected to by Congressman Charles Diggs (chairperson of the steering committee of the National Black Political Convention), Mayor Richard Hatcher of Gary, Indiana, and Amiri Baraka (RNA minister of culture). Again repressive behavior perceived as illegitimate and disproportionate created strange bedfellows. After spending ten months in jail, Tamu Sana Ana was released in May 1972, when the state dropped charges. The six others remained in jail for assorted lengths of time.

On August 22, there was an emergency session of the RNA (composed of the national cabinet with all ministers and vice presidents) to figure out what to do. In line with existing law within the RNA, Alajo Adegbalola was acknowledged as president, followed by Dara (the second vice president), Etherero Akinshegun (the third vice president), Choke Lumumba (the fourth vice president),

and Falani Adegbalda (minister of information). Given the importance of the
Midwest because of the role that both Detroit and Imari Obadele had played,
Choke assumed an especially important role in the RNA under siege – again.
While vowing to continue to "free the land" (i.e., continuing to build the land
base for the Republic) through solicitation of societal funds, tax collection,
newspaper sales, and nation-building classes, it was acknowledged that the
repressive behavior in Mississippi would change some things.

For example, it was argued that a "prisoner of war" fund should be created along with an enlistment program to immediately get more individuals
into new African security forces. In this discussion, "gossip" was identified as
especially damaging to the RNA during this phase of its existence. This was
defined as "any unauthorized idle or malicious conversation in which accusations are directed against any brothers or sisters" (Republic of New Africa
1971). To secure the organization, in an unprecedented move that restricted
individual freedom, all alcohol beverages were banned in all RNA facilities in
the Midwest. Moreover, it was ruled that "no citizen of the RNA in this region
[was] to put himself or herself in a drunken condition at any time either on
or off a premises." Finally, there was a ruling made that all consulates had
to produce monthly budgets so that the status of the RNA's financial situation could be better understood. All of this was done without the framing
efforts identified earlier. By this time, motivation was assumed, and following
the organizational changes mentioned earlier, there appeared to be little time
to reappraise anything. There were also hardly any meetings or events of any
kind and, in conjunction, few speakers. From the source material, most aspects
of the organization seemed to come to a halt. This said, anger and fear can
be found during this time (although, as we have shown, these were much less
consistently present than expected).

Interestingly, not only the usual suspects were involved during this period.
Other individuals who had played a role earlier began to reappear. They did
not rejoin the RNA but rather came to provide opinions about it in the public
domain. For example, asked about his opinion regarding what happened in
Mississippi, Gaidi Obadele, whose faction had completely demobilized by this
time,[8] simply responded, "We said very clearly that something like this would
happen because of [Imari's group's] overemphasis on the use of the gun and
their preoccupation with the military role in building a nation" (*Detroit News*
1971). Indeed, Gaidi maintained that it was inevitable when you had an undis-
ciplined group of "hooligans" with weapons. He was not completely without
compassion or ambition in the matter, however. In fact, one FBI document
noted that at some point, he offered his leadership to those who had mistakenly

---

[8] By early January 1971, the Gaidi Obadele faction of the RNA was reduced to a handful of
individuals, little discussion, and essentially no activity. Indeed, much of what they did was
listen to old recorded speeches of Malcolm or Gaidi and reflect about how they wished the RNA
would grow.

followed his brother. None took his offer, as everyone rallied around his fallen comrades. Even Gaidi would ultimately rally to Imari's side, offering his legal advice at the time of the trial, yet again trying to serve as the RNA's lawyer. However, fed up and/or scared, some individuals left. For example, on October 17, the minister of state resigned, and less ceremoniously, many just stopped showing up.

Lofton Mason (the owner of the land on which the RNA confrontation took place) also returned in the wake of the raid, shooting, and arrest. Specifically, he initiated proceedings to sue the RNA for $1 million (as printed in *South End* in 1971) to seek restitution for the RNA's slandering him when saying that he reneged on their deal, as well as to prevent the RNA from returning to his land. Consequently, the RNA was once again left landless.

As Zwerman and Steinhoff (2005) have suggested, new individuals also emerged on the scene who previously had little to no connection with the RNA. Unexpectedly, Imari's son, Imari Obadele II, who had increasingly participated after his father's ascension to power, began showing up at a larger number of functions. On September 5, 1971, he was arrested, accused of shooting an off-duty police officer following a holdup and resisting an attempted arrest. Two others, Rayford Johnson and Cicero Love, were accused and arrested at the time, again in Detroit. Also returning briefly into the story, Judge George Crockett (from the New Bethel Incident) ultimately dismissed all charges against the two for insufficient evidence.

Most surprisingly, and in direct violation of the RNA's law, despite incarceration, Imari Obadele still played a major role in the RNA. Indeed, from Hinds County Jail on October 29, 1971, and through Chokwe Lumumba, he sent a "Directive to Expedite Success of the Revolution" (Obadele 1971). Within this document, he resumed the role of chief executive, reminding all of the chain of command in the RNA; noting that all ministers, vice presidents, and consuls should provide him with a summary of activities, problems, and prognoses every week (effective immediately); and that all press releases and events needed to be overseen by the national minister of information, Sister Aisha, or a deputy designated by her, a vice president, or Imari himself. He ended with a promise to continue to work hard and an expression of faith in those whom he had selected and yet another request for donations to post bond for the RNA 11 (the number of which had obviously decreased but which was still used nevertheless).

Somewhat shocked at the announcement, the RNA leadership that was not imprisoned did not respond to this for a month. At that time, the People's Center Council (PCC) met in New Orleans to decide what to do about Imari's disregard for the RNA's law – for example, attempting to appoint individuals to diverse government positions, such as Rachi Malik Hekima and Chokwe Lumumba. After deliberating, the PCC rejected Imari's actions and decided that the procedure outlined in the Code of Umoja, which determined what should happen if anything like the incarceration of the president and first vice president took place, would be followed. With this response, Imari, Chokwe, and the PCC entered another constitutional crisis of contested leadership, a crisis that persisted for nearly a decade, invoking yet another faction from the splinter group.

Hearing the PCC's decision, Imari first attempted to challenge the RNA from within with the creation of the "People's Revolt Committee," continuing his objections from prison. Chokwe attempted to reduce presidential discretion by altering the Code of Umoja. Imari continued his challenge by creating the "Malcolm X Party" (drawing on the organization's roots), which also contested leadership from within the RNA, and later, he also held his own elections, denying the legitimacy of any other institution formalizing another schism. After numerous attempts by the RNA leadership to counter and curb Imari's actions, the membership became confused about what was going on, and in this light the RNA issued an order to ignore Imari, one of the organization's cofounders and by now a central figure in the organization's history. At this point, I argue that demobilization was complete: the individuals associated at the founding were largely absent, the institution had fractured irreparably, attendance had dropped to merely a fraction, and there were hardly any actions being taken to advance ideas that paradoxically stood much as they always had.

What accounted for the RNA's demise? Although the circumstances in which the organization found itself after the Mississippi raid, shooting, and arrest were directly attributed to state repression (with key members under arrest, property confiscated, others scared about what might happen next, and so on), some of the aftereffects are hard to attribute solely to this factor and push us to view an interaction between repression and internal dynamics as the most reasonable explanation. For example, the shift in leadership within the RNA after the arrest of the president and first vice president of the dissident organization makes sense given their approach to reappraisal. Indeed, as articulated within RNA law, this type of situation was well accounted for, as the RNA had developed clear instructions on what to do if anything happened to its leaders. At the same time, repression does not seem to account for Imari Obadele and those affiliated with him ignoring the RNA's law. Yes, Imari likely saw the organization was in a period of crisis, beset on all sides by U.S. political authorities and their coercive activity. Here repressive action is involved, but not as the existing literature thinks about it. Imari did not appear to be fearful of the repressive action; rather, he was fearful about what the repression could do to the RNA. Similarly, Imari was not angry about the repressive action, at least not to the extent that he was unable to think about how to adjust the SMO to address the weaknesses prompted by the government's behavior. There was no knee-jerk continuation or engagement in collective action pursued. Instead, there was an attempt to fix the organization (addressing vulnerabilities) and an interest in continuing the basic plan laid out before the government's coercive action devastated the organization. This does not, however, completely absolve Imari from guilt in ignoring the chain of command within the RNA and its law, with which presumably the U.S. government had no involvement. In fact, his actions in many ways reflected a lack of trust in those involved with the RNA, a position that would further hurt the organization.

Physically removing the two most important leaders of the time and one that had served as a catalyst for the RNA were not the only things done to the organization by the U.S. government. As Chokwe Lumumba (1980, 77) noted,

within 10 days after the August 18, 1971 assault 10 RNA citizens other than the 11 RNA – including RNA attorney William Miller – were summarily arrested on obvious fabricated charges, including traffic tickets, disorderly conduct, talking back to a police officer, possession of marijuana and possession of a concealed weapon. All were convicted of misdemeanors and served between one and four months in jail (with the exception of attorney William Miller who was released immediately after his arrest)... [Around September 1971 in Michigan,] New Afrikans Kimani Kali, Kojo Kambui and Gamba Kambui were arrested and convicted on alleged kidnap charges... In New Orleans, in January 1972 the RNA special Minister of the UN Kwablah Mthawabu was snatched off the street and imprisoned on a four year old conviction when he started highly successful organizing efforts in that city... In November of 1971 another police assailant accosted New Afrikans Fela Olatunji, Macheo Sundiata and Antar Rah in Albuquerque, New Mexico.

There were a few other events in the compiled data. On August 20, 1971, the RNA 11 faced a preliminary hearing on murder charges and declaring war against the state of Mississippi.[9] Under the relevant law, all individuals who "aid, abet, assist or encourage a felony are as guilty as the principal" (Umoja 2013, 203). On September 4, a grand jury was set to consider the charges against the RNA. On the edge, police across jurisdictions began to overwhelm the RNA with a wave of overt activity.

There were also issues that the group was working with internally, partially independent from but exacerbated by repressive behavior. For example, for the first time, the group was forced to try to go about its business with none of the Obadeles involved in any manner whatsoever. Now, it had been clear that Imari's absenteeism during Ocean Hill–Brownsville and later in Mississippi posed problems for the Detroit Consulate, but nevertheless he was still exerting influence (through directives or others) and would return to interact frequently. In this case, the organization was compelled to envision itself beyond Imari. This they began to do, but understandably one of its main concerns was their incarcerated comrades. In a sense, repressive behavior enacted an immediate cost on the RNA, extracting some of the organization's best and brightest.

---

[9] Interestingly, the cracks in the repressive machine showed during the hearings as the Mississippi attorney general noted that there would not have been any deaths had a U.S. attorney general done something earlier and had the FBI-paid informers not tipped off the RNA about the raid ahead of time. The claim of the tip seems unlikely, given that two of the leaders of the RNA were caught up in the raid and the subsequent arrest. It makes sense that if they had been tipped off, they would not have been in attendance.

Government coercion also exacted a longer-term cost by eating up resources and sucking up all of the organization's attention. These influences are not easily identifiable – especially in the current way that research on demobilization is done.

Interventions

As for the activities of the RNA during the postraid period, much involved legal issues brought about by the relevant repressive activities. Almost immediately, a prisoner of war fund was established in Detroit, which would be used for attorney fees and other expenses involved with gaining the release of the incarcerated members of the RNA. There were attempts to contact various Third World embassies as well as a rally to be held at Bethany United Methodist Church at 10301 Gratiot Avenue on Georgia Street in Detroit. On September 4, the Committee for Justice was created to generate money for the case, and a benefit was held for the RNA 11. On October 30, while all this was taking place, activity regarding developing the land claimed by the RNA came to an end. The Mason land would not be occupied again.

Ideas

With all effort and resources being spent on freeing the RNA 11, the various pillars of the Republic were essentially suspended. The social movement organization was in disarray as the core elements of its leadership were incarcerated or laying low; there was no plebiscite, as only limited work had been done in select locales within Jackson to prepare for them; reparations were refused by local, state, and federal authorities; and the land the RNA had struggled so hard to obtain was retaken by its original owner – alternatively, the potential black turncoat or swindled capitalist, depending on whom one consulted.

This situation was not lost on all members of the RNA. In jail, Imari Obadele (1972, 13) railed against the situation, noting,

A reduction in RNA programs to the level of POW work would be a fatal error; it would be to succumb to an old and familiar tactic of the enemy. It is as if you went to a store to buy a steak, and a bandage salesman cut you on the finger and you ended up buying nothing but bandaids. We started out in Mississippi to free the land by (1) building New Communities and (2) holding a plebiscite. The enemy's main effort is to stop us from freeing the land; to do this, he has given us a problem; people indicted and in jail ... If we stop the work of freeing the land, the enemy will accomplish his main purpose. We cannot do that. We must both free the land and free the RNA 11 (and our other political prisoners).

Such an approach further distanced the RNA from the very black community that they had sworn to represent and protect. Indeed, while members of the RNA fought for their freedom in Mississippi with significant assistance from the Detroit Consulate, black Detroiters were engaging in another battle over yet another incident of police malfeasance. Recall the earlier discussions of historically poor black-police relations, the policy of the "Big Four," as well as the "Blind Pig" incident that began the riot/rebellion of 1967. This time the policy of interest was called "STRESS: Stop the Robberies, Enjoy Safe Streets."

STRESS was initiated in January 13, 1971. The decoys, undercover work, and on-the-spot discretion very quickly led to about a dozen people (mostly black) being killed in STRESS-related operations. Although STRESS accounted for only 1 percent of the department's force, it accounted for 39 percent of police homicides in the city that led the nation in civilian killings by the police (STRESS 1971, 4). Following the deaths of two youths (Ricado Buck, age fifteen, and Craig Mitchell, age sixteen), the community had had enough, and on September 23, five thousand people protested, demanding the termination of the program. The size of this crowd exceeded any group that had attended any RNA event for quite some time, and with the RNA caught in the midst of trying to get its leadership out of jail as well as dealing with the major setback to its land campaign, it was completely disconnected from the event as well as its significance.

This was problematic for the RNA because the topic resonated loudly with the primary interests of the organization. The persistence of police brutality also served as a major force behind the election of Detroit's first black mayor, Coleman Young, in 1973. Young swore to eliminate such practices as well as change the makeup of the predominately white police force and the Red Squad itself. The RNA was an organization that consistently prided itself on being at the forefront of the black struggle, but during this period, it proved to be not only behind the curve but on a different track entirely. Inadequate reappraisal and an inability to readjust over time proved fatal to the black radicals.

To what degree was repression involved with the behavior of the RNA and its ideas after the Mississippi incident? I would maintain that the conventional way of addressing this question needs to be changed because there were few meetings recorded and even fewer emotional expressions of any kind that resulted in coded information. Despite this, it seems clear that the behavior and ideas of the organization were completely consumed by state repression. At this time, everything the organization did in mind, heart, and wallet had to do with government coercive action.

Did this need to be the case? In a sense, I would maintain that yes, it did. Following factionalization, with reduced trust and fear of informants, the organization had become top heavy in its governance, making it ripe for the picking. Although reappraisal had already prepared the organization for what transpired, it did not prepare them for the possibility that their preplanning would be overridden when the time arose – interestingly by one of the individuals historically believed to be the most steadfast revolutionary of them all, Imari Obadele.

This reveals the importance of the external-internal interaction. In the wake of the organization being left in shambles after earlier overt as well as covert repressive behavior and serious differences of opinion with regard to how to respond to such activity, Imari and those affiliated with him felt that they alone held the clue to the RNA's existence. There was some legitimacy to this position. They sustained the direct lineage to Malcolm X and they had developed the various ideas under which the organization struggled. Accordingly, they felt that they had the greatest claim to the mantle of leadership within the organization and the trust that that involved.

This position (the rightful and undisputed mantle of leadership) did not go unchallenged, especially after yet another failed instance of reappraisal following the Mississippi incident. Highlighting the lack of progress in achieving organizational goals and questioning the approach to getting there, others developed a different strategy. Unfortunately, given the structure of the RNA (top heavy and rigid), there was simply no way for there to be two strategies of governance within the RNA at the same time. In a sense, whoever held the helm controlled the ship as well as the voyage and the voyagers. Indeed, the structural deficiency would leave those in disagreement with but one strategy: factionalization/exit.

Interestingly, it would again be Imari Obadele, himself now on the "outside" of the organization (while physically in jail), who would lead an attempt to change the structure of the organization. He attempted to protect as well as continue the vision that he had believed in and to find a space for dueling political ideas within one organization. Unfortunately, he was too late, and not enough people bought into the idea. By this time, the RNA had effectively demobilized, and with that, the individuals, ideas, interventions, and institutions of the March 1968 cohort disappeared, transferred to other movement organizations, and/or went away for a while, only to come back later in a different organizational form, with slightly different ideas, different interventions, and different individuals. Indeed, although the organization created by the individuals who came together in March 1968 was effectively gone by the end of 1971, it is inaccurate to say that this is when the struggle waged by these individuals ended or that the institution of the RNA did not continue in some way.

Over time, the cohort of individuals who began the RNA withdrew and/or moved on to other struggles. Jaramogi Abebe Agyeman (previously Albert Cleage), who was associated with those who would create the RNA, went on to found and lead the Shrine of the Black Madonna, which is a Pan-African Orthodox Christian Church founded in 1970 and based on the principles of building black institutional, spiritual, and religious power – persisting to this day. After leaving the RNA, Gaidi Obadele (returning to his slave name, Milton Henry) founded Christ Presbyterian Church in Southfield, Michigan, and preached there until his death in 2006. Imari Obadele/Richard Henry continued to try to govern the RNA for several years, before and after going to prison. Later, he helped create the National Coalition of Blacks for Reparations in America (N'COBRA). This organization continued to call for compensation to all those formerly enslaved. In fact, the pioneering efforts of the RNA in raising the topic and the continuation of this work in N'COBRA were largely responsible for the later emergence of the topic in the United States. Imari was also engaged in varied struggles providing advice to different organizations and trying to find homes for various documents, right up until his death in 2010. Chokwe Lumumba went on to become a lawyer representing human rights cases not just in the United States but throughout the world. He also went on to become a councilman and mayor in Jackson, Mississippi, until his death in early 2014. There are many, many others, and in fact tracking down all of the different paths taken by former RNA members is the subject of another research effort entirely.[10] The point here is that many of the individuals who left the RNA stepped away from a grand discussion and plan of action, moving instead to address small parts of the problem in a more immediate way – as a lawyer, a teacher, a social worker. It would be wrong to say that these individuals have demobilized (at least not completely) because they have not ceased to concern themselves with the problems of their constituency. They have simply selected a different approach, a different venue within which to pursue change. As social movement scholars moved to explore everyday forms of resistance and periods of "abeyance," it is important to remember that while the revolution ends as an institution, the revolutionary continues. They may or may not join another institution, which is important to understand, but struggles continue in different ways, and researchers have been attentive to such dynamics, but we need to continue and extend this work looking at the children of activists, their children's children, and those who come in contact with them.

Looking over time, many of the ideas and interventions advocated by the RNA did not enjoy as much success as the reparations effort. For example, there has never been a national plebiscite of African Americans regarding their status, and given public opinion data concerning African American affiliations with the country, it is not likely to happen. Similarly, "electoral secession" (where a black group would elect politicians who would then use their powers to institutionalize the control of a black nation) and "expanded sovereignty" (where an African American organization would systematically seek to undermine and replace U.S. political sovereignty by directly administering to the unmet needs of blacks) have never been taken up – at least, not widely.

As for the RNA itself, it still also persists – to this day. The activities of the organization might not be newsworthy as they once were, but they still attempt to push forward the cause and claims of African American empowerment and equality.

---

[10] Please contact me if you know someone who worked with the RNA.

This lack of popularity and attention is especially intriguing given the fact that many of the problems that confronted the black community during the time of the RNA have not been resolved. In discussions of postracialism after President Barack Obama's victory, there has been a fundamental disregard for the raw data underneath this assertion. Has the number of employed African Americans relative to whites decreased? Has the number of African Americans poorly treated by the police decreased? Are blacks as likely as whites to be stopped on the street, arrested, convicted, and/or paroled? Have the wealth and income gaps been reduced over time? Is black self-esteem at levels comparable to white self-esteem? What is desired by African Americans as it relates to their citizenship, their identity? These are the questions and topics to which we are led when assessing the death and afterlife of the RNA. The case also makes individuals reflect on the subject of antiblack violence. For example, after the African American shock of the George Zimmerman verdict in the Trayvon Martin killing (the young black male shot by the older white Zimmerman, who felt threatened by the youth) and the growing awareness of the historically unlikely scenario that whites will be convicted for killing African Americans, it would not be surprising to see the antiblack violence issue in particular being raised in salience, but to date, there has been little effort in this regard. The 2014 shooting of Michael Brown and subsequent rioting in Ferguson, Missouri represents yet another opportunity for such a discussion.

Summary

Within the chapter, I discussed the demobilization of the SMO – the RNA – composed of those brought together in March 1968. As shown, the death as well as injury of police officers in Mississippi and the subsequent raid, shootout, and arrest of the core RNA leadership not only resulted in the removal of the organization's most dominant presence at the time and one of its cofounders (Imari Obadele) but also inaugurated a new power struggle within the RNA between the incarcerated leader and those who attempted to govern in his absence. Partial removal thus facilitated factionalization another intersection of the external and internal. Although the RNA had developed provisions for the leader's arrest and removal (reappraisal), it had not developed provisions for a leader trying to run the revolutionary organization from prison. In addition to this, sensing that the organization was "on the ropes," the U.S. government engaged in a series of arrests that essentially placed the RNA in full crisis mode, moving in and out of court and jail as well as the bail bondsman's office. In this context, under siege, with little to no confidence in the organization's ability to function, excluded from decision making, observing no movement toward the group's goals, and observing yet another battle over who led the organization, individuals departed, movement ideas went unfulfilled, and all actions became engrossed with freeing the imprisoned and away from the core objectives of the organization. In short, the RNA demobilized. This did not end the story, however, for movement termination sent the various elements of the claims-making effort formally initiated in 1968 to other, admittedly smaller, seemingly less newsworthy as well as dramatically transformative forms and formats. Here, modifying a famous phrase: governments might try to kill a revolutionary institution, eliminate some revolutionaries, and modify the revolutionary agenda, but it does not kill *the revolution* – at least not by itself. As found, revolutionaries have to assist in this process, because interestingly, even when the institutions, individuals, ideas, and interventions are changed, the spirit of change itself, the impetus to challenge authorities may continue. The revolutionary can just seek a different venue for expression. Or, they can just attempt to forget and disappear, ready to emerge again when worthwhile ideas, individuals, institutions and interventions arise. If/when they do, however, rest assured that there will be some government agents there trying to identify, confuse, intimidate, provoke, constrain and eliminate them. And, in this dynamic relationship, along with the lessons from prior interactions as well as the preparations that are made for what will likely transpire which are adopted by the relevant actors (if any), the struggle for change and order continues.

PART V

CONCLUSION

I2

Understanding the Death of Social Movement Organizations

In this book, I have attempted to shed some light on social movement demobilization (i.e., why individuals no longer associate with a political challenger
pursuing social change, why the ideas initially pursued by dissidents shift in
fundamental ways, why the activities selected by challengers are altered, and
why formal institutions cease to exist). While demobilization has been discussed
recently with specific attention given to al-Qaeda and the Iraqi insurgency as
well as the Arab Spring, these discussions have unfortunately been largely based
on little systematic scholarship. In part, this is because the existing literature
has been generally concerned with movement emergence and variations in the
conduct of challengers once they are under way. Newer work has explored
the outcomes of SMOs, but essentially little to nothing exists on the topic of
the processes of exactly how social movement organizations demobilize (i.e.,
how they die). The absence of this scholarship is also due to the fact that there
are significant data requirements necessary for such an investigation. To analyze this topic, one not only needs information about what SMOs do (e.g.,
meso-level information) but also who is present for the challenge, information
about what they say during their struggle with political authorities, some indication of what they feel (e.g., micro-level information), and what governments
do against them (again meso-level information). One needs this information
not simply during periods of repression but also in varied nonrepressive contexts – before (to establish a baseline), during (to know what happened), and
after (to assess effects over time). Part of the explanation is also due to the fact
that most research is dedicated to successful social movements (i.e., ones that
we like and that achieve remarkable things, such as democracy, regime change,
and decreased human rights violations). This focus has resulted in those concerned with the topic generally examining and understanding those who win
and those that result in happy outcomes. Although comforting, such a focus

does not always result in greater comprehension of the phenomenon in which we are interested.

Within this chapter, I first outline and review my theoretical argument concerning SMO death, discuss the case and the evidence used to examine the argument put forward, and then present some basic findings. Following this, I discuss some of the lessons from this research for challengers, authorities, and researchers interested in demobilization in particular and state-dissident interactions in general. I address some of the issues concerning case selection and sensitivity, thinking counterfactually about the trajectory that the RNA followed and how easily other paths and other outcomes could have been found.

Overview

To study state-dissident interactions and the outcomes of these exchanges, especially those concerning the demobilization of behavioral challengers, one has to explore the interaction between governments and challengers explicitly but also the internal dynamics that take place within challenging organizations themselves (i.e., their ideas, institutional structures, and individuals associated with them, bringing together the micro and meso). This is a somewhat different approach from that developed in most social science research – especially the quantitative literature, because it tends to divide and examine individually so-called *external* explanations (i.e., those factors outside of SMOs that are believed to influence them) from *internal* explanations (i.e., those factors inside of SMOs). To conduct the type of examination suggested earlier, I first discussed what we know about demobilization. Here I went through various arguments external or internal to SMOs, identifying which forces outside of behavioral challenges carry the explanatory weight as well as which forces within behavioral challenges carry the explanatory weight, respectively – but viewed distinctly. In line with a newer trend in the literature, I then discussed how these two factors combined to explain movement demobilization.

Essentially, my argument involved a coevolutionary dynamic composed of behavioral challengers – SMOs and political authorities. The former (the movement institution) attempts to recruit, socialize, and act on behalf of specific goals using a wide variety of tactics – specifically those viewed as being outside of the mainstream of political engagement and frequently with an element of coercion involved (e.g., contentious politics). The latter (authorities) attempts to intimidate, frustrate, scare off, and/or eliminate challengers with a wide variety of tactics, most notably overt and covert repressive activity. Coevolution becomes relevant because both sides of the conflict respond to each others' attempts at influencing them, and they do so in a way that attempts to simultaneously promote their own survival and their opponent's death or containment. The different actors are not simply shocked and perturbed by each effort, however, as currently perceived. Rather, I argue that attempts are made to reduce the impact of conflictual exchanges during the course of the conflict.

On one hand, SMOs realize that authorities attempt to disrupt them, and they try to prepare their membership for what could transpire, informing them about what will happen, what it will be like, and what they should do if and when it occurs. I called this *reappraisal*. In addition to this, movement organizations attempt to provide their members with enough social and psychological support, identity, and effectiveness in understanding what is going on and meeting the needs of constituents so that they can establish and retain *trust* (i.e., a willingness to put oneself into another's hands despite significant risk).

On the other hand, political authorities realize that SMOs attempt to counter their attempts at disruption, and thus they attempt to counter the counteractivity. One approach to this is what I called *overwhelming*, when authorities apply more repression than anticipated but of the same type. Alternatively, authorities can try *outwitting*, when they apply strategies that are different from what dissidents believe will be used against them. Governments also attempt to create *distrust*, but for this to actually work, challengers generally need to internalize and express their suspicions, thereby partially taking the responsibility for this movement problem. Toward this end, on some occasions, authorities can plant stories about infiltration, release information suggesting subversion, or make their agents easily identifiable to try to wield influence.[1]

Drawing on research often referenced as the conflict-repression nexus, this move-countermove approach leads to some important implications and expectations:

- First, when reappraisal is generally effective at identifying what governments do, challengers will likely be able to withstand repressive attempts to disrupt them (not falling victim to either rampant anger or fear, which existing research currently focuses on as the driving explanatory factors for subsequent behavior), and organizational trust is established and sustained; when reappraisal is generally ineffective in identifying what governments do, social movement organizations will not be able to withstand attempts at disruption, and trust is diminished.
- Second, governments with good intelligence can readily attempt to disrupt SMOs with *outwitting* and *distrust*, which is relatively inexpensive and requires little investment in any one strategy. Without good intelligence, however, they are more likely to engage in *overwhelming*;
- Third, using the wrong approach (i.e., one that does not appear to be proportional and appropriate) can be costly for governments, especially democratic ones, because the general citizenry may not look favorably on government

---

[1] Within my argument, it is not believed that political challengers can infiltrate governments to subvert them from the inside, and thus the model is largely asymmetrical.

repressive behavior, and the specific citizenry most directly connected to the SMO might rally around it following its persecution.

- Fourth, though reappraisal and trust are essential factors in understanding demobilization, other factors may be involved as well (e.g., factionalization, lost commitment, burnout, and limited resources).
- Fifth, demobilization is an iterative experience as governments and challengers go back and forth, until one has the advantage over the other – the government in the case of demobilization.[2]

Within this book, these hypotheses were explored through process tracing, using a unique data source that covered a group called the RNA and the efforts of the U.S. government to monitor, contain, and destroy this social movement organization. This interaction took place between 1968 and 1971. As conceived, the RNA pursued four objectives: (1) they wanted five states in the Deep South to be given to African Americans so that they could create their own nation (institutionalizing the one that already existed), (2) they wanted reparations for slavery, (3) they wanted a plebiscite to determine what should happen with blacks, and (4) they wanted a separate government. Although the group was national in its recruitment, membership, institutions, and behavior (involving numerous states), it was largely based in Detroit, Michigan; this was the locale for most of its members, its behavior, and its headquarters (for most of its existence) as well as the place on which most of the records focused.

Consulting more than ten thousand documents (including local, state, and federal police records; media reports from Detroit and national newspapers; and various records from the RNA itself), I carefully examined five periods during the relevant state-dissident conflict: (1) the founding of the RNA on March 28, 1968; (2) the implementation and development of its secessionist initiative in Ocean Hill–Brownsville, Brooklyn, in October 15, 1968; (3) the shooting, raid, and mass arrest at New Bethel Baptist Church in Detroit on March 28, 1969 (known as the "New Bethel Incident"); (4) the development of a faction within the organization on November 16, 1969; and finally, (5) the raid, shooting, and arrest in Jackson, Mississippi, of assorted members that occurred on August 18, 1971. These periods were specifically selected to identify distinct influences, that is, nothing taking place, exclusively externally driven state repression, exclusively internally driven RNA tensions unrelated to repressive action or some interaction between the external and internal environments. Identifying the individuals involved, the institutional structure in place, interventions undertaken (i.e., actions), and ideas advocated by the organization to understand the degree of demobilization, I examined all documents in the available archive (concerning events, utterances, and opinions) by the day

---

[2] Although there has been no global study taken over time, I would argue that historically, governments have vanquished most of the SMOs that have emerged within their territorial jurisdictions.

for the two-month period before the events in question to establish a baseline. I then examined the time of the event itself as well as the two-month period after the event was completed to assess effects. This approach allowed me to examine what changes (if any) took place and how long these lasted[3] – both over individual pre/event/post periods and across periods.

In line with my argument, the results disclosed that the demobilization of the RNA was connected with the organization's largely failed approach at reappraisal of repression, but this did not account for the RNA's demise by itself. Rather, it reinforced the loss of trust that resulted from the organization's failure to achieve pursued goals, including the protection of organizational members from state repressive action.[4] Generally preparing for overt repression, the organization was beset with a series of incidents involving covert action, which had been largely unanticipated. Overt behavior did exist, but the RNA was largely prepared for it, and thus it was somewhat less devastating for the group. It turned out that although some of the activity brought greater sympathy and more recruits to the organization, at the same time, many others were scared off by the actual overt behavior that took place – this was due to the overwhelming nature of some repressive behavior (e.g., the mass arrest and detention of everyone at New Bethel Baptist Church following an extensive shootout and raid was far more extreme than thought possible). Though it was only through replacement of members that the organization could sustain itself, over time, this became difficult. As anticipated, the inability to predict what form of repression would be used decreased trust within the organization.

Generally unanticipated and thus damaging to the organization's morale was the protracted length of time over which repression influenced SMOs. Along with most researchers in the current literature, I believed that the impact of repressive action would be either contemporaneous or short term. My investigation of the RNA, however, revealed that the dissidents talked or thought about and planned activity concerning previous repressive behavior for months, and occasionally for years, after relevant events occurred. In a sense, the analysis suggests that dissidents become carriers of repressive experiences, which they thereafter take with them into the social movement, affecting all who come across them.

Also generally unexpected was the greater importance of covert repressive action (largely neglected in existing literature) relative to more overt behavior

[3] In more explicitly quantitative work, I also explore more traditional time series investigations. Although useful in many ways, such an approach does not allow me to provide the sophistication and detail that I am able to provide with the approach applied here.

[4] For example, trust decreased because the group did not make significant progress toward its most important objectives (i.e., the plebiscite, reparations, and most importantly land); the leadership ceased to function following the fractionalization; and numerous decisions made within the organization seemed highly erratic and/or disconnected from the group's goals. Much of the lost trust was repression related.

(largely the focus of existing work). As found, the fear of informants and internal subversion proved to influence RNA (de)mobilization far more than anything else, in part because it turned every other member of the organization into a potential traitor. Once perceived, this is hard to overcome. In the U.S.-RNA case, when the leader of the organization became aware of this dynamic (of members seeing each other as potential traitors and shutting off from further contact or communication), the members attempted to reestablish trust by decreasing the number of individuals to only the most trustworthy and starting again. Not only was this inefficient as the activities of these individuals were infiltrated as well, but this inevitably alienated those who were not among the innermost circle, and it decreased the number of people involved with movement activity as the pool had been reduced.

In the end, the RNA was caught in a downward spiral in which repeated failures of reappraisal continued to reduce trust and, in turn, other internal dynamics beset the organization that are frequently highlighted by social movement scholars. One important negative influence was an organizational factor generally considered under the category of rigidity. Over time, a small clique of individuals (led by Gaidi Obadele/Milton Henry and Imari Obadele/Richard Henry) hindered the RNA's ability to adapt to changing personnel and circumstances because they largely dominated the RNA throughout the period under examination. Resource acquisition was a persistent source of tension as well, which fed into other organizational problems, both internal and external. Indeed, the more the RNA tried to do, the more money they tried to squeeze from their membership (especially the group in Detroit). This led to greater sacrifices, greater expectations about what would happen, and greater grievances when they did not.

Under all this weight, the individuals, institutions, and interventions largely demobilized. Although several individuals continued to engage in struggle, it seemed that ideas were the only elements of the claims-making effort that persisted. The dream of the black nation initially sparked by Malcolm X and later buoyed by Robert F. Williams within the relevant cohort of activists in Detroit continued, but nothing like how it was imagined.

General Lessons

What are the implications of this work for others? I think that there are several, and for different audiences.

For Challengers

The RNA versus U.S. government research teaches those interested in challenging political authorities a great deal about social movement demobilization. For example, guided by the preceding findings, if one were trying to mobilize, then one would need to be concerned with selecting individuals who are committed to an organization with a set of ideas and tactics but not so rigidly devoted to them that they are unable to adapt to situations around them. It is clear from the analysis that there needs to be some structure for engagement within the institution and rules for dealing with participants, but there also needs to be some flexibility. Furthermore, there need to be mechanisms for adjusting these institutions and roles in a transparent, easily understood manner.

Although this sounds reasonable, given the task of challenging political authorities, potentially with deadly violence, these requirements are not as easy to establish and maintain as it might seem. For example, only someone significantly committed to a cause would want to join an organization in which individuals could potentially be killed (i.e., so-called high-risk challengers). It should not surprise anyone that these people might not be excessively flexible when it comes to adjusting objectives and tactics. However, effective reappraisal necessitates the systematic and continuous analysis of repressive behavior, understanding how it influences social movement participants, behavior, and institutions as well as communicating this understanding to those in the movement. Such a process is crucial for establishing trust, which is determined by other things as well.

Indeed, my research shows that simply predicting repression correctly is not all that needs to be done. In the U.S.-RNA case, when overt repressive behavior occurred in line with movement expectations, this increased the trust of and reliance on the power of those contending with this type of repression, the military wing of the RNA (the Black Legion). This led the U.S. government to overwhelm as well as outwit the challengers, however, who seemed to realize that such a reliance revealed a particular vulnerability within the RNA. Specifically, as the role of the Black Legion increased, the role of others decreased, which in turn reduced general trust in the organization as more and more individuals were shut out. Once the struggle became a military one, only the military and those activities advocated by them were thought necessary.

Perhaps most important, the research discloses that individual members of SMOs are not only the physical embodiment of the revolutionary cause but potentially the embodiment of fear, paranoia, and duplicitous activity, which advances the government's agenda. Recruiting from tight networks is one way to address this problem, but these networks might not be big enough to replace individuals lost during the conflict either through death or departure.

A final point concerns reducing the potential for wedge issues being developed within challenging institutions and decreasing the potential for political authorities to exploit them. This involves maintaining a constant watch on topics over which group members are highly divided and attempting to diffuse the development or escalation of such tensions. Interestingly, such a position is very much in line with William Riker's argument in *The Art of Political Manipulation* (1986). While it might appear that openly discussing these issues is the most appropriate strategy for dealing with them, it is not clear that this is the most effective strategy in all cases, especially if informants and agents provocateurs are present.

For Governments

What does the current research have to say to and for political authorities who confront challengers? Essentially, the research suggests that political authorities interested in hindering or destroying behavioral challengers should get inside SMOs as soon as they can to better understand what takes place within them but also to better assess where the dissident organization would most likely be vulnerable to subsequent demobilization efforts. Governments have been shown to do precisely this historically, but the current book focuses on identifying not only individuals, institutional structure, ideas, and interventions but also SMO attempts at reappraisal and trust building, which need to be countered or subverted as well. Information of this sort can be used to guide repressive policies, influencing the selection and enactment of overwhelming and outwitting. In lieu of having inside information, the preceding research suggests that it makes sense for authorities to experiment with overwhelming to assess its impact on SMOs. I say this acknowledging that overwhelming could be politically risky (especially in a democracy) unless the government can convince the citizenry that the challengers didn't deserve it (Davenport 2007). Under these circumstances, there might not be any sanctions levied against political leaders; indeed, they might be rewarded for the coercive behavior.

For Researchers

What does the current study teach those of us interested in studying state-challenger interactions? Most importantly, the work here pushes those interested with understanding these interactions on the topic of source material. What emerges from this work is a simple question: how can one understand what is driving challenger (de)mobilization without having information from inside challenging institutions (e.g., their conversations, discussions, and meetings) as well as outside relevant challenges (e.g., their petitions, demonstrations, and marches as well as the government raids, arrests, and violence), realizing that most who study political conflict only have the latter and can only infer about demobilization from this source? After my analysis, the answer I develop is not likely to be satisfactory for many scholars. Nevertheless, it appears to be accurate.

From the investigation of the RNA's internal dynamics and what they were doing behaviorally, I would say that there is very little that can be understood about (de)mobilization and the role of repression on this outcome, viewing data on what social movement organizations and governments *do* exclusively. Without information about exactly who is participating (i.e., whether they were new or old to the organization); what role these individuals play and how SMOs process or counter what happens to them (i.e., gauging attempted reappraisal); and what individuals say or think regarding their perceptions about what is going on (i.e., if they have some understanding/preparation for what is happening to them and if they are scared/angry), protest and repression data themselves reveal very little about the processes that I discussed here.

For example, I can easily imagine that a SMO engages in dissent at time T, is repressed at time T + 1, and then engages in some more dissent at time T + 2. Does this mean that the group was not influenced negatively by repression? Within current approaches, it would. But, guided by the U.S.-RNA investigation, I would argue that a number of scenarios can explain this same exact behavioral pattern (e.g., Davenport and Sullivan 2014). In one, new dissidents come in as old ones leave to continue the struggle. Here there is essentially a new organization, and whatever calculi were presumed operative to influence the decision to engage in dissent earlier have been altered by the fact that new individuals are involved, not necessarily burdened with the experiences or expectations of the earlier cohort. In another scenario, all but those individuals engaged in a specific dissident tactic withdraw. Here the organization is severely weakened numerically, but behaviorally they would not lose a step. In another scenario, nothing changes in the organization, but individuals become angry about the repression and wish to retaliate. This is more or less in line with conventional wisdom. And in a final scenario, the dissident behavior at time T has essentially nothing to do with time T + 2 because one is directed against the court and the other against the police. Without getting inside the group, a strictly behavioral evaluation would reveal very little about how repressive behavior influences demobilization, as there are numerous explanations for the same phenomenon.

But what if one cannot get inside the group? In lieu of insider information like that used in the current book, perhaps researchers could employ something else. For example, in addition to behavioral data, scholars could consider what dissidents say within more public pronouncements like press statements, published diaries, or interviews, revealing differences of opinion about what happened or what should be done. Researchers would need to be precise about exactly who was engaging in what behavior by disaggregating across space, time, and perpetrators, comparing such information against who is speaking. This would reduce the likelihood of attributing someone's mobilization to someone else, which is possible when activities are highly aggregated. The simple presumption here is that groups who are able to consistently mobilize in some place and time are less influenced by repression and internal dynamics than organizations that are not able to do so. Of course, this does not address my earlier point that it might not be appropriate to make such an assumption because it presumes the dissidents *wish to* engage in the type of challenge being recorded, as opposed to undertaking some other form of action. This presumption of constancy (in interest) pervades existing work.

Until we get inside SMOs, however, systematically documenting what takes place there and why, we will not and should not feel comfortable discussing what influences them. Until we are inside SMOs, we will not truly understand why they demobilize, nor will we really understand why they are born. Related to this, and largely unexplored in the current manuscript, it could also be useful to get inside of government institutions to better understand not just the onset and escalation of repression (which I believe was touched on, albeit briefly) but also the termination of repressive action (which we know very little about).

Clearly I am not asking simply for ethnographic work here, which could be unsystematic. Rather, I am asking for a rigorous attempt at documenting the internal workings of those who challenge political authorities and the authorities themselves. Clearly we are not starting such an inquiry from scratch. There has been a great deal written about what takes place inside challenging institutions, and some regard what takes place inside repressive institutions. Unfortunately, much of this work has not then been systematically brought together, laying bare all compiled materials to be observed and examined with a set of common criteria. Such an effort is generally beyond one or a few scholars, unless they have a significant amount of time, resources, and/or sanity. Indeed, it would be wiser to develop a consortium to deal with the varied organizations, contexts, languages, and dynamics involved. Toward this end, I have placed all my documents at the Radical Information Project at http://www.radicalinformationproject.com and invite others to explore the material there. Relatedly, I have also created the Conflict Consortium[5] with Professor Will Moore to facilitate communication across projects and the sharing of research materials.

Thinking More (and Differently) About the Case

Within the research presented here, I do not ascribe to a position whereby the RNA is viewed as a unique case produced by a specific combination of circumstances that could not be repeated. The RNA existed in a particular time and place within the United States, but they share some elements with other movements in other times and places, something that merits comment. Despite my interest in generalizing beyond the case explored here, however, I am very sensitive to the issue of using the U.S.-RNA case to understand any other. Among American SMOs, the RNA was extreme in objectives but moderate in terms of tactics. For example, most of the RNA was involved with giving workshops, holding conferences and meetings, giving speeches, conducting petitions, and engaging in marches and demonstrations. The only thing "radical" about the group's tactics concerned the preparation for military confrontation with the U.S. government in the form of shooting practice, hand-to-hand combat, survival training, discussions of guerrilla activity as a second-strike capability, and secession. The group was not like the American Communist Party, trying to overthrow all of capitalism, but they clearly were more radical than the antitax activists who would rather avoid U.S. political authorities than take them on directly under any circumstances.

When it comes down to it, the RNA was also more radical than the Nation of Islam (NOI) and the Black Panther Party (BPP). Although the NOI discussed

---

5 http://www.conflictconsortium.com.

secession, they generally seemed content with carving out small sections of American cities and covertly having a presence. The NOI never overtly tried to challenge U.S. political authorities or overtly secede. Similarly, the RNA was far more ambitious than the BPP, which largely accepted the U.S. government, but in the end seems to have had a much more obvious and enduring impact on American politics and social life in general. The various elements of the RNA are worth contemplating, for it helps us understand what they can be reasonably compared to.

The RNA was interested in pulling the black "nation" out of the United States. By almost any measure, this would be viewed as a radical objective, thereby suggesting that perhaps the RNA should have adopted a less open structure. Some privacy and secrecy would have helped the organization engage in its activities without tipping off U.S. officials to what they were doing. In addition, it would have reduced suspicion as it would have been harder for unsympathetic individuals to gain entry.

Structurally, the RNA was semi-open, which seems to differ from movement organizations that maintained similar objectives within comparable political-economic contexts. Essentially, the RNA would let any African American attend their meetings, and they were relatively open to individuals joining after some minor hurdles were overcome (e.g., taking a few nation-building classes and doing some reading). This is a great approach if one is interested in trying to reach as wide an audience as possible. This approach is questionable, however, if there are concerns, such as those of the RNA, about infiltration and internal subversion.

Interestingly, the RNA generally disregarded the possibility that it could be infiltrated or overestimated its ability to operate in the midst of government agents and subversion. This error proved to be critical for the organization and for those studying their demobilization. For example, given the RNA's actual objective, it would have reduced the chances of infiltration and subversion and diminished trust had the RNA been more closed. At the same time, this could have made repression of the organization more legitimate in the eyes of the American audience, which tends to view closed organizations more skeptically – especially those of a radical nature. In fact, I would maintain that every step toward a more radical and/or military approach increased the government's interest in exploiting the organizational structure of the RNA. In contrast, if the RNA had moderated its objective, then it could have been semi- or even fully open.

The radical nature of the RNA's objective was countered by its rather conventional approach to achieving it, for example, a plebiscite would lead to an official declaration of nationhood, U.S. recognition, and negotiation for reparations and separation. The RNA needed mass support from the black population to make their declaration of sovereignty legitimate. Most African Americans, however, were not aware of the RNA. So the dissident organization had to make itself open not only to sympathetic blacks, who were not yet committed, but also to those who were just curious and/or wanted to listen, as well as to blacks who pledged allegiance to the U.S. government. This left the challenger vulnerable and makes comparisons somewhat complex. It is hard to find a challenger that completely matches the RNA on all dimensions, but I will maintain that this is not necessary to extract some useful information that can be employed to examine other cases.

Cases and Counterfactuals

Within research interested in identifying causal processes, there is frequently an attempt made to work through counterfactuals as a way to ascertain the robustness of one's claims. There are two ways that this could be done in the case studied here. First, one could attempt to understand what set the RNA on the particular path that it followed, believing that once established on a particular path, the dynamics and outcomes were basically fixed. For example, this would include assessing the specific details of reappraisal, why the RNA went public as a movement when it did, and why specific updating mechanisms were or were not put in place – thinking about what could have altered them. Second, one could try to ascertain alternative trajectories that the RNA could have taken. Here one would consider "plausible" counterfactuals (e.g., Fearon 1991) and assess why choices were or were not made as well as how easily they could have been altered. Each is explored in the following.

A Question of Alternative Origins

For the RNA, it was believed that state repression directed against them would most likely be overt as well as obvious in nature. The government in this view would not mount a full-on armed attack with clearly defined lines of confrontation. Rather, it would attempt something like the assaults seen on unarmed African American civil rights workers, attacked by dogs and night sticks – all under the watchful eye of others with guns, the media, and a viewing audience. Much of the self-defense rhetoric and planning of the black power movement was to prevent this from taking place. What would protect black folk from such an experience? The answer was simple: an effective, military-trained fighting force that, through its very existence or through its behavior, would deter such an attack and potentially engage in effective military behavior by inflicting significant damage on the opponent. Accordingly, when the RNA had the opportunity, they created an army – adorned in a full African-inspired uniform and engaged in shooting practice and other drills such as hand-to-hand combat. In addition to this, the RNA wrote about and to a lesser extent talked about something they referred to as "second-strike capability." Here the idea was that if the RNA and its citizens were overrun in some manner, then others would seek vengeance with "sleepers" (i.e., agents who would become active when needed) throughout the United States who would engage in guerilla warfare, rebellion, and/or random acts of terror. In a sense, the RNA took the fear that many whites had of every African American (i.e., the suspicion that deep down they might not like whites and that they were ready to strike out against them) and used it for their own purposes of appearing to magnify their strength.

This orientation was important for what happened to the RNA because the "defensive" posture they adopted was interpreted as "offensive" by authorities (like discussions of how weapons believed to be deterrent could be seen as provocative). In this view, the RNA was directly challenging the state's monopoly on the holding and wielding coercive power as well as the claim of sole legitimate use of this power within the relevant territorial jurisdiction. Such a situation is particularly interesting when thinking about current U.S. policies concerning the recent "Stand Your Ground" laws.

What else could the RNA have done? Well, in the beginning, the RNA was focused on the overt attack as the primary threat, and thus one could argue that they could have been more focused on covert repressive action. At a minimum, they could have at least conceived of a combination of the two. This would have introduced into the RNA some more detailed protocols for screening and accepting new members as well as developing sophisticated mechanisms for checking on individuals once they had entered into the organization (shifting their approach to reappraisal). The RNA attempted to do this after the New Bethel Incident, but this was much later in the organization's history, and indeed, one way around this for those who had already infiltrated the organization was their earlier presence in the SMO.

I maintain that it would have been difficult for the RNA to incorporate this different or, alternatively, more encompassing view of state repression into their reappraisal strategy, for the awareness of overt repressive activity was simply more well known and feared than anything else at the time. Many individuals had lived through or had known people who had lived through arrests, raids, and beatings within the earlier civil rights movement. Few had direct experience with informants and/or agents provocateurs. It is difficult to downplay the awareness of one reality for the possibility of the other. In addition to this, the position of the RNA was directly in line with the arguments of Malcolm X, Robert F. Williams, the RAM, the Deacons for Defense, and numerous other black nationalist organizations of the period. Some of these were connected to one another through social and political networks (e.g., Malcolm X and the RAM), but some were not (e.g., the Deacons for Defense). Thus numerous movement organizations at the same period had moved to a similar conclusion. Related, any black organization that was trying to mobilize people at the time had to address the issue of black victimization. Some kind of protection had to be offered to get people to overcome their very real fears of engaging in social struggle. The RNA took this task on directly. All of this leads me to believe that the RNA's path to reappraisal was not preordained but rather that it was strongly set on the path that was selected.

The one factor that might have changed the orientation was Malcolm X, but not necessarily in a way that would resolve the limitation identified earlier.

For example, had Malcolm X not died, it is possible that the particular approach adopted by the RNA would have been modified. Given the black leader's increasing pessimism regarding eliminating racism and inequality in America, toward the end of his life, he

foresaw the emergence of urban guerilla warfare as the natural alternative that would neutralize the superior military might of the racist forces and break the back of racism. (Sales 1999, 78)

As Malcolm X said himself,

modern warfare today won't work [by this a straight-up confrontation between distinct military forces]. This is the day of the guerilla . . . Nowhere on this earth does the white man win in a guerilla war. It's not his speed. Just as guerilla warfare is prevailing in Asia and in parts of Africa and in parts of Latin America, you've got to be mighty naïve, or you've got to play the Black man cheap, if you don't think some day he's going to wake up and find that its got to be the ballot or the bullet.[6] (as quoted in Sales 1999, 78)

Now, this would represent something of a shift from the RNA's initial position because it does not seem to be the case that the guerilla war would be fought by an armed, aboveground unit like the Black Legion (the military arm of the RNA). Indeed, just the opposite was the case. While resolving part of the problem in that it would remove an excuse for perceiving aggression and preemptive action, this would still not address the issue of covert repressive action.

The nature of trust building at the outset of the RNA is another topic of discussion. As conceived and practiced, the RNA was a relatively open institution with elements that were closed, it was politically socialistic as well as democratic in orientation and maintained very broad goals. This is important for trust in different ways. For example, the openness of the organization (to anyone of African descent) was useful in that it allowed individuals to enter the space and see what was going on, enhancing transparency. Many things were also hidden from the average member, however, such as how the leadership made the decisions that they did, which would not have been good for building trust. Although the leadership was initially appointed, which would have limited a sense of trust, they were selected as members of a "government," and thus they were expected to be accountable in some sense. The openness of the meetings (an important element of the RNA) generally followed the leftist nature of the political engagement, where all were able to participate or, at least, were allowed to at some level. This facilitated some connectedness but was countered by the generally hierarchically structured nature of the government. All power resided in the president and the cabinet, which established clear lines of command and accountability but also focused the attention of trust

---

[6] Interestingly, this is a point comparable to those of numerous political scientists (Arrequin-Toft 2005).

on a selected few individuals. Finally, the broadness and ambitiousness of the RNA's goals made actual delivery and success difficult, if not impossible, to achieve. Initially, it would not be expected that the movement could reach them, and there would be some amount of time given to the leadership before they would have to produce. In the long run, however, this would reduce trust, as it would not be possible to achieve the established objectives.

With regard to this aspect of the RNA's beginnings, I see a bit more flexibility with regard to trust and trust building than with regard to reappraisal. In a sense, the leadership was caught between organizational models that had been used throughout the black community at the time, and given the range being employed, they could have selected a different combination – one that might have cultivated more trust. Many of the organizational forms employed during the relevant period represented hybrid institutions with elements of distinct traditions found within them. Drawing from the GOAL and Malcolm X Society models (two earlier organizations created by the same cohort involved with the RNA), the individuals associated with the RNA could have officially selected a more closed, top-down type of structure with more clearly articulated and smaller-scale goals. This would have been something with which they were more familiar and would have reflected how the organization actually ran. Additionally, it would have reduced the degree of openness in the institution, which would have diminished the sense of accountability and made infiltration more difficult. As designed, more top-down organizational structures are accountable in some sense, but they are given more leeway in taking action than democratic leaders who are perceived to be much more responsive.

While available in theory, it is important to note that the rhetoric of the time was clearly more participatory in nature. Most black institutions were doing their best to connect and engage with "the people" – that is, the untapped masses who came out in droves during the riot/rebellion of 1967. In this context, it would have been difficult to openly push for a closed, elitist, "vanguard" institution like GOAL in 1968. Changing the approach to trust and trust building would have also been hindered by the relatively brief period that the RNA had before they went public at the founding. There was very little time between the Malcolm X Society and the RNA. Over a matter of months, there were numerous meetings taking place in several parts of the United States and a rather fast-paced effort to pull together a large number of different nationalist efforts that were under way. This is not to say that there was no thought or planning, for there was a great deal. This is to say, however, that several elements of the objectives pursued and how they would get there were not worked out as thoroughly as they could have been.

There were also some limitations in the organizational structure put forward that precluded effective adaptation, evolution, or updating later. As conceived, the RNA was hierarchically organized and even personalistic in nature given the amount of control held at the top of the institution. At the same time, there was some local autonomy but no real way for information to flow up with any efficiency or seeming impact. There was little accountability as well. For example, numerous contingencies were developed regarding what should be done if a member of the leadership were abducted, but these rules were not followed; indeed, over these types of issues, divisions and factions were more likely to form. An inability to take in new information, to develop an agreed-on policy, and an ability to enact that policy (i.e., rigidity) hindered the organization's ability to update their approach to mobilization.

This is in part a problem of the times. Many in the black nationalist movement were simultaneously attempting to deal with the idea of nationalism compared to the idea of integrationism, the tactical differences between nonviolent direct action and armed self-defense, guerilla warfare and nation building, the deaths or incarceration of some of the most prominent leaders and assorted aspects of socialism, but in direct practice day to day, not in the abstract.[7] Something new was desired, but it was not quite clear what that something would be, and a great number of individuals and groups were coming to similar conclusions, suggesting coordination or diffusion.

Weak and Strong Paths

In the preceding, I attempted to explore the origins of the RNA and to what degree it would have been possible to take any alternative routes in the creation of their social movement. As seen, the possibilities for selecting a different path at the beginning were somewhat limited. Here I wish to explore the choices that were made and not made across the various periods investigated. This will reveal the relative fragility of the causal sequence and provide some basis for understanding relevant comparisons to other state-dissident interactions.

Working chronologically, we begin with the beginning, as it were: the founding in March 31, 1968. According to the available documents, the organization began when it did for a variety of reasons. First, every moment without action following the death of Malcolm X and the riot/rebellion of 1967 seemed to reduce momentum of those interested in taking action (i.e., decreasing the legitimacy of those who sought to be seen as the heirs to Malcolm X's legacy and limiting the participation of those who were ready to join something following relevant events). Second, as noted earlier, several black nationalist efforts at the time began to discuss similar topics, and thus if the RNA was going to occupy a unique niche in the black social movement sector at that moment, they would have had to take some action – staking a claim as it were.

In this context, it is hard to imagine delaying, but this is possible, and it is worthwhile to think about what they would have gained from such a thing and what this might have influenced in terms of subsequent state-dissident interactions. Of course, just taking more time before coming forward (extending incubation and abeyance) is not the same thing as better developing ideas, institutions, and interventions (collective actions) in a way that would be more

---

[7] At the same time, topics like gender inequality and sexism were largely ignored.

effective, but this is somewhat implied. Given this type of delay, however, the impact seems like it would be significant. With a clearer idea of what they wanted to do and how they would do it, it is likely that the RNA would have been better at staying with what they set out to do. Greater time working out the ideological contours of the "New Afrikan" and the RNA would have helped them think through their membership, tactics, and organizational structure. Now, it is not clear that more time would have led to an adjustment in reappraisal (discussed earlier), as this appeared to involve a great many factors that do not readily seem alterable. The greater influence would have been seen in organizational trust (at least with regard to nonrepression and reappraisal issues). The group that formed the RNA had some reservoir of trust going into the social movement, but much of it rested on the backs of Malcolm X's memory, the presence of Robert F. Williams, and the existence of the RNA itself, as well as several years' worth of varied struggles. With high stakes and little time to pull things together, this put a tremendous amount of pressure on the dissident organization to deliver, but they had not quite worked out the end product. This said, they put forward an idea of what that end product could be and hoped that members of the "nation" would step forward to assist in its actualization.

Perhaps the most significant impact of the delayed founding and development of the RNA's ideas and structure concerns the next period of interest: the situation in Ocean Hill–Brownsville in Brooklyn, New York, around October 15, 1968. The principal reason for going to Ocean Hill–Brownsville was to push an extremely high-profile community toward secession, in line with the RNA's objective. The problem here was that up until that point, the dissident challenger had concerned itself with raising awareness about the black nation *and* taking action in the Deep South: Mississippi, Louisiana, Alabama, Georgia, and South Carolina. This was a very different context from Brooklyn and involved a significant shift in resources as well as commitment.

Had the organization stayed with the southern focus or continued to prepare for a plebiscite in Detroit without distraction, they might have been able to avoid the internal dissension that followed as well as sustain the trust that comes with consistent effort on a core aspect of an organization's goals. Both of these weakened the organization and rendered them vulnerable to subsequent government action. Of course, considering counterfactuals is tricky, for one is led to speculate about issues that were not often considered at the time, but the no Ocean Hill–Brownsville option was considered and inevitably defeated. The defeat may have less been about persuasion of the majority or popular will than about utilizing the top-down orientation of the organization, and thus the mixed amount of support that followed later made sense. At the time, neither Robert F. Williams (then president) nor Milton Henry/Gaidi Obadele (then first vice president) were running the institution as directly, and in the power vacuum, any impulse was likely to have an influence on the general direction of the institution. I do not exclusively put the blame

on these two individuals, however. Most of the people selected to be leaders in the RNA at the founding had other institutional affiliations as well as
projects on which they were working. This left a largely Detroit-oriented organization without the official ability to take action, which is what inevitably
happened.

Revealing the sequential nature of my argument, without Ocean Hill–
Brownsville and the problems that that raised for the RNA, the New Bethel
Incident (the shooting, mass raid, and arrest at the first national RNA conference in Detroit on March 28, 1969) would have had less of an impact. New
Bethel was devastating to the RNA in particular because it subjected the membership to a form of repression that they had been expecting (an overt assault)
but also to several that they had not been expecting (mass arrest, detention,
and interrogation as well as covert repressive behavior). Had the organization
had a larger degree of trust facilitated by not deviating from one of their primary objectives and locales, then they would have been able to better weather
the troubles brought from New Bethel. This said, there would still have been
some problems, for the approach to reappraisal adopted by the RNA up to that
time was different from what they experienced. This would have resulted in
some lost trust, but with the larger reserve, it may have been less devastating.
With greater trust and a more cohesive group, the RNA might have been better
able to take advantage of the press coverage and positive outreach from the
black community they received after New Bethel. The dissident organization
was not really able to take full advantage of these opportunities because they
had various internal issues to deal with. This also included dealing with the
new recruits they were receiving because of the increased attention.

Not contending with Ocean Hill–Brownsville is very different from creating
better protocols that allow an organization to deal with a wave of new recruits,
some of which were government informants. It is thus possible that the RNA
would still have been hit with a significant amount of infiltration and suspicion
following New Bethel, but I believe it is likely that the enhanced trust would
have limited some of this. A final change in the organization concerned the
acknowledgment that there needed to be a finer distinction made between
the "aboveground" (i.e., those who openly pushed for the new nation) and
the "underground" parts of the movement (i.e., those who would engage in
security and, if deemed necessary, guerilla warfare). This lack of clarity led to
a number of problems in the institution with regard to who should be doing
what.

Now, it should be clear, I think, that regardless of any other changes that
might have been made to the RNA past, the shooting, raid, and arrest of New
Bethel would still have happened. This was simply a policy choice that was
being made nationally at that time with regard to black nationalism, seemingly
with disregard for local context. It would be unreasonable to assume, therefore,
that this would not have taken place and also to assume what would follow
from it.

As for the two remaining periods of interest, I believe that the further one pushes forward into the RNA trajectory that was, the harder it is to assess counterfactuals because the sequence of events that did take place influenced later choices.

For example, the development of a faction within the RNA on November 16, 1969, was largely a function of the sequence as it actually took place. With the path not chosen (e.g., the survival and continued engagement of Malcolm X, the delayed founding, the better outlined and enforced plan of action, the active involvement of Robert F. Williams, and the increased and consistent focus on the South), I think that this scenario would have made the organization less vulnerable to divisionism. This clearly does not mean that they would be invulnerable. By this point, the organization had contended with a variety of issues; it was fighting for its soul and trying to figure out what should be done in the most effective manner possible. It makes sense that this could have been achieved more easily without internal dissension.

Rather than commit to separation, the two brothers and their respective supporters could have recommitted to unity and integration. Such an outcome would have been much easier had the alternative sequence been followed. Following the series of decisions made in the path that was selected, the respective factions could seemingly no longer fathom a world involved with the other. Trust was decimated, and it became redirected toward smaller subsets of the broader movement.

Similarly, the vulnerability of the RNA to a shooting, police raid, and mass arrest at the RNA's newly established capital in Jackson, Mississippi (which took place on August 18, 1971), would have been much lower had the actual sequence of events not taken place. Indeed, it is possible that the whole scenario with the RNA being there might have been altered. For example, one part of the factionalized RNA moved to New Orleans and then started to move to Mississippi. Rather than this being a small operation on a single farm, however, had the RNA substantively committed to this enterprise earlier, then they might have solidified a better connection with the local community and/or had a larger physical presence – lowering the possibility of an assault. The successful development of a land base in the South was somewhat far-fetched without the financial wherewithal and personnel willing to commit to such an enterprise, which they did not have at the time. These issues might have been less problematic with the alternative path (e.g., with a more engaged Robert F. Williams drawing more individuals to the RNA), or at least, this was the idea and why people pushed so hard for them.

Alternatively, the RNA could have followed its electoral secession strategy with trying to win the appointment of a police chief in a county where the black population was numerous and where they would be able to convince enough individuals to vote for a sympathetic candidate. Once appointed, the person could deputize the RNA members, and with this protection, they could then create part of the Republic. In a sense, the movement to Jackson was done more out of desperation and an attempt to get something done with as much fanfare and publicity as possible but with little mass/community support and limited RNA participation. In reality, the move was not undertaken out of a position of strength, and the signal sent was much more symbolic in nature as opposed to strictly based on the most effective approach to advancing the overall objective. This is not to downplay the importance of claiming land for the black nation, which was immense for a variety of reasons, for the RNA in particular but also for African Americans in general. It did not, however, correspond to the organization's ability to hold the land, something that was very quickly revealed by the shooting, raid, and arrest.

Rather than extending to the South, the group could have also recommitted to Detroit, but this was really determined by the bad blood created from the path that was selected. Had the organization begun from their base of operations and stayed engaged with it consistently from the founding, there would have been a somewhat different orientation to both Detroit and the South. This is not to say that had the RNA committed to Detroit more fully and more consistently, it would have worked. There were significant differences between the RNA and the average African American in Detroit on a number of items (e.g., on the perceived necessity for a black nation or the possibility of relying on a black politician from within the system). Furthermore, the Detroit chapter of the RNA attempted to do a great deal without much success in increasing participation, membership, or financial donations. This is to say, however, that such engagement could have reasonably gone a long way to building trust and community support.

With regard to the possibility that the U.S. government would have taken a different approach, I find this unlikely given the circumstances. In many respects, the RNA played to the strengths of the political authorities at the time in Detroit, Michigan, and the federal government. With the move to rural Mississippi, the RNA was no longer present within a sea of potential observers and sympathizers who could have born witness to what took place, such as at the time of the New Bethel Incident. Rather, they were in an isolated geographic locale – something that they feared in *War in America*. Moreover, the RNA provided probable cause with its discussion of nation building and secession. It was a small step from these concepts to the belief that potentially illegal weapons and explosives existed and that these might be used in some way, shape, or form against the government and/or whites in the area.

The Scope of Comparison

Given the previous discussion, to what would it be reasonable to compare the U.S.-RNA government case? Several possibilities emerge.

Clearly there should be a comparison of what happened to all of the different black nationalist organizations that emerged at the tail end of the civil rights conflict cycle, that is, the radical flank of the African American struggle. Across the United States, African Americans engaged in similar types of struggles involving similar ideas, individuals, institutions, and interventions (activities), but we know very little about the details of those struggling, that is, where they came from, what happened to them, and where the different groups ended up in comparison to one another as well as to the earlier civil rights movement.

Relatedly, I think it would be appropriate to look at specific political challengers in democratic societies with extremist objectives such as the Front de Liberation du Quebec of Canada or the Basques in Spain. Here researchers could investigate the similarities and differences in tactics and also try to assess the relative importance of repression and internal dissension to each movement's survival.

One could explore state-dissident interactions even more comparatively and quantitatively where the social movement sector is somewhat saturated, examining how government behavior and organizational survival covary across the range of different organizations. Although I think that the best RNA comparison would exist within democratic contexts, it is reasonable to expect that the basic idea could be explored in nondemocratic contexts as well.

Perhaps the broadest comparison could be made to ethnonationalist organizations globally. This type of research would involve seeing how government behavior did or did not interact with internal movement dynamics to influence the basic ideas, interventions (actions), institutions, and individuals. Such an examination would be especially difficult given the data requirements mentioned earlier (e.g., identifying individuals within challenging institutions globally), but it is possible to investigate a few of the claims (e.g., the influence of repressive behavior on public expressions of fear or anger, the expected differential influence of repression on groups that seek to advance their cause through dissident behavior as opposed to those that seek to advance their cause through education or some other means, or gauging how prerepressive evaluations of expected government behavior [reappraisal] influenced subsequent responses to repressive action).

These would all be lucrative areas for further examination, significantly advancing our understanding of demobilization in particular and contentious politics more generally.

References

Allen, Nathalie J., and John P. Meyer. 1990. "The Measurement and Antecedents of Affective, Continuance, and Normative Commitment to Organization." *Journal of Occupational Psychology* 63: 1–18.

Aronson, Eliot, Timothy Wilson, and Robin Akert. 2005. *Social Psychology*, 7th ed. Upper Saddle River, NJ: Pearson Education.

Arrequin-Toft, Ivan. 2005. *How the Weak Win Wars: A Theory of Asymmetric Conflict*. New York: Cambridge University Press.

Barkan, Steven E., Steven F. Cohn, and William H. Whitaker. 1993. "Commitment Across the Miles: Ideological and Microstructural Sources of Membership Support in a National Antihunger Organization." *Social Problems* 40: 362–73.

———. 1995. "Beyond Recruitment: Predictors of Differential Participation in a National Antihunger Organization." *Sociological Forum* 10: 113–34.

Barron, Barnett. 2004. "Deterring Donors: Anti-Terrorist Financing Rules and American Philanthropy." *International Journal of Not-for-Profit Law* 6(2), http://www.icnl.org/KNOWLEDGE/ijnl/vol6iss2/special_5.htm.

Berman, Eli. 2008. "Can Hearts and Minds Be Bought? The Economics of Counterinsurgency in Iraq." Working Paper 14606. National Bureau of Economic Research.

Biddle, Stephen. 2008. "The New U.S. Army/Marine Corps Counterinsurgency Field Manual as Political Science and Political Praxis – Review Symposium." *Perspectives on Politics* 6(2): 347–50.

Blaufarb, Douglas. 1977. *The Counterinsurgency Era: US Doctrine and Performance, 1950 to the Present*. New York: Free Press.

Bob, Clifford, and Sharon Nepstad. 2007. "Kill a Leader, Murder a Movement? Leadership and Assassination in Social Movements." *American Behavioral Scientist* 50(10): 1370–94.

Bopp, William. 1971. *The Police Rebellion: The Quest for Blue Power*. Chicago, IL: Charles C. Thomas.

Boykoff, Jules. 2006. *The Suppression of Dissent: How the State and Mass Media Squelch US American Social Movements*. New York: Routledge.

Brandt, Patrick T., T. David Mason, Mehmet Gurses, Nicolai Petrovsky, and Dasha Radin. 2008. "When and How the Fighting Stops: Explaining the Duration and Outcome of Civil Wars." *Defense and Peace Economics* 19(6): 415–34.

Brockett, Charles. 1993. "A Protest-Cycle Resolution of the Repression/Popular-Protest Paradox." *Social Science History* 17(3): 457–84.

Brown, Scott. 2003. *Fighting for Us: Maulana Karenga, the US Organization, and Black Cultural Nationalism.* New York: New York University Press.

Brubaker, Rogers. 1996. *Nationalism Reframed: Nationhood and the National Question in the New Europe.* Cambridge: Cambridge University Press.

Bueno de Mesquita, Ethan. 2005. "Conciliation, Counterterrorism and Patterns of Terrorist Violence." *International Organization* 59(1): 145–76.

Button, James. 1978. *Black Violence.* Princeton, NJ: Princeton University Press.

Byman, Daniel. 2006. "Do Targeted Killings Work?" *Foreign Affairs* 85(2): 95–111.

Carey, Sabine C. 2006. "The Dynamic Relationship between Protest and Repression." *Political Research Quarterly* 59(1): 1–11.

Carson, Clayborne. 1981. *In Struggle: SNCC and the Black Awakening of the 1960s.* Cambridge, MA: Harvard University Press.

Churchill, Ward, and James Vander Wall. 1988. *Agents of Repression: The FBI's Secret War against the Black Panther Party and the American Indian Movement.* Boston: South End Press.

Cleage, Albert. 1967. "Organizing for the Black Revolution." *Michigan Chronicle.*

———. 1968. "An Example of Organization." *Michigan Chronicle.*

Cohen, Eliot. 2010. *Mass Surveillance and State Control: The Total Information Awareness Project.* New York: Palgrave.

Collier, Paul. 2003. "The Market for Civil War." *Foreign Policy,* May/June, 38–45.

Collier, Paul, and Anke Hoeffler. 2002. "On the Incidence of Civil War in Africa." *Journal of Conflict Resolution* 46(1): 13–28.

Cone, James. 1992. *Malcolm and Martin and America: A Dream or a Nightmare.* New York: Orbis Books.

Connable, Ben, and Martin Libicki. 2010. *How Insurgencies End.* Washington, DC: National Defense Research Institute, Rand.

Conrad, Courtenay Ryals, and Will H. Moore. 2010. "Who Stops the Torture?" *American Journal of Political Science* 54(2): 459–76.

Council on Foreign Relations. 2002. *Terrorist Financing: Report of an Independent Task Force Sponsored by the Council on Foreign Relations.* New York: Council on Foreign Relations.

Cress, Daniel M., and David A. Snow. 1996. "Resources, Benefactors, and the Viability of Homeless Social Movement Organizations." *American Sociological Review* 61: 1089–1109.

Cronin, Audrey. 2006. "How Al-Qaida Ends: The Decline and Demise of Terrorist Groups." *International Security* 31(1): 7–48.

Cruse, Harold. 1967. *The Crisis of the Negro Intellectual: Historical Analysis of the Failure.* New York: William Morrow.

Cunningham, David. 2004. *There's Something Happening Here: The New Left, the Klan, and FBI Counterintelligence.* Berkeley: University of California Press.

Cunningham, Kathleen. 2011. "Divide and Conquer or Divide and Concede: How Do States Respond to Internally Divided Separatists?" *American Political Science Review* 105: 275–97.

Dalfiume, Richard. 1969. *Desegregation of the U.S. Armed Forces: Fighting on Two Fronts, 1939–1953.* Columbia: University of Missouri Press.

Davenport, Christian. 1995. "Multi-Dimensional Threat Perception and State Repression: An Inquiry into Why States Apply Negative Sanctions." *American Journal of Political Science* 38(3): 683–713.

———. 1996. "The Weight of the Past: Exploring Lagged Determinants of Political Repression." *Political Research Quarterly* 49(2): 377–403.

———. 1998. "Filling the Gap in Contentious Understanding: The Republic of New Africa and the Influence of Political Repression." Report SBR-9819274. Arlington, VA: National Science Foundation.

———. 2005. "Understanding Covert Repressive Action: The Case of the US Government against the Republic of New Africa." *Journal of Conflict Resolution* 49(1): 120–40.

———. 2007. "State Repression and Political Order." *Annual Review of Political Science* 10: 1–23.

———. 2010. *Media Bias, Perspective and State Repression: The Black Panther Party.* New York: Cambridge University Press.

Davenport, Christian, and Rose McDermott. 2011. "An Evolutionary Theory of State Repression." Manuscript.

Davenport, Christian, and Allan Stam. 2003. "Mass Killing and the Oases of Humanity: Understanding Rwandan Genocide and Resistance." Report SES-0321518. National Science Foundation.

Davenport, Christian, and Chris Sullivan. 2014. *If You Arrest a Revolutionary, Do You Arrest the Revolution? Resolving the 40 Year Debate about Repression's Impact on Political Challenges.* Manuscript.

Davis, Gerald, Doug McAdam, W. Richard Scott, and Mayer Zald, eds. 2005. *Social Movements and Organization Theory.* New York: Cambridge University Press.

Dawson, Michael. 2013. *Blacks in and out of the Left.* Cambridge, MA: Harvard University Press.

della Porta, Donatella. 1995. *Social Movements, Political Violence, and the State.* Cambridge: Cambridge University Press.

Detroit Area People against Racism. 1969. Untitled document. The Radical Information Project, University of Michigan.

Detroit Courier. 1968. "Mississippi Solon, Cleage, Henry Spark Meeting." March 30.

———. 1969. "Efforts Should be Made to Understand Separatists." April 3.

Detroit News. 1969a. "Goals of RNA Disavowed." April 18.

———. 1969b. "Senate Told of the RNA." June 26.

———. 1971. "Milton Says He Warned His Brother." August 19.

Detroit Police Department. 1968. Interoffice memorandum, Detective Division. Record 62. Radical Information Project, University of Michigan.

———. 1969. Interoffice memorandum, Detective Division. October 26. Record 62. Radical Information Project, University of Michigan.

Detroit Police Department – SIB. 1968. Confiscated RNA document dated October 4. Radical Information Project, University of Michigan.

———. 1969. Interoffice memorandum, Detective Division. Record 531. Radical Information Project, University of Michigan.

Detroit Urban League. 1967. *The People beyond 12th Street: A Survey of Attitudes of Detroit Negroes after the Riot of 1967.* Detroit: Detroit Urban League.

Dillard, Angela. 2003. *Faith in the City: Preaching Radical Social Change in Detroit.* Ann Arbor: University of Michigan Press.

DiMaggio, Paul, and Walter W. Powell. 1983. "The Iron Cage Revisited: Institutional Isomorphism and Collective Rationality in Organizational Fields." *American Sociological Review* 48: 147–60.

Donner, Frank. 1980. *The Age of Surveillance: The Aims and Methods of America's Political Intelligence System.* New York: Knopf.

———. 1990. *Protectors of Privilege: Red Squads and Police Repression in Urban America.* Berkeley: University of California Press.

Downton, James, and Paul Wehr. 1991. "Peace Movements: The Role of Commitment and Community in Sustaining Member Participation." *Research in Social Movements, Conflict, and Change* 13: 113–34.

———. 1997. *The Persistent Activist: How Peace Commitment Develops and Survives.* Boulder, CO: Westview Press.

Dryden, Charles. 2003. *A-Train: Memoirs of a Tuskegee Airman.* Tuscaloosa: University of Alabama Press.

Earl, Jennifer. 2003. "Tanks, Tear Gas and Taxes: Toward a Theory of Movement Repression." *Sociological Theory* 21(1): 44–68.

Earl, Jennifer, and Sarah A. Soule. 2006. "Seeing Blue: Going Behind the Baton to Explain Policing at Public Protest Events." *Mobilization* 11(2): 145–64.

Earl, Jennifer, and Sarah A. Soule. 2010. "The Impacts of Repression: The Effect of Police Presence and Action on Subsequent Protest Rates." *Research in Social Movements, Conflicts, and Change* 30: 75–113.

Earl, Jennifer, Sarah A. Soule, and John D. McCarthy. 2003. "Protest under Fire? Explaining Protest Policing." *American Sociological Review* 69: 581–606.

Edmondson, Amy. 1999. "Psychology Safety and Learning Behavior in Work Teams." *Administrative Science Quarterly* 44(2): 350–83.

Edwards, Robert, and Sam Marullo. 1995. "Organizational Mortality in Declining Social Movements: The Demise of Peace Movement Organizations in the End of the Cold War Era." *American Sociological Review* 60: 908–27.

Edwards, Robert, and John McCarthy. 2004. "Resources and Social Movement Mobilization." In *The Blackwell Companion to Social Movements*, ed. David A. Snow, Sarah A. Soule, and Hanspeter Kriesi, 116–52. London: Blackwell.

Einwohner, Rachel. 2003. "Opportunity, Honor and Action in the Warsaw Ghetto Uprising of 1943." *American Journal of Sociology* 109, no. 3: 650–75.

Elsbach, Kimberly, and Robert Sutton. 1992. "Acquiring Organizational Legitimacy through Illegitimate Actions: A Marriage of Institutional and Impression Management Theories." *Academy of Management Journal* 35(4): 699–738.

Farley, Reynolds, Sheldon Danziger, and Harry J. Holzer. 2000. *Detroit Divided.* New York: Russell Sage Foundation.

Fearon, James. 1991. "Counterfactuals and Hypothesis Testing in Political Science." *World Politics* 43, no. 2: 169–95.

Ferree, Myra. 2005. "Soft Repression: Ridicule, Stigma, and Silencing in Gender-Based Movements. In *Repression and Mobilization*, ed. Christian Davenport, Hank Johnston, and Carol Mueller, 138–54. Minneapolis: University of Minnesota Press.

Fine, Sidney. 2000. *Expanding the Frontiers of Civil Rights: Michigan, 1948–1968.* Detroit, MI: Wayne State University Press.

Finkle, Lee. 1973. "The Conservative Aims of Militant Rhetoric: Black Protest during World War II." *The Journal of American History* 60, no. 3: 692–713.

Fitzsimmons, Michael. 2008. "Hard Hearts and Open Minds? Governance, Identity and the Intellectual Foundations of Counterinsurgency Strategy." *Journal of Strategic Studies* 31(3): 337–65.

Foucault, Michel. 1995. *Discipline and Punish: The Birth of the Prison*. New York: Vintage.

Francisco, Ron. 1996. "Coercion and Protest: An Empirical Test in Two Democratic States." *American Journal of Political Science* 40(4): 1179–1204.

———. 2004. "After the Massacre: Mobilization in the Wake of Harsh Repression." *Mobilization* 9(2): 107–26.

Frey, R., T. Dietz, and L. Kalof. 1992. "Characteristics of Successful American Protest Groups: Another Look at Gamson's *Strategies of Social Protest*." *American Journal of Sociology* 98: 368–87.

Galaskiewicz, Joseph. 1984. "Interorganizational Relations." *Annual Review of Sociology* 11: 281–304.

Gamson, William. 1975. *The Strategy of Social Protest*. Homewood, NJ: Dorsey Press.

Gamson, William A., and David S. Meyer. 1996. "Framing Political Opportunity." In *Comparative Perspectives on Social Movements: Political Opportunities, Mobilizing Structures, and Cultural Framings*, ed. Douglas McAdam, John McCarthy, and Mayer Zald, 275–90. New York: Cambridge University Press.

Gartner, Scott Sigmund, and Patrick M. Regan. 1996. "Threat and Repression: The Non-Linear Relationship between Government and Opposition Violence." *Journal of Peace Research* 33(3): 273–87.

Gates, Scott. 2002. "Recruitment and Allegiance: The Microfoundations of Rebellion." *Journal of Conflict Resolution* 46(1): 111–30.

Giugni, Marco. 1998. "Was It Worth the Effort? The Outcomes and Consequences of Social Movements." *Annual Review of Sociology* 98: 371–93.

Goldstein, Robert Justin. 1978. *Political Repression in Modern America from 1870 to the Present*. Boston: GK Hall.

Goldstone, Jack. 1980. "The Weakness of Organization: A New Look at Gamson's *The Strategy of Social Protest*." *American Journal of Sociology* 85: 1017–42.

Goldstone, Jack, and Charles Tilly. 2001. "Threat (and Opportunity): Popular Action and State Response in the Dynamics of Contentious Action." In *Silence and Voice in the Study of Contentious Politics*, ed. Ronald R. Aminzade, Jack A. Goldstone, Doug McAdam, Elizabeth J. Perry, William H. Sewell Jr., Sidney Tarrow, and Charles Tilly, 179–93. Cambridge: Cambridge University Press.

Goodman, James. 1994. *Stories of Scottsboro*. New York: Pantheon Books.

Goodwin, Jeffrey. 2001. *No Other Way Out: States and Revolutionary Movements, 1945–1991*. New York: Cambridge University Press.

Grady-Willis, Winston. 1998. "The Black Panther Party: State Repression and Political Prisoners." In *The Black Panther Party (Reconsidered)*, ed. Charles Jones, 363–90. Baltimore, MD: Black Classic Press.

Grant, William. 1970. "Integration's Last Hurrah: 'Where Did Everyone Go To?'" *The New Republic*, September 12.

Greenhalgh, L. G. 1983. "Organizational Decline." *Research in the Sociology of Organizations* 2: 231–76.

Group on Advanced Leadership. 1964. Untitled document. Radical Information Project, University of Michigan.

———. 1965. "Who We Are." Radical Information Project, University of Michigan.

Gunaratna, Rohan. 2000. "The Lifeblood of Terrorist Organizations: Evolving Terrorist Financing Strategies." In *Countering Terrorism through International Cooperation*, 187–211. Vienna: United Nations.

Gupta, Devashree. 2002. "Radical Flank Effects: The Effect of Radical-Moderate Splits in Regional Nationalist Movements." Prepared for the Conference of Europeanists, Chicago.

Gupta, Dipak, and Y. P. Venieris. 1981. "Introducing New Dimensions in Macro Models: The Sociopolitical and Institutional Environments." *Economic Development and Cultural Change* 30(1): 31–58.

Gurr, Ted. 1970. *Why Men Rebel.* New York: Paradigm.

Gurr, Ted, and Will Moore. 1997. "Ethno-political Rebellion: A Cross-Sectional Analysis of the 1980s with Risk Assessments for the 1990s." *American Journal of Political Science* 41(4): 1079–103.

Haines, Herbert H. 1984. "Black Radicalism and the Funding of Civil Rights, 1957–1970." *Social Problems* 32(1): 31–43.

Hannan, Michael, and Glenn Carroll. 1992. *Dynamics of Organizational Populations: Density, Legitimation, and Competition.* New York: Oxford University Press.

Hannan, Michael, and John Freeman. 1989. *Organizational Ecology.* Cambridge, MA: Harvard University Press.

Hannan, Michael, Laszlo Polos, and Glenn Carroll. 2007. *Logics of Organization Theory: Audiences, Costs and Ecologies.* Princeton, NJ: Princeton University Press.

Henderson, Errol. 1997. "The Lumpenproletariat as Vanguard? The Black Panther Party, Social Transformation, and Pearson's Analysis of Huey Newton." *Journal of Black Studies* 28(20): 171–99.

Henrickson, Wilma Wood, ed. 1991. *Detroit Perspectives: Crossroads and Turning Points.* Detroit, MI: Wayne State University Press.

Henry, Milton. 1970. "Transcript, Milton Henry Oral History Interview by James M. Mosby Jr." RJB 699, Ralph J. Bunche Oral History Collection, Howard University. http://www.howard.edu/library/moorland-spingarn/civilh-l.html#HENRYM.

Hess, David, and Brian Martin. 2006. "Repression, Backfire and the Theory of Transformative Events." *Mobilization* 11(2): 249–67.

Hibbs, Douglas. 1973. *Mass Political Violence: A Cross-National Causal Analysis.* New York: John Wiley.

Hill, Lance. 2006. *The Deacons for Defense: Armed Resistance and the Civil Rights Movement.* Chapel Hill: University of North Carolina Press.

Hirsch, Eric. 1986. "The Creation of Political Solidarity in Social Movement Organizations." *The Sociological Quarterly* 27(3): 373–87.

———. 1990. "Sacrifice for the Cause: Group Processes, Recruitment, and Commitment in a Student Social Movement." *American Sociological Review* 55(2): 243–54.

Hirschman, Albert. 1970. *Exit, Voice, and Loyalty; Responses to Decline in Firms, Organizations, and States.* Cambridge, MA: Harvard University Press.

Humphreys, Macartan. 2005. "Natural Resources, Conflict, and Conflict Resolution: Uncovering the Mechanisms." *Journal of Conflict Resolution* 49(4): 508–37.

Humphreys, Macartan, and Jeremy Weinstein. 2007. "Demobilization and Reintegration." *Journal of Conflict Resolution* 51(4): 531–67.

Inman, Molly, and Christian Davenport. 2012. "The State of State Repression Research." *Terrorism and Political Violence* 24(4): 1–16.

Jaeger, David, and M. Daniele Paserman. 2009. "The Shape of Things to Come? On the Dynamics of Suicide Attacks and Targeted Killing." *Quarterly Journal of Political Science* 4: 315–42.

Jeffries, Lance, ed. 2007. *Black Power in the Belly of the Beast*. Chicago: University of Illinois Press.

Jenkins, Craig. 1983. "Resource Mobilization Theory and the Study of Social Movements." *Annual Review of Sociology* 9: 527–53.

———. 1998. "Channeling Social Protest: Foundation Patronage of Contemporary Social Movements." In *Private Action and the Public Good*, ed. Walter Powell and Elisabeth Clemens, 206–16. New Haven, CT: Yale University Press.

Jenkins, Craig, and Craig Ekert. 1986. "Channeling Black Insurgency: Elite Patronage and Professional Social Movement Organizations in the Development of the Black Movement." *American Sociological Review* 51(6): 812–29.

Jenkins, Craig, and Charles Perrow. 1977. "Insurgency of the Powerless: Farm Worker Movements (1946–1972)." *American Sociological Review* 42: 249–68.

Johnson, Ollie. 1998. "Explaining the Demise of the Black Panther Party: The Role of Internal Factors." In *The Black Panther Party (Reconsidered)*, ed. Charles Jones, 391–414. Baltimore: Black Classic Press.

Jones, Charles. 1988. "The Political Repression of the Black Panther Party 1966–1971: The Case of the Oakland Bay Area." *Journal of Black Studies* 18(4): 415–34.

Jordan, Jenna. 2010. "Leadership Decapitation and Organizational Resilience." Paper prepared for presentation at the annual meeting of the International Studies Association, New Orleans.

Joseph, Jeremy. 2007. "Mediation in War: Winning Hearts and Minds Using Mediated Condolence Payments." *Negotiation Journal*, July, 219–48.

Joseph, Peniel, ed. 2006. *The Black Power Movement: Rethinking the Civil Rights-Black Power Era*. New York: Routledge.

———. 2007. *Waiting 'til the Midnight Hour: A Narrative History of Black Power in America*. New York: Holt Paperbacks.

Kalyvas, Stathis. 2006. *The Logic of Violence in Civil Wars*. Cambridge: Cambridge University Press.

Kelley, Robin. 2002. *Freedom Dreams: The Black Radical Imagination*. Boston: Beacon Press.

Khawaja, Marwan. 1993. "Repression and Popular Collective Action: Evidence from the West- Bank." *Sociological Forum* 8: 47–71.

Klandermans, Bert. 1984. "Mobilization and Participation: Social-Psychological Expansions of Resource Mobilization Theory." *American Sociological Review* 49: 583–600.

———. 1993. "A Theoretical Framework for Comparisons of Social Movement Participation." *Sociological Forum* 8(3): 383–402.

———. 1997. *The Social Psychology of Protest*. Cambridge, MA: Blackwell.

Koehler, John. 1999. *Stasi: The Untold Story of the East German Secret Police*. Boulder, CO: Westview Press.

Koopmans, Ruud. 1993. "The Dynamics of Protest Waves: West Germany, 1965 to 1989." *American Sociological Review* 58(5): 637–58.

_____. 2004. "Protest in Space and Time: The Evolution of Waves of Contention." In *The Blackwell Companion to Social Movements*, ed. David A. Snow, Sarah A. Soule, and Hanspeter Kriesi, 19–46. London: Blackwell.

_____. 2005. "The Missing Link between Structure and Agency: Outline of an Evolutionary Approach to Social Movements." *Mobilization* 10(1): 19–33.

Koopmans, Ruud, and Paul Statham. 1999. "Political Claims Analysis: Integrating Protest Event and Political Discourse Approaches." *Mobilization* 4(2): 203–21.

Kurzman, Charles. 1996. "Structural Opportunity and Perceived Opportunity in Social-Movement Theory: The Iranian Revolution of 1979." *American Sociological Review* 61: 153–70.

Lahoud, Nelly. 2010. *The Jihadis' Path to Self-Destruction*. New York: Columbia University Press.

Larson, Jeff, and Sarah Soule. 2009. "Sector Level Dynamics and Collective Action in the United States, 1965–1975." *Mobilization* 14(3): 293–314.

Lee, Chris, Sandra Maline, and Will H. Moore. 2000. "Coercion and Protest: An EmpiricalTest Revisited." In *Paths to State Repression: Human Rights and Contentious Politics in Comparative Perspective*, ed. Christian A. Davenport, 125–44. Boulder, CO: Rowman and Littlefield.

Lee, Rensselaer. 2002. "Terrorist Financing: The U.S. and International Response." Report for Congress. http://www.law.umaryland.edu/marshall/crsreports/crsdocuments/RL31658_12062002.pdf.

Lichbach, Mark. 1987. "Deterrence or Escalation? The Puzzle of Aggregate Studies of Repression and Dissent." *Journal of Conflict Resolution* 31: 266–97.

_____. 1995. *The Rebel's Dilemma*. Ann Arbor: University of Michigan Press.

Lichbach, Mark, and Ted Gurr. 1981. "The Conflict Process – a Formal Model." *Journal of Conflict Resolution* 25(1): 3–29.

Lipset, Seymour, and Gary Marks. 2001. *It Didn't Happen Here: Why Socialism Failed in America*. New York: W. W. Norton.

Loveman, Mara. 1998. "High-Risk Collective Action: Defending Human Rights in Chile, Uruguay, and Argentina." *American Journal of Sociology* 104: 477–525.

Loyle, Cyanne, Chris Sullivan, and Christian Davenport. 2012. "The Coercive Weight of the Past: Temporal Dependence in the Conflict-Repression Nexus." *International Interactions* 38(4): 1–17.

Lumumba, Chokwe. 1980. "Statement in Support of Present Leadership of Provisional Government, Dara Abubakari President." Radical Information Project, University of Michigan.

Lyall, Jason. 2006. "Pocket Protests: Rhetorical Coercion and the Micropolitics of Collective Action in Semiauthoritarian Regimes." *World Politics* 58: 378–412.

Lyall, Jason, and Isaiah Willson. 2008. "Rage against the Machines: Explaining Outcomes in Counterinsurgency Wars." *International Organizations* 63: 67–106.

Martin, Andrew, and Marc Dixon. 2010. "Changing to Win? Threat, Resistance, and the Role of Unions in Strikes, 1984–2002." *American Journal of Sociology* 116(1): 93–129.

Marx, Gary. 1974. "Thoughts on a Neglected Category of Social Movement Participant: The Agent Provocateur and the Informant." *American Journal of Sociology* 80(2): 402–42.

———. 1979. "External Efforts to Damage or Facilitate Social Movements: Some Patterns, Explanations, Outcomes and Complications." In *The Dynamics of Social Movements: Resource Mobilization, Social Control, and Tactics*, ed. Mayer Zald and John McCarthy. Cambridge, MA: Winthrop.

Mason, T. David, and Dale Krane. 1989. "The Political-Economy of Death Squads: Toward a Theory of the Impact of State-Sanctioned Terror." *International Studies Quarterly* 33(2): 175–98.

McAdam, Doug. 1982. *Political Process and the Development of Black Insurgency, 1930–1970*. Chicago: University of Chicago Press.

———. 1986. "Recruitment to High-Risk Activism: The Case of Freedom Summer." *American Journal of Sociology* 92: 64–90.

McAdam, Doug, and W. Richard Scott. 2005. "Organizations and Movements." In *Social Movements and Organizational Theory*, ed. Gerald F. Davis et al., 4–40. New York: Cambridge University Press.

McCarthy, John, and Mayer Zald. 1977. "Resource Mobilization and Social Movements: A Partial Theory." *American Journal of Sociology* 82: 1212–39.

McKinley, William. 1993. "Organizational Decline and Adaptation: Theoretical Controversies." *Organization Science* 4(1): 1–9.

McLaughlin, Theodore, and Wendy Pearlman. 2012. "Out-Group Conflict, In-Group Unity? Exploring the Effect of Repression on Movement Fragmentation." *Journal of Conflict Resolution* 56(1): 41–66.

Meyer, John, and Nathalie Allen. 1991. "A Three Component Conceptualization of Organizational Commitment." *Human Resource Management Review* 1: 61–89.

Meyer, John, and Brian Rowan. 1977. "Institutionalized Organizations: Formal Structure as Myth and Ceremony." *American Journal of Sociology* 83: 340–63.

Michigan Chronicle. 1968a. "Black Government Parley Called." March 23.

———. 1968b. "Separatists Plan Convention Here." March 2.

———. 1968c. "Black Separatists Set Up Government." April 6.

Michigan State Police. 1968. Surveillance record 370. Radical Information Project, University of Michigan.

Minkoff, Debra. 1993. "The Organization of Survival: Women's and Racial-Ethnic Voluntarist and Activist Organizations, 1955–1985." *Social Forces* 71(4): 887–908.

———. 1999. "Bending with the Wind: Strategic Change and Adaptation by Women's and Racial Minority Organizations." *American Journal of Sociology* 6: 1666–1703.

Mishra, Aneil. 1996. "Organizational Responses to Crisis: The Centrality of Trust." In *Trust in Organizations: Frontiers of Theory and Research*, ed. Roderick Kramer and Tom Tyler, 261–87. London: Sage.

Moore, Will. 1998. "Repression and Dissent: Substitution, Context, and Timing." *American Journal of Political Science* 42(3): 851–73.

———. 2000. "The Repression of Dissent: A Substitution Model of Government Coercion." *Journal of Conflict Resolution* 44: 107–27.

Morris, Aldon. 1981. "Black Southern Sit-In Movement: An Analysis of Internal Organization." *American Sociological Review* 46: 744–67.

———. 1984. *The Origins of the Civil Rights Movement*. New York: Free Press.

Muller, Edward. 1985. "Income Inequality, Regime Repressiveness and Political Violence." *American Sociological Review* 50: 47–61.

Myers, Daniel. 1997. "Racial Rioting in the 1960s: An Event History Analysis of Local Conditions." *American Sociological Review* 62(1): 94–112.

Nepstad, Sharon. 2004. "Persistent Resistance: Commitment and Community in the Plowshares." *Social Problems* 51(1): 43–60.

Now!. 1965. "Community News." Radical Information Project, University of Michigan.

Obadele, Imari. 1968. *War in America: The Malcolm X Doctrine*. Detroit, MI: The Malcolm X Society.

———. 1969. Letter in response to Ocean Hill–Brownsville investigation. Radical Information Project, University of Michigan.

———. 1970a. *Revolution and Nation-Building: Strategy for Building the Black Nation in America*. Detroit, MI: House of Songhay.

———. 1970b. "Come to the Land." Radical Information Project, University of Michigan.

———. 1970c. Untitled manuscript. Radical Information Project, University of Michigan.

———. 1971. "Directive to Expedite Success of the Revolution." Radical Information Project, University of Michigan.

———. 1972. Letter to membership. Radical Information Project, University of Michigan.

———. 1975. *Foundations of the Black Nation*. Detroit, MI: House of Songhay.

———. 1982. *The Malcolm Generation and Other Stories*. Philadelphia: House of Songhay.

———. 1984. *Free the Land! The True Story of the Trials of the RNA-11 in Mississippi and the Continuing Struggle to Establish an Independent Black Nation in Five States of the Deep South*. Washington, DC: House of Songhay.

———. 1991a. *America the Nation-State: The Politics of the United States from a State-Building Perspective*. Baton Rouge, LA: House of Songhay.

———. 1991b. *The Macro-Level Theory of Human Organization*. Baton Rouge, LA: House of Songhay.

Obadele, Imari, and Sonny Carson. 1969. "The Situation in Ocean Hill–Brownsville." Radical Information Project, University of Michigan.

Oberschall, Anthony. 1973. *Social Movements*. New Brunswick, NJ: Transaction.

Oliver, Pamela, and Dan Myers. 2002. "The Coevolution of Social Movements." *Mobilization* 8(1): 1–24.

Olivier, Johan L. 1991. "State Repression and Collective Action in South Africa, 1970–1984." *South African Journal of Sociology* 22: 109–17.

Olson, Mancur. 1965. *The Logic of Collective Action*. Cambridge, MA: Harvard University Press.

Olzak, Susan, and Emily Ryo. 2007. "Organization Diversity, Vitality and Outcomes in the Civil Rights Movement." *Social Forces* 85(4): 1561–91.

O'Neill, Bard. 2005. *Insurgency and Terrorism: From Revolution to Apocalypse*. 2nd ed. Washington, DC: Potomac Books.

Opp, Karl-Dieter, and Christiane Gern. 1993. "Dissident Groups, Personal Networks, and Spontaneous Cooperation: The East German Revolution of 1989." *American Sociological Review* 58(5): 659–80.

Opp, Karl-Dieter, and Wolfgang Roehl. 1990. "Repression, Micromobilization, and Political Protest." *Social Forces* 69(2): 521–47.

Ortiz, David. 2007. "Confronting Oppression with Violence: Inequality, Military Infrastructure and Dissident Repression." *Mobilization* 12(3): 219–38.

Passy, Florence, and Marco Giugni. 2000. "Life-Spheres, Networks, and Sustained Participation in Social Movements: A Phenomenological Approach to Political Commitment." *Sociological Forum* 15(1): 117–44.

Pearlman, Wendy. 2008–9. "Spoiling Inside and Out: Internal Political Contestation and the Middle East Peace Process." *International Security* 33(3): 79–109.

Pearson, Christine M., and Judith A. Clair. 1998. "Reframing Crisis Management". *Academy of Management Review* 23(1): 59–76.

Pierskalla, Jan. 2009. "Protest, Deterrence and Escalation: The Strategic Calculus of Government Repression." *Journal of Conflict Resolution* 54(1): 117–45.

Pieth, Mark. 2006. "Criminalizing the Financing of Terrorism." *Journal of International Criminal Justice* 4(5): 1074–93.

Pinard, Maurice. 1971. *The Rise of a Third Party*. Englewood Cliffs, NJ: Prentice Hall.

Piven, Fox, and Richard Cloward. 1979. *Poor People's Movements*. New York: Vintage.

———. 1993. *Regulating the Poor*. 2nd ed. New York: Vintage.

Plain Dealer. 1968. "Black Nation Draft Constitution." April 1.

Podair, Jerold. 2002. *The Strike That Changed New York*. New Haven, CT: Yale University Press.

Poletta, Francesca. 2002. *Freedom Is an Endless Meeting: Democracy in American Social Movements*. Chicago: University of Chicago Press.

Pratkanis, Anthony, and Anthony Greenwald. 1989. "A Sociocognitive Model of Attitude Structure and Function." *Advances in Experimental Social Psychology* 22: 245–85.

Price, Bryan. 2010. "Removing the Devil You Know: An Empirical Analysis of Leadership Decapitation and Terrorist Group Duration." Paper at presented at the annual meeting of the International Studies Association, New Orleans, LA.

Radical Information Project. 1969. Anonymous police report. University of Michigan.

Radical Information Project. 2010. "Telegram from Milton Henry to Michigan Governor, Dated 1967." University of Michigan. http://www.radicalinformationproject.com.

Rasler, Karen. 1996. "Concessions, Repression, and Political Protest in the Iranian Revolution." *American Sociological Review* 61: 132–52.

Reddick, Lawrence. 1953. "The Relative Status of the Negro in the American Armed Forces." *The Journal of Negro Education* 22(3): 380–87.

Republic of New Africa. 1968a. "Objectives of Government through 30 October 1968." Radical Information Project, University of Michigan.

———. 1968b. "The Birth of Our Nation." Radical Information Project, University of Michigan.

———. 1969. Untitled document. Radical Information Project, University of Michigan.

———. 1970. "A Short History – The Republic of New Africa." Radical Information Project, University of Michigan.

———. 1971. Directive 00006. Radical Information Project, University of Michigan.

Republic of New Africa – Council of Political Policy and Action. 1969. Untitled document. Radical Information Project, University of Michigan.

Robinson, Sandra, Kurt Dirks, and Hakan Ozcelik. 2004. "Untangling the Knot of Trust and Betrayal." In *Trust and Distrust in Organizations: Dilemmas and*

Approaches, ed. Roderick Kramer and Karen Cook, 327–41. New York: Russell Sage Foundation Series on Trust.

Ron, James. 2005. "Paradigm in Distress? Primary Commodities and Civil War." *Journal of Conflict Resolution* 49(4): 443–50.

Ruef, Martin. 2000. "The Emergence of Organizational Forms: A Community Ecology Approach." *American Journal of Sociology* 106: 658–714.

Salanova, Marisa, and Susana Llorens. 2008. "Current State of Research on Burnout and Future Challenges." *Papeles del Psicologo* 29(1): 59–67.

Sales, William. 1999. *From Civil Rights to Black Liberation: Malcolm X and the Organization of Afro-American Unity*. Boston: South End Press.

Sambanis, Nicholas. 2004. "What Is Civil War? Conceptual and Empirical Complexities of an Operational Definition." *Journal of Conflict Resolution* 48(6): 814–58.

Scherer, K. R. 2001. "Appraisal Considered as a Process of Multilevel Sequential Checking." In *Appraisal Processes in Emotion: Theory, Methods, Research*, ed. K. R. Scherer, A. Schorr, and T. Johnstone, 92–120. Oxford: Oxford University Press.

Schertzing, Phillip. 1999. "Against All Enemies and Opposers Whatever: The Michigan State Police Crusade against the Un-Americans, 1917–1977." PhD diss., Michigan State University.

Schrecker, Ellen. 1998. *Many Are the Crimes: McCarthyism in America*. New York: Little, Brown.

Shellman, Stephen. 2006. "Process Matters: Conflict and Cooperation in Sequential Government-Dissident Interactions." *Security Studies* 15(4): 563–99.

Sherrill, Robert. 1968a. " . . . We Also Want Four Hundred Billion Dollars Back Pay: Separatism Command." *Esquire*, January.

———. 1968b. "Whitey's Reaction: From a Grudging Yes to an Oh, No, No, No to the Usual Confusion" *Esquire*, January.

Simon, Marc. 1994. "Hawks, Doves and Civil Conflict Dynamics: A 'Strategic' Action-Reaction Model." *International Interactions* 19(3): 213–39.

Smith, Ernest. 1963. "Why an All Black Party?" Freedom Now Party. Radical Information Project, University of Michigan.

Snow, David A., Louis A. Zurcher, and Sheldon Ekland-Olson. 1980. "Social Networks and Social Movements: A Microstructural Approach to Differential Recruitment." *American Sociological Review* 45: 787–801.

Soule, Sarah A., and Brayden King. 2008. "Competition and Resource Partitioning in Three Social Movement Industries." *American Journal of Sociology* 113(6): 1568–1610.

Spreen, Johannes, and Diane Holloway. 2005. *Who Killed Detroit? Other Cities Beware!* Lincoln, NB: iUniverse.

Suchman, Mark. 1995. "Managing Legitimacy: Strategic and Institutional Approaches." *Academy of Management Review* 20(3): 571–610.

Sugrue, Thomas. 2005. *The Origins of the Urban Crisis: Race and Inequality in Postwar Detroit*. Princeton, NJ: Princeton University Press.

Steedly, Homer, and John Foley. 1979. "The Success of Protest Groups: Multivariate Analyses." *Social Science Research* 8: 1–15.

Stryker, Sheldon. 2000. "Identity Competition: Key to Differential Social Movement Participation." In *Self, Identity, and Social Movements*, ed. Sheldon Stryker, Timothy Owens, and Robert White, 21–40. Minneapolis: University of Minnesota Press.

Tarrow, Sidney. 1994. *Power in Movement*. Cambridge: Cambridge University Press.

Taylor, Verta. 1989. "Social Movement Continuity: The Women's Movement in Abeyance." *American Sociological Review* 54: 761–75.

Thompson, Heather. 2004. *Whose Detroit? Politics, Labor, and Race in a Modern American City*. Ithaca, NY: Cornell University Press.

Tilly, Charles. 1978. *From Mobilization to Revolution*. New York: Paradigm Press.

———. 2000. "Processes and Mechanisms of Democratization." *Sociological Theory* 18: 1–16.

———. 2005. *Trust and Rule*. New York: Cambridge University Press.

———. 2006. *Regimes and Repertoires*. Chicago: University of Chicago Press.

Turrini, Joseph. 1999. "Phooie on Louie: African American Detroit and the Election of Jerry Cavanaugh." *Michigan History Magazine*, November/December, 11–17.

Tyson, Timothy. 1999. *Radio Free Dixie: Robert F. Williams and the Roots of Black Power*. Chapel Hill: University of North Carolina Press.

Umoja, A. O. 2013. *We Will Shoot: Armed Resistance in the Mississippi Freedom Movement*. New York: New York University Press.

U.S. Department of Justice. 1968. Untitled memo regarding the RNA. June 13. The Radical Information Project, The University of Michigan.

U.S. Department of Justice. 1969. "Mass Media, a Racist Institution: Coverage of the New Bethel Incident by the Detroit News and the Detroit Free Press, March 20–April 3, 1969." Ferndale, MI: Detroit Area People against Racism.

Van Deburg, W. L. 1992. *New Day in Babylon: The Black Power Movement and American Culture, 1965–1975*. Chicago: University of Chicago Press.

Walter, Barbara F. 2006. "Building Reputation: Why Governments Fight Some Separatists but Not Others." *American Journal of Political Science* 50(2): 313–30.

Weber, Max. 1946. *From Max Weber: Essays in Sociology*. New York: Oxford University Press.

Weede, Erich. 1987. "The Rise of the West to Eurosclerosis: Are There Lessons for the Asian-Pacific Region?" *Asian Culture Quarterly* 15(1): 1–14.

Weinstein, Jeremy. 2005. "Resources and the Information Problem in Rebel Recruitment." *Journal of Conflict Resolution* 49(4): 598–624.

———. 2007. *Inside Rebellion: The Politics of Insurgent Violence*. Cambridge: Cambridge University Press.

Weitzel, William, and Ellen Jonsson. 1989. "Decline in Organizations: A Literature Integration and Extension." *Administrative Science Quarterly* 34(1): 91–109.

White, Robert. 1989. "From Peaceful Protest to Guerrilla War: Micromobilization of the Provisional Irish Republican Army." *American Journal of Sociology* 94(6): 1277–302.

Widick, B. J. 1972. *Detroit: City of Race and Class Violence*. Detroit, MI: Wayne State University Press.

Williams, Robert. 1962. *Negroes with Guns*. Detroit, MI: Wayne State University Press.

Wood, Elisabeth. 2003. *Insurgent Collective Action and Civil War in El Salvador*. Cambridge: Cambridge University Press.

Woodard, Komozi. 1999. *A Nation within a Nation: Amiri Baraka (LeRoi Jones) and Black Power Politics*. Chapel Hill: University of North Carolina Press.

———. 2003. *Freedom North: Black Freedom Struggles outside the South, 1940–1980*. New York: Palgrave.

X, Malcolm. 1964. "The Ballot or the Bullet." Speech delivered in Cleveland, Ohio. http://www.hartford-hwp.com/archives/45a/065.html.

Zald, Mayer, and Roberta Ash. 1966. "Social Movement Organizations: Growth, Decay and Change." *Social Forces* 44: 327–41.

Zeile, Rachel. 2006. "Now We Have a Nation: The Republic of New Africa and Black Separatism in Detroit, 1968–1971." Honors thesis, Dartmouth College.

Zwerman, Gilda, and Patricia Steinhoff. 2005. "When Activists Ask for Trouble: State-Dissident Interactions and the New Left Cycle of Resistance in the United States and Japan." In *Repression and Mobilization*, ed. Christian Davenport, Hank Johnston, and Carol Mueller, 85–107. Minneapolis: University of Minnesota Press.

Zwerman, Gilda, Patricia Steinhoff, and Donatella della Porta. 2000. "Disappearing Social Movements: Clandestinity in the Cycle of New Left Protest in the U.S., Japan, Germany and Italy." *Mobilization* 5(1): 85–104.

Index

Books in the Series (*continued from page iii*)

Printed in the USA
CPSIA information can be obtained
at www.ICGtesting.com
CBHW022004230724
12043CB00001B/42

9 781107 613874